KT-549-198
061 339 9598

HANDBOOK ON THE PENTATEUCH

222.1
H221h

HANDBOOK ON THE PENTATEUCH

GENESIS
EXODUS
LEVITICUS
NUMBERS
DEUTERONOMY

NAZARENE THEOLOGICAL COLLEGE
LIBRARY

VICTOR P. HAMILTON

BAKER BOOK HOUSE
Grand Rapids, Michigan 49506

Copyright © 1982 by Baker Books
a division of Baker Book House Company
P.O. Box 6287, Grand Rapids, MI 49516-6287

ISBN: 0-8010-4259-3

Library of Congress Catalog Card Number: 82-70466

Twelfth printing, July 1994

Printed in the United States of America

Unless otherwise indicated, Scripture references are from the Revised Standard Version of the Bible, copyright 1946, 1952, 1971,1973.

To my wife Shirley

Contents

List of Abbreviations 9
Preface 11

Part ONE ***Genesis***

1 Creation and the Fall *(1–3)* 17
2 The Sequence after Creation and the Fall *(4–11)* 57
3 Abraham *(11:26–25:11)* 87
4 Jacob *(25:11–36:42)* 117
5 Joseph *(37–50)* 129

Part TWO ***Exodus***

6 The Emergence of Moses *(1–6)* 141
7 Plagues, Passover, and the Exodus *(7:1–15:21)* 163
8 Testing in the Wilderness *(15:22–18:27)* 185
9 Law and Covenant *(19–24)* 193
10 Tabernacle, the Golden Calf, and Covenant Renewal *(25–40)* 227

Part THREE ***Leviticus***

11 The Sacrificial System *(1–7)* 245
12 Priestly Ordination *(8–10)* 265
13 Clean and Unclean *(11–15)* 273
14 The Day of Atonement *(16)* 285
15 A Holiness Manifesto *(17–27)* 297

Part FOUR ***Numbers***

16 Preparations for Departure from Sinai *(1:1–10:10)* 315
17 From Sinai to Kadesh *(10:11–20:21)* 333
18 From Kadesh to Moab *(20:22–36:13)* 351

Part FIVE ***Deuteronomy***

19 Remember the Past *(1:1–4:40)* 377
20 Be Careful in the Future *(4:41–11:32)* 403
21 The Laws of Deuteronomy *(12–26)* 415
22 Blessings and Curses *(27–30; 31:1–6)* 455
23 Moses' Farewell *(31:7–34:12)* 465

Index of Authors 475
Index of Scripture Passages 481

List of Abbreviations

ABR	Australian Biblical Review
ANQ	Andover Newton Quarterly
AsSem	Asbury Seminarian
ASTI	Annual of the Swedish Theological Institute
ATB	Ashland Theological Bulletin
ATR	Anglican Theological Review
AUSS	Andrews University Seminary Studies
BA	Biblical Archaeologist
BAR	Biblical Archaeology Review
BASOR	Bulletin of the American Schools of Oriental Research
Bibl	Biblica
BJRL	Bulletin of the John Rylands University Library
BRes	Biblical Research
BS	Bibliotheca Sacra
BT	Bible Today
BTB	Biblical Theology Bulletin
BTrans	The Bible Translator
BZ	Biblische Zeitschrift
CBQ	Catholic Biblical Quarterly
ChrNIsr	Christian News from Israel
CT	Christianity Today
CTJ	Calvin Theological Journal
CTM	Concordia Theological Monthly
EncJud	Encyclopaedia Judaica
EQ	The Evangelical Quarterly
ETL	Ephemerides Theologicae Lovianienses
ExpT	The Expository Times
GJ	Grace Journal
HJ	The Heythrop Journal
HTR	Harvard Theological Review
HUCA	Hebrew Union College Annual
IDB	Interpreter's Dictionary of the Bible
IDBSuppl	Interpreter's Dictionary of the Bible Supplement
IEJ	Israel Exploration Journal
ILR	Israel Law Review
IndJT	Indian Journal of Theology
Intr	Interpretation
JAAR	Journal of the American Academy of Religion

JANES	*Journal of the Ancient Near Eastern Society*
JAOS	*Journal of the American Oriental Society*
JBL	*Journal of Biblical Literature*
JES	*Journal of Ecumenical Studies*
JETS	*Journal of the Evangelical Theological Society*
JJS	*Journal of Jewish Studies*
JNES	*Journal of Near Eastern Studies*
JNWSL	*Journal of Northwest Semitic Languages*
JQR	*The Jewish Quarterly Review*
JRelThot	*Journal of Religious Thought*
JSOT	*Journal for the Study of the Old Testament*
JSS	*Journal of Semitic Studies*
JTCh	*Journal of Theology and Church*
JTS	*Journal of Theological Studies*
Jud	*Judaism*
NT	*Novum Testamentum*
NTS	*New Testament Studies*
OTS	*Oudtestamentische Studien*
PEQ	*Palestine Exploration Quarterly*
RB	*Revue biblique*
RefR	*Reformed Review*
RelLife	*Religion and Life*
RestQ	*Restoration Quarterly*
RExp	*Review and Expositor*
RQu	*Revue de Qumran*
SBT	*Studia Biblica et Theologica*
SJT	*Scottish Journal of Theology*
Springf	*Springfielder*
SR	*Studies in Religion*
ST	*Studia Theologica*
StLukeJ	*St. Luke's Journal*
SVT	*Supplement Vetus Testamentum*
SWJT	*Southwest Journal of Theology*
TB	*Tyndale Bulletin*
TDig	*Theology Digest*
TDOT	*Theological Dictionary of the Old Testament*
TNN	*Theology News and Notices*
TToday	*Theology Today*
USQR	*Union Seminary Quarterly Review*
VT	*Vetus Testamentum*
WBE	*Wycliffe Bible Encyclopedia*
WTJ	*Westminster Theological Journal*
ZAW	*Zeitschrift für die altestestamentliche Wissenschaft*
ZPEB	*Zondervan Pictorial Encyclopedia of the Bible*

Preface

Few sections of the Old Testament have been treated as thoroughly by scholars as has the Pentateuch. A glance at any bibliographical reference volume covering biblical research will reveal immediately the vast amount of material produced in any given year on this portion of Scripture. Perhaps it is more accurate to say that Genesis and Exodus have been studied most copiously, with studies in Deuteronomy running a close second. Articles, monographs, and commentaries on Leviticus and Numbers, by contrast, lag far behind in terms of volume.

In spite of all this research there have been few studies of recent vintage that have tried to put all of the Pentateuch into a one-volume commentary. That is my purpose in the pages that follow. More specifically, I have tried to produce a book that may function as a text in English Bible classes at both the undergraduate and seminary levels.

At no point are my explorations of the biblical text exhaustive. To assist the student who desires to go beyond the reflections in this book, I have placed a bibliography at the end of each chapter. Two guidelines have controlled my selections. First, the entries in these bibliographies are limited mostly to studies that have appeared in the last ten years. Most of them will document more than adequately all previous research in that particular area. Second, I have limited my choices almost exclusively to studies that have appeared in English. The academic journals on the Continent and the European presses are constantly producing much that is valuable in biblical research, but few undergraduate students will be able to pursue and read technical articles in French, German, Italian, Spanish, and Swedish.

Readers will note immediately that I have omitted areas of possible analysis in which they might have great interest. For example, I have not touched the question of creation versus evolution in my discussion of the opening chapters of Genesis. This exercise I prefer to leave to the scientist, rather than to the biblical scholar.

I have not discussed some areas of historical import, such as the historicity of the patriarchs or the date of the exodus. It appears to me that the ground has been well covered here by both the critics and the traditionalists. For that same reason I have not devoted one major section of my manuscript to the question of the "origins" of the Pentateuch. Instead I have limited myself to a study, here and there, of some passages in the Pentateuch that are often cited as parade examples of multiple sources within the books of Moses.

As I wrote this book I had in mind the student not only as a scholar of God's Word, but also as a proclaimer of God's Word. Therefore I have attempted to write something that is as usable in the pastor's study as it is in the classroom, something that is as devotional as it is scholarly.

I am indebted to a host of biblical scholars from whose wells I have drawn much. Especially I would like to express my appreciation to Professors Brevard Childs and Jacob Milgrom, whose studies in Exodus, and Leviticus and Numbers respectively have made a profound impact on my own comprehension of the biblical text. Dr. Dennis Kinlaw, formerly my mentor in Old Testament studies at Asbury Theological Seminary, and Dr. Robert Traina, Professor of English Bible at Asbury Theological Seminary, have made decisive contributions to my own thinking in historical and inductive Bible study.

I would like to express my appreciation to both Professor John Hayes, editor of *JBL,* and Professor Bernhard Anderson for their permission to reproduce a chart by Dr. Anderson from the *Journal of Biblical Literature* 97 (1978): 38 that appears on page 76 of my book. I am similarly indebted to Father Albert Vanhoye, S. J., editor of *Biblica,* for his permission to reproduce portions of a chart by Dr. Anson Rainey from *Biblica* 51 (1970): 492–493 that appear on page 368 of my book.

It is a pleasure for me to thank the Committee on Faculty Research and Development of Asbury College for both a work leave and a financial grant, each of which contributed greatly to the implementation of this study.

Finally, I wish to acknowledge the indispensable role that my wife Shirley has assumed for the last several years, for really we have worked together. In addition to providing constant encouragement and stimulation, she has typed the entire manuscript and has offered many invaluable suggestions.

Part ONE

Genesis

1

Creation and the Fall

Genesis 1–3

There are numerous ways in which the first book of the Bible may be outlined. Perhaps the simplest is:

I. Primeval history—chapters 1–11
  A. The creation—chapters 1–2
  B. The fall—chapters 3–11
    1. The cause—chapter 3
    2. The effects—chapters 4–11
II. Patriarchal history—chapters 12–50
  A. Abraham—chapters 12–25
  B. Jacob—chapters 26–36
  C. Joseph—chapters 37–50

This outline accurately reflects the content of Genesis, but fails to suggest any relationship between the parts, or progression in emphases. It is preferable to allow Genesis to outline itself and follow the units suggested by the text. These units are readily discernible.

I. The story of creation (1:1—2:3)
II. The generations of the heavens and the earth (2:4—4:26)
III. The generations of Adam (5:1—6:8)
IV. The generations of Noah (6:9—9:29)
V. The generations of the sons of Noah (10:1—11:9)
VI. The generations of Shem (11:10–26)
VII. The generations of Terah (11:27—25:11)
VIII. The generations of Ishmael (25:12–18)
IX. The generations of Isaac (25:19—35:29)
X. The generations of Esau (36:1—37:1)
XI. The generations of Jacob (37:2—50:26)

Thus Genesis is composed of an introductory section, and ten other sections, each introduced with the phrase *these are the generations of*.

The movement in each of the last ten sections is from source to stream, from cause to result, from progenitor to progeny. That movement is described either through subsequent narrative after the superscription (points II, IV, VII, IX, and XI) or a genealogy which follows the superscription (points III, V, VI, VIII, and X).

The result created by this introduction—superscription—sequel pattern in Genesis is that of a unified composition, neatly arranged by the author (or the narrator or editor). Furthermore, the testimony of the text is to emphasize movement, a plan, something in progress and motion. What is in motion is nothing less than the initial stages of a divine plan, a plan that has its roots in creation. From the earth Adam will come forward. From Adam Abraham and his progeny will emerge. Eventually, out of Abraham Jesus Christ will emerge.

Creation (1–2)

The first thing that strikes the reader of the Bible is the brevity (just two chapters) with which the story of the creation of the world and man is told. The arithmetic of Genesis is surprising. Only two chapters are devoted to the subject of creation and one to the entrance of sin into the human race. By contrast, thirteen chapters are given to Abraham, ten chapters to Jacob, twelve chapters to Joseph (who was not a patriarch, and not the son through whom the covenantal promises were perpetuated). We face, then, the phenomenon of twelve chapters for Joseph, and two for the theme of creation. Can one man be six times more important than the world?

Nevertheless, we would all agree that our understanding of the Bible would be impoverished—rather, jeopardized—without these first two chapters. What are they

Figure 1

Day		Day	
1	light	4	luminaries (sun, moon, stars)
2	heavens	5	fish, birds
3	earth, vegetation	6	land animals, man

Day 7 the Sabbath

about? A skeletal outline of the contents of 1:1—2:3 is helpful. See Figure 1.

It is not difficult to see that the first six days fall into two groups of three. Each day in the second column is an extension of its counterpart in the left-hand column. Thus, on day one, God created light in general or light-bearers; on day four, there were specific kinds of light. On day two, the firmament separated waters above from waters below; on day five, God made creatures of sky and water. On day three, God created the earth; on day six, He made the creatures of land. The climax to creation is the seventh day, the day of rest for God. The preceding days He called good. This one alone He sanctified.

In addition to this horizontal literary arrangement, one can also observe a fundamental literary pattern throughout all of Genesis 1. Using the language of Claus Westermann, we note this pattern:[1]

1. announcement: "And God said"
2. command: "let there be/let it be gathered/let it bring forth"
3. report: "and it was so"
4. evaluation: "And God saw that it was good."
5. temporal framework: "And there was evening and there was morning"

An alternative pattern is:

1. introduction: "And God said"
2. the creative word: "let there be"

1. *Genesis* (Neukirchen-Vluyn: Neukirchener Verlag, 1974–), p. 7.

3. fulfillment of the word: "and there was/and it was so"
4. a description of the act in question: "And God separated/and God made/and God set/so God created"
5. a name-giving or blessing: "And he called/blessed"
6. the divine commendation: "and it was good"
7. the concluding formula: "there was evening and morning"

The Relationship of 1:1—2:3 (or 4a) to 2:4 (or 4b)–25

Frequently Genesis 2:4–25 is described as a second creation story. Further, it is suggested that not only is this a second story about creation, but also that it is from a different source than that of Genesis 1:1—2:3. Those who embrace the documentary hypothesis believe that the first creation story is the work of an anonymous priestly editor or editors (P) around the time of the Babylonian exile (sixth century) or immediately thereafter. By contrast, these scholars believe the second creation story is from a much earlier writer, usually designated as the Yahwist (J), again an anonymous writer or writers from Jerusalem in the time of David and Solomon (the tenth century).

The first reason for making this distinction is a different and, at points, contradictory account of the sequence of the orders of creation, the first sequence being vegetation, birds and fish, animals, man and woman; the second being man, vegetation, animals, woman. Second, in the first sequence the exclusive name for the deity is God (*Elohim*), but in the second it is Lord God (*Yahweh Elohim*). Third, in the first sequence God creates primarily by speaking, "And God said, 'let there be,' and it was," that is, creation by fiat. In the second sequence the emphasis is on God as potter or craftsman, "the Lord God *formed* man of dust" (2:7, italics mine); "out of the ground the Lord God *formed* every beast of the field" (2:19, italics mine); "and the rib ... he made into a woman" (2:22). Fourth, in the first sequence the emphasis is on cosmogony—whence this world? In the second sequence the emphasis is on anthropology—whence man?

Thus, the contention is that we are faced with two originally independent creation stories, in origin about five hundred years apart. The phenomenon of "doublets" we will encounter again in our discussion of the flood story where the unanimous opinion of literary and source critics is that originally there were two independent accounts of the deluge, again J and P, but with this one distinct difference. The redactor (or redactors) of these opening chapters juxtaposed the two creation stories, but spliced the two flood stories. The reason for this distinction has, to the best of my knowledge, not been satisfactorily explained, although attempts have been made.

To return to the creation stories, is it absolutely necessary to posit two mutually exclusive, antithetical accounts? Could not 2:4–25 be a continuation, not a break, of the creation story, "a close-up after the panorama of Genesis 1"?[2] The order of events in chapter 1 is chronological. The order of events in chapter 2 is logical and topical, from man to his environment. Most of the information in 2:4–25 is an amplification of 1:26–29. Chapter 1 is concerned with the world. Chapter 2 is concerned with a garden. One is cosmic, the other is localized. God's relationship to the world is in His capacity as *Elohim*. His relationship to a couple in a garden is in His capacity as *Yahweh Elohim*, the first suggesting His majesty and transcendence, the second His intimacy and involvement with His creation. Exactly why we must not posit a unity in Genesis 1–2 escapes me.

2. Leland Ryken, *The Literature of the Bible* (Grand Rapids: Zondervan, 1974), p. 37.

Theological Themes in Genesis 1–2

What the themes teach about God

The most obvious observation is the emphasis in these two chapters on God's oneness. Instead of encountering a host of deities one meets the one God. Unlike pagan gods, God has no spouse or consort. What is the significance of this? Can this be the Bible's way of saying that God needs nothing or no one outside of Himself to fulfill Him? All of the resources for self-fulfillment are within Him. Everthing else in the created order by itself is unfulfilled, and must look beyond itself or himself for fulfillment. It is God's oneness that alone makes sense of words such as "*uni*verse" or "*uni*versity."

A second truth affirmed by these chapters is that there is a line of distinction between God as creator and man as a creature that is never effaced. If one traces Mesopotamian chronologies back to their furthest point, as is done, for example, in the Sumerian King list (a document produced by Sumerian scribes shortly after 2000 B.C. and listing the names of rulers from the advent of kingship onward), the remote ancestors, it is discovered, are divine beings. The distinction between god and man has been erased. Genesis 1–2 traces the human race back as far as possible and still one finds Adam/man. Then comes the gulf. Through Hosea the Lord says succinctly, "I am God, and not man" (Hos. 11:9), and it is said in a context of hope, not haughtiness. If Israel's salvation is in man she is finished. If it is in God there is hope.

A third truth is that God is multiple in His nature. Genesis 1:26 says, "Let *us* make man in *our* image, after *our* likeness" (italics mine). On the basis of exegesis it would be impossible to say the reference is to the Trinity. At least six interpretations have been placed on the phrase *let us*. One of these interpretations is the mythological interpretation. One god, perhaps the chief god, speaks to the other deities and informs them of his intentions, or solicits their advice and help in some project, in this case the creation of man. The contention is that the writer of Genesis 1 failed to expurgate completely the mythological motifs he was borrowing. Another interpretation is that God is speaking to the creation, the earth. Earth then becomes a partner with God in the creation of man, and a constituent part of man's composite nature, balancing the divine inbreathing. A third possibility is that God is speaking to the angels, the heavenly court, and thus man bears certain resemblances to both God and the angels. This view implies that in the creation of man God had assistance from His angels. The fourth interpretation is that this is a plural of majesty, that is, God speaks of Himself and with Himself in the plural. (See also 11:7, "Come, let *us* go down," and Isaiah 6:8, "Whom shall I send, and who will go for *us*?" [italics mine].) The very name of God in chapter 1, *Elohim,* is plural, *-im* indicating masculine plural nouns. A fifth possibility is that the phenomenon here can be described as plural of self-deliberation, as in our English phrase, "let's see, what should I do?" Finally, I consider the most plausible explanation to be that which sees in the "us" a plural of fullness or plurality within the Godhead. Perhaps God is addressing His Spirit (already mentioned in 1:2). That God is triune is a fact that awaits the preachment of the New Testament revelation.

A fourth truth is that God is moral and holy. To Adam and Eve God said both "you may eat" and "you may not eat." One of the books most frequently alluded to in this area is *The Idea of the Holy,* by the German Protestant theologian and historian of religion, Rudolph Otto. Otto's book was first published in 1917 and translated into English in 1923. The essential theme of the book is the author's emphasis on the "holy" as the distinguishing feature of religious experience. To use Otto's phrase, the "holy" is *mysterium tremendum et fascinosum,* that is, that which elicits in the worshiper both fear and fascination, "lashed with terror, leashed with longing," to use the phrase of the poet Francis Thompson.

Important for Otto is his contention that the moral and the ethical are not identical with the holy. What Otto does not address is the fact that God's holiness gives the basis to His moral demands. The purpose of the Decalogue is to show Israel how to live with a holy God. Even in paradise there is the institution of law.

A fifth observation is the emphasis in these two chapters on God's sovereignty and majesty. Effortlessly He speaks into existence the created order, or He shapes it as a potter produces a masterpiece from clay. At no point does God encounter antagonism or resistance in His work of creation.

Two illustrations will suffice here. One is the way in which the creation of the sun, moon, and stars is delineated. The order of narration is interesting: sun, moon, stars. In the *Enuma elish*, the order is stars, sun, and moon. The stars are not created; they are considered independent realities. There is a divine aura about them. A second thing of interest about the sun and moon, given the adulation for these luminaries in the ancient world, is that they are simply called "the greater light" and "the lesser light." Third, the stars are given the skimpy observation, "he made the stars too." Fourth, the function of the sun and moon is explicitly spelled out to emphasize their position as servants, given their orders and duty by God.

A second illustration of divine sovereignty is the lack of any reference to God's confrontation with celestial monsters or opponents, a theme prevalent in the *Enuma elish*. The closest Genesis 1 or 2 comes is the reference to the "sea monsters" (1:21). What is of interest is the use of the Hebrew word *bara'*, used in 1:1, and three times in 1:27 in connection with the creation of man, to describe their origin. God "created" them. Whenever this verb is used in the Old Testament God is always the subject. Nor is the verb ever followed by the accusative of material, as in the phrase "[he] formed man of dust" (2:7), or "the rib . . . he made into a woman" (2:22).

For a good while it has been suggested that the reference to "the deep" (1:2; Hebrew *tehom*) is a veiled reference to Tiamat of Babylonian fame. Even if that is the case one would be hard pressed to see any obvious mythic allusions in the use of *tehom* by the author of Genesis 1:2. Absolutely no idea of the "deep" as the enemy of God emerges from the text. Rather, the "deep" is an inanimate part of the created order. In addition, very strong linguistic arguments militate against the equation of Tiamat and *tehom*.

Yet there are references in Scripture to God's doing battle with the monster. Isaiah 51:9 speaks of God's cutting Rahab in pieces and piercing the dragon. Psalm 74:13–14 says that God has broken the heads of the dragons in the waters and crushed the heads of Leviathan. Indeed, Isaiah 27:1 and 51:9 and Psalm 74:13 use the same Hebrew word for "dragon" or "sea monster" as does Genesis 1:21. But the dragon of Isaiah and the psalm is an adversary of God. The dragon of Genesis 1:21 is created by God and called "good."

What may be said about these references, outside of Genesis, to these monstrous antagonists of God? First, we have to assume that the allusions to Leviathan, Rahab, and the dragons would have to be intelligible to the hearers of these words before they could understand the forcefulness of the speaker's point. After all, would the psalmist's, "Thou didst crush the heads of Leviathan" mean anything if the mythical Leviathan were unknown by everyone else? We can surmise, therefore, that the people of God were familiar with the mythological literature of their neighbors.

Second, the language and motifs of mythology find their clearest expression not in the opening chapters of Genesis, where one might expect them, but rather in prophetic literature and the Psalter. More importantly, the context in which these "battles" take place is redemption, not creation. For example, cutting Rahab into pieces and piercing the dragon (Isa. 51:9) is parallel with God's parting of the Red Sea "for the redeemed to pass over" (Isa. 51:10). Similarly, crushing the heads of Leviathan and breaking the heads of the dragons (Ps. 74:13–14) appear in a psalm of lamentation in which the author prays for deliverance from his enemies. The deliverer is God who is "working salvation in the midst of the earth" (Ps. 74:12).

Deliberately the biblical writers use these mythical allusions not in the setting of creation but in the context of redemption. There is no evil inherent in the world God has made. Where is evil conquered? In creation? No! Rather, evil and chaos and disruption are conquered within time, in the redemption of God's people.

The climax of creation is the Sabbath (Gen. 2:1–3). This episode too may be seen as an extension of the implicit emphasis here on divine sovereignty and majesty. God's rest on this day is not to renew His strength after combat with turbulent forces of evil. The day's purpose is to provide rest for God after a week's work of creation. Rest supersedes the act of creation. There is silence before creation, before God speaks. After creation there is silence again. This silence God has sanctified (Gen. 2:3).

What the themes teach about man

The pattern of creation by fiat in Genesis 1 is broken by the observation that God's act of creation of man is preceded by an act of self-deliberation and a statement of divine intention (1:26a).

Specifically, we are told that God created man in his own "image" and "likeness." This is the only place in the Old Testament where these two nouns appear in connection with each other, and one immediately asks about their relationship. Are they interchangeable, an example of the penchant for listing synonyms that is so prevalent in biblical Hebrew? Two observations may support this. In 1:26, referring to God's decision to create, both words are used. But in verse 27, which deals with the actual work of creation, only "image" is used. In 5:1, "he made him in the likeness of God," the Hebrew word for "likeness" is translated in the Septuagint not by the usual *homoiōsis,* but by *eikōn,* normally the Greek equivalent for the Hebrew word for "image."

A second possibility is that the word *likeness* modifies the word *image.* The function then of "likeness" would be to limit the meaning of "image." Such qualification, it is suggested, helps to avoid the implication that man is a precise copy of God. Some credence may be lent to this view by the fact that "likeness" appears in the Old Testament twenty-four times and fourteen of these are in chapters 1 and 10 of Ezekiel. In these passages, the prophet is careful never to say he saw God or His entourage, but only the likeness of God.

A third suggestion is the reverse of the second suggestion. Thus, "likeness" does not soften the concept about "image," but rather amplifies it. Man is not simply an image of God but a likeness-image. That is, man is not simply representative, but representational, of the invisible God.

Whatever the best explanation may be on this technical matter, it is plain to see that man is set apart from the rest of creation and indeed is placed on a pedestal. Unlike the pagan accounts we will examine, man is not created as an afterthought, nor is he consigned to the work of drudgery as a substitute for recalcitrant deities. Manual labor is a God-given privilege, not a sentence or a penalty.

Genesis 1 also affirms that man was created to "subdue" and "have dominion" over the earth and over living creatures of the sea, land, and air. Some scholars have suggested, in light of the wording of 1:26, that it is precisely man's domination of the world that constitutes the image of God (although the relation is more a consequence than a definition).

But what does it mean to subdue and have dominion over? The latter verb is used twenty-four times in the Old Testament, normally to denote human relationships: a master over a hired servant (Lev. 25:43); chief officers over laborers (I Kings 5:16); a king over his subjects (Ps. 72:8); the rule of one nation over another (Lev. 26:17). Several of these passages (Lev. 25:43; Ezek. 34:4) suggest that dominion is to be exercised with care and responsibility. Nothing destructive or exploitative is permissible. Presumably the same nuance is present in Genesis 1:28. The same verb applied to man in 1:28 is applied to the sun and moon in 1:16—"to rule," respectively, the day and the night—and certainly no concept of indiscriminate or manipulative action is included there. It is not incidental that in Genesis 1 both man and animals are vegetarians, each being given access to one element of vegetation (1:29–30).

It is remarkable that a large section of the creation story is given over to a separate and distinct account of the creation of woman. By implication Eve is referred to in the "them" and "female" of 1:26–29, with the specific mention found in 2:18–25. Such a separate narration of woman's creation is without parallel in ancient Near Eastern literature.

The long-overdue emphasis on women's rights has, in our time, stimulated many scholars to restudy the opening chapters of Genesis for essential clues on the identity of woman, and for principles determining male-female relationships. Such a study reveals, as examples, the following. First, both man and woman are made in the image of God. Sexual identification is irrelevant, certainly not a qualifying factor. Thus the command to rule and have dominion is directed to both male and female. Second, the origins of both man and woman are similar, that is, both owe their existence to raw material—rib and dirt. Neither is actively involved in the creation of the other. Third, woman is described as a "helper fit" for Adam. What Eve is (2:19), the animals are not (2:20). Interestingly, the writer has described Eve with a word which preponderantly is applied to God elsewhere in the Old Testament. The "helper" par excellence is God. The helper who is invoked for assistance normally is stronger than the one who stands in need. Fourth, on first seeing Eve, Adam says: "this at last is bone of my bones and flesh of my flesh" (v. 23a). Similar words appear in Genesis 29:14, Judges 9:2, and II Samuel 5:1 and 19:12–13, where a case could be made for the fact that the phrase *your bone and your flesh* is not simply an affirmation of kinship but of loyalty. Thus the phrase would be the equivalent of our commitment "in sickness and in health." That is, circumstances will not dictate or determine a relationship previously agreed to by both parties, and certainly adverse circumstances will not undermine it.

The follow-up to this also bears examination. A man is "to leave" his father and mother and "cleave" to his wife (2:24). The verb "to leave" may also be translated "forsake" with God as object (as in Jer. 1:16), that is, terminate a loyalty. The second Hebrew verb, "to cleave," may also describe one's covenantal commitment to God (as in Deut. 10:20; 11:22). The marriage relationship is then an oath, a covenant, never an arbitrary relationship of convenience.

A fifth observation we may make about male-female relationships is that quite clearly Genesis sets subordination of the woman to the man not in the context of creation, but in the context of the fall (see 3:16).

I have already suggested that according to Genesis 1 and 2 man is unique, set apart from everything else God created. He alone bears God's image and he alone is subduer. But the same passage of Scripture that underlines man's uniqueness (Gen. 1:26–31) also modifies that uniqueness (Gen. 2:15–17). Man is not autonomous, but lives under a divine law. There are boundaries.

Man is placed in a garden, "put" there (Gen. 2:8) by God Himself. The location of the garden is not easy to fix, but it is to be found "in the east" (Gen. 2:8). The presence of the Tigris and Euphrates (Gen. 2:14) suggests Mesopotamia. If that is the case, the first sin (Gen. 3) and the last sin of primeval history (Gen. 11) both had their setting in Mesopotamia. Additionally, Eden is distinctly placed outside the limits of Palestine, a further illustration of the international and universal emphases within Genesis 1–2.

In the garden man has a dual responsibility: to till the soil (Gen. 2:15), and to abstain from eating of "the tree of the knowledge of good and evil" (Gen. 2:17). The penalty for transgressing these commands is death, which in this instance I interpret to mean mortality. This seems to me to be the best explanation of why later in the narrative God prohibits further access by Adam and Eve to the tree of life (Gen. 3:22).

No small amount of debate has centered around the meaning of "the knowledge of good and evil." What does this oblique phrase imply? Can "evil" be inside the garden too? Does the "knowledge of good and evil" designate either omniscience or sexual awakening? Those are the two interpretations most commonly offered by the scholars. But there are problems with both, especially the latter one, in light of Genesis 3:22.

Perhaps we should limit ourselves to the observation that in Eden God placed limits on man's freedom. As we shall shortly see, Genesis 3–11 points out that the act of sin often consists of precisely this: overstepping divinely-imposed limits.

The First Verse of the Bible

At least two problems cluster around Genesis 1:1: how should the verse be translated and what is its relationship to 1:2 and to 1:3ff.? First, how should the verse be translated? Two possibilities exist. One is to treat verse 1 as a dependent, temporal clause. The translation then could be, "when God began to create the heaven and the earth . . ." or "in the beginning, when God made heaven and earth. . . ." In modern times this translation is as old as Moffatt's translation (1922), and is reflected in even more recent translations such as the Jewish Publication Society version, the New English Bible, and the translation of Genesis by E. A. Speiser in the Anchor Bible commentaries.

The more traditional translation renders Genesis 1:1 as an independent clause: "In the beginning God created the heavens and the earth." This is reflected in the KJV, RSV, NASB, NIV, and the Jerusalem Bible.

If the first possiblity is followed—that 1:1 is a dependent clause—then the additional facts are that verse 2 is a parenthetical comment, set off by hyphens from what precedes and follows; and the main clause appears in verse 3, "And God said. . . ." The result is an unusually long, rambling sentence, in itself not unheard of, but quite out of place in this chapter, laced as it is with a string of staccato sentences.

As far as the biblical evidence itself is concerned, the problem of translation originates with the first word of the Bible, *bᵉrē'shîṫ* (KJV, RSV, "in the beginning"; NEB, JPS, "when").

In biblical Hebrew, nouns are classified, in terms of syntax, as being either in the construct case or the absolute case. To illustrate, in the phrase *the word of the Lord*, "word" is in the construct state, for it is dependent upon the next word, "the Lord." It cannot stand by itself and make any sense. A word in the construct case does not take a definite article, although an article may be placed in a translation for sense and smoothness. Conversely, "Lord," in the absolute state, is independent and stands alone. The question is: is *bᵉrē'shîṫ* in the absolute or the construct state? If it is absolute then Genesis 1:1 is an independent clause. If it is construct then 1:1 is a dependent clause.

Although this is not a source of relief to the reader, it must be pointed out that grammatically *bᵉrē'shîṫ* can be defined, as it stands, as either in the absolute or the construct case. The preference should be given, however, to the absolute case. At least, this is how all the ancient versions understood it. Those opting for the temporal interpretation of the verse point out, in protest, that if this were the case, one would expect a reading *barē'shît*. The difference in Hebrew between *b^{e}rē'shît* and *barē'shît* is that the latter includes the definite article, "in *the* beginning" (italics mine). The objection is not fatal, however. The counterargument for the traditional translation is the observation that time designations in adverbial expressions do not need the article, seldom use the article, and occur in the absolute state.

Gerhard von Rad, in his celebrated commentary on Genesis, states that "syntactically perhaps both translations are possible, but not theologically."[3] Brevard Childs says, "to read verse 1 as a temporal clause does not take seriously enough the struggle which is evidenced in this chapter."[4] Keeping in mind the pagan emphasis on creation out of eternal and pre-existent matter (Tiamat's corpse, for example), and the emphasis on confrontation, struggle, and manipulation as antecedents to creation, one cannot miss the fact that the Scripture writer in this opening declaration is repudiating that very concept.

Further confirmation of this is found in the verb employed by the writer in 1:1 (Hebrew *bārā'*). It is used again in verses 21, 27 (three times), 2:3, 5:1–2 (three times), 6:7, and elsewhere in the Bible. Two things may be said about this verb. First, the subject of *bārā'* is never anybody but God. Thus such activity is exclusively divine activity. Second, whenever this verb is used the direct object that follows is always the product created, never the materials used as the means in creation. To quote von Rad again, "it is correct to say that the verb *bārā'* 'create' contains the idea both of complete effortlessness and *creatio ex nihilo*, since it is never connected with any statement of the material. The hidden grandeur of this statement is that God is Lord of the world."[5] Childs says, "the omission of

3. *Genesis, a Commentary*, Old Testament Library, rev. ed. (Philadelphia: Westminster, 1973), p. 48.

4. *Myth and Reality in the Old Testament*, Studies in biblical theology, no. 27 (London: SCM Press, 1962), p. 41.

5. *Genesis, a Commentary*, p. 49.

the accusative of material along with the simultaneous emphasis on the uniqueness of God's action could hardly be brought into a smooth harmony with the fact of a pre-existent chaos. World reality is a result of creation, not a reshaping of existing matter."[6]

All of this brings us to the second major problem, the relationship of 1:1 to what immediately follows, especially verse 2. At least three major views have been propounded. These are summarized in Table 1.

The first view has been called the "gap" or "restitution" theory.

Nonbiblical Creation Stories

Every ancient civilization produced its own corpus of mythical literature in which the general topic was either the origins and behavior of the gods (properly called myths) or the exploits of ancient heroes (properly called legends). In the myths the exclusive actors are the gods. In the legends the actors are primarily people, but the gods also assume major roles in the stories.

Of course not every piece of ancient literature has survived or has been excavated by an archaeological expedition. It is, for example, a moot question whether there was a strong emphasis on creation theology among the Canaanites. That question is spawned by the fact that no specific creation story has yet been discovered in the literature from Ras Shamra. Ras Shamra, located on the eastern shore of the Mediterranean, is the modern Arabic name for ancient Ugarit. From 1929 to the present, large amounts of Canaanite texts, to say nothing of texts in other languages, have been discovered there. The general subject of these texts is either economic or political concerns, but a good number of the texts also have had a religious dimension, either myths (Baal and Anat versus Mot or Yamm) or legends (Daniel and King Keret).

6. *Myth and Reality*, p. 41.

Table 1

Verse \ Theory	1	2	3
1	original creation	original creation	superscription, or summary statement of everything developed in the following verses. The phrase *the heavens and the earth* may be a biblical rhetorical device known as merismus, a means of expressing totality through the use of antonyms (e.g., "I've been through thick and thin" or "I've looked up and down for the paper"). The statement then affirms that all that is owes its existence to God.
2	gap, indeterminable in terms of length—"the earth *had become* without form and void" (italics mine; due to Satan's expulsion from heaven?)	condition of the earth at its inception: formless and void; dark; the Spirit of God moved over the waters	situation before creation, the preprimeval period. Almost cryptically, the phrases *without form and void, darkness, deep,* and *waters* stand alone and without explanation or commentary. F. Derek Kidner correctly captures the contrast: "the sombre terms of 2a throw into relief the mounting glory of the seven days."[7] To assume, however, that these terms are reflective of a chaos, outside of God's creation and antagonistic to His divine plan, finds no justification in the text.
3ff	God's second act of creation, or the divine act of re-creation	gradual order and symmetry were imposed on the formless cosmos, the movement being from imperfection to perfection, incompletion to completion	sequential narration of creation

7. *Genesis* (Chicago: Inter-Varsity, 1968), p. 44.

It does not need to be debated whether these myths and legends, both those produced inside and outside of Canaan, were known to God's people Israel. I have already argued that references in the Old Testament to Rahab, Leviathan, and the dragon presuppose an intelligent awareness on the part of the worshipers of Yahweh of the traditions surrounding these suprahuman beings. Furthermore, one section of the Gilgamesh Epic, a Mesopotamian deluge story, has been discovered at the Israelite city of Megiddo in an indubitable archaeological setting.

What is the contribution of these stories to our further knowledge and understanding of the Old Testament? In other words, why should we study them, apart from any information they may add to our awareness of ancient religions and cultures?

Obviously one does not need an extensive or even a superficial knowledge of mythology in order to understand the message of Genesis 1–2. And yet I am persuaded that the implications of the creation story of Genesis emerge most dramatically when it is compared with the creation literature of, for example, Mesopotamia (be that literature Sumerian, Assyrian, or Babylonian). For it is in the comparison of literature of identical general theme that the distinctiveness of biblical faith and message appears.

We need to remember that Genesis 1–2 was not produced by the nation called Israel, in the sense that these chapters are the mature reflections of some individual (or individuals) on the questions of origins. Rather, they are the result of divine revelation, truth that man could not know unless it was revealed to him from above.

A study of mythology helps the believer to see how ancient man tried to answer ultimate questions about life and reality when the light of revelation had not dawned upon him. Interestingly, the answers provided to those questions by ancient man are not all that different from the answers provided by modern but unredeemed man.

In the study that follows I limit myself to material from Mesopotamia, the *Enuma elish* (the first two words in the poem, which may be translated as "when on high . . ."), and pertinent sections of the Atrahasis Epic.

There are several reasons for limiting my study to compositions from that part of the world. In the first place, the stories I shall discuss are among the most remarkably preserved specimens of ancient literature. They are relatively free from problems of translation and from large gaps in the text. Often there are multiple copies, as later generations copied the story out for themselves.

Second, it is precisely these stories from Mesopotamia that are thought by many scholars to provide the source of the biblical material in Genesis 1–2 and 6–9. The scriptural stories, so goes this theory, are adaptations of pagan myth, with appropriate editorial revisions and deletions. I shall respond specifically to this in my discussion of the flood episode.

Third, we know that Abraham came from Ur of the Chaldeans. It is more than likely that the stories I am about to discuss were part of his upbringing. If nothing else, a knowledge of these particular myths and legends will help us to understand something of the world out of which God called Abraham. The shift was nothing short of radical. That shift was as much theological and philosophical as it was geographical.

The *Enuma Elish*

As I have said, there are two stories from Mesopotamia in which creation is a prominent theme. Since its publication in the nineteenth century the better–known one is the *Enuma elish*. Two critical questions, apart from interpretation, are open to debate in any discussion of the *Enuma elish*. One is the date of composition and the other is the degree to which the epic is typical of Mesopotamian (a period covering three thousand to four thousand years) belief about creation. Is it normative or is it exceptional? Concerning date, two opinions exist. Although no available copies of the epic are earlier than the first millennium B.C., cuneiformists such as E. A. Speiser and T. Jacobsen believe, on the basis of internal evidence, that the epic was first produced in the Old Babylonian period, that is, the early part of the second millennium B.C. (Speiser), or sometime during the middle of the latter half of the second millennium B.C. (Jacobsen). On the other hand, another cuneiformist, W. G. Lambert, is of the opinion that the story is not earlier than 1100 B.C. He also states that *Enuma elish* is not typical of Sumerian or Babylonian cosmology, but rather is a sectarian and aberrant account. Apparently the Assyrians in the first millennium did not find it aberrant, and so did not hesitate to borrow the epic from the Babylonians, making only such changes as necessary for the story to fit its new milieu (for example, the hero is no longer Marduk, but the Assyrian god Ashur).

What of the contents of the story? Before the creation of anything there were two divine beings, Apsu, the male divine personification of fresh waters, and Tiamat, the female divine personification of marine waters. Through their mingling (or mating) a second generation is produced, Lahmu and Lahamu, both perhaps to be associated with the silt produced by these waters. Then comes a third generation, Anshar and Kishar, the horizon. And from them comes Anu the god of heaven, and from him Ea (Enki).

The senior deity Apsu is, however, unable to sleep because these younger deities are making too much noise. Over the protests of his wife Tiamat, but at the prompting of Mummu his servant, Apsu plans to remedy the problem by killing these boisterous gods. But before he can implement his plan Ea places a magic spell on Apsu, and then kills him.

Aroused and indignant over her husband's unfortunate

end and spurred on by some sympathetic supporters, Tiamat vows to carry out Apsu's plan of theocide. She takes as her second husband Kingu.

At this point the major character of the story, Marduk the son of Ea, emerges. He is charged with the responsibility of leading and defending those earmarked for execution by Tiamat, a challenge he accepts with the qualification that, if successful, the gods will make him their head. After being suckled by goddesses he is ready for battle (theomachy).

Marduk swiftly eliminates Tiamat, and captures Kingu and the rest of the entourage. Marduk then splits Tiamat in two, making heaven from one half of her cadaver, and from the other half the earth. The imprisoned gods he subsequently charges with the responsibility of building him a permanent home, Babylon.

Further reflection and an outburst of protest by the employed gods leads Marduk to relieve the gods of this manual work by a second creation, the creation of man. He does this by having Kingu killed and using his blood to create man. The story concludes with a royal banquet at which Marduk formally receives permanent kingship, and finally the listing of his fifty names, each of which extols Marduk.

The Atrahasis Epic

The second account to be considered is the Atrahasis Epic, dating originally to no later than 1700 B.C., from which the earliest surviving copies come. Though dealing eventually and more extensively with the flood, I shall limit myself here to those parts dealing with creation. The epic begins with a description of the world as it was before man was created. The three supreme gods had partitioned among themselves the universe. Anu rules over heaven, Enlil over earth, and Enki over all bodies of water. The focus in the epic is on the earth, the overseeing of which is a mixed blessing, more to be endured than enjoyed. Specifically, Enlil is in charge of the gods whose primary job is to dig the Tigris and Euphrates rivers. But as is true in many modern labor disputes, the employees refuse to work and rebel against Enlil, to the point where even Enlil is alarmed by the violence of these mutineers, even though they are his own children. Observing how intransigent his children are, Enlil starts to weep and threatens to tender his resignation and retire to heaven to live with Anu.

The arbiter is Enki. He is sympathetic to the complaints of the hard-pressed, overworked gods. His suggestion is to create man and thus free the gods from their toil. At Enki's suggestion the gods kill one of their own, We-ila (the perpetrator of the rebellion?). From his blood and flesh, along with clay, man is created, through the help of the birth goddess Nintu(r)/Mami. In appreciation the gods confer on her the honorific title, Mistress of all the gods. In all, seven males and seven females are created.

The Epics compared

There are, to be sure, other creation accounts in cuneiform literature. I have outlined the two that best parallel the Old Testament. The following observations may be made.

First, the primary function of the *Enuma elish* is not to describe the creation of the world or the creation of man. At best, that is a subplot. Its primary purpose is theogonic, that is, to explain the origin of the gods, and especially Marduk. How did a relatively minor deity (Marduk) climb from virtual obscurity to become the chief god of Babylon? In that sense the story is an etiology of Babylon's patron god.

Second, the epic was composed with religious functions in mind. Evidence indicates that the *Enuma elish* was recited in Babylon annually at the Akitu festival, the beginning of the new year. Tiamat was associated with the forces of chaos, Marduk with the forces of order. As in the myth Marduk triumphed over Tiamat, so for the coming year the ritual recitation of the text, it was hoped, would go a long way in guaranteeing the victory of order over chaos in the unpredictable world of nature. The idea is that the right words in the right places at the right times implement the most desirable results. We ought to observe Lambert's cautious note, however, that too much has been made of the cultic reading of the epic, and that nothing in the content of the story unequivocally implies a specific cultic function.

Third, both stories are set within the framework of a polytheistic system. According to the *Enuma elish,* in the beginning there were two gods, Apsu and Tiamat. Marduk, the creator god, is a sixth-generation god. See Figure 2.

Figure 2

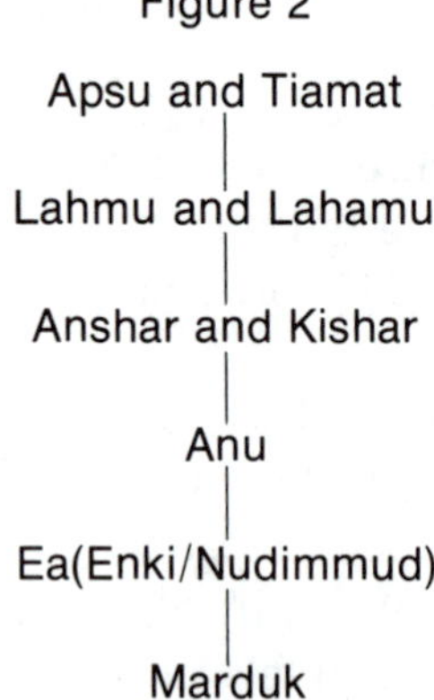

How the Babylonians portrayed their gods is interesting. Both of the epics serve as a window for us into these people's concept of gods: origin, character, and destiny. Creation is told in terms of procreation. In the beginning there were two, not one. Through the "mingling" of these partners a part of the created order appears. (In Sumerian there is one word for water and semen.) Anu, the numinous power in the sky and thus the source of rain, has as his spouse Ki, the earth. Through impregnating her Anu produces vegetation (and a host of demons and gods). Thus the gods are products of sex, and are subject by their nature to sexual needs. The pagan could see no future for his world and for his gods apart from a sexual relationship.

The needs, characters, and destinies of the gods are not markedly different from those of humans. Apsu is annoyed because he is deprived of sleep. He is also tossed betwixt and between listening to his spouse Tiamat, who urges against the plan for execution, and Mummu, his vizier and counselor, who urges its implementation. Faced with mutually exclusive advice Apsu opts for Mummu's directive over that of his consort. The god, unable to act independently, is swayed by his counselor.

Apsu, although divine, is subject to magic, and is successfully immobilized by Ea's spell and subsequently killed. If myth is the poetic expression of pagan religion, magic is its practical expression, and it can be called on in situations of god against man, man against god, or god against god. The reason for this is the concept in paganism of a realm transcending even the powers of the deities, a realm to which they may be subservient. The late Israeli scholar, Yehezkel Kaufmann, called this area the "meta-divine." In this sense no god is sovereign and without limitations, not even Apsu.

Gods can be killed and can attempt to kill simply out of impulsive anger or very selfishly motivated reasons. The attempt to murder may be motivated by revenge (e.g., Tiamat).

Fourth, in the *Enuma elish* heaven and earth are not spoken into existence by the creative word of one majestic god, but are formed from the corpse of a slain god, Tiamat. The created order is thus divine, more a "thou" than an "it."

Fifth, both in the *Enuma elish* and the Atrahasis Epic man is created to relieve the gods of the necessity of manual labor, a chore about which the latter soon complained and felt beneath their dignity. In the *Enuma elish* man is created from the blood of a rebellious god, Kingu; in the Atrahasis Epic, from the blood of We-ila (mixed with clay). In no sense can the creation of man be termed climactic, nor is there any unique dignity conferred on him. He is created as servant, not as king. Perhaps it is too speculative to see a Mesopotamian doctrine of original sin in the above, but may not the episodes serve as an etiology to account for man's proclivity to evil? He was made that way, and man is thus the product of an inscrutable determinism.

The Fall (3)

Chapter 3 of Genesis raises tantalizing questions in the mind of the reader, but for these questions an answer is not supplied. For example, no detailed account is given of the serpent at this point. Certainly he is not called Satan. If he is indeed a cosmic antagonist to God, once in the angelic host but now expelled, Genesis 3 does not pause to tell us that. To be sure, the New Testament unequivocally refers to "that ancient serpent, who is called the Devil and Satan, the deceiver of the whole world" (Rev. 12:9; 20:2).

The Serpent

About the etymological origin of the Hebrew word for "serpent" there is doubt. The Hebrew word is *nāḥāsh*. Is it to be related to the Hebrew *n^{e}ḥōshet*, "copper, bronze," suggestive perhaps of something luminous ("an angel of light")? Indeed, in the wilderness Moses made a bronze serpent (Num. 21:9), only to have it demolished centuries later by Hezekiah when the image itself became a fetish and an object of worship (II Kings 18:4). Or may the word for "serpent" be related to the Hebrew verb *nāḥash,* "to practice divination"?

It needs to be pointed out that information in the Old Testament about Satan, and for that fact the whole world of demonology, is at a precious premium. And for good reason. It is as unlikely that the Old Testament will address itself to this issue at any length as it is that it will address itself in depth to an explication of the Trinity. When one remembers that Israel was surrounded by nations whose religious ideas about forces supernatural included a belief not only in gods but in hosts of demons as well, then it is easy to see why the Old Testament rarely mentions demonology.

As a matter of fact, the word *satan* is employed in a number of ways (but never in Genesis 3). It refers, surprisingly, to the angel of the Lord, who may be an "adversary" (Num. 22:22, 32); to another person who also functions as an "adversary" (I Sam. 29:4; II Sam. 19:22; I Kings 5:4; 11:14, 23, 25; Ps. 109:6); to Satan, opponent of God and intruder into the angelic host (Job). In this last category the word occurs eighteen times (fourteen of them in Job 1–2). What is interesting is that in all but one of these eighteen occurrences (the exception is I Chron. 21:1), "satan" has attached to it the definite article, "the satan." This indicates "the satan" is a title, not a personal name. Satan is not who he is, but what he is. He does not merit a name, and in antiquity, not to have a name was to be reduced to virtual nonexistence.

All that the chapter says, then, about this serpent was that he or it was one of the wild creatures that the Lord God had made. That is, the serpent was a created being, neither eternal nor divine. Also, the serpent was more "subtle" than any other animal. This in itself is not pejorative. The same word is used in Proverbs eight times (12:16, 23; 13:16, 14:8, 15, 18; 22:3; 27:12), and translates there as "the prudent [man]," who is contrasted with the "fool" in the first four of these references, and with the "simple" or "naïve" in the remaining four. It is no wonder that Jesus said we are to be as wise as serpents (Matt. 10:16).

On the other hand, the word is translated as the "crafty" whom God loathes (Job 5:12; 15:5), the opposite in tone of the passages in Proverbs. Similarly the feminine counterpart to this word translates as "prudence" in Proverbs (1:4, for example) but, by contrast, in Exodus 21:14 it means "treachery."

It should also be pointed out that the Hebrew word for "subtle" that is used here—*ᶜārûm*—sounds very much like the word for "naked" in the last verse of chapter 2—*ᶜărûmîm*. No great theological conclusion should be gleaned from that. However, the use in consecutive verses of two words which are written alike and sound alike, but mean two different things, is an indication of the author's use of key words to tie together the narratives. In this case chapter 2 is linked nicely with chapter 3 of Genesis.

The Temptation

If Genesis 3 is unconcerned with amplification about the identity of the serpent, it is equally unconcerned with answering another question that intrigues the modern reader: why did the serpent tempt the woman and not the man, or both at the same time?

It seems fair to suppose that the narrator does not intend to have the reader suppose Adam and Eve are in two different places when the dialogue is in progress. The "you shall not eat" of verses 1 and 3, the "you die" of verse 3, and the "you shall not die" of verse 4 are all plural verbs. Adam and Eve are the subjects. Also, the KJV rendering of 3:6b is quite clear: "and [she] gave also to her husband *with her*" (italics mine). This is to be preferred over the RSV's "and she also gave *some* to her husband" (italics mine).

Answers to the question about why it was Eve who was

tempted are legion. At one extreme is the view that the temptation aimed initially at the woman is reflective of women as the weaker sex, the one more inclined to engage in fanciful speculation. Thus, the respected scholar von Rad hastens to generalize that it is women, more than men, who have "shown an inclination for obscure astrological cults" (biblically, is von Rad referring to the likes of Ezekiel 8:14?).[8] At the other end of the spectrum are feminists like Phyllis Trible, who suggest that in the story as presented Eve is the more challenging of the two. She is theologian-philosopher-aggressive rationalist-God's defense attorney all in one. If the serpent can make her capitulate, so will her silent, uninvolved mate.

The apostle Paul states that "Adam was not the one deceived; it was the woman who was deceived and became a sinner" (I Tim. 2:14, NIV). And in that emphasis Paul correctly lists the chronology of the trespass: first Eve, then Adam. She leads; he assents. But the apostle does not attempt to raise the issue of why Eve was tempted first.

The prohibition about not eating from the tree of the knowledge of good and evil was addressed to man (2:16–17). Nowhere are we clearly informed how Eve learned of the prohibition. Presumably she learned of it from her husband, for it is obvious she knows quite well about the prohibition once her dialogue with the serpent commences (3:2–3).

Possibly then the serpent chose Eve because she received the command from God only through an intermediary, that is, her husband. One who had received God's command directly would be less likely to acquiesce. (As an example of this in another context, who yielded to the temptation to idolatry and built the golden calf—Moses, God's spokesman, or the people and Aaron, who received God's word through Moses?)

8. *Genesis, a Commentary*, p. 90.

It is, perhaps, something of a surprise that the snake and Eve are able to converse at all without an interpreter. This observation is not made tongue-in-cheek. Granted there are parallels in ancient literature, such as the Egyptian Shipwrecked Sailor, who, alone surviving a wreck at sea and then being cast upon an island, finds himself engrossed in conversation with the island's lone occupant, a snake. But is the ability of the woman and the animal to converse simply mythological window-dressing? Might modern man's ability to communicate with his pets be a remnant of a situation that once indeed did prevail? Because of sin Adam's relationship to God, to Eve, and to the ground was ruptured. May we include also his relationship to the animal world? How interesting it is that animals are accountable for their actions and behavior (Gen. 9:5). The post-flood covenant is made with animals too (Gen. 9:9), not just mankind. Isaiah sees ahead to the messianic age in which the wolf shall become lamblike or the lamb shall become wolflike (are these metaphors for the nations of the world?).

If all of this is incidental, some elements in the text are quite clear and present themselves to the reader with forcefulness and precision. To use J. R. W. Stott's outline, there is here:[9]

1. a permission to eat of every tree in the garden
2. a prohibition not to eat from one tree
3. a penalty for disobedience

How does the serpent attempt to undercut all of this? What is the essential intent of the temptation, and how far is it paradigmatic for the rest of the Bible, whenever the actions of the evil one are delineated?

9. "The Subtlety of Satan," *CT* 9 (1965), p. 741.

The intent of the temptation is twofold. First the temptation raises questions in Eve's mind about the integrity of God. Her mental image of God is attacked. God is portrayed more as fiend than friend. The method here is to exaggerate the prohibition: you shall not eat *of any tree* of the garden. How cruel and vicious of God. The serpent implied, "You may observe them with the eye, work among them with the hands, but not partake of them with the mouth." In this context, we might change the title of J. B. Phillips's interesting book from *Your God Is Too Small* to *Your God Is Too Mean.* Stott's words here are perceptive: "God's provision for Adam and Eve was perfect. They lacked nothing in the Garden of Eden. God knew that their happiness lay in enjoying what he had permitted and abstaining from what he had prohibited. His permission and his prohibition both issued from his sheer goodness and love."[10] This concept, however, the serpent must distort.

Second, the temptation encourages Eve to declare autonomy, quite apart from any guidance God may have given, which is to be considered absurd and irrelevant. "You will not die . . . when you eat of it your eyes will be opened, and you will be like God, knowing good and evil" (vv. 4–5).

Von Rad has summarized correctly what these words mean: "the serpent holds out . . . the independence that enables a man to decide for himself what will help him or hinder him . . . God had provided what was good for man, and had given him complete security. But now man will go beyond this to decide for himself."[11] The temptation, then, is for man to overstep his limits. The difference between Adam and Eve in the garden and Jesus in the

10. *Ibid.*, p. 743.
11. *Genesis, a Commentary*, p. 89.

wilderness is that the former acquiesced. For Jesus, obedience to the Father's will was paramount.

What is next after Adam and Eve cross their Rubicon? Shame (v. 7), guilt (vv. 8–11), and looking for a scapegoat (vv. 12–13). Then God speaks, not in the dialogue of verses 8–13, but in a monologue: first to the serpent (vv. 14–15), then to the woman (v. 16), climactically and more extensively to the man (vv. 17–19).

It is, I believe, an incorrect interpretation which sees in these words of God to Adam and Eve primarily a punitive message: pain in pregnancy, disruption in the family, minimal returns for manual labor. The writer is not picturing God as a petulant deity, sulking, determined to teach these rascals a lesson which they will not soon forget. Like a surgeon who cuts with his scalpel only that he may heal, God initiates a means of redemption to reclaim the prodigals. His plan? To place at the respective point of highest self-fulfillment in the life of a woman and a man problems of suffering, misery, and frustration. These "sentences" are not the prescribed impositions of a volatile deity. Rather, they are gifts of love, strewn in the pathway of man, to bring him back to God. One may recall that the late C. S. Lewis, while reflecting on the ills and problems in the world, came to the conclusion that his reasons for not believing in God were actually much better reasons for believing in God, and thus was begun Lewis's pilgrimage into faith and his "surprise by joy."

Commentators, in trying to salvage at least a ray of light out of this chapter, have usually focused on either verse 21, "the LORD God made for them garments of skin, and clothed them" or verse 15, sometimes called the *prot(o)evangelium,* literally, "the first good news." It is tempting to see atonement in verse 21, or at least to contrast God's covering with the manmade type (v. 7). And if this is not atonement, at least it is preservation, a gauge of God's concern and compassion.

The First Word of Promise

Genesis 3:15 has traditionally been viewed by Christians as the first word of promise—in a prophetic sense—of deliverance from sin. The provision of a covering for Adam and Eve is immediate atonement. Verse 15 by contrast places atonement in an eschatological context. Its concern is the future, not the present.

Not all commentators, however, give their endorsement to the christological interpretation of Genesis 3:15. On the contrary, many biblical scholars eschew any messianic message in the verse. For example, Westermann attempts to crush under his own exegetical feet all who support the time-honored interpretation, beginning with Luther.[12] For him such an analysis fails to respect the original meaning of the verse, and reads into the text something totally alien from the author's intention. I find it impossible to follow Westermann and others like him for reasons I shall delineate.

The Hebrew verb for "bruise" or "crush" is *shûp.* Outside of Genesis 3:15 it is found only in Job 9:17, "he crushes me with a tempest," and Psalm 139:11, "let only darkness cover me." The serpent will crush the heel of the woman's seed (a temporary and healable injury), but the seed of the woman will crush the head of the serpent (a fatal injury).

The older versions of the Old Testament have interesting translations of this verb. The Septuagint translates both occurrences by a verb meaning "to watch, guard (lie in wait for?)." The Vulgate translates the actions of the woman's seed ("*she* will . . .") with a verb meaning "to crush," and the actions of the serpent and his seed with a verb meaning "to lie in wait for."

In the New Testament, this verse does not appear anywhere except in Paul's comment, "then the God of peace will soon crush Satan under your feet" (Rom. 16:20). Key

12. *Creation* (Philadelphia: Fortress, 1974), p. 100.

words and phrases are, however, highlighted elsewhere. In the Old Testament, clustering around David, are the promises of God that David is but the start of something new, something that God will perpetuate through David's "seed" (II Sam. 7:12; Ps. 89:4, 29, 36). Whoever tries to oppose David and/or his seed God will "crush" (Ps. 89:23, but not the same verb as in Gen. 3:15). In a prayer for the king (Ps. 72:9) the one petition asks that the king's enemies "might lick the dust." This is analogous to the king's enemies viewed as the "king's footstool" (Ps. 110:1). Jesus, the seed of David (Rom. 1:3), and "one born of a woman" (Gal. 4:4), "must reign until he has put all his enemies under his feet" (I Cor. 15:25).

There are at least three phenomena in Genesis 3:15 which have all too frequently been ignored by many commentators. And it is precisely the glossing over of these facts that has resulted in de-emphasizing the messianic import of the verse. First, this is the only place in the Old Testament that the Hebrew word for "seed" or "descendant" occurs with a third-person, feminine, pronominal suffix—"her seed." The uniqueness of the construction becomes even more apparent in the Septuagint with its reference to the woman's sperm—"her sperm(a)"! (Where is the man, the father?)

Almost 100 percent of the times in the Old Testament, descent is through the male. The son is the seed of his father rather than of his mother. Exceptions are rare, as in the case of Hagar's seed (Gen. 16:10), or Rebekah's seed (Gen. 24:60), but both references, by context, clearly point to individuals, not an individual. (Eve will refer later to Seth as her "other seed," Gen. 4:25.)

Second, the Septuagint translation of the "he" in "he shall bruise your head" is the masculine form of the pronoun, whose antecedent is the word *seed,* which is neuter in gender, not masculine. Of the more than one hundred uses of the pronoun "he" in the Greek translation of Genesis, this is the only instance where the "he" does not agree in gender with its antecedent where literal translation is involved. That is to say, the translators could easily have used "it" instead of "he," for Greek does have three genders, unlike Hebrew, which has only masculine and feminine. The Septuagint, then, emphasizes the "heness" of the woman's seed, not the seed's "it-ness" or "they-ness" in some collective sense.[13]

Third, the first part of the verse boldly proclaims that this future confrontation is not an accident of history, an event which catches God unawares. He is actually the producer of this warfare: "I will put enmity between you and the woman." It is an event as foreordained as the incarnation of Jesus. Interestingly, the passage anticipates not the crushing of the head of the serpent's seed, but the crushing of the head of the serpent himself: "he shall crush your head."

For these reasons I believe that any reflection on Genesis 3:15 that fails to underscore the messianic emphasis of the verse is guilty of a serious exegetical error. There is no doubt but that the ultimate significance failed to occur to Eve. Did she think that Cain was that promised seed (Gen. 4:1)? Then again, who would care to suggest that Abraham saw the long-range significance of the promise he was to receive in Genesis 12, a promise that would take at least four hundred years for its implementation, or two millennia for its full implementation?

Thus far I have suggested that in Genesis 3, at least in the last half, God's concern is redemption. This concern is manifest in the provision of a covering, the promise of a seed of the woman, and the pronouncement of words of judgment which are redemptive and not vindictive in purpose.

13. Walter C. Kaiser, Jr., *Toward an Old Testament Theology* (Grand Rapids: Zondervan, 1978), pp. 36–37.

Expulsion from the Garden

May another evidence of this emphasis on redemption be found in man's expulsion from the garden, to which re-entry is blocked by cherubim and flaming sword (3:22–24)? Parents are aware that if they have in their home a particularly delinquent child in the late teens or twenties, perhaps the healthiest thing they can do for that son or daughter, however difficult it may be, is to expel him from the home. Something as simple as a shift in geography can be in itself a motivation for change. Why should one want to abandon his sins if he can have both his sins and the presence of God?

So man is sent out of the garden. But to do what? The answer is provided in 2:23b: "to till the ground from which he was taken." We read in 2:5b that "there was no man to till the ground." Further on in the narrative we are informed that the Lord put man in the garden of Eden precisely to fill that void: "to till it and keep it" (2:15). We are, therefore, confronted by a man who is indeed expelled from God's presence, but who is not barred from continuing the vocation for which he was created. He is still tiller of the soil, but a soil that is now cursed.

Just prior to the announcement of expulsion Adam has named his wife "Eve," a word connected with the Hebrew word for "life" or "living" (3:20). But in the context almost every event narrated points to death. Relationships with God, spouse, and soil are all fractured. But here is life. Westermann comments, "despite man's disobedience and punishment, the blessing given with the act of creation remains intact . . . man who is now far from God is always man blessed by God."[14]

It is interesting that the characters in Genesis 3 are not mentioned again until the New Testament, first in the Lucan genealogy of Jesus (Luke 3:38), then in some of the

14. *Creation*, p. 104.

Pauline epistles (Rom. 5:12ff.; I Cor. 15:22). One might expect this incident to be a natural one from which the prophets might draw in order to drive home their point about the consequences of disobedience, as they did, for example, with the episode about Sodom and Gomorrah. But it was left untouched.

The verses from Paul are, of course, the linchpin in what is commonly called the doctrine of original sin. Both the Old and New Testaments affirm the doctrine (Gen. 6:5; I Kings 8:46; Ps. 51:5; Rom. 5:19; Eph. 2:3), but do not explain it in terms of theological origins. Lest we are prone to dismiss the idea as too medieval, too negative, or absurd, let us recall G. K. Chesterton's comment in chapter 2 of his biography of Saint Francis of Assisi: "there is a bias in man and Christianity was the discovery of how to correct the bias . . . it is profoundly true to say that the glad good news brought by the Gospel was the news of original sin."[15] Bad news may be good news!

Bibliography

Commentaries

Cassuto, U. *A Commentary on the Book of Genesis*. Translated by Israel Abrahams. 2 vols. Jerusalem: Magnes Press, the Hebrew University, 1961.

Kidner, F. D. *Genesis*. Chicago: Inter-Varsity, 1968.

Rad, G. von. *Genesis, a Commentary*. Revised edition. Philadelphia: Westminster, 1973.

Sarna, N. "Genesis, Book of." In *EncJud* 7: 386–398.

———. *Understanding Genesis: The Heritage of Biblical Israel*. New York: United Synagogue Commission on Jewish Education, 1966.

Schaeffer, F. *Genesis in Space and Time*. Downer's Grove, IL: Inter-Varsity, 1972.

Speiser, E. A. *Genesis*. New York: Doubleday, 1964.

15. *Saint Francis of Assisi* (New York: Doubleday, 1957), p. 28.

Vawter, B. *A Path Through Genesis*. New York: Sheed and Ward, 1956.

Westermann, C. *Genesis*. Neukirchen-Vluyn: Neukirchener Verlag des Erziehungsvereins, 1974–.

Genesis 1–3

Anderson, B. W. "A Stylistic Study of the Priestly Creation Story." In *Canon and Authority*. Edited by George W. Coats and Burke O. Long. Philadelphia: Fortress, 1977, pp. 148–162.

Bailey, J. "Initiation and the Primal Woman in Gilgamesh and Genesis 2–3." *JBL* 89 (1970): 137–150.

Barr, J. "The Image of God in the Book of Genesis—A Study of Terminology." *BJRL* 51 (1968): 11–26.

______. "Man and Nature—The Ecological Controversy and the Old Testament." *BJRL* 55 (1972): 9–32.

______. "Themes from the Old Testament for the Elucidation of the New Creation." *Encounter* 31 (1970): 25–30.

Blenkinsopp, J. "The Structure of P." *Bibl* 38 (1976): 275–292.

Brueggemann, W. "From Dust to Kingship." *ZAW* 84 (1972): 1–18.

______. "Of the Same Flesh and Bone (GN 2, 23a)." *CBQ* 32 (1970): 532–542.

Carlson, G. I. "The Two Creation Accounts in Schematic Contrast." *BT* (April 1973): 1192–1194.

Childs, B. *Myth and Reality in the Old Testament*. Studies in biblical theology, no. 27. London: SCM Press, 1962, pp. 31–50.

Clark, W. M. "A Legal Background to the Yahwist's Use of Good and Evil." *JBL* 88 (1969): 266–278.

Clines, D. J. A. "The Image of God in Man." *TB* 19 (1968): 53–103.

Davies, J. D. *Beginning Now: A Christian Exploration of the First Three Chapters of Genesis*. Philadelphia: Fortress, 1971.

Duncan, R. "Adam and the Ark." *Encounter* 37 (1976): 189–197.

Fisher, L. R. "A Ugaritic Ritual and Gen. 1:1–5." *Ugaritica* 6: 197–205.

Foh, S. T. "What Is the Woman's Desire?" *WTJ* 37 (1975): 376–383.

Fretheim, T. E. *Creation, Fall and Flood*. Minneapolis: Augsburg, 1969.

Gehrke, R. "The Biblical View of the Sexual Polarity." *CTM* 41 (1970): 195–205.

Gilbert, M. "One only flesh." *TDig* 26 (1978): 206–209.

Habel, N. C. *Literary Criticism of the Old Testament*. Philadelphia: Fortress, 1971, pp. 18–28.

Hanson, R. S. *The Serpent Was Wiser: A New Look at Genesis*. Minneapolis: Augsburg, 1972.

Hasel, G. F. "The Polemic Nature of the Genesis Cosmology." *EQ* 46 (1974): 81–102.

______. "Recent Translations of Gen. 1, 1." *BTrans* 22 (1971): 154–168.

______. "The Significance of the Cosmology in Genesis 1 in Relation to Ancient Near Eastern Parallels." *AUSS* 10 (1972): 1–20.

Higgins, J. M. "The Myth of Eve: The Temptress." *JAAR* (1976): 639–647.

Joines, K. R. "The Serpent in Genesis 3." *ZAW* 87 (1975): 1–11.

Kapelrud, A. "The Mythological Features in Genesis I and the Author's Intention." *VT* 24 (1974): 178–186.

Kikawada, I. M. "Two Notes on Eve." *JBL* 91 (1972): 33–37.

Lewis, C. "From Adam's Serpent to Abraham's Ram." *Jud* 22 (1973): 392–396.

Limburg, J. "What Does It Mean—Have Dominion Over the Earth?" *Dialog* 10 (1971): 221–226.

Martin, R. A. "The Earliest Messianic Interpretation of Genesis 3:15." *JBL* 84 (1965): 425–427.

Mendenhall, G. E. "The Shady Side of Wisdom: The Date and Purpose of Genesis 3." In *A Light unto My Path: Old Testament Studies in Honor of Jacob H. Myers*. Edited by Howard N. Bream et al. Gettysburg Theological Studies, no. 4. Philadelphia: Temple University Press, 1974, pp. 319–334.

Miller, J. M. "In the 'Image' and 'Likeness' of God." *JBL* 91 (1972): 289–304.

Mondin, B. "Original Sin in Contemporary Thought." *TDig* 26 (1978): 145–149.

Moran, W. L. "The Creation of Man in Atrahasis I, 192–248." *BASOR* 200 (1970): 48–56.

Naidoff, B. "A Man to Work the Soil: A New Interpretation of Genesis 2–3." *JSOT* 5 (1978): 2–14.

Neiman, D. "The Supercaelian Sea." *JNES* 29 (1969): 243–249.

Nielsen, E. "Creation and the Fall of Man: A Cross-Disciplinary Investigation." *HUCA* 43 (1972): 1–22.

Phipps, W. E. "Adam's Rib: Bone of Contention." *TToday* 33 (1976): 263–273.

Piper, J. "The Image of God: An Approach from Biblical and Systematic Theology." *SBT* 1 (1971): 15–32.

Rice, G. "Cosmological Ideas and Religious Truth in Genesis One." *JRelThot* 23 (1966): 15–30.

Ruger, H. P. "On Some Versions of Genesis 3:15, Ancient and Modern." *BTrans* 27 (1976): 105–110.

Ryken, L. *The Literature of the Bible.* Grand Rapids: Zondervan, 1974, pp. 33–42.

Sawyer, J. "The Meaning of 'In the Image of Elohim,' in Genesis I–XI." *JTS* 25 (1974): 418–426.

Scullion, J. J. "New Thinking on Creation and Sin in Genesis i–xi." *ABR* 22 (1974): 1–10.

Shanks, H. "How the Bible Begins." *Jud* 81 (1972): 51–58.

Shea, W. H. "Adam in Ancient Mesopotamian Traditions." *AUSS* 15 (1977): 27–41.

Snaith, N. H. "The Image of God." *ExpT* 86 (1974): 24.

Stott, J. R. W. "The Subtlety of Satan." *CT* 9 (1965): 740–744.

Thompson, P. "The Yahwist Creation Story." *VT* 21 (1971): 197–208.

Trible, P. "Ancient Priests and Modern Pollutors." *ANQ* 12 (1971): 74–79.

______. "Eve and Adam: Genesis 2–3 Reread." *ANQ* 14 (1972): 251–258.

Trudiger, L. P. " 'Not Yet Made,' 'Newly Made,' A Note on Gen. 2:5." *EQ* 47 (1975): 67–69.

Waltke, B. "The Creation Account in Genesis 1:1–3." *BS* 132 (1975): 25–36, 136–144, 216–228, 327–342.

Westermann, C. *Creation.* Philadelphia: Fortress, 1974.

______. *The Genesis Accounts of Creation.* Philadelphia: Fortress, 1964.

Wifall, W. "The Breath of His Nostrils." *CBQ* 36 (1974): 237–240.

______. "Genesis 3:15—a Protoevangelium?" *CBQ* 36 (1974): 361–365.

Williams, A. J. "The Relationship of Genesis 3:20 to the Serpent." *ZAW* 89 (1977): 357–374.

Wilson, S. G. "The Image of God." *ExpT* 85 (1974): 356–361.

Woudstra, M. H. "Recent Translations of Genesis 3:15." *CTJ* 6 (1971): 194–203.

2

The Sequence after Creation and the Fall

Genesis 4–11

Genesis 3 sets in motion a series of events, all of which have their root in the activities in Eden. In chapter 3, man sins and violates a vertical relationship, his communion with God. In chapters 4–11, man violates a horizontal relationship, his fellowship with his brother. The movement then is from cause to effect. What all these malignant activities have in common (Gen. 3–11) is a demonstration of man's desire to be like God. Having once overstepped his imposed limits, he subsequently surrenders his standards. The results are:

1. fratricide engendered by jealousy—4:8, Cain kills Abel
2. polygamy and retaliation—4:23–24, Lamech
3. titanic lust—6:1–4, sons of God and daughters of men
4. corruption and violence in the earth—6:5, 11–12
5. incest (?)—9:20–27, the curse on Canaan
6. a tower to the heavens—11:1–9, Babel

Undoubtedly the spread of sin is described in these chapters, as these six events testify. In the description of chapter 3, however, we observed a mixture of sin and grace, a divine word of both judgment and promise. I suggest that the same dual emphases continue throughout chapters 4–11. We shall see in operation both sin and judgment and grace and promise. Neither the sin of individuals (Cain, Lamech, and Ham) nor of groups (sons of God and daughters of men, the whole earth, and the builders of the tower) eclipses completely the mercy and sovereignty of God. Here too, where sin abounds grace much more abounds.

Fratricide (4:8)

Obviously there is no break between chapters 3 and 4 of Genesis. The narrative is to be read as a continuous whole. This continuity is emphasized by the repetition in both chapters of key vocabulary: for example, "and they knew they were naked" (3:7) and "Now Adam knew his wife" (4:1); "your desire shall be for your husband" (3:16) and "sin is couching at the door; its desire is for you" (4:7); "but he shall rule over you" (3:16) and "but you must master it" (4:7; the same Hebrew verb as "rule" in 3:16); "he drove out the man" (3:24) and "thou hast driven me this day away from the ground" (4:14); "and at the east of the garden of Eden he placed the cherubim" (3:24) and "then Cain . . . dwelt in the land of Nod, east of Eden" (4:16).

Interestingly, but not without later parallel, history's first recorded crime of man's inhumanity to man has its context in an act of worship. Two brothers, apparently spontaneously, bring to the Lord an offering. Cain offers part of his agricultural produce. Abel, the second-born, presents one of the firstlings of his flock. From here on the story is well known. God accepts the offering of Abel, but rejects that of Cain. Unable to accept graciously God's decision on the matter, Cain gives way to sulking and anger, and eventually kills his own brother.

The intriguing question is why the Lord accepted the

offering of Abel, but refused that of Cain. Was it because Abel's involved a blood sacrifice? But the Old Testament allows for nonblood sacrifices when such sacrifices are not primarily expiatory (Lev. 2, and even Lev. 5:11ff. allows for the use of fine flour with the sin offering in certain circumstances). Even the Hebrew word for Cain's "offering" is the same as for the "cereal offering" of Leviticus 2.

Did Abel present his best, but Cain only what was conveniently available? Is the difference one of attitude in that Abel offered his by faith (Heb. 11:4)? Was Cain's offering rejected because it was not matched by an inner righteousness (I John 3:12; Jude 11)? Perhaps this idea is hinted at in God's word to Cain, "if you do well, will you not be accepted?" (Gen. 4:7). Several times, especially in prophetic literature, we are informed that God's reason for rejecting a sacrifice or offering was usually that religious ritual became a substitute for obedience and holy living.

Can we move backward from the prophets to the incident in Genesis 4 and assume the same inconsistency in the life of Cain that the prophets saw in the lives of their contemporaries? In light of God's word to Cain in Genesis 4:7 I am inclined to say yes, but cannot be dogmatic. May the Bible not be as wise in its reservations as it is in its revelations?

Cain has the opportunity to talk with God after his sin. The dialogue swiftly degenerates into sarcasm on Cain's part. He answers God's question—"Where is Abel your brother?"—with a question of his own—"am I my brother's keeper?" (Gen. 4:9).

The answer to Cain's question is an emphatic no. God never meant for Cain, or anybody, to be his brother's keeper. "To keep" means "to control, to regulate and rule"—"the Lord God took the man and put him in the garden to . . . keep it" (Gen. 2:15). Zoos, bees, and prisons have keepers. Here activities must be regulated and supervised. Not without reason is God consistently called in

Scripture "Israel's keeper." That is His role for He is their Lord. Cain was indeed called to love and respect his brother, but never was he called to keep his brother.

As with Adam and Eve, the punishment for Cain is banishment or exile from the presence of the Lord (4:16). But again, as with Adam and Eve, there is a manifestation of mercy just prior to the manifestation of judgment. Before Adam and Eve are expelled (3:22–24), they are provided clothing (3:21). Before Cain is expelled (4:16), God places a mark on his forehead to spare him from becoming a victim of someone's vengeance (4:15). As David J. A. Clines has said, "God's grace . . . is not only revealed in and after the judgement, but even *before* the execution of judgement."[1]

Polygamy and Retaliation (4:23–24)

For the first but not the last time, God's pattern of one man for one woman and one woman for one man breaks down. No particular verse in the Old Testament prohibits polygamy, but the crucial point is that there is hardly a polygamist whose life is not extremely complicated and bruised. Witness Abraham with Hagar and Sarah. Witness Jacob with Leah and Rachel, or the fiascos in the lives of David and Solomon.

Added to Lamech's violation of the marriage pattern is his unchecked penchant for revenge and violence. He glories in macabre statistics (4:23–24).

It is something of a paradox that the descendants of Cain emerge as the heralds of culture and industry (4:21–22), specifically, farming and herding (Jabal), music (Jubal), and metallurgy (Tubal-cain). They are all sons of Lamech.

1. *The Theme of the Pentateuch*, Journal for the study of the Old Testament: Supplement series (Sheffield: Department of Biblical Studies, University of Sheffield, 1978), p. 63.

Yet none of these novelties, however noble they may be, restrains the diabolical tendencies of man. The announcement of this cultural history comes between the account of Lamech's polygamy and his spiteful song of revenge. Secular culture, then, is advanced by the line of Cain, but it is through the line of Seth (4:25—5:32) that God's plan of redemption will move.

Nothing is said about the life span of the descendants of Cain (4:17–22), but for each of the descendants of Seth (5:1–32) a life span is given, and one that is spectacularly long in each instance. It is not wide of the mark, I believe, to interpret both the notation of life span and the longevity of those life spans as a reflection of God's unique blessing on the seed of Seth, as opposed to the seed of Cain. To be sure, none of them escaped death, with the exception of Enoch (5:24), for the possibility of "living forever" ceased with the announcement of Genesis 3:22. Still, the sons of Seth were "being fruitful, multiplying, and filling the earth." Not only does the notice about life span distinguish the line of Seth from that of Cain, but so does the constant inclusion of the refrain "and he had other sons and daughters" for the representative Sethites.

The tenth individual in the Sethite genealogy is Noah. His name is connected here with the verb "bring relief or comfort" (5:29). This word is the same Hebrew verb, but in a different form, that is used in Genesis 6:6–7 to express God's regret and repentance over conditions in His earth. Father Lamech predicts—and the source of his foreknowledge is not revealed—that his son Noah "shall bring relief from our work and from the toil of our hands because of the ground which the LORD hath cursed" (5:29, KJV).

The language in this verse is reminiscent of language in Genesis 3:17, ". . . cursed is the ground [in 5:29, too] because of you; in toil [the same word as the "toil" of 5:29] you shall eat of it." The curse placed in Adam's time is now to be lifted, or significantly diminished, in the tenth generation. Genesis 3:17 gives way to Genesis 5:29. A new day is dawning.

The "Sons of God" and the "Daughters of Men" (6:1–4)

Few passages in Scripture have appeared so enigmatic to the interpreter as Genesis 6:1–4. The thorniest problem is the identification of the "sons of God" and "daughters of men." Again we note that the Scriptures introduce these two groups without fanfare or explanation. No commentary on their origin or specific identification is offered.

Three possibilities for the identification of the villains and victims in the story enjoy popularity among the commentators. In the first place a number of both modern and ancient exegetes see in the "sons of God" a reference to the descendants of Seth, and in the "daughters of men" a reference to the descendants of Cain. The particular sin is an unfortunate mingling in marriage between the godly Sethite line and the ungodly Cainite line.

The immediate advantage to this explanation is that it takes cognizance of the material in the immediately preceding chapters, especially chapters 4 and 5, in which the line of Cain is contrasted with the line of Seth. Furthermore, there are some explicit parallels in the activities of Sethites and Cainites and the two groups mentioned in Genesis 6:1–4. For example, the sudden mention of "daughters of men" (6:2) possibly finds its antecedent in the daughters of the various Sethites, the only other reference so far in Scripture to daughters (5:4, 7, 10, 13, 16, 19, 22, 26, 30). Another example of parallelism might be found in the sons of God "taking wives" for themselves (6:2) and the Cainite Lamech who "took two wives" (4:19).

If one pursues these parallels, however, it will be quickly observed that they equate the sons of God with the Cainites (the Cainite Lamech took wives for himself, as did the sons of God for themselves) and the daughters of men with the Sethites, that is, the reverse of a time-honored explanation.[2]

The objection has been made that this theory is untenable, for it must posit one meaning for "man" in 6:1 (mankind in general), but a restricted meaning for "man" in 6:2 (either Sethites or Cainites). In response I would say that it is possible for one word to assume several distinctive meanings within one chapter. I cite as an example II Samuel 7—the institution of the Davidic covenant—in which "house" has four different nuances. "House" designates a temple in verses 5, 6, 7, 13; a palace in verses 1 and 2; a dynasty in verses 11, 16, 19, 25, 26, 27, 29; and reputation or status in verse 18.

A second interpretation of the narrative suggests that the sons of God are ancient dynastic rulers and the daughters of men are their royal harems, as inviting to the rulers as was the forbidden fruit to Eve (see the articles by M. Kline, cited in the bibliography). This interpretation moves the identification from Cainites and Sethites to something more ambiguous, a group of regal individuals whose existence has not yet been mentioned in the opening chapters of Scripture. Presumably if the sons of God are heads of state the narrative would then refer to a limited number of individuals. And yet God's penalty is aimed at mankind. We would then be faced with the imbalance between sin in limited places—but in high places—and judgment that will reach almost cosmic proportions. This is not impossible, however. Witness the 70,000 who died in Israel because of the sin of their monarch David at the census taking (II Sam. 24:15, 17).

A third interpretation suggests that the sons of God are angels. The expression *sons of God* is indeed a name for the angelic host in Job 1:6, 2:1, 38:7, and Psalms 29:1 and

2. L. Eslinger, "A Contextual Identification of the *bene ha'elohim* and *benoth ha'adam* in Genesis 6:1–4," *JSOT* 13 (1979): 65–73.

89:6. The sin then is cohabitation between supernatural and natural beings. Some support for this may be found in Jude 6 and 7 (perhaps also I Peter 3:19–20 and II Peter 2:4). If the function of verse 7 is to compare the immorality and unnatural lust of Sodom and Gomorrah with similar behavior of the angels in verse 6, then much credence is lent to this interpretation. On the other hand, if the purpose of verses 6 and 7 is to provide two illustrations of divine judgment on different forms of sin at the angelic level and the human level, then Jude 6 and 7 have no bearing on Genesis 6:1–4.

Moreover, the reference in Genesis does not appear to be to rape or the indulgence of unbridled lust, but to marriage—"and they took to wife such of them as they chose." The sin is not sexual violation, but the establishment of an illicit marital relationship in which the two partners cannot possibly become one flesh. And Jesus reminds us that angels do not marry (Mark 12:25).

It is suggested sometimes that the most serious flaw in this explanation is that the perpetrators of the crime are nonhuman beings, but the recipients of judgment are human beings—"my spirit shall not abide in man . . . he is flesh, but his days shall be a hundred and twenty years." While I do not accept the explanation that the passage refers to angels or divine beings, neither do I find the preceding criticism all that forceful. For if one is prepared to decipher an inconsistency and non sequitur here, what will he do with the next few verses in Genesis 6: "the wickedness of man was great . . . the Lord was sorry he had made man . . . I will blot out man . . . man and beast and creeping things and birds of the air" (6:5–7)? The criminal is man. The victims are both man and animals.

Can we detect here a voice of grace, however faint it may be? I suggest we can hear that voice, and the clue is to be found in 6:3, "but his days shall be a hundred and twenty years." Once again the interpretation of this part of verse 3 is anything but unanimous. There are two possibilities. The 120 years refer either to the diminished life span God will now impose on mankind, or to a period of grace (preceding the flood) in which God's hand of judgment will be restrained.

Either way, it appears to me that the notation suggests grace. If the reference is to the former—a shorter life span—then it is obvious that this enforcement is not immediate but long-range. Noah, introduced before this episode, lives 950 years. Abraham's father, Terah, lives for 205 years, and Abraham himself lives for 175 years. In the Book of Genesis, only Joseph fails to surpass the 120-year maximum. God had said to Adam, if you eat the forbidden fruit, you will die. He ate, but he did not die immediately.

On the other hand, if the reference is to a period of respite in which God voluntarily restrains Himself—an interpretation I find quite natural—then again grace is easy to discern. A parallel to that exercise of self-restraint on the part of the Deity would be Jonah's message to Nineveh—"Yet forty days, and Nineveh shall be overthrown!" (Jonah 3:4). The best parallel is in the New Testament (II Thess. 2). Before the coming of Jesus Christ will be the coming of "the man of lawlessness." The withdrawal of the restraint on this "son of perdition" will release him from his confinement. Until now, however, he is being held in check. Thus the opportunity to receive and offer grace is available.

The Flood (6:5, 11–12)

Paramount in this whole section is the description of the flood. Two well-preserved extrabiblical accounts of an ancient flood are from Mesopotamia: the Gilgamesh Epic and the Atrahasis Epic.

The Gilgamesh Epic

Named after Gilgamesh, king of Uruk (Erech in Gen. 10:10) around 2600 B.C., this epic dates to approximately 1600 B.C., according to Thorkild Jacobsen. As king Gilgamesh is tyrannical and brutal, causing deep resentments among his subjects. To topple him the people solicit one of their gods to create an antagonist. The one formed is named Enkidu. He is "humanized" or "civilized" only after a week-long spirited orgy with a prostitute. A fight follows between Enkidu and Gilgamesh. It produces neither a victor nor a victim. Rather the combatants become colleagues, battling all sorts of celestial, maleficent monsters. In the process the mortal Gilgamesh is proposed to by none other than the stunning goddess Ishtar, but he spurns her, primarily because of her poor record in marital fidelity!

Because of effrontery to Ishtar, Enkidu dies, setting off a pathological fear of death in Gilgamesh's own life. His mind is at least clear enough to recall that one of his ancestors—Utnapishtim—had bypassed death and gained immortality. If Gilgamesh can find Utnapishtim maybe he can learn the secret and save his own life. A tortuous trip through the various parts of the underworld follows. At last he meets Utnapishtim. And this is the story Utnapishtim tells Gilgamesh.

One day the god Ea told Utnapishtim that Enlil was preparing to destroy humanity with a flood. Utnapishtim, if he is wise, should build a boat, on board which he is to take members of his family, cattle, some valuables, and professional seamen. The storm begins, and continues for seven days and nights, only to have Utnapishtim's boat snag on a mountaintop. After the abating of the waters, he leaves his boat and worships his gods. Subsequently it comes to Enlil's attention that two mortals have escaped drowning. To finish his job of ridding the earth of humanity, he confers immortality on Utnapishtim and his wife.

But Utnapishtim's experience is unique, and thus produces further chagrin for Gilgamesh. After additional frustrating experiences, Gilgamesh returns to his home of Uruk, resigned to reality. Denied personal immortality, he will at least live on in the minds of his people through impressive Uruk he has built. Immortality thus is the work of his hands.

The Atrahasis Epic

I have already traced the Atrahasis Epic through the account of creation. After their creation, humans multiply so swiftly and make so much noise that Enlil has insomnia. He plans to reduce the population with a plague. Suddenly Atrahasis is introduced, who, with the guidance of his god Enki, manages to have the plague averted.

The problem is rectified, but after twelve hundred years the land is "bellowing like a bull." Enlil's plan this time is a drought, and once more Atrahasis has drought brought to a speedy end by placating the offended deity. Then the cycle starts a third time, and the punishment this time is a renewal of the drought.

Exasperated that this does not work either, Enlil orders a flood. What follows is much like the Gilgamesh Epic, except the hero is Atrahasis, not Gilgamesh. On Enki's advice Atrahasis builds a boat to weather the storm, destined to last seven days and nights. So devastating was the storm and so thorough was the annihilation of humanity that even the gods had serious questions about the sagacity of Enlil's plan.

After disembarking, Atrahasis, like Utnapishtim, offers a sacrifice to the gods for his preservation, and none too soon, for they have been without food for the duration of the flood. Their source of food, the food sacrifices of mortals, has been dissipated.

Permanent countermeasures are then invoked which will put a ceiling on the ever-increasing world population. The plan is birth control: the creation of some permanently barren women, the creation of a demon whose function is to "snatch the baby away from the lap of her who bore it," and the creation of several categories of priestesses for whom childbearing is prohibited.

The Epics Compared

If one compares the Gilgamesh Epic and the Atrahasis Epic with Genesis 6–9 the similarities in details surrounding the catastrophic flood are undeniable. Does this mean, however, that the Hebrews borrowed, and then edited, the story from Mesopotamian literature, with only the names changed to protect the innocent? May not stories be shared by the Bible and surrounding cultures because they are both based on a historical event? Both Scripture and Mesopotamian literature mention a flood because there was a flood.

If that is the case it is as interesting, if not more so, to contrast as it is to compare how two different traditions handled the same material, the same event. Such a contrast uncovers crucial differences in mentality and world outlook. One of the benefits to the believer who reads mythology is an understanding of how ancient man answered ultimate questions about life without the light of revelation.

For example, the Gilgamesh Epic is virtually silent about a motive for the flood. The only pertinent line is "that city was ancient, [as were] the gods within it/When their heart led the great gods to produce the flood." After the flood, Ea remonstrates with Enlil: "thou wisest of gods, thou hero, How couldst thou, unreasoning, bring on the deluge? On the sinner impose his sin, on the transgressor impose his transgression!" (11:179–181). In the Atrahasis Epic it is the noise of the multitudes that triggers Enlil's anger and vengeance. And most cuneiformists are convinced that the words used for noise indicate simply that, rather than moral turbulence.

Enlil, then, acts out of anger, selfishness, and caprice. His judgment is totally punitive; for the masses this judgment certainly is not therapeutic. But can one of the pantheon impose a catastrophe on humanity because of the sins of the latter? After all, the gods themselves fall short of being puritans.

Also, it is equally difficult to discern a reason that one mortal is saved. In the Gilgamesh Epic it is Ea who warns Utnapishtim of Enlil's scheme, and in the other it is the divine Enki who informs Atrahasis. Again the closest the literature comes to a saving of one who is righteous is in the Sumerian account of the deluge. There, the one saved from drowning is Ziusudra, a pious, reverent king, although even here the nexus between his character and his salvation is not underscored.

Further, the dimensions of the ship built by the heroes are strange: "equal shall be her width and her length," that is, cubic, as later lines in the epic confirm. Along with his family and animals, the hero takes aboard professional seamen. It is human skill and ingenuity that will keep this ship afloat. In addition, Utnapishtim takes aboard copious amounts of silver and gold, a little nest egg with which to start over if indeed he ever comes out of this nightmare alive.

Finally, both pagan stories lack a clear didactic function. What are they trying to say, and what is the significance of their theme? Does either story intricately involve the reader? The concern of the Gilgamesh Epic is more with Gilgamesh than it is with Utnapishtim, and more with the former's epic wanderings than the latter's escape from drowning. One might conceivably extract from the story this principle: be satisfied with what you have and where you are, and don't try to overstep your limits (Genesis 3?). Precious little, however, in the dialogue of the text firmly establishes this.

The ending of the Atrahasis Epic is even more dour. Having failed three times, Enlil delivers an ultimatum: close the wombs, let any births be stillbirths, impose celibacy. This is obviously not a note designed to engender respect in mortals for their gods. Fear and suspicion, perhaps, but not love and trust.

The Epics Contrasted with the Genesis Account

Something of the uniqueness of the biblical account can be demonstrated by pursuing the above-mentioned four points of contrast into the deluge story in Genesis.

Genesis affirms that the impetus for the flood comes from the sin of humanity. Enough of this has been indicated in the narratives of chapters 3–5, and the first four verses of chapter 6. To this will be added: "the wickedness of man was great in the earth, . . . every imagination of the thoughts of his heart was only evil continually" (6:5); "Now the earth was corrupt . . . filled with violence" (6:11); "all flesh had corrupted their way upon the earth" (6:12).

Although it cannot be reflected in English translation, one who reads the Hebrew text will observe that the "corrupt" of verses 11 and 12 (two times) is built from the same Hebrew root as the "I will destroy" of verse 13b. Is this one way God destroys? Rather than interrupt and impede, He allows the evil started by man to run to its inevitable conclusion. "The iniquity of the Amorites is not yet complete" (Gen. 15:16). Similarly, in Romans 2, Paul, in speaking of the expression of God's wrath against sin, employs the phrase "God gave them up" (2:24, 26, 28), surely more passive than active, more gentle than raging.

Yet, lest one draw the conclusion that God is simply an

unmoved spectator to this morass, observe that God Himself suffers emotional pain—God was "grieved" (6:6). How interesting that the Hebrew word here is from the same root as the word "pain" which Eve will experience in childbirth (3:16), and which man will confront in his working and attempting to make productive the soil (3:17). Man's pain has become God's pain!

Noah is not spared on the basis of caprice or favoritism. On the contrary, he "was a righteous man, and blameless . . . Noah walked with God" (6:9; also 7:1). Character, either way, does determine destiny.

To be more precise, Noah is told to build not a boat, but an ark (6:14), more a chest than a ship. Its dimensions (approximately 450′ x 75′ x 45′), far from being nonsensical, are quite worthy of a seagoing vessel. No sailors accompany Noah aboard, nor is there reference to any type of navigational equipment (unless one counts the window in the ceiling for following the stars, or the birds as the mariner's homing pigeons). Salvation will be from God alone. No material possessions are to be packed away either. Noah is no more entitled to this than was Achan.

Far from being a hair-raising but irrelevant story sung around campfires in generations to come, the deluge story relates profoundly to successive generations. First of all there is a retraction by God of the curse placed on the ground (8:21; cf. 3:17), evidenced by the story of Noah's vineyard, in itself a verification of the abrogation of the curse (9:20ff.). Connecting 8:21 with 6:5, Gerhard von Rad writes, ". . . v. 21 is one of the most remarkable theological statements in the Old Testament: it shows the pointed and concentrated way in which the Yahwist can express himself at decisive points. The same condition which in the prologue [viz., 6:5] is the basis for God's judgment in the epilogue reveals God's grace and providence. The contrast between God's punishing anger and his supporting grace

. . . is here presented . . . as an adjustment by God towards man's sinfulness."[3]

This promise is then followed by the institution of a covenant with Noah in chapter 9. What God had once said to Adam (1:28) He now says to Noah (9:1). Thus, there is a second start, a second chance for humanity, albeit with qualifications (9:2–6).

What this covenant does is to establish not uniqueness but precedence. Noah is the first in a series with whom God is making this commitment. What is unrepeatable is another flood (9:11). This covenant is God's responsibility at the point of maintenance. Note that the rainbow in the sky is for God's benefit (9:12–17). God Almighty writes Himself a memo! Such is the extension of this story into the lives of its readers.

Two Flood Stories?

I have had previous occasion to draw attention to the documentary hypothesis or source criticism in dealing with the creation account. Genesis 6–9 is an example thought to substantiate once and for all the validity of this approach. A surface reading of Genesis 6–9, say the source critics, demonstrates palpably that these four chapters are not a homogeneous work. Several observations are culled to buttress this idea.

The first category includes blatant inconsistencies. One of these is the number of animals to go aboard. According to 6:19–20 and 7:9, 15, the number is set at two of every kind, male and female. But 7:2 says that Noah is to take with him "seven pairs" of clean animals, one pair of unclean animals, the male and his mate ("man" and "woman" are the words used here, as in 2:23).

A second example is the mention of conflicting dura-

3. *Genesis, a Commentary,* Old Testament Library, rev. ed. (Philadelphia: Westminster, 1973), p. 123.

tions for the flood. One section established the length as forty days and nights (7:4, 12, 17; 8:6). Another tradition has the flood lasting 150 days (7:24).

Another example is the nature of the flood. Was it rain from above (7:4, 12), or was it a bursting open of the subterranean waters (7:11)?

The second category that the source critics cite is a distinctive shift in the use of the divine name. They list these examples:

(a) 6:5—"the Lord saw"; also 6:6–8
(b) 6:9—"Noah walked with God"; also 6:11, 12, 13, 22
(a) 7:1—"the Lord said to Noah"; also 7:5
(b) 7:9—"as God had commanded"; also 7:16a
(a) 7:16b—"the Lord shut him in"
(b) 8:1—"but God remembered Noah . . . God made a wind"; also 8:15
(a) 8:20—"Noah built an altar to the Lord"; also 8:21
(b) 9:1—"God blessed Noah"; also 9:6, 8, 12, 16, 17

A third category is that the account points to two different conclusions: one, Noah's offering, God's inhaling of its pleasant odor, and the lifting of the curse on the ground (8:20–22); two, God's blessings to Noah and the institution of the Noahic covenant (9:1–18).

The fourth category is that the account features two distinctive styles and modes of expression. For instance, God is at one time pictured very much in human terms—He repents, is grieved, inhales a sacrificial odor, has second thoughts; at another point in the story He is pictured as the completely other-worldly, all-powerful supernatural force standing over the world.

The conclusion drawn from all this is that there were originally two flood stories, one traceable to a writer or writers in approximately the tenth or early ninth centuries B.C. (the Yahwist), the other produced about four hundred years later (the Priestly account, anytime between 550–450 B.C.). Subsequently the two stories were spliced by an editor or editors. In the text as we have it, Genesis 6–9 can be divided this way:

6:5–8	J	7:12	J	8:3b–5	P
6:9–22	P	7:13–16a	P	8:6–12	J
7:1–5	J	7:16b–17	J	8:13a	P
7:6	P	7:18–21	P	8:13b	J
7:7–8	J	7:22–23	J	8:14–19	P
7:9	P	7:24–8:2a	P	8:20–22	J
7:10	J	8:2b–8:3a	J	9:1–17	P
7:11	P				

Not a few voices of protest have been raised against this division of the flood story, and for that fact the entire Pentateuch, into originally composite sources. The works of modern scholars such as Umberto Cassuto, Cyrus H. Gordon, and Kenneth A. Kitchen take the theory to task on several grounds. For Cassuto such fragmentation of the pericope fails to do justice to the literary structure of the text. Heterogeneity raises more problems than it solves. For Gordon and Kitchen source division is suspect on the grounds that similar phenomena exist in the ancient literature of the Mediterannean world, but to draw from this a multiple-source theory is ludicrous.

We may make the following observations, particularly concerning the flood section of Genesis.

First, some of the supposedly telltale evidences of confluence in the text may not be all that evident. Are "two pair" and "seven" mutually exclusive? Why cannot the "two" of 6:19–20 and 7:9, 15 be the standard number of animals (a male and female for breeding—even the unclean animals are preserved!) taken into the ark? "Seven" would apply only to sacrificial animals, that is, animals in a category by themselves. Is this solution any less probable than applying "two" to J and "seven" to P? Again, does the text indicate an inconsistency in the duration of the flood, 40 versus 150 days? Was not the actual downpour 40 days and nights, followed by five months (150 days) of rising water until the water level peaked?

Second, the Scandinavian scholar, Eduard Nielsen, has called into question, on the basis of the principles of oral tradition, the splitting of the flood account. To illustrate, Nielson points out that 7:9 is, on this theory, from P. The reason? The name "God" occurs in this verse, a sure sign of P: "two and two . . . went into the ark with Noah, as God had commanded." But just a few verses later (7:15, ascribed by all critics also to P) exactly the same thing is said, "They went into the ark with Noah, two and two. . . ." Duplication in the same document! Before one is ready to explain verse 15 as an editorial insertion let him be reminded of Nielsen's rejoinder: "it is reassuring and sometimes necessary to have a Redactor up one's sleeve."[4]

Third, on the basis of an examination of the grammatical structure of the text, Francis Andersen is able to isolate and identify units which have been scissored by the source critics.[5] Thus, grammatically, 7:6–17 is a unit with a distinct and clearly identifiable structure; yet the documentary hypothesis will have this section seesaw from P to J and back at least seven times. To quote Andersen, "if the documentary hypothesis is valid, some editor has put together scraps of parallel versions of the same story with scissors and paste, and yet has achieved a result which, from the point of view of discourse grammar, looks as if it has been made out of whole cloth."[6]

Fourth, writers such as B. W. Anderson and G. J. Wenham are convinced that in treating the text of the flood in

4. *Oral Tradition* (Chicago: Alec R. Allenson, 1954), p. 98.
5. *The Sentence in Biblical Hebrew* (The Hague: Mouton, 1974), pp. 124–126.
6. *Ibid.*, p. 40.

Figure 3*

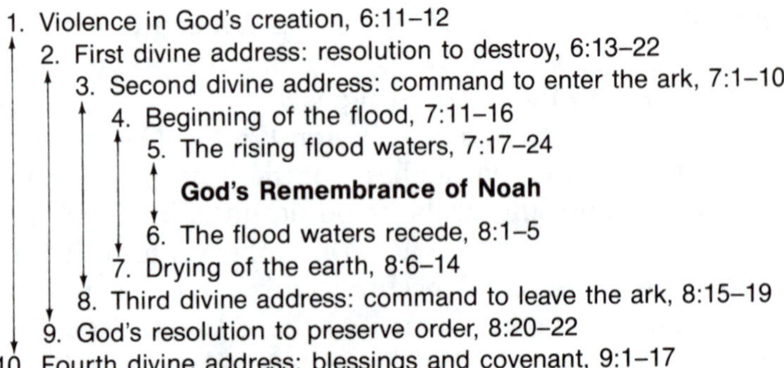

*From B. W. Anderson, "From Analysis to Synthesis: The Interpretation of Genesis 1–11," *JBL* 97 (1978), p. 38. Used by permission.

Scripture we must go beyond the analytical probing (dissect the whole to recover the original parts), beyond the diachronic probing (how did the parts converge to form the whole?), to the synchronic dimensions of the text (what is observable about the final form of the text?). Thus, in scrutinizing the flood narrative, Anderson produces the overall interesting design shown in Figure 3.

Anderson is not attempting to use this chart in any way to establish Genesis 6–9 as a unified work. It certainly does not rule out originally independent stories. But does this smoothness in the account not raise the possibility that Genesis 6–9 is from one source? After producing his own palistrophe on these chapters, Wenham states: "the documentary hypothesis may yet be defended if one is prepared to posit a most ingenious and thorough redactor who blended J and P into a marvellous and coherent unity."[7] But is that the more likely explanation?

7. "The Coherence of the Flood Narrative," *VT* 28 (1978), pp. 347–348.

The Curse on Canaan (9:20–27)

At least two problems are present here: the nature of the crime committed by Ham against his father, and why Noah placed a curse upon Ham's son Canaan, and not upon Ham himself.

It is true that the drunkenness of Noah is not made the focal point of any exhortation, even though the actions of Ham presumably would not have taken place if his father had been sober. When one recalls, however, that the two explicit incidents of drunkenness recorded in Genesis—here and Genesis 19:30–38—became occasions for the obnoxious, then perhaps the scenarios that follow each incident are sufficient commentary on overindulgence. (One might also compare Laban's giving to Jacob Leah instead of Rachel in Genesis 29:23. The text does not state how the father-in-law managed this deceit, but more than likely Jacob was so drunk by this time in the wedding celebration that he would be unable to distinguish one sister from another. Notice that when he finally wakes up he says to Laban: "What is this you have done to me?" [Gen. 29:25]. That is very close to ". . . and knew what his youngest son had done to him" [Gen. 9:24].)

Ham's sin is described in verse 22: "he saw the nakedness of his father." Is Ham's sin simply the accidental viewing of his naked father which subsequently he related to his brothers? The text implies more, for upon awakening Noah "knew what his youngest son *had done* to him" (italics mine). How he knew it was his youngest son we do not know.

The suggestion has been made (see the journal article by F. W. Basset, in the bibliography) that Ham's sin was incest. While Noah was asleep Ham slept with his mother, and a child, Canaan, was produced by this incestuous relationship. This explains why Noah's curse is on Canaan. There are two other clarion instances in Genesis of incest:

Reuben with his father's concubine (Gen. 35:22; 49:3–4), and Lot with his daughters, from which relationship sons are born (Gen. 19:30–38).

Support for this interpretation may be found in sections of the Pentateuch which deal with forbidden sexual relations. Leviticus 18 and 20 repeatedly use the phrase "you shall not uncover the nakedness of ______" in dealing with cases of possible incest, and the relationship is always heterosexual, never homosexual. Thus, to uncover the nakedness of one's father is to have sexual intercourse with one's mother. The verb that is used consistently in these legal sections is "uncover" (see Gen. 9:21 for Noah, who was "uncovered" before the trespass), except for Leviticus 20:17 which speaks of "seeing" the nakedness of one's sister.

There are three problems with this interpretation, as plausible as it is. First, the story in Genesis presupposes the birth of Canaan *before* the episode, not as a result of the episode, unless one is prepared to say that the reference to Canaan in 9:18 is an explanatory gloss by the narrator of Genesis, but without chronological significance. That is possible.

Second, taken at face value, the story suggests that Noah was made aware shortly after he recovered from his hangover of what Ham had done to him, and immediately pronounced the curse on the grandson. The incest theory would necessitate Noah learning of his wife's pregnancy, the birth of Canaan nine months later, and the imprecation then put on Canaan.

The third weakness in this theory is that it fails to provide a rationale for the actions of Ham's two brothers, Shem and Japheth. What is involved in their "walking backward and covering the nakedness of their father"? By explaining Ham's action as a case of incest, this can only mean that the brothers refrained from imitating their younger brother's folly.

The second major problem—why the grandson is cursed—also avoids a watertight solution. I have already mentioned one possibility in the preceding paragraphs: Canaan is the offspring of an incestuous relationship.

One can easily say that the words "Ham, the father of" in verses 18 and 22 are later insertions by a redactor.[8] This nicely eliminates the problem, but at the expense of the subjective deletion of parts of the text. It was Canaan who saw his (grand)father's nakedness, and thus it is he who is cursed.

Perhaps the curse is placed on Canaan because he is the youngest son of Ham (10:6), as Ham is the youngest son of Noah (9:24). We have already seen instances in our study of Genesis in which the innocent suffer because of the guilty: the ground is cursed because of Adam and Eve's sin; if the sons of God are angels, then it is man who is punished for the sin of the angels; most animals and birds are drowned in the flood because of the sins of mankind.

This is the only negative event in Genesis 3–11 in which God does not say a word. Or as an extension of that, this is the first time in Scripture that one person places a curse on another person. God has placed a curse, but now so does Noah.

In that word of Noah there is in addition to curse a word of blessing. What have thus far been divine prerogatives are now assumed by a mortal. Noah's announcements must have as much validity and carry as much force as similar announcements made by God. By what possible logic could one see blessings and curses in God's mouth as actual decisions, but limit the same words in Noah's mouth to simple wishes?

Noah's first word is to Shem: "blessed be the LORD, the God of Shem" (RSV, alternate translation). Of special inter-

8. Von Rad, *Genesis, a Commentary*, p. 135.

est here is the fact that for the first time in the Bible God is called the God of a particular individual, or the larger group that emerges from that individual. We will have to wait for a parallel to "the God of Shem" until we meet Abraham's servant speaking of "the God of my master Abraham" (Gen. 24:12, 42, 48).

Crucial to the interpretation of verse 27—"God enlarge Japheth, and let *him* dwell in the tents of Shem"—is the identification of "him." Is the subject Japheth or God? Is Noah's prophecy one in which Japheth will dwell in the tents of Shem, that is, the ingathering of Gentiles to the fold of God's people? Or is Noah's prophecy one in which God Himself will dwell in the tents of Shem? The majority of ancient commentators identify "him" as God, and most contemporary writers opt for Japheth (but with little agreement on precisely what the phrase means).

Most recently Walter C. Kaiser, Jr. has argued, convincingly to my mind, for the translation, "But He [God] will dwell in the tents of Shem."[9] The prophecy may then be taken as a further narrowing of the family line through which God's plan of redemption and word of promise is transmitted. Ultimately this family will produce Abraham.

The Tower at Babel (11:1–9)

Several of the incidents in Genesis 4–11 are bracketed by similar genealogical notes. The account of the sons of God and daughters of men, 6:1–8, is preceded and followed by a note about Noah's three sons, 5:32 and 6:9–10. The flood account is surrounded by the same reference to Noah's progeny, 6:9–10 and 9:18–19. The tower of Babel incident has as its forerunner and follow-up the genealogy of Shem, 10:21–31 and 11:10–32.

There has been a strong emphasis on the east in these

9. *Toward an Old Testament Theology* (Grand Rapids: Zondervan, 1978), p. 82.

opening chapters of Genesis. The garden of Eden is in the east (2:8). At the east of the garden of Eden God placed the cherubim to block re-entry to the garden (3:24). Cain dwells in the land of Nod, east of Eden (4:16). Several of Shem's descendants lived "in the hill country of the east" (10:30). This story about the tower opens with the migration of men from the east (11:2), to the plain of Shinar. Once again the geographical milieu of our story is placed outside of the land of Palestine.

The sin of the people does not lie in the desire to build a city, which is a neutral, amoral act. It is the motivation behind this undertaking that is most prominent—"let us build *ourselves* a city, and a tower with *its top in the heavens,* and *let us make a name for ourselves*" (Gen. 11:4; italics mine). This is the pagan concept of immortality. Long after the decease of the artist, the sculptor, the poet, the musician, the architect, and the author, memories of them will be perpetuated by their productions. Immortality is based on an achievement. One lives on in perpetuity because of his skills.

God does not embrace that idea, however. For our narrative tells us that the antics of these builders goaded God into action. Their titanic project grinds to a halt when God "confuses the language" and disperses those who insisted on becoming more sedentary. Babel (v. 9), "the gate of God," had instead become "Babbleville."

The narrative begins by saying that the earth had "one language and few words." Does this imply that up until this time the earth had been linguistically unific? Hardly so! For we simply have to read the "table of nations" in the preceding chapter where not once but three times (vv. 5, 20, 31) we are told that the sons of Japheth, Ham, and Shem were divided "by their families, their languages, their lands, and their nations."

One can see a conflict between these two chapters, as do proponents of the documentary hypothesis. In that system there are two explanations for the scattering of mankind: the P source—chapter 10—in which the scattering is a sign of blessing; and the J source—chapter 11—in which the scattering is a sign of divine dissatisfaction, a penalty.

It is possible also to explain the juxtaposition of these two chapters by suggesting that two different linguistic aspects are under discussion here. Chapter 10 refers to individual dialects or languages. By contrast the "one language" of chapter 11 refers to a lingua franca, an international language that makes cooperation and interchange possible among people of different languages.

The point of chapter 11, then, would not be that God divided one language into many languages, but that He made incomprehensible the one common language understandable to all engaged in the building program.[10]

A third suggestion has been offered by Clines. He says, "If the material of ch. 10 had followed the Babel story, the whole Table of Nations would have to be read under the sign of judgement; where it stands it functions as the fulfillment of the divine command of 9:1."[11] This last interpretation has the advantage in my estimation in that it provides another example of a constant element we have seen in Genesis 3–11. That element is the voice of God in both judgment and redemption, wrath and mercy. In all things God is working for good, annoyed by the stupidity of some, but swayed from His plan by none.

Bibliography

Andersen, F. *The Sentence in Biblical Hebrew.* The Hague: Mouton, 1974.

Anderson, B. W. "From Analysis to Synthesis: The Interpretation of Genesis 1–11." *JBL* 97 (1978): 23–39.

10. Cyrus H. Gordon, *Before Columbus: Links Between the Old World and Ancient America* (New York: Crown Publishers, 1971), pp. 107, 165–166.

11. *The Theme of the Pentateuch*, pp. 68–69.

Barnard, A. N. "Was Noah a Righteous Man? Studies in Texts: Genesis 6, 8." *Theology* 74 (1971): 311–314.

Basset, F. W. "Noah's Nakedness and the Curse of Canaan, A Case of Incest?" *VT* 21 (1971): 232–237.

Baumgarten, A. L. "Myth and Midrash: Genesis 9, 20–29." In *Christianity, Judaism and other Greco-Roman Cults; Studies for Morton Smith at Sixty*. Edited by Jacob Neusner. 4 vols. Leiden: E. J. Brill, 1975, pp. 55–71.

Brow, R. "The Curse on Ham—Capsule of Ancient History." *CT* 18 (1973): 76–78.

Brueggemann, W. "David and His Theologian." *CBQ* 30 (1968): 156–181.

———. "Kingship and Chaos (A study in Tenth Century Theology)." *CBQ* 33 (1971): 317–332.

———. "Weariness, Exile, and Chaos." *CBQ* 34 (1972): 19–38.

Cassuto, U. "The Episode of the Sons of God and the Daughters of Men (Genesis vi: 1–4)." In *Biblical and Oriental Studies*, vol. 1. Translated by Israel Abrahams. 2 vols. Jerusalem: Magnes Press, the Hebrew University, 1973.

Childs, B. *Myth and Reality in the Old Testament*. London: SCM Press, 1962, pp. 50–59.

Clark, W. M. "The Flood and the Structure of the Pre-patriarchal History." *ZAW* 83 (1971): 184–211.

———. "The Righteousness of Noah." *VT* 21 (1971): 261–280.

Clines, D. J. A. "Noah's Flood: I: The Theology of the Flood Narrative." *Faith and Thought* 100 (1972–73): 128–142.

———. "Themes in Genesis 1–11." *Bibl* 38 (1976): 483–507.

Coats, G. W. "The God of Death: Power and Obedience in the Primeval History." *Intr* 29 (1975): 227–239.

Fisher, E. "Gilgamesh and Genesis: The Flood Story in Context." *CBQ* 32 (1970): 392–403.

Fukita, S. "Theology of Hope in Genesis 1–11." *BT* (November 1975): 519–527.

Habel, N. C. *Literary Criticism of the Old Testament*. Philadelphia: Fortress, 1971, pp. 29–42.

Hartmann, T. C. "Some Thoughts on the Sumerian King List and Genesis 5 and 11b." *JBL* 91 (1972): 25–32.

Hasel, G. "The Genealogies of Gen 5 and 11 and Their Alleged Babylonian Background." *AUSS* 16 (1978): 361–374.

Kensky, T. F. "The Atrahasis Epic and Its Significance for Our Understanding of Genesis 1–9." *BA* 40 (1977): 147–155.

______. "What the Babylonian Flood Stories Can and Cannot Teach Us about the Genesis Flood." *BAR* 4 (1974): 32–41.

Kessler, M. "Rhetorical Criticism of Genesis 7." In *Rhetorical Criticism: Essays in Honor of James Muilenburg.* Pittsburgh Theological Monograph series, no. 1. Edited by Jared J. Jackson and Martin Kessler. Pittsburgh: Pickwick Press, 1974, pp. 1–17.

Kikawada, I. "The Shape of Genesis 11:1–9." In *Rhetorical Criticism.* Pittsburg: Pickwick Press, 1974, pp. 18–32.

Kline, M. "Divine Kingship and Genesis 6:1–4." *WTJ* 24 (1962): 187–204.

______. "Oracular Origin of the State." In *Biblical and Near Eastern Studies.* Edited by Gary Tuttle. Grand Rapids: Eerdmans, 1978, pp. 132–141.

Lambert, W. G. "A New Look at the Babylonian Background of Genesis." *JTS* 16 (1965): 287–300.

Larson, G. "Chronological Parallels Between the Creation and the Flood." *VT* 27 (1977): 490–492.

Laurin, R. B. "The Tower of Babel Revisited." In *Biblical and Near Eastern Studies.* Edited by Gary Tuttle. Grand Rapids: Eerdmans, 1978, pp. 142–145.

Longacre, R. "The Discourse Structure of the Flood Narrative." *SBL Seminar Papers,* 1976, pp. 235–262.

McEvenue, S. E. *The Narrative Style of the Priestly Writer.* Rome: Biblical Institute Press, 1971, pp. 22–89.

Millard, A. R. "A New Babylonian 'Genesis' Story." *TB* 18 (1967): 3–18.

Miller, J. M. "The Descendants of Cain: Notes on Genesis 4." *ZAW* 86 (1974): 164–174.

Nielsen, E. *Oral Tradition.* Chicago: Alec R. Allenson, 1954.

Olson, W. S. "Has Science Dated the Biblical Flood?" *Zygon* 2 (1967): 274–278.

Petersen, D. L. "The Yahwist on the Flood." *VT* 26 (1976): 438–446.

Riemann, P. "Am I My Brother's Keeper?" *Intr* 24 (1970): 482–491.

Sandmel, S. "Two Living Traditions." *HUCA* 32 (1961): 19–29.

Sasson, J. "A Genealogical 'Convention' in Biblical Chronography." *ZAW* 90 (1978): 171–185.

______. "Word Play in Gen 6:8–9." *CBQ* 37 (1975): 165–166.

Smith, G. V. "Structure and Purpose in Genesis 1–11." *JETS* 20 (1977): 307–319.

Weeks, N. "The Hermeneutical Problem of Genesis 1–11." *Themelios* 4 (1978): 12–19.

Wenham, G. J. "The Coherence of the Flood Narrative." *VT* 28 (1978): 336–348.

Wickham, L. R. "The Sons of God and the Daughters of Men: Gen VI 2 in Early Christian Exegesis." *OTS* 19 (1974): 135–147.

3

Abraham

Genesis 11:26—25:11

Only two chapters are devoted in the opening book of the Bible to the story of creation, and the narration of the fall of man from sinlessness into sin is limited to one. Yet the story of Abraham covers thirteen chapters in Genesis, and parts of two other chapters. May we find a clue here about the essential purpose of Scripture? Its primary function is not to address itself to philosophical, metaphysical questions which engage, properly, the mind of modern man. If pressed for a definition of God, or how one may know that God works in history, the Hebrew's answer would be like that of the late jazz artist Louis Armstrong, who replied, when asked to define jazz, "Man, if you don't know now, you'll never know."

The Old Testament is more theological than it is philosophical. How do God and men ever reach an agreement and become compatible? The answers are in the Book of Leviticus, and a substantial part of Exodus. How does God encourage a person amid the most forbidding circumstances? Look to Joseph's story. How does God call one person out of anonymity and use that life to challenge and change the world? Consider Abraham's life.

Still, we do not find, in the technical sense, a biography of Abraham in Genesis. We are not able to trace his life in detail. However, certain events of his life are highlighted, and a particular section of his life is emphasized. Table 2 reveals this. We have no information about Abraham for

Table 2

Scripture	Age of Abraham	Event
12:4	75	Abraham departs from Haran
16:16	86	birth of Ishmael
17:1	99	the covenant
21:5	100	birth of Isaac
23:1	137	death of Sarah
25:7	175	death of Abraham

the first seventy-five years of his life, and minimal information about the last seventy-five years of his life. The crucial twenty-five years are those from Abraham's seventy-fifth to one hundredth years.

From Adam through Noah's progeny (1–11) models of faithlessness have easily outnumbered the models of obedience. With these unpromising individuals Abraham is set in contrast. One cannot miss, for example, the contrast between "let us make a name for ourselves" (11:4) and "I will make your name great" (12:2). Human machinations contrast with divine initiative.

The transition from prepatriarchal to patriarchal history is marked by the opening words of Genesis 12. Hans W. Wolff categorizes correctly the grammatical parts of the passage:[1]

1. an imperative—"go!" (12:1)
2. five imperfect verbs, with God as subject—"I will make . . . I will bless . . . I will make great . . . I will bless . . . I will curse."
3. one perfect verb—"by you all the families of the earth [Gen. 10–11?] shall be blessed" or "shall bless them-

1. Walter Brueggeman and Hans W. Wolff, *The Vitality of Old Testament Traditions* (Atlanta: John Knox, 1974), p. 47.

> selves." (It will strike the reader as interesting that a promise for the future is put in the perfect. Is one's future ahead of or behind one? Does one walk into or back into the future?)

Within these three verses the word *bless(ing)*, as verb or noun, appears five times. Wolff contrasts this fivefold use of "bless(ing)" with the fivefold use of "curse" in Genesis 1–11:[2]

1. 3:14, "cursed are you above the cattle"
2. 3:17, "cursed is the ground because of you"
3. 4:11, "you are cursed from the ground"
4. 5:29, "the ground which the Lord has cursed"
5. 9:25, "cursed be Canaan"

   (8:21 uses a different Hebrew verb than do these five)

One might also be inclined to link the blessings of Genesis 12:1–3 on God's lips with a similar number of blessings in Genesis 1–11: 1:22, "And God blessed them"; 1:28, "And God blessed them"; 2:3, "So God blessed the seventh day"; 5:2, "male and female . . . he blessed them"; 9:1, "And God blessed Noah." Source critics, however, would not allow the equation, for, they say, Genesis 12:1–3 is J, and these five are all from P.

What events then follow in Abraham's life?

1. Abraham travels to Egypt with Sarah because of famine, 12:10–20
2. Back from Egypt, Abraham and Lot must parcel the land between themselves, 13:1–18
3. Abraham rescues Lot from his captors, 14:1–17, 21–24, and in the process confronts Melchizedek, 14:18–20
4. God makes the covenant with Abraham (15), a cove-

2. *Ibid.*, p. 54.

nant that is sealed with circumcision (17); Ishmael is born (16)
5. God judges Sodom and Gomorrah, 18–19
6. Abraham, away from home, again tries unsuccessfully to deceive a king by calling Sarah his sister, 20
7. Isaac is born and subsequently offered, 21–22
8. Sarah dies, 23
9. Abraham sends his servant back home to obtain a bride for Isaac, 24 (Note that the longest chapter in Genesis deals with the subject of marriage.)
10. Abraham dies, 25:1–11

The Theme of Promise

Our knowledge about Abraham is limited to what we find in Scripture. As is true of the majority of biblical personalities, there are no extrabiblical references to him in any extant literature from the patriarchal age. There are individuals who had (approximately) the same name, for example, at ancient Ebla—a fact that bears witness to the antiquity of the tradition. But none of these persons are the biblical Abraham.

One reference to the patriarch Abraham—or Moses, for that matter—in a cuneiform or hieroglyphic text would be sufficient to squelch much of the speculation that has swirled around these early characters. The absence of such a reference, however, has unleashed the imagination of much of modern scholarship in the search for the "historical Abraham." Even those scholars who have, based on archaeological discoveries, underscored the authentic cultural background of the patriarchal traditions would not admit that here one has an illustration of pure history. Even for them, historical reporting in its sterling sense does not emerge until the "objective" account of David and his family in the so-called Succession Narrative (II Sam. 9–20; I Kings 1–2).

In addition, those critics who have expressed a conservative historical judgment on the patriarchs would also, by and large, affirm that the stories—mixtures of fact and legend or saga—are products of Israel and Judah from the period of the monarchy's establishment down to the return from exile (1000–500 B.C.). As such, all of the narratives about the patriarchs were part of a long oral tradition, and subsequently underwent a process of collection, revision, and editing in which many of the stories were far removed from their original context and purpose. Compatible with this emphasis is the suggestion that some of the patriarchal stories are sheer inventions of a later age, stories which were artificially set in an earlier period.

This approach obviously minimizes, or ignores, the crucial role placed on the patriarchs in Genesis. That role is to be the initial channels through which God's promises for the future are launched. In the words of Geerhardus Vos, "if according to the Bible they [the patriarchs] are real actors in the drama of redemption, the actual beginning of the people of God . . . then the denial of their historicity makes them useless."[3] Instead they become either murky figures from an ancient and undecipherable past, or parabolic persons (for example, more like the prodigal son in Jesus' parable than John the Baptist) from which any generation may extract timeless truths to be applied to its age.

The significant part played by the patriarchs in redemptive history is made most prominent in Genesis by the constant emphasis on divine promise. Everything starts with Abraham, Isaac, and Jacob, but nothing ends with them. All three of these individuals are means to an end that reaches well beyond their lifetimes. They are all catalysts and not conclusions. Thus, we read the accounts of Abraham in Genesis not primarily to gain a perspective

3. *Notes on Biblical Theology* (Grand Rapids: Eerdmans, 1948), p. 67.

on daily life in the second millennium B.C., but to become informed of the promises of God for the future. Ultimately our interest is prophetic, not historical.

As we shall observe, the life of Abraham appears as an interesting amalgamation of faith and folly, movements forward and movements backward. At most points the reader will have no problem in applauding the Abraham of faith. But several incidents will reveal the absence of faith.

What is it that puts both the positive and the negative events in perspective? Gerhard von Rad has answered that question for us: "the whole has nevertheless a scaffolding supporting and connecting it, the so-called promise to the patriarchs. At least it can be said that this whole variegated mosaic of stories is given cohesion of subject-matter . . . by means of the constantly recurring divine promise."[4] Brevard Childs similarly suggests that the promises provide "the constant element in the midst of all the changing situations of this very chequered history."[5]

Moreover, these promises are absolute and not conditional. This emphasis shifts the promises away from the idea of a reward (something earned), to the idea of a gift (something unsolicited). We can see this point made rather strongly in the very first instance of a promise to Abraham, 12:1–3 (a promise of both blessing and increase). First is the divine imperative—"go!" (v. 1). Then comes the divine promise—"I will" (vv. 2–3). Then the human response—"so Abraham went" (v. 4). The entire intent of the passage would have been changed radically had verse 4 preceded verses 2–3. If it had, then the promises could only be read as a result of Abraham's obedience. The divine word would

4. *Old Testament Theology*, trans. D. M. G. Stalker, 2 vols. (New York: Harper and Row, 1962), vol. 1, p. 167.

5. *Introduction to the Old Testament As Scripture* (Philadelphia: Westminster, 1979), p. 151.

then have been reduced from an initiating word to a responding word.

Precisely the same structure is found in the second reference to promise, 13:14–18: the divine imperative—"lift up" (v. 14); the divine promise—"I will" (vv. 15–17); the human response—"so Abram moved his tent," (v. 18). The third reference to promise demonstrates the same, 15:1–6: the divine imperative—"Look" (v. 5a); the divine promise—"so shall your descendants be" (v. 5b); the human response—"and he believed the Lord" (v. 6).

This is not to say that Abraham is absolved of all responsibility. He is "to walk before God and be blameless" (17:1). He must "keep the covenant" (17:9). He is to do "righteousness and justice; so that the LORD may bring to Abraham what he has promised him" (18:19). A causal nexus between obedience and fulfillment is suggested by "*because* you have done this . . . I will indeed bless you . . . *because* you have obeyed my voice" (22:15–18; italics mine). The same nuance is present in 26:4–5—"I will multiply your descendants . . . because Abraham obeyed my voice. . . ." This last passage, however, promises multiplication of Isaac's descendants because of Abraham's—not Isaac's—obedience!

My point is not that human responsibility is obliterated. After all, even in a unilateral covenant there must be some reciprocity. What if Abraham had not gone out as the Lord told him? What if he had not believed? What if he had chosen consistently not to walk before God and be blameless? These options must have been open to Abraham unless we are prepared to say that as the chosen of the Lord (18:19) God's grace was irresistible. My point is that human reponsibility is repeatedly subordinated to God's word of promise.

The first stipulation, in terms of conduct, is placed on Abraham (17:1) only after he has already been, on numerous occasions, the recipient of a promissory word (12:1–3,

7; 14–17; 15:1–6, 7–21). In terms of chronology God's first word of promise was spoken to Abraham in his seventy-fifth year (12:4). God's first word to Abraham in terms of conditionality is in Abraham's ninety-ninth year (17:1), almost a quarter of a century later.

The promises of God to the patriarchs cover the following areas: the birth of a son; the increase of descendants; land; divine presence; blessing. Some of these may occur by themselves (". . . Sarah your wife shall have a son," 18:10; "to your descendants I will give this land," 12:7) but normally they occur in clusters. To illustrate, 22:15–18 includes a promise of blessing ("I indeed will bless you"); a promise of the increase of descendants ("I will multiply your descendants as the stars of heaven"); a promise of land ("your descendants shall possess the gates of their enemies"); and a second promise of blessing ("and by your descendants shall all the nations of the earth bless themselves").

More promises are made to Abraham than to either his son or grandson. In listing the promise of descendants, David J. A. Clines cites nineteen passages from Genesis. Thirteen of them are directed to Abraham, while there is only one to Hagar (21:18), two to Isaac (26:4, 24), and three to Jacob (28:14; 35:11; 46:3). Clines lists thirteen passages from Genesis about the promise of land. Nine of these are addressed to Abraham, one to Isaac (26:3), and three to Jacob (28:13, 15 [also 48:4]; 35:12; 46:4).[6]

In connection with the promise of land we note variations even in how the promise is given. In 12:7 God is to give this land "to your descendants." In 13:15 God gives the land "to you and to your descendants. . . ." In 13:17 God is to give the land "to you." Even the tense "I will

6. *The Theme of the Pentateuch*, Journal for the study of the Old Testament: Supplement series (Sheffield: Department of Biblical Studies, University of Sheffield, 1978), pp. 32–33.

give" in these verses may shift to "I give" (15:18, literally, "I have given").

Abraham, of course, never possessed the land as did the Israelites under Joshua. His "possession" is limited to staking out the land—"arise, walk through the length and breadth of the land"—which his seed will one day occupy. At least that is how we see it in retrospect. There is no indication in any early text that Abraham himself saw it that way. Ostensibly he was anticipating a more immediate fulfillment of the promise when it was first announced to him in 12:7. Only a divine indication of a four-hundred-year hiatus (15:12–16) put to rest any questions Abraham may have entertained. On several occasions he does ask God: where is my heir? But never does he ask God: where is my land? Living in tents was for him fully satisfying (Heb. 11:9–10).

It is easily observed that most of the promises God gave to Abraham, and to Isaac and Jacob, could not be fulfilled during the lifetime of the patriarch. This is certainly true for the two promises that appear most frequently, the promise of a vast number of descendants and the gift of land. God begins with Abraham a process whose climax is in the distant future.

But what about Abraham? He has a son, or two, but not a myriad of descendants. He has a tent and wealth, but no land, except for the purchase of a tiny bit of property on which to bury his wife (Gen. 23). And during the last seventy-five years of his life how many families of the earth are blessed in him?

One rich blessing Abraham has. True, he does not have, in terms of personal realization, all the promises of God. But he does have the God of all the promises. God Himself is his shield and his reward (15:1). The giver, and not the gifts, is Abraham's highest reward and his consuming obsession. Not without reason, therefore, is Abraham referred to three times in the Bible as "the friend of God" (II Chron.

20:7; Isa. 41:8; James 2:23). They enjoyed each other's company.

Abraham, Man Without Faith

Through all the experiences recorded in Genesis 12–25 Abraham emerges as an individual of great obedience and trust. His pilgrimage begins (chap. 12, "go") and climaxes (chap. 22, "offer Isaac") at the point of being tested by God. In between he appears as the paragon of patience, promised an heir at the age of seventy-five, and willing to wait a quarter of a century before he first gets the chance to change diapers. Like the suffering servant whom Isaiah describes (53:12), Abraham too makes intercession for the transgressor. Although he does not condone them, he at least tolerates the quirks of his will-o'-the-wisp nephew Lot.

However, all is not perfect. Looming large in Abraham's story are some questionable activities on the part of the hero. In this way Abraham becomes the prototype for Jacob, Moses, and David, a curious mixture of the sacred and the profane, the lofty and the languid.

Abraham is weak enough to use his wife, Sarah, to save his own life. Caught in a threatening situation, he persuades Sarah to identify herself to the Egyptians as the sister, not the wife, of Abraham (12:10–20). One may explain the tactics of Abraham by appealing, as has commentator E. A. Speiser, to Hurrian documents (a territory where Abraham spent a part of his life, 11:31c), in which marriage is followed by adoption. The woman becomes first wife, then sister, to cement the relationship.

One would be hard pressed to read that into the narrative. Moreover, Abraham's culpability is enforced by the fact that he is silent throughout the whole episode. He is only listener, not conversationalist. To be sure, he obtains wealth (12:16) for his sinister part in the episode, but not as an evidence of God's blessing. We have not yet gone beyond the "I will bless" of 12:3 to the "Lord had blessed" of 24:1.

Abraham stores away in his mind the strategy used on this occasion, perhaps to be used again if dire circumstances prevail. A second trip away from home provides such an opportunity (20:1ff.). This time, among the neighboring Philistines, Sarah is once again prevailed on to deceive the king, and make herself vulnerable for her husband's sake.

Unlike the incident in chapter 12, where it appears, or is at least hinted, that the Pharaoh and Sarah had a sexual relationship (12:15b), here adultery is averted before it can begin (20:4a, 6b). Once again Abraham is materially enriched (20:14–16), but primarily as a vindication for Sarah. His philosophy in ethics is unchanged: the end justifies the means. The end? Nothing must happen that will throw a cloud of uncertainty over God's promises (a great nation, seed). The means? If necessary, use Sarah as a pawn.

Alas, like father, like son. Isaac resorts to the same subterfuge (26:1ff). Robert Polzin draws attention to the way in which the innocent monarch in each instance was apprised of the woman's real identity. In 12:17 it is through plagues. In 20:3 it is through a dream. In 26:8 it is through the king's observing Isaac fondling Rebekah. One is the acting of God in history (the Torah?); the second is the revelation of God through visions and dreams (the prophets?); the third is through the use of one's eyes (the emphasis on wisdom?).[7]

It may well be that Abraham's rascality is prompted not just by a desire to save himself. The larger issue is the promise that God had given earlier (blessing and descendants). First of all is the famine in the land. Later Old

7. "The Ancestress of Israel in Danger," *Semeia* 3 (1975), p. 93.

Testament literature (for example, Deut. 28:17–18, 22–24) saw famine as one of the manifestations of God's displeasure with disobedience. The question in Genesis 12 is: will Abraham survive the famine? If so, how?

The second question in Genesis 12 is: will Abraham survive Egypt? Perhaps Abraham's own question is: will God's promises survive? For if there is no Abraham there can be no subsequent great nation. If that is his thinking at this point, and thus the explanation for his attempted ruse, then Abraham becomes the standard-bearer for many other believers who felt God needed a little assistance in extricating Himself from a potentially damaging and embarrassing situation.

The story does indeed illustrate an immediate fulfillment of one part of God's earlier promise to Abraham: him who curses you I will curse. Taking another man's wife, even innocently, brings catastrophic repercussions. This one part of the first promise of God to Abraham illustrates an important distinction between the covenant with Abraham and the covenant with Israel at Sinai. In the latter God's curse is directed at the Israelite who disobeys. In the former God's curse is directed at the non-Israelite who attempts to damage God's covenant people.

Still, the reader of Abraham's odyssey to Egypt wonders where is Abraham's Nathan with his "you are the man," unless it is the Pharaoh himself. Through deceit Abraham has become rich. He exits from Egypt with his coffers full, his wife tainted, and without any demonstrable tinge of remorse. To compound the issue, God apparently ignores Abraham's foolhardiness.

Does divine silence imply divine approval? I suggest the silence is to be explained not as an insinuation of God's approbation of duplicity, but by the desired emphasis the story wishes to make. That emphasis is not to comment on Abraham's behavior, however despicable it may be, but to use the story as a graphic illustration of divine providence. God's promise to Abraham cannot be voided even when the greatest threat to that promise is the bearer of the promise.

Not unlike Job, Abraham is both patient and impatient; once relaxing, then fretting; once passive, then manipulative. Still not quite sure that God is able to implement His promise, or at least frustrated because God is not on his timetable, Abraham is prepared to adopt his servant Eliezer as his heir (15:2–3). I recognize that such a contrivance finds analogy in the fifteenth-century B.C. cuneiform texts from Nuzu. In the event of childlessness a slave might be adopted as one's legal heir. But in the Abrahamic cycle the event becomes simply another illustration of God's testing the venerable patriarch.

Similarly, Sarah's presentation of Hagar to Abraham as a surrogate (16:3) because of her own infertility finds precedent in cuneiform literature. If in the preceding episodes it was Abraham who initiated the scheme, with Sarah as the go-between, here it is Sarah herself who initiates. Abraham, rather than protesting, acquiesces. The Eve-Adam mentality is not difficult to discern (16:2b). Unable to see the long-range implications of their action, Abraham offers no resistance.

What is the sequel? There is obvious divisiveness between Hagar and Sarah. As sin had separated Adam from Eve, Cain from Abel, Noah from his (grand)son, it now puts a wedge between Hagar and Sarah. Hostility and mutual recrimination loom large, resulting in Hagar's fleeing her mistress's home precipitously, pregnant at that. More than a decade later, the animosity has only intensified, not evaporated (21:9ff.). This time Hagar leaves not on her own but is summarily dismissed together with Ishmael.

This is another narrative thought by the critics to be a prima facie case for source detection. We are told that there are three sources behind the Hagar-Ishmael stories. The text breaks down as follows:

16:1	P	16:4–14	J
16:2	J	16:15–16	P
16:3	P	21:9–21	E

Fundamentally, say the critics, the two stories are in conflict and cannot therefore both be true in their facts. To illustrate, in chapter 16 Hagar is haughty and contemptuous toward Sarah. In chapter 21 she is more victim than villain. In 16:6 Abraham willingly turns Hagar over to Sarah, and does not interfere. In 21:11, on the other hand, far from being passive, Abraham finds his wife's reactions nauseating. For Hagar's trek into the wilderness Abraham makes sure she is provided for with physical sustenance (21:14).

But most palpable of all is the picture we get of Ishmael in chapter 21. By this time Ishmael must be, at a minimum, thirteen years old (17:25). He is born when Abraham is eighty-six (16:16). Abraham is one hundred when Isaac is born (21:4), which means Ishmael is fourteen or fifteen. Yet, along with bread and water, Abraham places on the shoulder of Hagar her teen-age son (21:14)! Facing certain death in the desert, she "casts" the child under a bush (21:15), a child about to die of thirst. Is this a picture of a teen-ager or a helpless infant?

In defense of the unity of chapters 16 and 21, and any lack of consistency between the two, I make the following remarks.

Does 21:14 support the idea that Abraham did indeed load Ishmael onto Hagar's shoulders? The verse reads literally: Abraham "took bread and water and gave them over to Hagar, there upon her shoulder, and the child." Nothing in this translation demands that the child was carried on the mother's shoulder.

If one is prepared to favor the translation "gave" as "place" or "set," let him recall that the same Hebrew word, *nātan*, also means "to deliver" in the sense of "commit, entrust" as in Exodus 22:7, 10. May Abraham not be "placing" the items on Hagar's shoulder but "entrusting" Ishmael to Hagar's guardianship?

The translation "cast" in 21:15 is unfortunate. Ishmael certainly is not being thrown to the ground, be he infant or adolescent. H. C. White observes that the Hebrew verb used here, *shālak*, almost always refers to the placing of a dead body into the grave, if the object of the verb is a person.[8] "They took Absalom and *threw* him into a great pit" (II Sam. 18:17, italics mine); "the man was *cast* into the grave of Elisha" (II Kings 13:21, italics mine); Ishmael "*cast* them [the bodies of the men he had slain] into a cistern" (Jer. 41:7; italics mine). It may also apply to a person who is being placed in what presumably will be his grave (Gen. 37:20, 22, 24; Jer. 38:6). What sane mother would throw her feeble child like a ball under a tree?

Abraham, Man of Faith

Although momentarily sidetracked by the lapses described in the preceding section, it is to the credit of Abraham that he rises above these negative experiences. Such experiences were intrusions into and momentary interruptions of God's plan for his life. It may be more than incidental that almost all the individuals assembled by the author of Hebrews 11 to illustrate faith have somewhere in their life a fatal flaw, and sometimes more than one. The person who adamantly rejects God's will for his life has his request honored. But for the person who at least stumbles and falls forward in the direction of God's

8. "The Initiation Legend of Ishmael," *ZAW* 87 (1975), pp. 287, 302.

will there is a divine resource and promise from God. The mosaic of faith includes the following examples.

Genesis 12. How does God break into a man's life where there have been few or no John the Baptists to prepare the way? Abraham has been cradled in a world of polytheism and idolatry. His father Terah appropriately traveled from Ur to Haran, for both were ancient centers for the worship of the moon god Sin. Genesis does not even record as directly and plainly as does Acts 7:2 that God appeared to Abraham when "he was in Mesopotamia, before he lived in Haran" (unless one translates the "said" of 12:1 as "had said").

In a sense, then, God's voice comes to Abraham without warning. The patriarch is perceptive enough to recognize that voice the first time he hears it. Not only is he perceptive enough to hear, but he also is perceptive enough to obey: "so Abram went, as the LORD had told him" (12:4). Abraham's adventure is made even more risky for he is simply pointed in the right direction by that voice, with a minimum of directions and explanations: "go . . . to the land I will show you" (12:1). The direction is plain. The exact destination is unknown.

Genesis 13. Abraham returns to Canaan, not because the famine is past, but because he has worn out his welcome in Egypt (12:20). He receives from the Pharaoh orders to return to the place from which he came. Does he learn any lesson from his mistake? Are there any indications of subsequent change in his life? Chapter 13 answers those questions affirmatively.

The focus in this chapter is on the strife that developed between Abraham's and Lot's herdsmen. There is almost as much material about Lot in these narratives as there is about his uncle. The crucial chapters describing the covenant with Abraham—15 and 17—are framed by stories about Lot: his herdsmen (chap. 13) and his capture (chap. 14) on one side; and his connection to Sodom and

Gomorrah on the other (chaps. 18–19). At no point does Lot emerge as a worthy and creditable person. More often than not he is an albatross around Abraham's neck. Lot's herdsmen cannot "dwell" together with Abraham's (13:6), but each can safely dwell with the Canaanites and Perizzites (13:7). Getting along together within the family is more difficult than getting along with those outside the family.

In the contention that developed between their employees, Abraham might easily have solved the situation by asserting his authority over his nephew. After all, he was the elder, the head of the clan. Instead, he is content to let Lot choose which pasturage he desires for his cattle.

But what if Lot chooses the land God is going to give to Abraham? Maybe Abraham needs to be more self-assertive, more insistent on his rights. The matter, however delicate, can be left in God's hands. No move by Lot can thwart the promise of God. Unfortunately Abraham had not lived by that philosophy while he was in Egypt.

Genesis 14. In many ways the incident in Genesis 14 is the most unusual one recorded in Abraham's life. The first half of the chapter—a battle between four powerful kings from the east and five minor kings in the Dead Sea area—is not about Abraham at all. Only the capture of Lot brings Abraham into the narrative. In chapter 13 the emphasis had been on family strife. Here the emphasis is on international strife.

With characteristic brevity the chapter records Abraham's victory—with the help of 318 "servants"—over these four titanic kings. In theory, all the odds went against Abraham with his miniscule army. But God has said to him, "those who curse you I will curse." Will God keep that promise? Just as Sarah was "taken" (12:15)—with resulting plagues on the takers—now Lot is taken (14:12) by outsiders. The consequence for their action is equally as devastating as it was for the Egyptians—a humiliating defeat (v. 15, "and routed them") at the hands of a peanut-sized group of men.

Even Melchizedek, the king of Salem, gives this quick but accurate analysis of the incident: "blessed be God . . . who has delivered your enemies into your hands" (v. 20). It is not without interest that the Hebrew word for "deliver" used here (*miggēn*) is from the same root as "shield" (*māgēn*) of 15:1. This is another illustration of identical vocabulary used at key points to link individual stories within the larger unit.

From Melchizedek Abraham accepts a minimal gift, a meal, if it can even be called that (v. 18). But the offer of booty from the king of Sodom he refuses (vv. 21–24). God will supply all his needs, but not this way. Once only too eager to accept a purse from Pharaoh, Abraham has now learned to exercise restraint in accepting handouts. For he is now seeking grace, not graft.

Genesis 15, 17. These two chapters describe the actual institution and confirmation of the Abrahamic covenant. For a good reason the promises of God to Abraham are more abundant in these two chapters than elsewhere. There is the promise of a son, 15:4; 17:16, 19; the promise of descendants, 15:5, 13, 16, 18; 17:2, 4–8, 19; the promise of land, 15:7, 8, 16, 18–21; 17:8; the promise of blessing, 17:16.

It would be difficult to describe these two chapters as serious dialogue. Abraham's conversational role is limited to two questions (15:2, 8) and one exclamatory comment (17:18). By contrast, God speaks repeatedly: "the word of the LORD came to Abram in a vision" (15:1); "and behold, the word of the LORD came to him" (15:4); "and he . . . said. . . . then he said to him" (15:5); "and he said to him" (15:7); "he said to him" (15:9); "then the LORD said to Abram" (15:13); "on that day the LORD made a covenant with Abraham, saying" (15:18); "the LORD appeared to Abram, and said to him" (17:1); ". . . and God said to him"

(17:3); "and God said to Abraham" (17:9); "and God said to Abraham" (17:15); "God said" (17:19).

Abraham's response to these grand promises of God is summed up tersely with these words: "and he believed [in] the LORD; and he reckoned it to him as righteousness" (15:6). God's responsibility is promise and performance. Man's responsibility is belief. Von Rad is correct in his observation that "Abraham's righteousness is not the result of any accomplishments. . . . Rather it is stated programmatically that belief alone has brought Abraham into a proper relationship to God."[9]

This is not the only illustration of faith in Genesis, but it is the only place in Genesis where there is an explicit reference to faith. We do not read, in so many words, that Isaac, or Jacob, or Joseph believed in the Lord and such belief was reckoned to them as righteousness. The promises given to Abraham are essentially repeated to Isaac and Jacob. The faith of Abraham is all that is accentuated. The emphasis then falls on God's faithfulness from generation to generation with His renewed promise, rather than upon each successive generation's appropriation of that promise in faith.

The remainder of chapter 15 is God's ceremonial ratification of this covenant. After Abraham arranges the animal remains in parallel columns, God Himself passes between the two rows in fiery manifestation. The intent of the ritual could hardly be more daring. God is obligating Himself to Abraham and his seed to the degree that He places Himself under a potential curse. Should this God of promise prove to be unreliable, then may His fate be dismemberment, as with these animals.

It is impossible to know the age of Abraham in chapter 15. Between chapters 16 and 17 there is thirteen years

9. *Genesis, a Commentary*, Old Testament Library, rev. ed. (Philadelphia: Westminster, 1973), p. 185.

(16:16, Abraham is eighty-six; 17:1, he is ninety-nine). Thus, between Abraham's receiving the covenant and his own name change and circumcision there is a decade and a half.

The source critics are almost unanimous in their identification of the traditions behind these two chapters. Normally 15:1–6 is assigned to E, 15:7–21 to J, and 17:1–27 to P. Evangelical scholars have usually countered with the suggestion that the narrative in chapter 17 is not a duplicate of that in chapter 15, but rather it is a reconfirmation by God to Abraham of His promises. Abraham is still not even a father!

There is more here, however, than reconfirmation. Two new items enter the covenant promises in chapter 17. In the first place "Abram" becomes "Abraham." Only one verse—verse 5—is devoted to this shift. This new name universalizes Abraham's experience with God. He is to be "the father of a multitude of nations."

The second new item is the introduction of circumcision. This particularizes Abraham's experience with God. He is to be the father of the Jews. Nine verses are devoted to this innovation (17:9–14), plus five more (17:23–27) for Abraham's actual circumcision, and that of Ishmael and the other males in Abraham's house.

This mark, cut into the flesh so that it is ineradicable, now becomes a witness to identity with Yahweh and Yahweh's people. That the female has no corresponding mark on her body is not to be understood as a reflection of a male chauvinist mentality. On the contrary, now that two have become "one flesh" (2:24), a mark on only one is necessary.

Clearly chapter 17 is occupied more with Abraham's circumcision than it is with his name change. Why is the institution of this rite delayed? Could Abraham's circumcision have been recorded in chapter 15 instead? I suggest that the chronological gap between the institution of the covenant and Abraham's circumcision is to put divine promise and human obligation in perspective. The later is subordinated to the former. Circumcision surfaces only once again in Genesis (that of Isaac, 21:4), except for the debacle described in chapter 34. The covenant promises of God, by contrast, continue as a chorus through the rest of Genesis.

Genesis 18–19. Informed of God's intention to obliterate Sodom and Gomorrah because of their extensive sensual (19:1–11; Ezek. 16:50) and social (Ezek. 16:49) sins, Abraham becomes the intercessor for the transgressor. Rather than rejoicing in evil (I Cor. 13:6) Abraham goes boldly to God to plead mercy. The prayer presupposes a belief and faith in a God who is merciful as well as just, compassionate as well as holy, tender as well as stern, a God who, to quote Pascal, "lends to His creatures the dignity of causality."

Genesis 20. Introduced in chapter 18 to Abraham the intercessor, the reader confronts the patriarch again in a similar role. Because of the prayers of Abraham the Lord restores fertility to the wife and concubines of a pagan king, Abimelech (v. 17). Is it not ironic that Abraham's prayers result in the opening of wombs of Philistine women, but still his own wife is unable to conceive?

Genesis 21–22. A quarter of a century of waiting terminates with the birth of Isaac. We have followed Abraham, chronologically, from septuagenarian (12:4) to centenarian (21:5). Despite setbacks, unwise moves, and frustrations, Abraham has never lost sight of the original promise he received from God, "a great nation" (12:2). The incredible has become real.

But then the incredible surfaces again. Incredible that Sarah may yet need the services of an obstetrician? Yes. Incredible too, at least for Abraham (and maybe the reader as well?), that God will now ask Abraham to offer Isaac, "your son, your only son, Isaac whom you love?" Yes.

One would like to know something about the time between Isaac's birth and his offering. Was he a helpless child, an inquisitive adolescent, or a consenting adult? The Isaac of chapter 22 is referred to as a "lad" (22:5, 12), a Hebrew word covering a male from infancy (the baby Moses, Exod. 2:6) to a teen-ager (seventeen-year-old Joseph, Gen. 37:2), to men old enough to serve in such capacities as spies (Josh. 6:23). Indeed the same word applied to Isaac in this chapter is also applied to the two servants father and son took with them (22:3, 5). Isaac carries the wood for the fire himself (22:6, thus "bearing his own cross," John 19:17). He is able to ask intelligent questions (22:7).

In his *Antiquities of the Jews*, book 1, chapter 13, Josephus states that Isaac was twenty-five at this time. Although Josephus does not explain the source of his information, the figure may be a reference to the minimum age for active military service (i.e., twenty-five) at the close of the second temple period (five more years than the minimum "twenty" of Scripture, Num. 1:3, 45). The Jewish Midrash on Genesis (*Genesis Rabbah* 56:8) states that Isaac was thirty-seven on this occasion! This figure is based on Sarah's age of ninety at the birth of Isaac, and her death thirty-seven years later at the age of 127 (Gen. 23:1), precipitated by the false announcement of her son's death! In any event, the Isaac of this chapter is anything but a child.

In chapters 18–19 we met the loquacious Abraham, trying to make God to reconsider, asking questions, demanding answers, becoming audacious. By contrast, here he is silent, passive, following divine directions. Or is he?

Of Abraham George W. Coats says, "he appears in superhuman, unemotional, somewhat unrealistic dress. He never objects to the unreasonable, slightly insane commandment to sacrifice his son, as the Abraham of Genesis 12 or Genesis 16 most certainly would have done. To the contrary, he seems to move about his grim task with silent resignation, as if he were an automaton."[10] On the other hand, A. W. Tozer, in his *Pursuit of God,* says, "the sacred writer spares us a close-up of the agony that night on the slopes near Beersheba when the aged man had it out with his God, but respectful imagination may view in awe the bent form and convulsive wrestling alone under the stars. Possibly not again until a Greater than Abraham wrestled in the Garden of Gethsemane did such mortal pain visit a human soul."[11]

Chapter 22 is introduced as a testing from God for Abraham. Certainly the patriarch's faith is being tested (v. 12, "now I know that you fear God"), but it is then only another in a series of divine testings at the point of faith, a faith which was challenged as early as chapter 12: go forth!

Ultimately the episode is more revealing about God than it is about Abraham. The climax is: "So Abraham called the name of that place The Lord will provide" (v. 14). The name draws attention to God, not Abraham. It is not Abraham-has-performed, but God-will-provide. Faith then is ultimately based on God's character and the reliability of His word.

Although Abraham will live a good bit beyond this event, and although his life will cover two and a half chapters of Scripture yet to come, never again is there any dialogue between God and Abraham. For the last time Abraham receives the promise of many descendants, the promise of land, and the promise of blessing to the nations in his seed (vv. 15–18).

Genesis 24. God will provide. Abraham discovered this at Moriah. He provided a ram. Now will He provide a wife for Isaac? The longest chapter in Genesis is devoted to answering this question. For Abraham there is no question

10. "Abraham's Sacrifice of Faith: A Form-Critical Study of Genesis 22," *Intr* 27 (1973), p. 397.

11. (Harrisburg, PA: Christian Publications, 1948), p. 25.

but that the answer to this is an unqualified yes (v. 7). Inspired by his master's faith, the servant too places the search in God's hand (vv. 12–14). Nothing of chance or coincidence is allowed to intrude. For this union God has "appointed" a wife (vv. 14, 44).

Abraham in the New Testament

Surprisingly, the New Testament nowhere connects explicitly Abraham's near-sacrifice of Isaac with the offering of Jesus. Perhaps the closest analogy is in Paul's words about God "who did not spare his own Son but gave him up for us all" (Rom. 8:32).

What the New Testament, and especially Paul, does with Abraham is to elevate him as the paragon of faith. Involved in a clash with proponents of works-righteousness, Paul refers to Abraham, a pre-Sinaitic (pre-legal) model, and then bases his whole argument for justification by faith around his life.

Toward the end of Romans 3, Paul affirms that it is through faith, and faith alone, that one is justified (3:22, 27, 28, 30). Chapter 4 is then a test case of this thesis. Justification is not through works (4:1–8). Justification is not through circumcision (4:9–12). Justification is not through keeping the law (4:13–15). It is by faith (4:16ff.). As proof, consider Abraham, who believed and was justified (apart from works, circumcision, and the law).

What is faith, though? How did it operate in Abraham's case? How is he illustrative of the principle? Paul proceeds to list nine characteristics of Abraham's faith (4:17–20).

1. It is theistic, "in the presence of God in whom he believed"—a God who gives life to the dead (resurrection) and who calls into existence things that do not exist (creation). This is precisely what God must

do with the womb of Sarah and the loins of Abraham, both of which have lost their capacity to procreate. He must create or resurrect their life-producing power.

2. It is suprarational, "In hope he believed against hope." Faith is not against reason (i.e., irrational), but it goes beyond reason. Behind the human realities of the situation are divine realities. If there is a God He can do this. This God transcends human resources.
3. It is purposeful, "that he should become the father of many nations as he had been told." Abraham's desire is not just a normal urge for a child, but to realize the implementation of God's plan for his life.
4. It is intelligent and realistic. "He did not weaken in faith when he considered his own body." Facts are faced, not avoided. But such facts never become dominating or intimidating.
5. It is unwavering. "No distrust made him waver." Abraham did not hold faith. Faith held him.
6. It is well-grounded, "concerning the promise of God." It is not faith in faith, or faith in feelings, but faith in God's promise.
7. It is strengthening. "He grew strong in his faith." Character was the by-product.
8. It is worshiping, "as he gave glory to God."
9. It is assuring, "fully convinced. . . ."

This is the kind of faith, then, that justified Abraham. It is interesting that in this mosaic of faith, Paul nowhere draws per se on the offering of Isaac. Instead, he concentrates on the other aspect of Abraham's life, his inability to father a child, although God had promised an innumerable seed. In a more limited way Paul presents a similar argument to that of Romans, in Galatians 3:6ff.

The writer of Hebrews, on the other hand, gives more of an overview of Abraham's odyssey (11:8–22).

1. By faith Abraham *obeyed* (v. 8) when he was called, although the final destination of his journey remained unknown.
2. By faith he *sojourned* (v. 9), living in tents.
3. By faith he *offered* up Isaac (v. 17), convinced in advance of a resurrection for the son. James (2:21–23) also uses Genesis 22 to buttress his observation that in offering Isaac Abraham was justified by works. He was justified by a faith that works. Works as a *merit* for salvation? No! Works as a *mark* of salvation? Yes.

If the reader of Scripture is somewhat surprised by Paul's omission in Romans and Galatians of any clear reference to Abraham's offering of Isaac as an example of faith, then he must be similarly surprised by the omission in Hebrews of any clear reference to Abraham's one great act of faith recorded in Genesis 15:6. There is no "by faith he believed" in Hebrews 11.

There is good reason for the deletion by both authors. Paul uses Abraham's faith as an illustration of the necessity of faith in becoming a child of God. Hence, he focuses on Abraham's faith as it relates to the problems surrounding Isaac's birth.

The writer of Hebrews is using Abraham's faith as an illustration of faith in the daily walk of the child of God. Hence, he focuses not on one incident at the beginning of Abraham's pilgrimage, but chooses instead to give a kaleidoscopic view of Abraham's life, starting with God's first imperative to Abraham and concluding with God's last imperative to Abraham.

Bibliography

Archer, G. L. "Old Testament History and Recent Archaeology—From Abraham to Moses." *BS* 127 (1970): 3–25.

Bonneau, N. "The Woman at the Well—John 4 and Genesis 24." *BT* (November, 1975): 519–527.

Brueggemann, W., and Wolff, H. W. *The Vitality of Old Testament Traditions*. Atlanta: John Knox, 1974.

Charny, I. W. "And Abraham Went to Slay Isaac: a Parable of Killer, Victim, and Bystander in the Family of Man." *JES* 10 (1973): 304–318.

Clifford, R. J. "The Word of God in the Ugaritic Epics and in the Patriarchal Narratives." In *The Word in the World: Essays in Honor of Frederick L. Moriarty S. J.* Edited by Richard J. Clifford and George W. Mac Rae. Cambridge, MA: Weston College Press, 1973, pp. 7–18.

Coats, G. W. "Abraham's Sacrifice of Faith: A Form-Critical Study of Genesis 22." *Intr* 27 (1973): 309–400.

Davies, P. R., and Chilton, B. D. "The Aqedah: A Revised Tradition History." *CBQ* 40 (1978): 514–546.

Emerton, J. A. "The Riddle of Genesis XIV." *VT* 21 (1971): 403–439.

______. "Some False Clues in the Study of Genesis XIV." *VT* 21 (1971): 24–27.

Fox, M. V. "The Sign of Covenant. Circumcision in the light of priestly *'ot* Etiologies." *RB* 81 (1974): 557–596.

Freedman, R. D. " 'Put Your Hand under My Thigh'—The Patriarchal Oath." *BAR* 2 (1976): 3–4, 42.

Gammie, J. G. "Loci of Melchizedek Tradition of Genesis 14, 18–20." *JBL* 90 (1971): 385–396.

Gevirtz, S. "Abram's 318." *IEJ* 19 (1969): 110–113.

Ginsberg, H. L. "Abram's 'Damascene' Steward." *BASOR* 200 (1970): 31–32.

Gordon, C. H. "Where Is Abraham's Ur?" *BAR* 3 (1977): 20–21, 52.

Grayson, A. K., and Van Seters, J. "The Childless Wife in Assyria and the Stories of Genesis." *Orientalia* 44 (1975): 485–486.

Greengus, S. "Sisterhood Adoption at Nuzi and the 'Wife-Sister' in Genesis." *HUCA* 46 (1975): 5–31.

Habel, N. C. "The Gospel Promise to Abraham." *CTM* 40 (1969): 346–355.

______. *Literary Criticism of the Old Testament*. Philadelphia: Fortress, 1971, pp. 43–57.

Hauge, M. R. "The Struggle of the Blessed in Estrangement." *ST* 29 (1975): 1–30, 113–146.

Kline, M. "Abram's Amen." *WTJ* 31 (1968): 1–11.

Loewenstamm, S. E. "The Divine Grants of Land to the Patriarchs." *JAOS* 91 (1971): 509–510.

Longenecker, R. "The 'Faith of Abraham' Theme in Paul, James and Hebrews: A Study in the Circumstantial Nature of New Testament Teaching." *JETS* 20 (1977): 203–212.

McCarthy, D. J. "Three Covenants in Genesis." *CBQ* 26 (1976):179–189.

McEvenue, S. E. "A Comparison of Narrative Styles in the Hagar Stories." *Semeia* 3 (1975): 64–77.

______. *The Narrative Style of the Priestly Writer.* Rome: Biblical Institute Press, 1971, pp. 145–178.

Mitchell, J. J. "Abram's Understanding of the Lord's Covenant." *WTJ* 32 (1969): 24–48.

Myers, J. "The Way of the Fathers." *Intr* 29 (1975): 121–140.

Neff, R. "The Annunciation in the Birth Narratives of Ishmael." *BRes* 17 (1972): 51–60.

______. "The Birth and Election of Isaac in the Priestly Tradition." *BRes* 15 (1970): 5–18.

Peck, W. J. "Murder, Timing, and the Ram in the Sacrifice of Isaac." *ATR* 58 (1976): 23–43.

Polzin, R. "The Ancestress of Israel in Danger." *Semeia* 3 (1975): 81–98.

Premsager, P. "Theology of Promise in the Patriarchal Narratives." *IndJT* 23 (1974): 112–122.

Rogers, C. L. "The Covenant With Abraham." *BS* 127 (1970): 241–256.

Rotenberry, P. "Blessing in the Old Testament." *RestQ* 2 (1958): 32–36.

Roth, M. W. "The Wooing of Rebekah." *CBQ* 34 (1972): 177–187.

Ryken, L. *The Literature of the Bible.* Grand Rapids: Zondervan, 1974, pp. 45–52.

Schultz, J. P. "Two Views of the Patriarchs: Noahides and pre-Sinai Israelites." In *Texts and Responses: Studies Presented to Nahum N. Glatzer on the occasion of his seventieth birthday by his students.* Edited by Michael A. Fishbane and Paul R. Flohr. Leiden: E. J. Brill, 1975, pp. 43–59.

Smith, R. H. "Abram and Melchizedek (Gen. 14:18–20)." *ZAW* 77 (1965): 129–153.

Swindell, A. C. "Abraham and Isaac: An Essay in Biblical Interpretation." *ExpT* 87 (1975): 50–53.

Thompson, T. L. *The Historicity of the Patriarchal Narratives: The Quest for the Historical Abraham*. New York and Berlin: W. de Gruyter, 1974.

Van Seters, J. *Abraham in History and Tradition*. New Haven: Yale University Press, 1975.

Wagner, N. E. "Abraham and David." In *Studies in the Ancient Palestinian World*. Edited by J. Wevers and D. B. Redford. Toronto: University of Toronto Press, 1972, pp. 117–140.

Weeks, N. "Man, Nuzi, and the Patriarchs: A Retrospect." *Abr–Nahrain* 16 (1975–76): 73–82.

White, H. C. "The Divine Oath in Genesis." *JBL* 92 (1973): 165–179.

______. "The Initiation Legend of Ishmael." *ZAW* 87 (1975): 267–306.

Wiseman, D. J. "Abraham in History and Tradition." *BS* 134 (1977): 123–130, 228–237.

______. "They Lived in Tents." In *Biblical and Near Eastern Studies*. Edited by Gary Tuttle. Grand Rapids: Eerdmans, 1978, pp. 195–200.

4

Jacob

Genesis 25:11—36:42

For twenty years Isaac and Rebekah lived together, but with no children. Married at the age of forty (25:20), Isaac does not father a child until he is sixty (25:26). Like her mother-in-law, Rebekah has had to endure an extended period of barrenness, but unlike her mother-in-law and her own daughter-in-law (30:3), she offers no substitute to Isaac.

Abraham's prayers result in the cessation of barrenness for other women (20:17), but not for his own wife. In the case of the third generation, Rachel's inability to conceive produces only friction, and sarcasm on Jacob's part (30:2). In contrast with both father Abraham and son Jacob, Isaac's prayer for his wife results in Rebekah's pregnancy (25:21).

The prayer was doubly answered. At least Isaac and Rebekah got more than they bargained for—twins! At the birth of Jacob and Esau, grandfather Abraham is 160 years old, and still has fifteen years to live. But nowhere do the Scriptures hint of any meeting or relationship between the old patriarch and the grandchildren.

The three most important women in Genesis—Sarah, Rebekah, and Rachel—all experienced problems in producing children. A period of extended barrenness was a common frustration for all. This particular problem relates especially to God's promise to the patriarchs of many descendants. For how can God's promise be fulfilled when one encounters example after example of female sterility?

Add to the problems created by an infertile womb the other exasperating situations described in Genesis, and the outlook for the implementation of God's promises becomes dim indeed.

Not one major character in this part of Scripture flies through history on "flowery beds of ease." Sometimes, of course, the problems are the direct result of an act of folly on the part of the patriarch. At other times, however, the problems are the result of situations over which the patriarchs have no control. This would include the barrenness of the wives, and the various famines that sent Abraham and Isaac scurrying hither and yon for food.

These kinds of events merely happen. They are not punishments sent by God. But each of them does represent a "threat" to God's redemptive plan for mankind. A deceased and childless Abraham or an infertile Sarah is a sentence of death over that divine plan. Surely these potentially disruptive circumstances serve as background material for illustrations of God's power to overcome obstacles and hurdles. And wherever the challenge is the greatest, God is there to enable the individual to weather the crisis.

In a recent stimulating study of Jacob's story, Michael A. Fishbane has examined chapters 25–36 of Genesis from the perspective of the symmetry of the whole. His conclusion is that there is a remarkable consistency in the arrangement of the narrative material in the story, even to the point that the story is framed by the genealogies of two individuals who are not a part of the chosen line (Ishmael's descendants, 25:12–18, and Esau's descendants, 36:1–43).[1]

This suggests that the most fruitful investigation of Jacob's history, in terms of theological analysis, is not to

1. "Composition and Structure in the Jacob Cycle (Gen 25, 19–35, 22)," *JJS* 26 (1975): 15–38; subsequently revised and included as chapter 3 in *Text and Texture: Close Readings of Selected Biblical Texts* (New York: Schocken, 1979).

extract out of the whole the individual strands (if indeed such did ever exist) and then look for a J emphasis, an E emphasis, or P's genealogical, chronological framework and editorial insertions. One can become dizzy following the weaving back and forth of these sources in the text. Thus, to illustrate, in listing the different sources of Genesis 25–28, one discovers this mosaic (following scholarly consensus):

25:19–20	P	27:1–45	J	28:17–18	E
25:21–26a	J	27:46	P	28:19	J
25:26b	P	28:1–9	P	28:20–21a	E
25:27–34	J	28:10	J	28:21b	J
26:1–33	J	28:11–12	E	28:22	E
26:34–35	P	28:13–16	J		

Whether this account was originally composite and then edited, or whether it was originally a homogeneous work, we must deal with the unit as a whole as we have it in the text.

To get an overview of the Jacob cycle we may summarize it in Table 3.

Need for Transformation (25:19—28:9)

Genesis 25:19–26. Like the older Jacob who will not let go of his divine assailant (32:26) until a blessing is forthcoming, the infant Jacob, after an *in utero* struggle, emerges

Table 3

Reference	Description
25:19—28:9	need for transformation
28:10—32:21	preparation for transformation
32:22–32	transformation
33:1—36:40	results of transformation

into this life clasping his brother's heel. The Hebrew for "heel" is *ʿēqeb*, a play on the name *Jacob*, *yaʿăqōb*. The phrase "he had taken hold of Esau's heel" is not explained, but the implications seem clear. It is obviously not a gesture of friendship, a hearty welcome extended to his twin brother. Even in infancy Jacob is a self-centered, self-oriented individual. The name is given to him proleptically (cf. "call his name Jesus, for he will save. . . ."), indicating a lifestyle ahead that is not commendable.

Genesis 25:27–34. Capitalizing on his brother's hunger, Jacob solicits from his brother the birthright in return for some food. A cup of broth or red pottage has become a bargaining tool. Esau may be a skillful hunter, but Jacob is a skillful opportunist. Like the later Israelites who would have gladly surrendered their spiritual credentials (although in the wilderness) in return for three meals a day in Egypt (although it means the forfeiture of freedom), so Esau is glad to barter away his spiritual birthright to satisfy his gastronomic needs. And Jacob is more than willing to oblige. An oath clinches the transaction (v. 33).

Genesis 27:1ff. To exploit one's own brother is bad enough. To deceive deliberately one's own father, now senile and physically incapacitated, is to stoop even lower.

Rebekah is not much more of a saint than were Sarah or Eve. It is she who initiates the scheme of Jacob impersonating Esau. Jacob readily cooperates. Once the aggressive initiator, he is now follower. Isaac, the deceiver in chapter 26, is about to become the deceived.

Further, under the pretext of concern for maintaining purity in the line of descent, Rebekah reminds her husband of the compromising Esau (27:46). Wanting to avoid this at all costs, Isaac blesses Jacob and sends him on his way to find a wife in Paddan-aram (28:1–9).

It will be observed from the preceding chart on sources in chapters 25–28 that the critics assign 27:1–45 to J and 27:46—28:9 to P. The reason? The two episodes are irreconcilable. In J Jacob deceives his father, Esau discovers the intrigue, and Jacob flees home with a price placed on his head by Esau. In P Isaac blesses Jacob, there is no reference to deception, and Jacob's purpose for leaving is to obtain a wife. But our analysis of the passage shows this to be a misreading of the text. Far from being a contradiction to what precedes, 27:46—28:9 narrates a second scheme of Rebekah's—this time to get Jacob away from Esau. Guile worked once. Why not again?

Preparation for Transformation
(28:10—32:21)

Genesis 28:10–22. It is inaccurate to say that these episodes in Jacob's life are meant to put a premium on deceit. Ethically there is no question about the impropriety of Jacob's behavior. Here is a classic example of one who takes God's will into his own hands. That Jacob was predestined to surpass his brother (25:23) is granted. That this gives him the right to become manipulative, exploitative, and deceitful, a thousand times no. The end does not justify the means.

The chapters about Abraham were introduced with God speaking to the patriarch: "now the Lord said to Abram" (12:1). By contrast, a number of episodes take place in Jacob's life before God enters the picture directly. All through the affair with Isaac, Esau, and Rebekah, God does not speak. Nor does He enter during the first part of Jacob's flight.

This changes at Bethel. For the first time God confronts Jacob directly (in a dream). Jacob's response upon waking is unusual, but not unexpected: "and he was afraid" (28:17), afraid of God. He is afraid of Laban (31:31) and of Esau (32:7, 11), too.

What makes this response unusual is that it contrasts with that of Jacob's father and grandfather and even Lot, who, when confronted by God or angels, greeted them. On occasion, the angels might even be offered food and overnight lodging! The antecedent to Jacob's fear is Adam's "I heard the sound of thee in the garden, and I was afraid" (3:10). It is the fear spawned by a guilty conscience.

The divine presence is sufficient to score the point. At no juncture does God take Jacob to task. There are no lectures, no fulminations by God, no Nathan's "you are the man." On the contrary Jacob found:

1. the gift of divine friendship. He was lonely and alone.
2. the grace of divine forgiveness. The guilt in his life is heavier than the stone on which his head rests.
3. the goal of a divine purpose. In verses 13–15 he receives the same covenantal promises made to Abraham, and is thus a link in God's chain.

Genesis 29–31. In this preparation for transformation God has first of all showed Jacob Himself. Now He will show Jacob himself. The method is to let Jacob spend the next twenty years living with a person whose character is much like his own, that is, Laban.

At first Laban is the gracious host (29:13). He sounds almost like Adam when he first cast eyes on Eve, "surely you are my bone and my flesh" (29:14). He is a generous employer (29:15). He desires his nephew and employee to become his son-in-law (29:19).

But this perpetrator of deceit is about to become the victim of deceit at the hands of Laban. The irony is hard to miss. Jacob will see himself in Laban. The unsuspecting Jacob discovers, to his chagrin, that he has slept with Leah, not Rachel. Was the trick possible because it was at night, or Leah was heavily veiled, or Jacob was too drunk to know or care who his bed partner was?

If the providence of God has intruded into the theophany at Bethel, similarly here out of chaos "God moves in a mysterious way His wonders to perform." The third and fourth children mothered by Leah are Levi and Judah respectively (29:34–35). From Levi comes the line of priests. From Judah comes one line of kings, and eventually Jesus. Two of the most significant institutions in the Old Testament have their origin in an unwanted marriage, initiated only by duplicity! As Gerhard von Rad says, "God's work descended deeply into the lowest worldliness and there was hidden past recognition."[2]

That Jacob is still the supplanter, the trickster, is evidenced by the narrative of 30:25–43. In an attempt to outwit Laban, he concocts a plan to take a good number of Laban's flocks back with him to Canaan. Jacob's animals will be those multicolored ones he breeds from Laban's monochromatic animals, a rarity indeed (at least Laban thinks so!). Whether Jacob believed the rods in the watering trough made a difference (30:37–39), or whether the rods were just a decoy,[3] the plan is laced with deception.

To be sure, Jacob says to his wives, "God has taken away the cattle of your father, and given them to me" (31:9), an idea seconded by the wives (31:16). He even lends credibility to his actions by appealing to divine attestation (31:12).

But is Jacob making assumptions? Are the cattle a blessing from God to Jacob because of Jacob or in spite of Jacob? Compare Abraham's ill-gotten wealth from the Pharaoh (12:16). Surely God does not lend His imprimatur to all the wily schemes of His children.

The narrative in 31:22–55 shows at least that Jacob and Rachel deserve each other! Laban outwits Jacob. Jacob outwits Laban. Rachel outwits Laban by stealing the house-

2. *Genesis, a Commentary*, Old Testament Library, rev. ed. (Philadelphia: Westminster, 1973), p. 291.

3. M. L. Gabriel, "Biology," in *EncJud* 4, pp. 1024–1027.

hold gods (31:30, 34–35), resulting in a confrontation between Jacob and Laban.

Is it possible here to read between the lines? Laban and Jacob reconcile, and Laban then goes home. But what about the gods upon which the menstruating Rachel has been sitting? Presumably Rachel confessed to her husband after her father's departure. Can we see Jacob contentedly tolerating the presence of false gods in his entourage?

Genesis 32:1–21. Time does not heal broken relationships. Often it intensifies them. Hurts die slowly. Although twenty years have passed, Esau still resents Jacob's bold moves—at least Jacob thinks so. To that end Jacob lays out another stratagem. Not yet convinced that his security is not in himself, but in God, the carnal Jacob goes into action.

First there is an advance mission (vv. 3–5), then a plan to avoid total obliteration by Esau (vv. 6–8), then a prayer of desperation with no expression of repentance, unless it is found in verse 10 (vv. 9–12), then an attempt to buy Esau's forgiveness (vv. 13–21). Does Jacob need to meet Esau or God? The next section will answer that question for us.

Transformation (32:22–32)

Twenty years earlier Jacob, alone then too, was confronted by God at Bethel. In the blackness of night God and man met. Now this will happen again. Jacob is not the seeker, but the sought.

God, in the form of a "man," engages Jacob in a wrestling match, one that lasts through the night, almost until dawn (v. 24b). One is reminded of the nocturnal conversation between Jesus and Nicodemus (John 3) in which the Lord broke down systematically and thoroughly all of Nicodemus's defenses, verbally wrestled with Nicodemus, and went to the heart of the problem, which was Nicodemus's heart.

At least three distinguishing characteristics of Jacob surface here which separate him from the pre-Peniel Jacob:

1. a consciousness of weakness: "and Jacob's thigh was put out of joint as he wrestled with him" (v. 25b). The victor in his wrestlings with Esau, Isaac, and Laban, Jacob is now victim, not wrestling but clinging.
2. a consuming hunger for God: "I will not let you go unless you bless me" (v. 26b). The blessing of Isaac is meaningless unless accompanied by the blessing of God.
3. a confession of unworthiness: " 'What is your name?' And he said, 'Jacob' " (v. 27). His problem is his nature. (Cf. "And Jesus asked him, 'What is your name?' He replied, 'My name is Legion,' " Mark 5:9.) The name *Jacob* is what he is, as much as it is who he is.

That, then, is Jacob's response. What are the results?

1. a new name and character: "Your name shall no more be called Jacob, but Israel, for you have striven [Hebrew *śrh*] with God [Hebrew *'ēl*] and with men and have prevailed" (v. 28). (One might parallel the objects of Jacob's striving with the words that "Jesus increased in . . . favor with God and man," Luke 2:52.)
2. a new power: ". . . you have prevailed" (v. 28b)
3. a new blessing: "And there he blessed him" (v. 29b)
4. a new testimony: "I have seen God face to face, and yet my life is preserved" (v. 30)
5. a new day, a new start: "The sun rose upon him" (v. 31a)
6. a new reminder of his own weakness: "limping upon his thigh" (v. 31b). The name is changed, but the leg is not healed.

Results of Transformation (33–36)

Genesis 33. Reconciliation with God must be followed by reconciliation with one's brother. Observe the difference between the pre-Peniel Jacob who is in the rear of his company ("Pass on before me," 32:16) and the post-Peniel Jacob who now leads the procession to Esau ("He himself went on before them," v. 3a). And there is not only the demonstration of a new courage, but also a new humility, "bowing himself to the ground seven times" (v. 3b). Then there is a new generosity, "accept my present from my hand . . . accept my gift" (vv. 10–11). His motives in giving the gift to Esau are genuine. He no longer connives.

Genesis 34. This chapter records a vicious incident in the life of one of Jacob's children, Dinah, his only daughter. She is raped by Shechem, the son of Hamor. What will the "blessed" Jacob do now? Will he seek revenge? Will he attempt to take justice into his own hands (which is what the commandment "thou shalt not kill" prohibits)?

We discover what Jacob's sons will do—at least two of them, Simeon and Levi. Through deceit (v. 13)—the same Hebrew word applied to Jacob himself in 27:35 and to Laban in 29:25—Simeon and Levi lure the guilty parties to their death.

But what of Jacob? His first reaction to the news about Dinah is that he "held his peace" (v. 5). Was it because his peace held him? Upon learning of his sons' macabre war of revenge he lashes out at Simeon and Levi (v. 30), reserving even harsher words for a later period (49:5–7). Their actions are unjustifiable. The end does not justify the means, although Jacob had once subscribed to this philosophy.

Genesis 35. The false gods brought by Rachel from her father's household must be disposed of (vv. 2–4). The spiritual sensitivity of Jacob shows here. Their continued presence is incompatible with the worship of the one Lord.

For a second time Jacob comes to Bethel, where, more than twenty years earlier, God first met him (vv. 5–8). But now we see a Jacob who has gone from Bethel to El-Bethel, from the house of God to the God of the house of God (v. 7). God now is first. His house is second.

To reaffirm the transaction at Peniel (chap. 32), God again informs Jacob that he is now Israel (vv. 9–10). Fishbane comments correctly, "to be sure, Jacob had won the name of Israel earlier (32:29). But perhaps the narrative seeks to indicate that it is only *after* the resolution of his conflict with Esau (Gen. 33) that Jacob was, indeed, Israel."[4]

The death of his wife Rachel (vv. 16–21), the incest committed by his eldest son Reuben (v. 22), or the death of his father (vv. 27–29) do not prostrate Jacob. The conclusion to the chapter is appropriate. Isaac is buried by "his sons Esau and Jacob." Alienation has been replaced by proximity.

Genesis 36. The "generations of Esau" (KJV) are introduced by a description of the final parting of Esau and Jacob. We began in chapter 28 with Jacob fleeing from Esau. Here it is Esau who leaves Jacob. Much like a parting earlier between Abraham and Lot (13:5ff.), Esau and Jacob bid each other adieu, and go their separate ways amicably.

Bibliography

Albright, W. F. "From the Patriarchs to Moses." *BA* 36 (1973): 19–26.

Anderson, B. W. "An Exposition of Genesis XXXII." *ABR* 17 (1969): 21–26.

Clarke, E. "Jacob's Dream at Bethel as Interpreted in the Targums and the New Testament." *SR* 4 (1974/75): 367–377.

Coote, R. "The Meaning of the Name Israel." *HTR* 65 (1972): 137–142.

Fensham, F. C. "Gen XXXIV and Mari." *JNWSL* 4 (1975): 15–38.

4. "Composition and Structure," p. 28.

Fishbane, M. "Composition and Structure in the Jacob Cycle (Gen 25, 19–35, 22)." *JJS* 26 (1975): 15–38.

Fisher, L. R. "Literary Genres in the Ugaritic Texts." In *Ras Shamra Parallels*. Vol 2. Edited by L. R. Fisher. Rome: Pontifical Biblical Institute, 1975.

Fokkelman, J. P. *Narrative Art in Genesis*. Amsterdam: Van Gorcum, 1975.

Frankena, R. "Some Remarks on the Semitic Background of Chapters XXIX–XXXI of the Book of Genesis." *OTS* 17 (1970): 53–64.

Fretheim, T. E. "The Jacob Traditions, Theology and Hermeneutic." *Intr* 26 (1972): 419–436.

Greenberg, M. "Another Look at Rachel's Theft of the Teraphim." *JBL* 81 (1962): 239–248.

Houtman, C. "Jacob at Mahanaim. Some remarks on Genesis XXXII 2–3." *VT* 28 (1978): 37–44.

______. "What did Jacob see in his dream at Bethel? Some remarks on Genesis XXVIII 10–22." *VT* 27 (1977): 337–351.

Kessler, M. "Genesis 34—An Interpretation." *RefR* 19 (1965): 3–8.

Lewis, J. "Gen 32:23–33, Seeing a Hidden God." *SBL Seminar Papers*, 1972, 1, 449–457.

McKenzie, J. L. "Jacob at Peniel: Gn 32, 24–32." *CBQ* 25 (1963): 71–76.

Miscall, P. D. "The Jacob and Joseph Stories as Analogies." *JSOT* 6 (1978): 28–40.

Rast, W. E. *Tradition History and the Old Testament*. Philadelphia: Fortress, 1972, pp. 33–56.

Roth, M. W. "Structural Interpretations of 'Jacob at the Jabbok' (Genesis 32:22–32)." *BRes* 22 (1977): 51–62.

Tucker, G. M. *Form Criticism of the Old Testament*. Philadelphia: Fortress, 1971, pp. 41–54.

Van Seters, J. "Jacob's Marriages and Ancient Near Eastern Customs." *HTR* 62 (1969): 377–395.

White, H. C. "French Structuralism and OT Narrative Analysis: Roland Barthes." *Semeia* 3 (1975): 99–127.

5

Joseph

Genesis 37–50

The story about Joseph opens ominously: "Now Israel loved Joseph more than any other of his children, because he was the son of his old age" (37:3). It portends trouble as surely as did "Isaac loved Esau . . . but Rebekah loved Jacob" (25:28). The father supplies the son with "a coat of many colours" (KJV) or "long robe with sleeves" (RSV), according to 37:3. The brothers' reactions are envy, jealousy, and anger.

A Young Man with a Dream

To make matters worse, at least from the brothers' perspective, Joseph tells them about two of his dreams. In one the sheaves of his brothers bowed before his (37:5–7). In the second the luminaries bowed before him (37:9). How shall we gauge Joseph's motives here? Does he, to quote George W. Coats, "dream grandiose dreams and freely flaunt them and their obvious significance to all members of the family"?[1]

I believe not. Joseph's behavior is not unlike that of the youthful David who is willing to take on Goliath (I Sam. 17:26, 31), over the protestations of his older brothers and Saul. The dreams are from God. To teen-age Joseph the

1. *From Canaan to Egypt: Structural and Theological Context for the Joseph Story* (Washington: Catholic Biblical Association of America, 1976), p. 82.

revelation means at least one thing: God has a plan for this young man's life, and that plan includes some type of leadership. Here then is a teen-ager with a sense of destiny, divine destiny. This fact is shared out of enthusiasm, not out of brashness. "Here am I, Lord, send me." But the brothers cannot tolerate this.

Unsavory Experiences (37:9–36; 39–41)

Joseph has not yet seen everything in God's plan for his life. Some of it is about to appear.

Genesis 37. To dismiss Joseph as a fraud and ignore him is insufficient. He must be eliminated. After having second thoughts about killing their brother outright, the brothers sell him to some traders going to Egypt. These latter are called within one verse (v. 28) both "Midianites" and "Ishmaelites." Along with other facts in the narrative, this phenomenon is interpreted as an indication of two originally independent stories about Joseph, a J story ("Ishmaelite"), and an E story ("Midianites"). That Judges 8:22 expressly identifies the Midianites and the Ishmaelites as one and the same, and that dual names for individuals and groups were usual in antiquity are sufficient to undercut the credibility of this source division.[2]

To return to the narrative, what, may we ask, are Joseph's thoughts through all this nightmare? Intended for a leadership role, he finds himself sold as a slave by his own brothers to total strangers traveling to a land about which Joseph knows nothing! What about God's plan? How does this fit in?

Genesis 39. All goes well for a while. Joseph has security, a good job, and a respectable employer. But only for

2. F. Derek Kidner, *Genesis* (Chicago: Inter-Varsity, 1968), pp. 184–186, and Kenneth A. Kitchen, *Ancient Orient and Old Testament* (Chicago: Inter-Varsity, 1966), pp. 119, 123.

a while! In her husband's absence Potiphar's wife propositions Joseph. Previously a victim of jealousy and anger, Joseph is about to become a victim of a vicious lie. For a crime of which he is totally innocent Joseph will go to prison. But what about the dreams, and God's plan for his life?

Almost all commentators have observed the similarity between this story and the Egyptian "Tale of Two Brothers" from the thirteenth century B.C. An unmarried brother, Bata, lives with his older brother, Anubis, and his wife. In the husband's absence the wife attempts to seduce her brother-in-law: "come, let's spend an hour sleeping [together]." Bata emphatically refused and ran away "like a leopard." The wife's attempt to put the blame on Bata succeeded for a while. Only a miracle by Re, the sun god—putting a body of water filled with crocodiles between the two—saved Bata from Anubis. When Anubis discovers that it was his own wife who was initiator, "he reached his house, and he killed his wife, and he threw her out to the dogs."

One of the major differences between the two stories is the fate of the temptress. We do not know what happens to Potiphar's wife. N. Sarna suggests that "the reason for this disinterest is that our story was not intended for entertainment purposes and was not told for its own sake. The focus of attention is on Joseph's reaction. . . ."[3]

Genesis 40. In prison Joseph befriends two of Pharaoh's employees who have fallen out of favor with the king, the chief butler and the baker. He also interprets their dreams for them. His one request for assistance is directed to the butler: please tell the Pharaoh I am here unjustly and want my release (vv. 14–15). However, "the chief butler did not remember Joseph, but forgot him" (v. 23). And for two

3. *Understanding Genesis: The Heritage of Biblical Israel* (New York: United Synagogue Commission on Jewish Education, 1966), p. 216.

more years (41:1) Joseph remained incarcerated. Where is God in all of this?

Might there not be a "subtle serpent" around who will suggest to Joseph: "Did not God say your brothers will bow before you? Is this how your God treats you in return for your obedience to Him?" All of the temptations are there, the temptation to be angry, bitter, resentful, cynical, self-pitying.

Genesis 41. Pharaoh's dual dreams, unsettling to say the least, provide the opportunity for Joseph's release from prison. As in the case of the dream of the chief butler and baker (40:8), Joseph is quick to disclaim any innate gift for interpretation of dreams (41:16).

After interpreting the dream, Joseph counsels the Pharaoh to appoint someone (is he hinting?) to oversee the stockpiling of food for the lean years ahead. To be forewarned is to be forearmed. Joseph is Pharaoh's choice (v. 41) for this office.

We have now followed Joseph from the age of seventeen (37:2) to the age of thirty (41:46). What began as something exhilarating for Joseph turned into a nightmare that was to last thirteen years. But the light is now beginning to dawn. If Joseph had to endure thirteen years of bewilderment, it is only half of what his great-grandfather had to suffer through. Abraham received God's promise of a child at the age of seventy-five, but had to wait until he was one hundred before he became the father of the child of promise.

In All Things God Works for Good
(42–50)

The remaining chapters of Genesis describe the trips between Egypt and Canaan by Joseph's brothers in an attempt to procure grain. These trips climax in Joseph's self-disclosure to his brothers, reconciliation with them, and a final chance to be with his father. It has been at least twenty years since Joseph has seen his brothers: thirteen years in Egypt, followed by the seven good years. In chapter 37 he went to see his brothers. In chapter 42 his brothers come to see him.

What will Joseph's response be? Will he meet them with open arms? Will he let bygones be bygones? Joseph's greeting may surprise us. He first accused them of being spies, which they were not (42:9). Second, he put them in prison, and offered release only if one would return to Canaan and bring back the youngest brother (42:15–17). Third, Simeon is put in jail while the other brothers return to fetch Benjamin. Meanwhile, Joseph loaded their sacks with grain and also put their money back inside the sacks. Not only spies, but thieves too (42:18ff.)? Fourth, with Benjamin present Joseph sent his brothers back to Canaan again, secretly putting his own valuable silver cup into Benjamin's sack (44:1ff.). Judah begs Joseph to take him as slave instead of Benjamin (44:14–34).

For a parallel to these machinations of Joseph, Cyrus H. Gordon refers to the Middle Egyptian story called "The Complaints of the Eloquent Peasant." A peasant loses his donkeys to a rogue on the basis of a trumped-up charge of trespassing. The peasant complains eloquently to both the Pharaoh and the man on whose property he allegedly trespassed. These two individuals listen carefully to the peasant and eventually decide in his favor, but all the time this is going on, make sure that his wife and family are adequately provided for in terms of food and basic supplies.[4]

In the context of the biblical story, however, how shall the reader judge Joseph at this point? Is he ruthless, mer-

4. *The Common Background of Greek and Hebrew Civilizations* (New York: Norton, 1965), pp. 113, 229.

cilcss? Is he toying with his brothers? Is Joseph acting as Jacob once had?

I grant that the language is rough and the tactics forceful (see 42:7). But may not such measures be ultimately redemptive? Joseph did speak to his brothers "roughly," but no more roughly than God spoke to Adam and Eve in Eden. And God's ultimate design in Eden is to restore these two. Rough words are redemptive words.

Joseph's refusal to accept adulation from his brothers, as the story concludes, is indicated by the words: "Fear not, for am I in the place of God?" (50:19). B. Dahlberg, in attempting to link themes of the narrative about Joseph with similar ones in Genesis 1–11, contrasts this word of Joseph with the word of the serpent, "you will be like God" (3:5). He also contrasts the words of Joseph, "you meant evil against me; but God meant it for good" (50:20), with the serpent's "knowing good and evil."[5] Such comparisons, among others, again are illustrative of the literary artistry throughout this first book of the Bible.

How does Joseph overcome his temptations to which we alluded? Simply he related all his experiences in life, both benign and malignant, to the sovereign plan of God for his life. "God sent me before you to preserve life . . . it was not you who sent me here, but God" (45:5–8). Or again, "as for you, you meant evil against me; but God meant it for good" (50:20). Already the sentiment expressed in Romans 8:28 has surfaced. We will see it again with Daniel (see Dan. 6:10), and Paul (see Phil. 1:12–14).

One may ask what is "the life that is preserved" (45:5), or who are the "many people kept alive" (50:20) by Joseph's extended presence in Egypt? In one sense the reference is to the residents of Egypt. Had it not been for Joseph's wise counsel to prepare for the years of leanness, the Egyptians would have been decimated by the prolonged famine.

5. "On Recognizing the Unity of Genesis," *TDig* 24 (1976), p. 363.

The text has informed us that Joseph already has been the means of blessing on one Egyptian and his house (39:5). Is he now a means of blessing on all Egyptians and their houses? If so, then the providential sparing of these unbelievers becomes a graphic illustration of how God's word of promise to Abraham is fulfilled: "those who bless you I will bless." We have already seen a dramatic fulfillment of "those who curse you I will curse" in Genesis 12. A patriarch's wife taken into the Pharaoh's harem becomes the occasion for an eruption of plagues in the Pharaoh's house. Conversely, Abraham's great-grandson, now taken into the highest echelons of Egyptian administration, becomes the occasion for Egypt's salvation from a devastating crisis.[6]

Primarily the "preserved life" and the "many people" of whom Joseph makes mention to his brothers must be a reference to the descendants of Abraham. We have observed many instances in Genesis where God's people have been threatened with extinction. And if the family which bears the covenant promise is annihilated does this mean that all the promises of God evaporate into thin air?

In an exhibition of tangible, spiritual maturity Joseph sees himself and his experiences in Egypt as the divinely appointed means of perpetuating the promises of God for the people of God. The Joseph story is linked not only with Genesis 1–11 (Dahlberg), but also more importantly with the theme of divine promise that begins with Abraham. The story also links Genesis with Exodus. For both this story and the opening chapters of Exodus highlight the same theme: potential threats to the divine promise.

There is no reservation, however, in Joseph's mind about whether the divine plan will succeed. About its implementation he is totally convinced. God will indeed "visit"

6. See further Hans W. Wolff, *The Vitality of Old Testament Traditions* (Atlanta: John Knox, 1974), pp. 41–66, especially p. 59.

his brothers (50:24–25) as He "visited" Sarah (21:1), and then bring them to the land of Abraham, Isaac, and Jacob.

Judah and Tamar (38)

Obviously Genesis 38 interrupts the flow of Joseph's story. One can read chapters 37 and 39, avoiding chapter 38 entirely, without destroying the continuity of the story. Some commentators, such as Sarna and Eric I. Lowenthal, ignore the chapter altogether.

The chapter is about Judah, son of Jacob, brother of Joseph. He fathers, by a Canaanite woman, three sons: Er, Onan, and Shelah. Er, the oldest, marries Tamar. Er dies, leaving Tamar as a childless widow. It then becomes the responsibility of the second oldest son, Onan, to father a child by his sister-in-law, thus preserving the name of the deceased first-born (see Deut. 25:5–10 for the Mosaic legislation of the levirate marriage; *levir* is Latin for "brother-in-law"). Onan refuses by practicing a method of birth control, coitus interruptus (v. 9). For refusing to accept responsibility Onan dies. Judah sends Tamar back to her own father, and promises to summon her when Shelah is old enough to have sexual intercourse with her.

The promise, however, is never honored. Taking matters into her own hands, Tamar dresses as a prostitute, eventually seduces her father-in-law Judah, and bears twins by him. But how do we relate this to Joseph?

Donald B. Redford states, "The only reasonable explanation of the present order of the chapters must be chronological. Chapter 38 could not follow the Joseph Story, since Judah is then in Egypt for the rest of his life, while the setting of 38 is in Palestine. It could not precede the Joseph Story for Judah is an old grandfather at the close of 38, while at the outset of the Joseph Story he is still a young man."[7]

7. *A Study of the Biblical Story of Joseph (Genesis 37–50)*, supplement to *Vetus Testamentum* 20 (Leiden: E. J. Brill, 1970), p. 17.

Apart from the chronological necessity one cannot miss the vivid contrasts this event presents with the Joseph story. In chapter 37, Jacob is deceived; in chapter 38, Judah is deceived, both by members of the family. In chapter 37, the bloodied coat of Joseph is the evidence to Jacob of his son's death; in chapter 38, Tamar's possession of Judah's personal seal, cord, and staff is the evidence of the latter's culpability.[8] The adulterous Judah of chapter 38 contrasts with the faithful, noncompromising Joseph of chapter 39. Tamar is successful, Potiphar's wife is not.

Chapter 38 is in microcosm what chapters 37 and 39–50 are in macrocosm. God works His plan even in unsavory circumstances. Joseph survives hostility and becomes the physical salvation of his family. Zerah and Perez, twins in the messianic line (Matt. 1:3), have their origin in an incestuous relationship between father-in-law and daughter-in-law.

Both of the incidents of chapters 37 and 38 are heartaches for Jacob. In one a son is mauled to death, so the father thinks. In the other, another son becomes an adulterer. In light of these kinds of experiences one can understand why Jacob is later to say, "few and evil have been the days of the years of my life" (47:9).

Bibliography

Albright, W. F. "From the Patriarchs to Moses." *BA* 36 (1973): 26–33.

Battenfield, J. R. "A Consideration of the Identity of the Pharaoh of Genesis 47:11." *JETS* 25 (1972): 77–85.

Cassuto, U. "The Story of Tamar and Judah." In *Biblical and Oriental Studies*. Translated by Israel Abrahams. 2 vols. Jerusalem: Magnes Press, the Hebrew University, 1973, vol. 1, pp. 29–40.

Coats, G. W. *From Canaan to Egypt: Structural and Theological Context for the Joseph Story*. Washington: Catholic Biblical Association of America, 1976.

8. George W. Coats, "Redactional Unity in Gen 37–50," *JBL* 93 (1974), p. 17.

______. "Redactional Unity in Gen 37–50." *JBL* 93 (1974): 15–21.

______. "The Joseph Story and Ancient Wisdom: A Reappraisal." *CBQ* 35 (1973): 285–297.

______. "Widow's Rights: A Crux in the Structure of Gen. 38." *CBQ* 34 (1972): 461–466.

Dahlberg, B. "On Recognizing the Unity of Genesis." *TDig* 24 (1976): 360–367.

Emerton, J. A. "An Examination of a Recent Structuralist Interpretation of Genesis XXXVIII." *VT* 26 (1976): 79–98.

______. "Some Problems in Genesis XXXVIII." *VT* 25 (1975): 338–361.

Gevirtz, S. "Of Patriarchs and Puns: Joseph at the Fountain, Jacob at the Ford." *HUCA* 46 (1975): 33–54.

______. "The Reprimand of Reuben." *JNES* 30 (1971): 87–98.

Goldin, J. "The Youngest Son or Where Does Genesis 38 Belong." *JBL* 96 (1977): 27–44.

Kitchen, K. A. "Joseph." In *New Bible Dictionary*. Edited by J. D. Douglas. London: Inter-Varsity Fellowship, 1962, pp. 656–660.

Lowenthal, E. I. *The Joseph Narrative in Genesis: An Interpretation*. New York: Ktav, 1973.

Peck, W. J. "Note on Genesis 37, 2 and Joseph's Character." *ExpT* 82 (1971): 342–343.

Rad, G. von. "The Joseph Narrative and Ancient Wisdom." In *The Problem of the Hexateuch and Other Essays*. Translated by Rev. E. W. Trueman Dicken. Edinburgh and London: Oliver and Boyd, 1966, pp. 292–300.

Redford, D. B. *A Study of the Biblical Story of Joseph* (Genesis 37–50). *Supplement to Vetus Testamentum* 20. Leiden: E. J. Brill, 1970.

Seybold, D. A. "Paradox and Symmetry in the Joseph Narrative." In *Literary Interpretations of Biblical Narratives*. Edited by Kenneth R. R. G. Louis et al. Nashville: Abingdon, 1974, pp. 59–73.

Whybray, R. N. "Joseph Story and Pentateuchal Criticism." *VT* 18 (1968): 522–528.

Wright, G. R. H. "Joseph's grave under the tree by the omphalos at Shechem." *VT* 22 (1972): 476–486.

Part TWO

Exodus

6

The Emergence of Moses

Exodus 1–6

It is possible to outline the Book of Exodus in one of the following ways:

I. Oppression 1:1—12:36
II. Liberation 12:37—15:21
III. Itineration 15:22—19:25
IV. Divine revelation 20:1—24:18
V. Divine veneration 25:1—40:38

I. In Egypt 1:1—15:21
II. To Sinai 15:22—19:2
III. At Sinai 19:3—40:38

I. God's Saving Act: Deliverance Out of Distress: 1–14
  A. The distress, chapters 1–11
  B. The deliverance, chapters 12–14
II. Man's Response in Praise: 15:1–21
III. God's Action: Preservation: 15:22–18:27
  A. From thirst, chapter 15:22–27; 17:1–7
  B. From hunger, chapter 16
  C. From despair, chapter 17:8–16; 18:1–27
IV. Man's Response in Obedience: 19–31
V. Transgression and Renewal: 32–40[1]

1. Claus Westermann, *Handbook to the Old Testament,* trans. Robert H. Boyd (Minneapolis: Augsburg, 1967), pp. 55–56.

Regardless of what language one uses in outlining Exodus, the basic divisions in the structure of the book are fairly clear. Unlike the Book of Genesis (the patriarchal section), which focuses on several human actors, Exodus highlights only one, Moses. Also unlike the Book of Genesis (again chaps. 12–50), which spans a considerable period of time—at least four generations—Exodus 19–40 covers only about a year. The Israelites reached Sinai three months after their exit from Egypt (19:1). About eleven months later (Num. 10:11) the Israelites leave Sinai for Canaan. Thus Exodus, chronologically, follows the pattern in Table 4.

As is true of the Genesis account about Abraham, the Exodus narrative is deliberately selective in showing us Moses. The second chapter of Exodus deals with the first two-thirds of Moses' life. And even here only meager detail is recorded: he is born, put in a basket in a river, and reared by the Pharaoh's daughter. Forty years later (Acts 7:23) he kills an Egyptian and is forced to live in exile in Midian. Four decades later, as an octogenarian (Acts 7:30), Moses begins his ministry with the incident of the burning bush. George E. Mendenhall, using the incident of Moses slaying the Egyptian for an insight into the question about the exercise of force, says, "the great importance of this narrative for the origins of the religious ideology of ancient Israel is indicated by the fact that it is the only story pre-

Table 4

Chapter	Duration	Reference
1	400 years	(Gen. 15:13)
2—15:21	80 years	(Acts 7:23, 30)
15:22—19:2	3 months	(Exod. 19:1)
19:3—40:38	11 months	(Num. 10:11)

served about Moses between infancy and his experience at the burning bush."[2]

Moses As Infant and Refugee (1–2)

One cannot help but notice the difference between the end of Genesis and the first few verses in Exodus in terms of divine activity. With his life in jeopardy, Joseph bears witness to God's protection of his life. The story is as much about God as it is about Joseph.

Then follow the first seven verses of Exodus, a period covering no less than four hundred years. During this hiatus there is no explicit reference to the activity of God (apart from what is implied in Israel's preservation and population explosion in Egypt, 1:7). No great figure emerges on whom Scripture's spotlight will shine. These are four centuries over which the Scriptures pass in silence. The gulf is comparable to the period between Noah and Abraham. There are times when God is near (Isa. 55:6), and times when His presence is veiled.

Preservation by God

Still, we should not pass the first seven verses of Exodus too quickly. It is of interest that Exodus 1:1 does not begin where Genesis 50:26 ended. Instead the narrative tape is rewound, and the reader of Exodus 1:1 is taken back to Genesis 46:8, "these are the names of the descendants of Israel, who came into Egypt. . . ." Both genealogies introduce Jacob's sons as the "sons of Israel," not as the sons of Jacob. The covenant line is through the new covenant name given to Jacob at Peniel. Those who do multiply in Egypt are Israelites rather than Jacobites.

2. *The Tenth Generation: The Origins of the Biblical Traditions* (Baltimore: Johns Hopkins Press, 1973), p. 20.

This four-hundred-year period is the time in which God's promises to the patriarchs continue toward fulfillment, especially the promise of numerous progeny. In Egypt Israel was "fruitful and increased greatly; they multiplied and grew exceedingly strong" (Exod. 1:7). Not only is there a new king over Egypt who does not know Joseph, but also there now is a host of Israelites who do not know Joseph, at least as a contemporary.

Like indigenous populations in countries today who are suspicious of growing minorities in their cities, the Egyptians began to fret over the presence of ever-increasing Israelites. To that end, the unnamed Pharaoh ordered the institution of a plan to remedy the situation. To prevent both their escape and the possibility of the Israelites becoming fifth columnists in time of siege, the Pharaoh has them perform excruciatingly difficult manual labor (1:8–14). The intent is to demoralize them, to impress on them their role of servitude, and to diminish as much as possible any likelihood of insurrection.

But the Egyptians only discovered (as have, for example, the Russians with Christian or Jewish believers in the Soviet Union) that physical punishment brings out only the best in its religious minorities. Resiliency, not capitulation, is the result.

Subsequently, a second plan (1:16) and a third plan (1:22) are ordered by the Judophobic Pharaoh. The second stratagem is to kill at birth all Hebrew males. Commenting on this strange ultimatum, Moshe Greenberg remarks that, if successful, "Israel would have been gradually reduced entirely to females. Insurrection would have been impossible, the people would have been dissolved, leaving to Egypt their women-power and reproductive capacity."[3] This time the malicious attempt at genocide is frustrated by the midwives. The fear of God is a deterrent sufficient

3. *Understanding Exodus* (New York: Behrman, 1969), p. 29.

to put restrictions on unquestioned obedience to the dictates of a superior.

Throughout this whole first chapter there is contrasted, by implication, the struggle between one king to eliminate God's people through various pogroms, and another King who is bent on preserving His people.

If chapter 1 is devoted to a narration of God's saving His people as a whole, chapter 2 is devoted to a narration of God's saving one of His people, Moses. Both the group (chap. 1) and the individual (chap. 2) are in His hands.

Significant Events in Moses' Life

Three things of long-range significance are to take place in Moses' life:

1. his birth and conferment of his name, 2:1–10
2. his attempt to act as law enforcer, then peacemaker, the latter resulting in personal rebuff, 2:11–15a
3. his flight to Midian and his eventual marriage, 2:15b–22.

Each of these events is a harbinger of Moses' career, although it will not begin for eighty more years.

Much as Joseph had earlier found himself in the Pharaoh's employment, Moses is to find himself as adopted son of the Pharaoh's daughter. The climax surrounding Moses' rescue from drowning is the name he receives, "Moses." Apart from the connection of "Moses" with the similar verbal element in Pharaonic names (Ah*mose*, Thut*mose*, Ra*mses*, borne by Egyptian kings in the eighteenth and nineteenth dynasties, i.e., from the sixteenth to the twelth centuries B.C.), we are interested in the meaning attached to "Moses" by Scripture. The Bible (Exod. 2:10) connects "Moses" with the Hebrew verb *māsha*, "to draw out." "Moses" is an active participle, in Hebrew *mōshe*, of this verb; hence, the literal meaning of *mōshe* is "one who draws out" or "a drawer out."

As with Jacob, Moses is not only who he is, but also what he is. His name is his mission. He is to "draw out" his people from Egypt and lead them to Canaan. Here then is an illustration of the premium placed on the name by Hebrews.[4]

Although acting out of good intentions (as Abraham had done with Sarah, also in Egypt), Moses takes the law into his own hands by murdering an Egyptian who was violently assaulting his kinsman (2:11–12). The man of God is following his natural instincts. We are interested here in observing Moses in the role of defender of the oppressed. Here Moses steps in between one Egyptian and one Hebrew. Both antagonists and protagonists will be multiplied later.

That Moses is shunned by his own people (2:14) the next day "foreshadows the truculence and perverse ingratitude that Moses will experience from this people decades later."[5] It also anticipates a rejection by his own people of the One greater than Moses (Acts 7:35, 52).[6]

In the land of Midian (in Arabia) Moses again is propitiously placed in the role of arbitrator. Observing some shepherds monopolizing access to the well for water, and thus making it difficult for seven women to draw their share of water, Moses comes to the rescue of these women (2:17). Once again Moses has championed and become the salvation of individuals who themselves are unable to retaliate against the harassers.

Thus God prepares His vessel for his life vocation. To Abraham God spoke a direct word. For Jacob, the divine

4. But observe the caution by J. Barr, *BJRL* 52 (1969), pp. 20–21, that this principle is not absolute in the Old Testament.

5. Greenberg, *Understanding Exodus*, p. 45.

6. Brevard Childs, *The Book of Exodus: A Critical, Theological Commentary*, Old Testament Library (Philadelphia: Westminster, 1974), p. 34.

word was announced to the mother. Joseph learned something of his future through dual dreams. Moses is plunged into the arena of experience. He is in the right place at the right time to do the right thing.

Moses Meets God (3–5)

Pursuant to these experiences and prior to Moses' commissioning is the incident of the burning bush (3:1–6).

Parallels in Moses' and Jacob's Experiences

So much of what is happening to Moses parallels experiences of Jacob.

Both are younger brothers who replace in revelational significance an older brother: Jacob over Esau, Moses over Aaron.

Unusual circumstances surround the birth, or the days immediately thereafter, of both. Jacob enters this world grasping the heel of his brother. At three months of age Moses is set afloat in an ark.

Both manage to offend a brother, one through exploitation, one through the usurpation of mediatorial power.

The result in each case is a forced exile.

At some point in this exile God confronts the person: through a dream for Jacob, through a burning bush for Moses.

At the human level, the first response is fear. "And he was afraid" (Gen. 28:17); "Moses hid his face, for he was afraid to look at God" (Exod. 3:6).

In both the fear is engendered by guilt. Both have acted out of God's will: Jacob in taking advantage of Esau, Moses in killing the Egyptian.

In neither episode does the divine being draw attention to the criminal behavior of the person. To the contrary, the word that both receive from God is positive and challenging. See Genesis 28:13–15 and Exodus 3:7–10.

On both occasions the initiative for confrontation is taken entirely by God. There is no indication in the text that either individual is aggressively seeking God. Jacob is a refugee, running from home. Moses is idling his time and observing the sheep nibbling on the grass. God is the furthest thing from their thoughts. No other person is present.

In subsequent history the site at which the theophany occurred becomes sacrosanct—Bethel and Sinai.

Moses' theophany is preceded in the record by a marriage (Exod. 2:21); Jacob's is followed by a marriage (Gen. 29:28). The first scene for both eventual marriages is at a well (Gen. 29:2–10; Exod. 2:15b–17). The marriages are consummated while the husband is in a strange land, Jacob in Paddan-aram, and Moses in Midian.

In the life of Jacob and Moses the first meeting with God is followed eventually by a second meeting. For Jacob Bethel is followed by Peniel. Moses also needs a confirming word from God (Exod. 6:1—7:7). Note that between these experiences of divine visitation and revelation there are interludes that are less than successful and spectacular. What Laban is to Jacob the Pharaoh is to Moses. Jacob is deceived, and manages to escape his father-in-law only by a trick of his own. In Moses' case the Pharaoh taunts Moses and Moses' God (Exod. 5:2). Because Moses spoke to the Pharaoh requesting release the monarch responded by intensifying the work load of the Hebrews (5:4–18). As a result Moses' own people turn against him (5:19–21), bringing Moses close to the point of complete despair (5:22–23).

First theophany	Jacob at Bethel (Gen. 28:10–22)	Moses in Midian (Exod. 3:1–6)
Interlude	Genesis 29:1—32:21	Exodus 3:7—5:22
Second theophany	Jacob at Peniel (Gen. 32:22–32)	Moses in Egypt (Exod. 6:1—7:7)

Moses Makes Excuses to God

Far from being nerved by his experience at the burning bush, Moses is prepared with a series of excuses that he believes disqualify him as God's choice. Perhaps God has made a mistake in judgment! These excuses are:

inadequacy or self-belittlement—"Who am I that I should go to Pharaoh?" (3:11)

ignorance—"If I come to the people of Israel . . . and they ask me, 'What is his name?' what shall I say to them?" (3:13)

incredibility—"But behold, they will not believe me or listen to my voice, for they will say, 'The LORD did not appear unto you' " (4:1)

inarticulateness—"Oh, my Lord, I am not eloquent . . . but I am slow of speech and of tongue" (4:10)

insubordination—"Oh, my Lord, send, I pray, some other person" (4:13)

Childs appropriately comments, "the progression of the dialogue is more visceral than rational."[7]

It is, happily for Moses, a long-suffering God with whom he is conversing. God counters Moses' excuses at each point.

Inadequacy. The common denominator in Moses' various responses is that in all of them he is thinking in terms of his resources, not His resources. To correct him, then, and to reply to the first excuse, God says, "I will be with you" (Exod. 3:12). That is to say, for Moses the ultimate question is not "who am I?" but "*whose* am I?" (Cf. Paul's, "this very night there stood by me an angel of the God to whom I belong," Acts 27:23.) As a guarantee God provides

7. Ibid., p. 71.

a "sign" (3:12a). But to Moses' chagrin the sign will become evident only *after* Moses risks his life (3:12b). What he wants is a sign before, not after; not just the word of the Lord, but a tangible sign from the Lord.

Ignorance. Moses anticipates he will be asked a question which he will not be able to answer satisfactorily. It is perhaps not an accident that the Scripture never records an instance of anyone asking such a question. Nevertheless, God does not dismiss Moses' question as illusory.

Out of God's response comes God's own name, Yahweh, or as it is often called, the tetragrammaton (i.e., it is composed of four Hebrew letters: y-h-w-h). The number of biblical scholars who have addressed themselves to this issue is legion. For beginners we can take y-h-w-h as the third-person singular imperfect form of the verb h-w/y-h, "to be," that is, "he is" or "he will be." The rendering in verse 14 of *'ehyeh '^{a}sher 'ehyeh* is usually "I am who I am," although a few (Cyrus H. Gordon and C. Isbell) scholars have suggested that this phrase is third person, not first person, and thus read "He is who He is."

But what is the significance of God's answer? Is it an evasion, an abasement of Moses who has no more right to ask the holy name than did Jacob (Gen. 32:29)? The point of verse 14b—"Say this to the people of Israel, 'I AM has sent me to you' "—demonstrates that the answer is not an evasion. This is a sufficient and satisfying answer for Moses to give to the people if the issue is ever broached.

In Hebrew syntax, when the verb in the subordinate clause is the same as the verb in the principal clause two possible translations present themselves. And that is what one has here: I AM WHO I AM (3:14). To illustrate, Exodus 4:13 reads, "send whom thou wilt send" (KJV), that is, "send somebody else, anybody except myself." I Samuel 23:13 says, "David and his men . . . arose and departed . . . and they went where they went" (literal), that is, "they went wherever they could go" (RSV). In these latter two illustrations the speaker in one and the writer in the other are deliberately general. Relating then this idiom to 3:14, Martin Noth, for example, says, "that kind of indefiniteness is expressed which leaves open a large number of possibilities ('I am whatever I mean to be')."[8]

The same idiom can convey not only indeterminacy but also intensity and actuality. To illustrate, Exodus 33:19, "I will be gracious to whom I will be gracious, and will show mercy on whom I will show mercy," suggests not indefiniteness but actuality. Again, Ezekiel 12:25, "But I the LORD will speak the word which I will speak," means the Lord cannot be hushed or muted. A New Testament analogy would be Pilate's "What I have written I have written" (John 19:22). The word is unchangeable and inerasable.

In this sense, then, "I AM WHO I AM" means "I am there (with you, wherever you are), I really am." Something of this nuance is suggested by the Septuagint's translation of the phrase as "I am the one who is." To return again to Hebrew syntax, the subject of the relative clause must be the same in number and gender as that of the principal clause. Thus, Exodus 20:2 literally reads, "I am the Lord your God, who *I* brought you out of the land of Egypt." In English syntax, of course, "who" alone would be the subject of the verb, but in Hebrew "who" is only a connecting word joining a principal and subordinate clause. So then, an exact English equivalent of "I AM WHO I AM" is "I am he who is." And because He is, He is present, even in the imbroglio in Egypt.

Incredibility. Still haunted by the possibility of personal rejection, Moses suggests that his credibility will be attacked by his own people. The people of God are more of a thorn in the flesh than the enemies of God.

Three signs from God are granted to Moses as empirical

8. *Exodus, a Commentary*, Old Testament Library (Philadelphia: Westminster, 1962), p. 45.

evidence of his divine calling: a rod is changed into a snake, then back into a rod; a healthy hand becomes leprous, then is restored; a cup full of water from the Nile poured on the ground becomes blood (4:2–9). The first two, for Moses at least, would cause no little anxiety. George A. F. Knight says, "God must shake Moses out of his selfish rationalizings. Moses must learn that it is God who is calling him to do the absurdly difficult thing."[9]

Inarticulateness. To perform an unusual act is one thing. But what happens if the person has to speak too and is afraid he will be tongue-tied or will jumble his words? Would such verbal blundering wipe out any good effects the signs may have on the audience?

It is interesting to observe that Stephen draws attention (Acts 7:22) to a Moses "who was instructed in all the wisdom of the Egyptians, and he was *mighty in his words* and deeds" (italics mine). Either Stephen is deliberately using hyperbole or Moses is parading a false humility, that is, denying a gift that God has indeed given him. It may be, however, that Moses did indeed suffer from some kind of speech impediment (see the article by J. H. Tigay in the bibliography), which was thus a cause for concern at the beginning.

Insubordination. Moses' attempt to avoid his duty reaches its climax in his fifth objection, "send some other person." God reluctantly cooperates with Moses' request, suggesting the appointment of Aaron as Moses' surrogate. Aaron's credentials? "He can speak well" (4:14). How well? At least well enough to solicit support and funds for the apostate act of building the golden calf (Exod. 32)!

Satisfied that God has at least provided him with an assistant, Moses returns to his father-in-law to bid him

9. *Theology As Narration: A Commentary on the Book of Exodus* (Edinburgh: Handsel Press, 1976), p. 28.

farewell (a little different than Jacob's departure from Laban!), then goes on to Egypt.

Next we read about what is perhaps the strangest event narrated in the Book of Exodus. Before reaching his destination Moses is met by the Lord, who seeks to kill him. The passage bristles with problems. Why does the Lord seek to kill Moses just after He has commissioned him? In the phrase, "the LORD . . . sought to kill him" (4:24), who is the "him," Moses or one of his two sons, and if a son, which of the two? How does Zipporah, a pagan Midianite, know how to respond immediately to the crisis? In the phrase, "and she touched his feet with it" whose feet are touched? Moses', the son's, or even the divine assailant's? (The RSV freely inserts "Moses" in the phrase.) What is the meaning of Zipporah's words, "you are a bridegroom of blood" ("a bloody husband," KJV)?

It is possible that the phrase "the LORD . . . sought to kill him" is an early way of stating that Moses became violently ill.[10] Such wording would be analogous to "the LORD hardened his heart." Both sickness and an act of disobedience are subsumed under one ultimate cause, God. To attempt, however, to take the stinger out of this difficult phrase by understanding it as a reference to physical sickness, nothing more, seems to be taking extreme liberty with language.

Moses is assailed by the Lord, ostensibly for neglecting to circumcise one of his sons (Gershom, the older one?). Zipporah reacts spontaneously. She circumcises her son with a flint and then touches somebody's feet (a euphemism for the genitalia?) with the foreskin. Because of the wife's alert behavior Moses is saved.

The obvious fact stressed by the story is the importance of circumcision as a sign of the covenant. It is a rite not to be done only when convenient. The worshiper is not

10. See Childs's objection, *The Book of Exodus*, p. 103.

consulted as to whether he considers this appropriate and relevant. Circumcision is a divine mandate. Ministry to one's family takes precedence over ministry to one's congregation. Of this incident Gordon says, "It is designed to warn the Hebrews of every generation: 'Don't fail to circumcise your sons! If Moses couldn't get away with it, how can you?' "[11]

The narrative, however, serves as more than an object lesson to later generations. We have already seen that circumcision is the sign of God's special covenant with Abraham and his seed (Gen. 17). As the covenant mediator, Moses has to observe the covenant sign. Furthermore, Zipporah's circumcision of her son identifies both the son and Moses as among the descendants of Abraham. God's covenant with Abraham includes Moses as a child of Abraham. Any attempt to draw rigid distinctions between the covenant with the patriarchs and the covenant at Sinai is defused by matching Moses' covenant obligations with those of Abraham.

Greenberg connects the story thematically with Jacob's experience at Peniel. A divine assailant attacks an unsuspecting person under the cover of darkness. Jacob is anticipating reconciliation with Esau. Moses is returning to Egypt to be reunited with his fellow Hebrews, and to face the Pharaoh. The shedding of blood here, resulting in Moses' deliverance, presages Israel's deliverance from Egypt, but not without bloodshed too.[12]

For this episode there are other parallel themes in Genesis and Exodus. For example, the Lord delivers, then commissions, then seeks to kill Moses. Similarly, the Lord delivers, then commissions, then seeks shortly thereafter to wipe out His people (Exod. 32:10). The judgment is pro-

11. *The Ancient Near East* (New York: Norton, 1965), p. 138.
12. Greenberg, *Understanding Exodus*, p. 111.

voked in both instances by a violation of the covenant. Zipporah's quick actions save Moses, and Moses' intercessory prayer saves the Israelites.

Just as shrewd action by Rachel saved Jacob from Laban, so alertness by Zipporah saves Moses from God. Knight raises some interesting questions: "Did Zipporah . . . glimpse this idea about the Covenant more clearly than her husband? Did she believe that the union of a man and woman under God within the covenant reflected the significance of the divine covenant itself, and so had she come to believe that her husband had dishonoured both her and God? Had Zipporah intuitively glimpsed the great reality of revelation that there is no redemption . . . without the shedding of blood?"[13]

At least for the immediate future Moses' life will not become one bit more pleasant. He has gone through a contentious dialogue with God (3:1—4:17), then found himself at the precipice of death (4:18–26). He has met God as debater, then God as holy aggressor. There is something of a momentary reprieve (4:27–31), as Moses is welcomed back, and together all of God's people join in a service of worship and praise.

But Pharaoh is obstinate. He is totally unsympathetic to the pleas of Moses (5:3). Pharaoh's words, "I do not know the LORD,"(5:2) mean "I do not acknowledge His authority."

To make matters worse the workload of the Hebrews was unrealistically increased (5:4–18). Inevitably there is only deep resentment on the part of the Hebrews toward their alleged liberator (5:19–21). What a difference in reception. One day, adulation; the next, rejection. About another Liberator the people were to say one day, "hosanna," but the next, "crucify him."

13. *Theology As Narration*, p. 35.

Moses' Call Reconfirmed (6)

Just as Jacob received a confirmation of the events at Peniel (cf. Gen. 32:28 with 35:10), so Moses is now about to receive a confirmation of the events at the burning bush. To be sure, the old objections do not die easily (cf. 6:12, 30). In the first exchange of challenge and rejection Moses had emphasized his own inabilities. What troubles him here is that it is a much more formidable assignment to speak to the Pharaoh than it is to speak to his own people. On this latter assignment he had failed. How, then, can he possibly make his message register with the Pharaoh? ("If you have raced with men on foot, and they have wearied you, how will you compete with horses? And if in a safe land you fall down, how will you do in the jungle of the Jordan?" Jer. 12:5.) Moses is still too conscious of results.

For response God gives Moses seven encouraging "I will"s which are ringed by two "I am"s. See Table 5.

At least two critical matters are located in this chapter. One is verse 3, "I appeared to Abraham, to Isaac, and to Jacob, as God Almighty, but by my name the LORD I did not make myself known to them." But what about those passages in which the Lord identifies Himself to one of

Table 5

Response	Verse	
→ "I am the LORD"	6	
1. "I will bring you out"	6	redemption
2. "I will deliver you"	6	
3. "I will redeem you"	6	
4. "I will take you for my people"	7	adoption
5. "I will be your God"	7	
6. "I will bring you into the land"	8	settlement
7. "I will give it to you for a possession"	8	
→ "I am the LORD"	8	

the patriarchs by precisely that name? Thus, Genesis 15:7, "And he said unto him [i.e., Abraham], 'I am the LORD. . . .' " Or those passages in which the narrator describes the Lord speaking to Abraham as Lord: "Now the LORD said to Abraham . . ." (Gen. 12:1)? Or those passages which indicate some familiarity with the Lord? So, Genesis 12:8, "there he built an altar to the LORD and called on the name of the LORD."

It is unwarranted to assume, however, that all of the above flatly contradict Exodus 6:3. It may simply be the Lord's way of saying to Moses that the patriarchs never understood the full significance of God's personal name. To be sure, they knew it, used it, and recognized it as a vocable. Gleason L. Archer states, ". . . Exodus 6:3 teaches that God, who in earlier generations had revealed Himself as El Shaddai (God Almighty) by deeds of power and mercy, would now in Moses' generation reveal Himself as a covenant-keeping Jehovah by His marvellous deliverance of the whole nation of Israel."[14]

But did Moses, his peers, and successors grasp the significance of the name? Would such a breakthrough have to wait until Jesus could say, "I have manifested thy name to the men whom thou gavest me out of the world" (John 17:6)?

The second problem surrounds the genealogy given in 6:14–27. We are particularly interested in the line of descent to Moses and Aaron. See Figure 4.

Moses and Aaron are, then, the great-great-grandsons of Jacob. To phrase it differently, there are four generations between the descent into Egypt and the exodus from Egypt. The duration of that period of time is given as 430 years in Exodus 12:40–41, as 400 years in Genesis 15:13, and as "the fourth generation" in Genesis 15:16. Are four generations enough to cover four centuries?

14. *A Survey of Old Testament Introduction* (Chicago: Moody, 1973), p. 113.

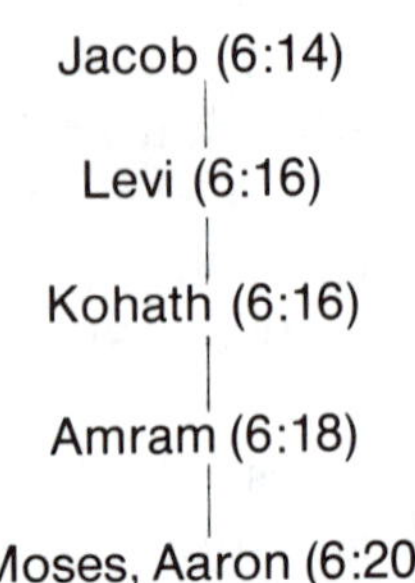

Furthermore, Exodus plainly says (1:6) that the death of Joseph antedated the birth of Moses. Genesis 50:23 tells us that Joseph lived long enough to see his own great-grandchildren (Joseph, Ephraim, Machir, and unnamed children). These fourth-generation children would be as removed from Jacob as were Moses and Aaron, and probably younger than Moses and Aaron.

Two responses may be made. One is that we must assume that the genealogy of Moses and Aaron in Exodus 6:14–20 is selective, not complete or continuous. This is not unheard of in either the Bible or other literature of the Mediterranean world.[15] Also, other portions of Scripture posit a minimum of ten generations between Joseph and Joshua. For example, I Chronicles 7:20–29 lists (Joseph), Ephraim, Rephah, Resheph, Telah, Tahan, Ladan, Ammihud, Elishama, Nun, and Joshua. This latter fact then confirms the selectivity of Exodus 6:14–27.

It is of interest that this genealogy discusses Aaron's children (v. 23) and one of his grandchildren (v. 25). Yet nothing is recorded of Moses' progeny. Moses, whose descent goes back to Levi, is followed by Joshua, whose descent goes back to Joseph. No caste is here inaugurated

15. Kenneth A. Kitchen, *Ancient Orient and Old Testament* (Chicago: Inter-Varsity, 1966), pp. 54–55.

in which God chooses His leader on the basis of heredity. Kings and priests, yes. But prophetic spokesmen, no.

Bibliography

Commentaries and Monographs

Beegle, D. *Moses, the Servant of Yahweh.* Grand Rapids: Eerdmans, 1972.

Cassuto, U. *A Commentary on the Book of Exodus.* Jerusalem: Magnes Press, the Hebrew University, 1967.

Childs, B. *The Book of Exodus: A Critical, Theological Commentary.* Old Testament Library. Philadelphia: Westminster, 1974.

Clements, R. E. *Exodus.* Cambridge Bible Commentary. Cambridge: At the University Press, 1972.

Coats, G. W. *Rebellion in the Wilderness: The Murmuring Motif in the Wilderness Traditions of the Old Testament.* Nashville: Abingdon, 1968.

Cole, R. A. *Exodus.* Tyndale Old Testament Commentaries. Downers Grove, IL: Inter-Varsity, 1973.

Gilmer, H. W. *The If-You Form in Israelite Law.* SBL Dissertation Series. Missoula, MT: Scholars Press for the Society of Biblical Literature, 1975.

Greenberg, M. "Exodus, Book of." In *EncJud* 6: 1050–1067.

______. *Understanding Exodus.* New York: Behrman, 1969.

Gutzke, M. G. *Plain Talk on Exodus.* Grand Rapids: Zondervan, 1974.

Huey, F. B., Jr. *Exodus: A Study Guide Commentary.* Grand Rapids: Zondervan, 1977.

Hyatt, J. P. *Commentary on Exodus.* New Century Bible. London: Oliphants, 1971.

Knight, G. A. F. *Theology As Narration: A Commentary on the Book of Exodus.* Edinburgh: Handsel Press, 1976.

Maimonides, M. *The Song at the Sea: Being a Commentary on a Commentary in Two Parts.* Translated by Judah Goldin. New Haven: Yale University Press, 1971.

Napier, B. D. *The Book of Exodus.* Laymen's Bible Commentary. Richmond: John Knox, 1959.

Nicholson, E. W. *Exodus and Sinai in History and Tradition.* Richmond: John Knox, 1973.

Noth, M. Exodus, *a Commentary*. Old Testament Library. Philadelphia: Westminster, 1962.

Ramm, B. *His Way Out: A Fresh Look at* Exodus. Glendale, CA: Regal, 1974.

Schmidt, W. H. Exodus. Neukirchen-Vluyn: Neukirchener Verlag, 1974–.

Exodus 1–6

Ackermann, J. S. "The Literary Context of the Moses Birth Story (Exodus 1–2)." In *Literary Interpretations of Biblical Narratives*. Edited by Kenneth R. R. G. Louis et al. Nashville: Abingdon, 1974, pp. 74–119.

Albright, W. F. "From the Patriarchs to Moses. Part II: Moses Out of Egypt." *BA* 36 (1973): 48–76.

Archer, G. L. "Old Testament History and Recent Archaeology—from Moses to David." *BS* 127 (1970): 99–115.

Bretscher, P. "Exodus 4, 22–23 and the Voice from Heaven." *JBL* 87 (1968): 301–311.

Brownlee, W. H. "The Ineffable Name of God." *BASOR* 226 (1977): 39–46.

Bush, F. " 'I am Who I am': Moses and the Name of God." *TNN* 23 (1976): 10–14.

Butterworth, M. "Revelation of the Divine Name." *IndJT* 24 (1975): 45–52.

Campbell, E. F., Jr. "Moses and the Foundations of Israel." *Intr* 29 (1975): 141–154.

Childs, B. *Myth and Reality in the Old Testament*. Studies in biblical theology, no. 27. London: SCM Press, 1962, pp. 59–65.

Coats, G. W. "Moses in Midian." *JBL* 92 (1973): 3–10.

______. "A structural transition in Exodus." *VT* 22 (1972): 129–142.

Cohen, C. "Hebrew *tbh*: Proposed Etymologies." *JANES* 4 (1972): 36–51.

Dumbrell, W. "Exodus 4:24–26: A Textual Re-examination." *HTR* 65 (1972): 285–290.

Eakins, J. E. "Moses." *RExp* 74 (1977): 461–471.

Feliks, J. "Burning Bush." *EncJud* 4 (1971): 1528–1530.

Freedman, D. N. "The Burning Bush." *Bibl* 50 (1969): 245–246.

Gager, J. G., Jr. "Moses and Alpha." *JTS* 20 (1969): 245–248.

Gordon, C. H. "He is Who He Is." In *Joshua Finkel Festschrift*. New York: Yeshiva University Press, 1974, pp. 61–62.

Hamlin, E. J. "The Liberator's Ordeal. A Study of Exodus 4:1–9." In *Rhetorical Criticism: Essays in Honor of James Muilenburg*. Pittsburgh Theological Monograph series, no. 1. Edited by Jared J. Jackson and Martin Kessler. Pittsburgh: Pickwick Press, 1974, pp. 33–42.

Harris, R. L. "The Pronunciation of the Tetragrammaton." In *The Law and the Prophets*. In honor of O. T. Allis. Edited by John H. Skilton. Nutley, NJ: Presbyterian and Reformed, 1974, pp. 215–224.

Isbell, C. "Initial 'alef-yod Interchange and Selected Biblical Passages." *JNES* 37 (1978): 227–236.

Janzen, J. G. "What's in a Name? 'Yahweh' in Exodus 3 and the Wider Biblical Context." *Intr* 33 (1979): 227–239.

Jensen, J. "What Happened to Moses?" *CBQ* 32 (1970): 404–417.

Kitchen, K. A. "From the Brickfields of Egypt." *TB* 27 (1976): 137–147.

______. "Moses: A More Realistic View." *CT* 12 (1968): 920–923.

Kline, M. "Old Testament Origins of the Gospel Genre." *WTJ* 38 (1975): 1–27.

Lachs, S. T. "Exodus IV, 11: evidence for an emendation." *VT* 26 (1976): 249–250.

Magonet, J. "The Bush That Never Burnt (Narrative Techniques in Exodus 3 and 6)." *HJ* 16 (1975): 304–311.

Martens, E. A. "Tackling Old Testament Theology." *JETS* 20 (1977): 123–132.

McCarthy, D. J. "Exod 3:14: History, Philology and Theology." *CBQ* 40 (1978): 311–322.

Nixon, R. "New Wine in Old Wine-skins VII. Exodus." *ExpT* 85 (1973): 72–75.

Orlinsky, H. M. "Moses." In *Essays in Biblical and Jewish Culture and Bible Translation*. New York: Ktav, 1973, pp. 5–38.

Plaut, W. G. "The Israelites in Pharaoh's Egypt—A Historical Reconstruction." *Jud* 27 (1978): 40–46.

Rand, H. "Figure-Vases in Ancient Egypt and Hebrew Midwives." *IEJ* 20 (1970): 209–212.

Tigay, J. H. " 'Heavy of Mouth' and 'Heavy of Tongue.' On Moses' Speech Difficulty." *BASOR* 231 (1978): 57–64.

Uphill, E. P. "Pithom and Raamses: Their Location and Significance." *JNES* 28 (1969): 15–39.

Zimmerli, W. *Old Testament Theology in Outline*. Translated by David E. Green. Atlanta: John Knox, 1978, pp. 17–58.

7

Plagues, Passover, and the Exodus

Exodus 7:1—15:21

This section of Exodus is devoted principally to a description of the plagues God sent on Egypt (7:14—11:10; 12:29–32), and the exodus from Egypt via the Red (or Reed) Sea. Moses receives from the Lord, as preparation, this astounding word: "I make you as God to Pharaoh" (7:1). But before elation can set in He also says, "Pharaoh will not listen to you" (7:4). A God who will not be listened to!

The Plagues (7–11)

The function of the plagues goes back to the word of Pharaoh (5:2): "I do not know the LORD." The key word here is "know." It appears in:

- 6:7: "and you [Israel] shall know that I am the LORD your God"
- 7:5: "and the Egyptians shall know that I am the LORD"
- 7:17: "By this you [Pharaoh] shall know that I am the LORD" (the first plague)
- 8:10: "that you [Pharaoh] may know that there is no one like the LORD our God" (the second plague)

8:22: "that you [Pharaoh] may know that I am the LORD in the midst of the earth" (the fourth plague)

9:14: "I will send all my plagues . . . that you [Pharaoh] may know that there is none like me in all the earth" (the seventh plague)

9:29: "I [Moses] will stretch out my hands . . . there will be no more hail, that you [Pharaoh] may know that the earth is the LORD'S" (also the seventh plague)

10:2: ". . . what signs I [the Lord] have done among them [Egyptians], that you [Moses and Israel] may know that I am the LORD" (the eighth plague)

11:7: "that you [Moses and Israel] may know that the LORD makes a distinction between the Egyptians and Israel" (the tenth plague)

14:4: "and I will get glory over Pharaoh . . . and the Egyptians shall know that I am the LORD" (crossing the sea)

14:18: "and the Egyptians shall know that I am the LORD, when I have gotten glory over Pharaoh, his chariots, and his horsemen"

The use of this idiom continues in Exodus beyond this pericope, as indicated by 16:6, 12. In the wilderness Israel shall "know" that He is the Lord God through His miraculous provisions.

The Purpose of the Plagues

This emphasis on knowing the Lord lifts the plagues beyond the function of chastisement. The plagues are not God's revenge on Pharaoh. The Lord's intention is not to leave behind in Egypt a bruised and bloodied Pharaoh, nor is He interested in leaving the Egyptian king breathless via an exhibition of miracles.

The divine purpose is that the Pharaoh and his people—to say nothing of the Israelites—will indeed acquire knowledge of the true God. It will be knowledge based on observation and confrontation and not on hearsay. To know the Lord as Lord means to recognize and then submit to His authority. This is the choice the Pharaoh needs to make and is invited to make.

Ten plagues are recorded:

1. 7:14–25, water to blood
2. 8:1–15, swarms of frogs
3. 8:16–19, gnats (or lice)
4. 8:20–32, swarms of flies (Hebrews spared, 8:22)
5. 9:1–8, plague upon cattle (Hebrews' livestock spared, 9:4, 6)
6. 9:8–12, boils on man and beast
7. 9:13–35, hail, thunder, and lightning (except in the portion of territory assigned to the Hebrews, 9:26)
8. 10:1–20, plague of locusts
9. 10:21–29, three days of thick darkness
10. 11:1—12:36, the death of the first-born, both people and cattle (the Hebrews exempted if the necessary preparations were taken, 12:7, 13)

The suggestion has often been made that these plagues are each aimed directly at some aspect of Egyptian religion. In several instances this is quite possible, but in others the connection is difficult to make. Indeed, Exodus 12:12 has the Lord saying, "and on all the gods of Egypt I will execute judgments." That does apply to some of the plagues:

1. Hapi, the god of the Nile, bringer of fertility
2. Hek/qet, the frog-headed goddess of fruitfulness
4. Kheper(a), in the form of a beetle (if that may be included among "swarms of flies"). He symbolizes the daily cycle of the sun across the sky.

5. Many Egyptian gods and goddesses are pictured in the hieroglyphs zoomorphically: Hathor, a cow-headed goddess, or a goddess with a human head adorned with horns or cow's ears; Khnum, a ram-headed male figure; Amon, king of the gods and patron deity of the Pharaohs, a male figure with a ram's head, or a ram wearing a triple crown; Geb, god of the earth, a goose or a male figure with his head surmounted by a goose; Isis, queen of the gods, a cow's or ram's horns on her head
7. Nut, the sky goddess, also protectress of the dead
8. Serapia, protector from locusts
9. Re, the personification of the sun, king of the gods, and father of mankind
10. Possibly Taurt, goddess of maternity, who presided over childbirth; later a protective household deity

It needs to be pointed out that the biblical text gives no indication that the plagues are to be associated with Egyptian religion and deities. The similarities may, therefore, be only coincidental.

Z. Zevit has looked for analogies to the plagues elsewhere. He has discovered similar terms and language in the pericope about the plagues and in the creation narratives of Genesis, and suggests Genesis 1–2 is the background, thematically, for the plagues. Thus, as an example, in the plague of blood the phrase "all their pools of water" (7:19) is literally "every gathering of their waters" and is a parallel to the "waters that were gathered together" of Genesis 1:10. Zevit also connects the ten plagues with the tenfold "and he [God] said" of Genesis 1:3, 6, 9, 11, 14, 20, 24, 26, 28, 29.[1]

1. "The Priestly Redaction and Interpretation of the Plague Narrative in Exodus," *JQR* 66 (1976), p. 211.

The Hardening of Pharaoh's Heart

Terms used to describe Pharaoh's heart

Terminology about the hardening of Pharaoh's heart appears twenty times in Exodus 4–14, and three different Hebrew verbs are used—*kābēd, ḥāzaq, qāshâ* — to describe the act of hardening. The basic meaning of *kābēd* is "to be heavy." In addition to describing the heart, the word *kābēd* may describe the eyes (Gen. 48:10), the ears (Isa. 6:10), or the mouth and the tongue (Exod. 4:10). All these references are to the malfunction of a particular organ, the malfunction being caused either by age or disease (Gen. 48:10; Exod. 4:10). R. R. Wilson, therefore, says that in these passages the writer is "referring to an organ of perception that is no longer receiving outside stimuli."[2]

The verb *ḥāzaq* means "to be strong, hard." The root is in the name *Hezekiah*, that is, "the Lord is my strength," and in *Ezekiel*, that is, "may the Lord strengthen." Put in a negative context, perhaps our closest English equivalent is "bullheaded." *Qāshâ* means "to be hard, difficult, severe."

Following are the passages from Exodus that use one of these Hebrew verbs. After each reference is a listing of the particular verb that is used, and an indication of what stem that verb assumes there, the basic *Qal* stem or the *Piel* or *Hiphil* stems. (Put most simply, the *Qal* describes a state, "to be . . ."; the *Piel* and *Hiphil* describe a condition or situation that is caused, "to make. . . .") The translation is that of the RSV. I include parallels from the Jerusalem Bible (JB) and the New English Bible (NEB) if they are different from the RSV. These two modern versons of Scripture—which I consider to be among the best—show flexibility in choice of translation for one of the three Hebrew verbs listed above. Whenever a verse number is put in

2. "The Hardening of Pharaoh's Heart," *CBQ* 41 (1979), p. 22.

brackets, this is the number of the verse in the Hebrew text, which is at variance with the English text.

1. 4:21, "I will harden his heart"; "make him obstinate" (NEB); *ḥāzaq* in the Piel
2. 7:3, "I will harden Pharaoh's heart"; "I will make Pharaoh's heart stubborn" (NEB, JB); *qāshâ* in the Hiphil
3. 7:13, "Still Pharaoh's heart was hardened"; "Pharaoh, however, was obstinate" (NEB); "stubborn" (JB); *ḥāzaq* in the Qal
4. 7:14, "Pharaoh's heart is hardened"; "obdurate" (NEB); "adamant" (JB); *kābēd* in adjectival form
5. 7:22, "Pharaoh's heart remained hardened"; "remained obstinate" (NEB); "was stubborn" (JB); *ḥāzaq* in the Qal
6. 8:15[11], "Pharaoh . . . hardened his heart"; "he became obdurate" (NEB); "became adamant" (JB); *kābēd* in the Hiphil
7. 8:19[15], "Pharaoh's heart was hardened"; "remained obstinate" (NEB); "was stubborn" (JB); *ḥāzaq* in the Qal
8. 8:32[28], "Pharaoh hardened his heart"; "became obdurate" (NEB): "was adamant" (JB); *kābēd* in the Hiphil
9. 9:7, "the heart of Pharaoh was hardened"; "he remained obdurate" (NEB); "became adamant" (JB); *kābēd* in the Qal
10. 9:12, "the LORD hardened the heart of Pharaoh"; "made Pharaoh obstinate" (NEB); "made Pharaoh's heart stubborn" (JB); *ḥāzaq* in the Piel
11. 9:34, "he hardened his heart"; "became obdurate" (NEB); "became adamant" (JB); *kābēd* in the Hiphil
12. 9:35, "the heart of Pharaoh was hardened"; "remained obstinate" (NEB); "was stubborn" (JB); *ḥāzaq* in the Qal
13. 10:1, "I have hardened his heart"; "I have made him obdurate" (NEB); "stubborn" (JB); *kābēd* in the Hiphil
14. 10:20, "the LORD hardened Pharaoh's heart"; "made

Pharaoh obstinate" (NEB); "made Pharaoh's heart stubborn" (JB); *ḥāzaq* in the Piel

15. 10:27, "the Lord hardened Pharaoh's heart"; "made Pharaoh obstinate" (NEB); "made Pharaoh's heart stubborn" (JB); *ḥāzaq* in the Piel
16. 11:10, "the LORD hardened Pharaoh's heart"; "made him obstinate" (NEB); "made Pharaoh's heart stubborn" (JB); *ḥāzaq* in the Piel
17. 13:15, "Pharaoh stubbornly refused to let us go"; "proved stubborn and refused to let us go" (NEB); "stubbornly refused to let us go" (JB); *qāshâ* in the Hiphil
18. 14:4, "I will harden Pharaoh's heart"; "make Pharaoh obstinate" (NEB); "make Pharaoh's heart stubborn" (JB); *ḥāzaq* in the Piel
19. 14:8, "the LORD hardened the heart of Pharaoh"; "made obstinate" (NEB); "made . . . stubborn" (JB); *ḥāzaq* in the Piel
20. 14:17, "I will harden the hearts of the Egyptians"; "make obstinate" (NEB); "make . . . stubborn" (JB); *kābēd* in the Piel

Of the three verbs then, *ḥāzaq* is used most frequently (eleven times), followed by *kābēd* (seven times), and *qāshâ* (two times).

Analyses of the Terminology

It is interesting to arrange these twenty verses on the basis of the subject of the verb. See Table 6.

From these analyses at least several observations may be made. To be sure, there is the word from God to Moses in 4:21 and 7:3 that "I will harden Pharaoh's heart." Twice Moses hears this before the commencement of the plagues. But neither time does the announcement elicit either protest or a demand for an explanation from Moses. And we have already seen in the Exodus narrative that Moses occasionally protests or presses God for additional facts. Here, however, he is compliant.

Table 6

God as subject (10 references)		
kābēd	**ḥāzaq**	**qāshâ**
10:1 Hiphil 14:17 Piel	4:21 Piel 9:12 Piel 10:20 Piel 10:27 Piel 11:10 Piel 14:4 Piel 14:8 Piel	7:3 Hiphil
Pharaoh as subject (4 references)		
kābēd	**ḥāzaq**	**qāshâ**
8:15[11] Hiphil 8:32[28] Hiphil 9:34 Hiphil		13:15 Hiphil
Pharaoh's heart as subject (6 references)		
kābēd	**ḥāzaq**	**qāshâ**
7:14 adjective 9:7 Qal	7:13 Qal 7:22 Qal 8:19[15] Qal 9:35 Qal	

Is this then an indication that Moses has accepted his responsibilities and is confident enough that he does not question God? Or may we assume that on hearing such an enigmatic word from God, Moses engaged in even further remonstrations with God? May not such announcements be considered God's declaration of the outcome?

On examining the description of the plagues, one notices that references to God's hardening of Pharaoh's heart emerge only late in the narrative. Thus:

1. "Pharaoh's heart is hardened" (7:14)
2. "he hardened his heart" (8:15[11])
3. "Pharaoh's heart was hardened" (8:19[15])
4. "But Pharaoh hardened his heart" (8:32[28])
5. "But the heart of Pharaoh was hardened" (9:7)

6. "But the LORD hardened the heart of Pharaoh" (9:12)

7. "So the heart of Pharaoh was hardened" (9:35)

8. "I have hardened his heart" (10:1)
   "But the LORD hardened Pharaoh's heart" (10:20)
9. "But the LORD hardened Pharaoh's heart" (10:27)
10. "The LORD hardened Pharaoh's heart" (11:10)

What is noticeable is that there is no reference to God's hardening the heart of Pharaoh until after the sixth plague is well under way. There is only one reference (9:34) to Pharaoh hardening his own heart after God's hardening is done.

Can this be fortuitous? Or is the Scripture implying that Pharaoh, now so impervious to God, has forfeited his right to choose consciously and independently? May freedom be abrogated? At least for a while Pharaoh had control over his own choice, but never did he exercise control over the consequences of his choice.

With all of our concentration on the hardening of Pharaoh's heart we may miss the several clear ways in which God attempted to soften his heart:

1. by the prayers of Moses: 8:8[4], 28[24]; 9:28; 10:17, "entreat the LORD"
2. by the testimony of his own magicians: "this is the finger of God" (8:19[15])
3. by moving him to partial obedience: "I will let the people go to sacrifice to the LORD" (8:8[4]); "go, sacrifice to your God within the land . . . I will let you go . . . only you shall not go very far away" (8:25–28[21–24]); "Go . . . only let your flocks and your herds remain behind" (10:24)
4. by moving him to partial penitence: "I have sinned this time; the LORD is in the right, and I and my people are in the wrong" (9:27); "I have sinned against the LORD your God, and against you. Now

therefore, forgive my sin . . ." (10:16). Putting together the "I have sinned" of 9:27 and the "he sinned yet again" of 9:34, Moshe Greenberg says, "he acknowledged guilt but went right on being guilty."[3] The Pharaoh needs to hear the word of Matthew 3:8, "prove your repentance by the fruit it bears" (NEB).

5. by continually giving Pharaoh another chance: God is as long-suffering with Pharaoh as He was with Moses after the burning bush. Moses' repeated "I will not go" is matched by the Pharaoh's repeated "I will not let you go." That God had to act ten times before Pharaoh acquiesced is not unexpected or surprising. After all, in terms of long-range effectiveness, or even for the first few generations after the deluge, how successful was the flood, another act of divine judgment?

Explanations about the hardening of Pharaoh's heart

Addressing himself to the issue of the hardening of Pharaoh's heart, and similar events, Walther Eichrodt says,

> The remarkable thing, however, is that his never led to a flat determinism, depriving Man of the responsibility for his actions. At all times the capacity for self-determination is insistently retained. The whole ethical exhortation of the prophets is based on the conviction that decision is placed in the hands of men. But the Law too . . . rests on this presupposition. The fundamental postulate of moral freedom is thus found in equal force alongside the religious conviction of God's effective action in all things; and no attempt is made to create a harmonizing adjustment between them. It is testimony to the compelling power of the Old Testament experience of God that it was able to affirm both realities at once, and to endure the tension

3. *Understanding Exodus* (New York: Behrman, 1969), p. 161.

> between them, without discounting anything of their unconditional validity.[4]

What God has joined together, let no man put asunder!

In the New Testament it is in Romans 9–11 that one finds further explanation of the motif. There is reference to the hardening of Pharaoh's heart (9:17–18) and to the hardening of Israel (11:7, 25). Following Eichrodt, we will observe that the New Testament, no less than the Old, also holds in tension God's divine sovereignty and man's moral freedom. This is precisely what emerges out of this Pauline passage.

Contending that physical descent from Abraham is insufficient to qualify one as a spiritual child of Abraham, Paul will buttress his case by appealing to Genesis. Both Isaac and Ishmael were physical sons of Abraham, but only one was the child of promise (9:7–9). Both Jacob and Esau were children of Isaac, but Esau was passed over in favor of Jacob (9:10–13). Thus, Paul has addressed himself to the questions of God's fidelity (9:6) by showing in operation in patriarchal history God's principle of selectivity.

But if God is selective, does this imply injustice on God's part (9:14)? Were Ishmael and Esau indiscriminately rejected? To respond to that objection Paul turns to Exodus and essentially says, "If you maintain that the God of the patriarchs is unjust, you must maintain the same about the God of Exodus." Here, too, selectivity was in operation. On Israel He showed mercy. Pharaoh's heart He hardened. (Note that in Romans "mercy" appears eleven times, nine of which are in 9–11: 9:15 [two times], 16, 18, 23; 11:30, 31[two times], 32.)

Crucial here is 9:17: "I have raised you [Pharaoh] up for

4. *Theology of the Old Testament*, 2 vols., translated by J. Baker (Philadelphia: Westminster, 1967), vol. 2, pp. 178–179.

the very purpose of showing my power in you. . . ." This verse is a quotation of Exodus 9:16. The equivalent in Exodus to "I have raised you up" (in Romans) is "I have let you live." "Raising up" then has nothing to do with being born or created. Rather, it means, "I have not destroyed you" or "I have allowed you to continue to live." The raising up is itself an expression of God's mercy. And His mercy and His hardening are both expressions of His sovereignty (9:18).

To underscore this idea of a sovereign God, Paul appeals to creation (God as potter), plus several quotes from Hosea and Isaiah (9:19–29).

Where then does all of this place man? This is the concern of 9:30—10:21. It is important that we not stop with 9:29. God is sovereign, yes, but this does not negate human freedom. If there are Jews who are not justified it is not because their unbelief was predetermined, but because they have "stumbled over the stumbling stone" (9:32). There has been no lack of invitation on God's part: "All day long I have held out my hands to a disobedient and contrary people" (10:21). Thus, we have side by side divine sovereignty (9:6–29) and human privilege and personal responsibility (9:30—10:21).

Turning from comments on Jews as individuals, Paul progresses to discussion of Jews as a people, a community (11:1ff.). Although God has rejected individual Jews, He has never rejected His people in toto (11:2). In 11:7–25 Paul compares implicitly the hardening of Pharaoh and the hardening of Jews. In each case God uses the hardening redemptively. He hardened Pharaoh. The result? The Israelites were delivered from Egypt. He has hardened the Israelites. The result? Gentiles are allowed to enter God's kingdom. What then of the Jews, not just the remnant? Is the hardening permanent? Paul's answer is an emphatic no. "All Israel will be saved" (11:26), a tantalizing expression on which Paul does not elaborate.

The Passover (12:1—13:16)

Exodus 12 spells out the procedures in the observance of Passover. Further information may be found in the cultic calendars of the Pentateuch: Leviticus 23:5–8; Numbers 28:16–25; Deuteronomy 16:1–8. In these three passages, as well as in Exodus 12, Passover is closely linked with the feast of unleavened bread. The Old Testament records the observance of five particular Passovers besides the original one: in the wilderness, Numbers 9:1–14; at Gilgal after entering Canaan, Joshua 5:10–12; that celebrated by Hezekiah, II Chronicles 30:1–27 (but no parallel to this in Kings); that celebrated by Josiah (an abbreviated account in II Kings 23:21–23, and an extended account in II Chron. 35:1–19); that celebrated in the post-exilic community, Ezra 6:19–22.

The Hebrew word for "Passover" is *pesaḥ*. There is also a verb (*pāsaḥ*, "to pass over") used three times in this chapter: 12:13, "when I see the blood I will pass over you"; 12:23, "the LORD will pass over the door"; 12:27, "It is the sacrifice of the LORD'S passover, for he passed over the houses of the people of Israel in Egypt."

What does the phrase "the LORD will pass over" mean, however? Does it mean He will by-pass the houses over whose door the blood is smeared? The clue is found in 12:23, "the LORD will pass over the door and will not allow the destroyer to enter your houses to slay you." To "pass over," then, means "to protect," or as NEB suggests in a footnote, "or stand guard over." The Lord Himself will block the entry of the destroyer. He will be a protective covering for His people. Their security is in His presence.

Most important here is the use of the blood. That blood is to be extracted from the lamb's body, then smeared over the doorposts and the horizontal beam atop the door (12:7, 13). Failure to take this action will result in disaster.

It is no wonder, then, that Moses, in relating God's word

to his people (12:21–27), focuses exclusively on the role of the blood. As Brevard Childs says, "The literary effect of Moses' speech is one of tremendous telescoping."[5] He says nothing about the meal in the home, the quality of the lamb to be chosen, when it is to be killed, how the meat is to be prepared, how much of it is to be eaten, what type of clothing the people are to wear—all of which are included in God's directions to Moses (12:1–13).

Exodus 12 is concerned not only about the *when* of Passover, the *why* of Passover, the *how* of observing it, but also about *who* may participate (12:43–49). The observance of Passover is not an indiscriminate invitation to everyone. Who may? The congregation of Israel (v. 47); the slave (v. 44), if circumcised, who has the same privileges as a Hebrew; the stranger (v. 48), the non-Israelite who has become a believer in Yahweh. Who may not? The foreigner (v. 43), the pagan unbeliever; the sojourner (v. 45), either the resident alien or the visitor who will settle temporarily on Israelite soil; the hired servant (v. 45), one belonging to another nation but working in Israel. These distinctions are necessary because of the "mixed multitude" (12:38) leaving Egypt.

Deliberately the New Testament writers move from the lamb to the Lamb, from the type to the antitype, for this is the fullness of God's plan. The prison is now a kingdom of darkness and not slavery in Egypt. The captive who is called forth is not Israel, but the world. Redemption is an ethical change rather than a geographical change.

As with the lamb in Egypt (Exod. 12:46), so not one bone of Jesus the Lamb was broken (John 19:36). The two explicit references in the epistolary literature of the New Testament to Christ the Passover Lamb are in I Corinthians 5:7 ("Christ, our paschal lamb") and I Peter

5. *The Book of Exodus: A Critical, Theological Commentary*, Old Testament Library (Philadelphia: Westminster, 1974), p. 200.

1:19 ("a lamb without blemish or spot"). What is of interest in these passages is that both Paul and Peter are concerned more with the implications of redemption by the Lamb for holy living than they are in formulating a theological discourse on soteriology. That is, the apostles move beyond salvation and into sanctification.

The immediate sequel to the Passover is Moses' transmission of further instructions to the Israelites about the feast of unleavened bread (13:3–10) and the consecration of the first-born (13:11–16). Each of these two sections stresses that God's redemption is both *from* and *into*. It is from Egypt, but into the land of the Canaanites (vv. 5, 11). Israel's possession of her new land will be the fulfillment of God's promises to the fathers. Suddenly the reader is taken back as far as Genesis 12:7. But once in the land Israel must share her testimony with the sons God will give her (vv. 8, 14). God's faithfulness reverberates over three periods: the past—your fathers; the present—you; the future—your sons.

The Exodus (13:17—15:21)

Exodus 12:37 informs us that 600,000 men, besides women and children, left Egypt. The total number of Israelites leaving would be in excess of two million. This same number is repeated substantially in Exodus 38:26; Numbers 1:46; 2:32; 26:51. What shall we do with such an astronomical number? Exodus 23:29–30 suggests that God will drive out the Canaanites gradually because Israel's population is too meager to repopulate Canaan: "little by little I will drive them out from before you, *until you are increased*" (italics mine). (See also table 12, page 316.)

The Population of Israel

Not a little discussion has surrounded the total number of those counted in the census: 603,550. This number excludes the Levites, all women, and all children under twenty years of age. The total number of the congregation would be approximately two million people.

Various explanations from the critics among biblical scholars have been offered. One suggestion is that the figures are nothing short of fabulous, and without any historical value. That is, they represent the unrestrained imagination of a later writer given to hyperbole. A second suggestion is that the numbers are of historical value, but reflect a later census made during David's reign.

A third suggestion surrounds the translation of the Hebrew word *'élep*, whose normal translation is "thousand." As early as 1905 the eminent archaeologist, Sir Flinders Petrie, suggested that the word should not be translated "thousand" but as "family."[6] In this he has been seconded in more modern times by Jacob Milgrom.[7] Verses cited to support this thesis include Judges 6:15, "behold my clan (*'élep*) is the weakest in Manasseh"; Numbers 1:16, "the ones chosen . . . the leaders . . . the heads of the clans (*'élep*) of Israel" (KJV has here "heads of thousands in Israel"); I Samuel 10:19, ". . . Now therefore present yourselves before the Lord by your tribes (*šēbeṭ*) and by your clans (*'élep*)" (JB, NIV; "thousands," RSV, KJV); I Samuel 10:21, "He brought the tribe (*šēbeṭ*) of Benjamin near by its families (*mišpāḥah*). . . ." These latter two verses would seem to indicate that "clan" and "family" are synonyms. Thus, according to this system Judah does not have a population of 74,600. Rather, it totals 74 families and 600 people.

A third suggestion is much like that of Petrie. George E. Mendenhall suggests that the word *'élep* designates not "family," "clan," or "tent," but a military unit (see Num. 1:3).[8] Following this interpretation, we would para-

6. *Researches in Sinai* (London: J. Murray, 1906), pp. 209–211.
7. "Priestly Terminology," *JQR* 69 (1978), pp. 79–80.
8. "The Census Lists of Numbers 1 and 26," *JBL* 77 (1958): 52–66.

phrase Numbers 1:26–27 as, "Of the people of Judah registered by lineage in clans and ancestral homes: when all the males of twenty years or more who were fit for military service were polled, *74 units* of the tribe were recorded, and from these *600* men were enrolled for military service."

In either case the conclusion is the same. The number of men (twenty years or older) in the wilderness is reduced from 603,550 to 5,550. Evangelical scholars have in many instances accepted the rendering of *'élep* as "military unit" or "family."

An additional support for the decreased number may be found in the military records from the ancient Near East. If Ramses II (1304–1234 B.C.) is the Pharaoh of the exodus—a possibility, but still not a totally accepted suggestion—then it is interesting to observe that at the Pharaoh's famous battle at Kadesh in Syria, both the Pharaoh and Muwatallis, the Hittite king, fielded approximately 20,000 troops each.[9] And these are the armies of the two titans of that day! By contrast Israel would have had, as she left Egypt, a group of males (twenty years and older) who would number approximately one-fourth the size of the Egyptian and Hittite armies.

But is all of this explaining or explaining away the integrity of the biblical narrative? James Barr, focusing on this very section of Exodus and the opening chapters of Numbers, asks whether the modern conservative "is boldly upholding the accuracy of the Bible, relying on the power of God to sustain this great multitude by miraculous feedings? Not in the slightest. On the contrary, he is doing all he can to find a way to cut the numbers down."[10] Lest the reader believe that all evangelical Old Testament scholars have abandoned the traditional translation—one that is

9. J. H. Breasted, *Ancient Records of Egypt: Historical Documents from the Earliest Times to the Persian Conquest* (1906; reprint ed. New York: Russell and Russell, 1962), vol. 3, pp. 127, 129.

10. *Fundamentalism* (Philadelphia: Westminster, 1978), p. 250.

retained in all modern Bible versions—let him read the comments by Gleason L. Archer in defense of the credibility of the high figures.[11] A sufficiently large number of Israelites must be assumed to make sense of the Pharaoh's, "Behold, the people of Israel are too many and too mighty for us" (Exod. 1:9). Also, the approximately six and one-half tons of precious metal donated to the tabernacle project by the Israelites (Exod. 38:21–31) presupposes a rather large base of people as contributors, to say nothing of how this was carried out of Egypt and into the wilderness.

The Crossing of the Reed Sea

The crossing of the Reed Sea (to be preferred to "Red Sea," which is based not on the Hebrew, but on the Greek *eruthra thalassa* and the Latin *mare rubrum*) is described miraculously. The people of God pass through on dry land between two walls of water, walls of water which subsequently converged and submerged the retreating Egyptians.

To have the Red Sea divided would be no insignificant event. Today the Red Sea is approximately 1,200 miles in length (excluding the gulfs of Aqaba and Suez at the north). Its width varies from 124 to 155 miles. Its average depth is a bit more than 1,600 feet. Minimum depth is 600 feet and maximum depth is 7,700 feet. In addition, the name "Sea of Reeds" (or, "Rushes") presupposes fresh water, not salt water, in order for reeds to grow.

We conclude then that the Hebrews crossed not the Red Sea or the gulf of Suez, but rather some freshwater lake in northern Egypt (perhaps the southern tip of modern Lake Manzalah near modern Port Said). This does not, in any way, undercut the supernatural element in the story. Six hundred Egyptians were drowned, a fact not impossible given this general area's proneness to earthquakes and

11. *A Survey of Old Testament Introduction* (Chicago: Moody, 1973), pp. 234–238.

possible tidal waves.[12] Whether passage was through a sea, a lake, or a lagoon, God had delivered His people from the paws of the largest lion in the world, Egypt.

One might suspect that such a distinctive divine working would erase any suspicions the Israelites might have entertained about God's ability to deliver them and Moses' ability to lead them. Such was not the case. As early as 16:2–3, the people of God, recently liberated, are yearning for Egypt. Freedom and pioneering are not as promising as bondage with the guarantee of three meals a day.

Chapter 14 concludes by observing that "the people feared the LORD; and they believed in the LORD and in his servant Moses" (v. 31). But such belief must be verbalized. For impression without expression leads to depression. Moses is coupled with the Lord at the end of chapter 14. But in the song of chapter 15 Moses is conspicuously absent.

It is fitting in this litany of praise that it is primarily as Yahweh that God is addressed. Ten times the tetragrammaton is used: 1, 3 (two times), 6 (two times), 11, 16, 17, 18, 21. One time there is an abbreviated form of Yahweh—*yah* in verse 2; one time the use of *adonay*, verse 17; and two times *el* (v. 2). The hymn is then an affirmation of His lordship.

In speaking of God, the hymn begins in the third person (vv. 1–5), shifts into the second person (vv. 6–17), then returns to and concludes with the third person (vv. 18–21). Preponderantly, then, this is a hymn addressed directly to God, the God "who dwells in the praises of His people."

The emphasis is primarily on what God has done. Israel does serve a God who acts, and acts decisively. To tamper with God's people is no small risk. As early as Genesis 12

12. See G. A. F. Knight, *Theology as Narration. A Commentary on the Book of Exodus* (Edinburgh: Hardsel Press, 1976), pp. 104–105, and K. A. Kitchen, "Red Sea," in *ZPEB*, 5, p. 47.

an Egyptian Pharaoh discovered that truth. To wound the body is to wound the head. Paul found that to persecute the church was to persecute Christ.

The hymn celebrates not only the great acts of God, but also His nature, who He is. He is "majestic in holiness" (v. 11). He is a God of covenant, mercy love (v. 13). He is incomparable (v. 11).

So then, both God's acts and God's nature lend a predictibility to the future (vv.13–18). The Philistines, the Edomites, the Moabites, and the Canaanites too will fall as have the Egyptians. No exterior force can restrain the forward march of God's people. Only sin and disobedience can loom as a deterrent.

Bibliography

The Plagues Account

DeVries, S. J. "The Time Word *maḥar* as a Key to Tradition Development." *ZAW* 87 (1975): 66–73.

Eakin, F. E., Jr. "The Plagues and the Crossing of the Sea." *RExp* 74 (1977): 473–482.

Elder, W. E. H. "The Passover." *RExp* 74 (1977): 511–522.

Greenburg, M. "Plagues of Egypt." *EncJud* 13 (1971): 604–613.

______. "The Redaction of the Plague Narrative in Exodus." In *Near Eastern Studies: In Honor of William Foxwell Albright*. Edited by Hans Goedicke. Baltimore: Johns Hopkins Press, 1971, pp. 243–252.

Haran, M. "The Passover Sacrifice." *SVT* 23 (1972): 86–116.

Jocz, J. "Passover." In *ZPEB*, 4, pp. 605–611.

Kuyper, L. J. "Hardness of Heart According to Biblical Perspective." *SJT* 27 (1974): 459–474.

Loewenstamm, S. E. "Number of Plagues in Psalm 105." *Bibl* 52 (1971): 34–38.

______. "An observation on source-criticism of the plague pericope." *VT* 24 (1974): 374–378.

Margulis, B. "Plagues tradition in Ps. 105." *Bibl* 50 (1969): 491–496.

MacIntosh, A. A. "Exodus VIII 19, distinct redemption and the Hebrew roots *pdh* and *pdd*." *VT* 21 (1971): 548–555.

McCarthy, D. J. "Moses' Dealing with Pharaoh: Exodus 7:8—10:27." *CBQ* 27 (1965): 336–347.

———. "Plagues and the Sea of Reeds: Exodus 5—14." *JBL* 85 (1966): 137–158.

McKay, J. W. "The Date of Passover and its Significance." *ZAW* 84 (1972): 435–447.

Ogden, G. S. "Moses and Cyrus. Literary Affinities between the Priestly Presentation of Moses in Exodus vi–viii and the Cyrus Song in Isaiah xliv 24–xlv 13." *VT* 28 (1978): 195–203.

Ramm, B. "The Theology of the Book of Exodus: A Reflection on Exodus 12:12." *SWJT* 20 (1977): 59–68.

Riggs, J. R. "The Length of Israel's Sojourn in Egypt." *GJ* 12 (1971): 18–35.

Wilson, R. R. "The Hardening of Pharaoh's Heart." *CBQ* 41 (1979): 18–36.

Zevit, Z. "The Priestly Redaction and Interpretation of the Plague Narrative in Exodus." *JQR* 66 (1976): 193–211.

The Exodus Account

Brisco, T. "The Sinai Peninsula and the Exodus." *SWJT* 20 (1977): 23–32.

Childs, B. "A traditio-historical study of the Reed Sea tradition." *VT* 20 (1970): 406–418.

Coats, G. W. "An exposition for the wilderness traditions." *VT* 22 (1972): 288–295.

———. "History and Theology in the Sea Tradition." *ST* 29 (1975): 141–154.

———. "The Song of the Sea." *CBQ* 31 (1969): 1–17.

Cohen, C. "Studies in Early Israelite Poetry I: An Unrecognized Case of Three-Line Staircase Parallelism in the Song of the Sea." *JANES* 7 (1975): 13–17.

Craigie, P. C. "Yahweh as a Man of Wars." *SJT* 22 (1969): 183–188.

Cross, F. M. *Canaanite Myth and Hebrew Epic; Essays in the History of the Religion of Israel*. Cambridge, MA: Harvard University Press, 1973, pp. 121–144.

———. "Song of the Sea and Canaanite Myth." *JTCh* 5 (1968): 1–25.

Dahood, M. "Exodus 15, 2 *'anwēhû* and Ugaritic *śnwt*." *Bibl* 59 (1978): 260–261.

Francisco, C. T. "The Exodus in Its Historical Setting." *SWJT* 20 (1977): 3–20.

Freedman, D. N. "Strophe and Meter in Exodus 15." In *A Light unto My Path: Old Testament Studies in Honor of Jacob M. Myers*. Edited by Howard N. Bream et al. Gettysburg Theological Studies, no. 4. Philadelphia: Temple University Press, 1974, pp. 163–203.

______. "Divine Names and Titles in Early Hebrew Poetry." In *Magnalia Dei: The Mighty Acts of God*. Essays on the Bible and Archaeology in Memory of G. Ernest Wright. Edited by Frank M. Cross, Werner E. Lemke, and Patrick D. Miller, Jr. Garden City, NY: Doubleday, 1976, pp. 57–61.

Good, E. "Exodus xv 2." *VT* 20 (1970): 358–359.

Gronigen, G. Van. "That Final Question." In *The Law and the Prophets*. In honor of O. T. Allis. Edited by John H. Skilton. Nutley, NJ: Presbyterian and Reformed, 1974, pp. 253–271.

Kitchen, K. A. "Red Sea." In *ZPEB*, 5, pp. 46–49.

Klein, M. "The Targumic Tosefta to Exodus 15, 2." *JJS* 26 (1975): 61–67.

Loewenstamm, S. E. "The Lord is my strength and my glory." *VT* 19 (1969): 464–470.

Mann, T. W. "The Pillar of Cloud in the Reed Sea Narrative." *JBL* 90 (1971): 15–30.

Miller, P. D. *The Divine Warrior in Early Israel*. Cambridge, MA: Harvard University Press, 1973, pp. 113–117.

Parker, S. B. "Exodus XV 2 again." *VT* 21 (1971): 373–379.

Patrick, D. "Traditio-history of the Reed Sea account." *VT* 26 (1976): 248–249.

Reist, I. W. "The Theological Significance of the Exodus." *JETS* 12 (1969): 223–232.

Sabourin, L. "The Biblical Cloud. Terminology and Traditions." *BTB* 4 (1974): 290–311.

Soltis, T. "Scientific Theology and the Miracle at the Red Sea." *Springf* 38 (1974): 55–59.

Tomes, R. "Exodus 14: The Mighty Acts of God." *SJT* 22 (1969): 455–478.

Waldman, N. "Comparative Note on Exodus 15:14–16." *JQR* 66 (1976): 189–192.

Walsh, J. T. "From Egypt to Moab: A Source-Critical Analysis." *CBQ* 39 (1977): 20–33.

8

Testing in the Wilderness

Exodus 15:22—18:27

The three-month journey from Egypt to Sinai was not carefree, either for Moses or for the Israelites. During this brief part of their itinerary they confronted at least four crises: the bitter waters at Marah (15:22–27); the need for sufficient quantities of food (16:1–36); a lack of drinking water at Rephidim (17:1–7); the invasion of the Amalekites (17:8–16). A fifth crisis might be the state of Moses' health. He is evidently overtaxed. Can he continue at such a pace indefinitely? Might Israel lose her leader, now dangerously close to the point of complete physical exhaustion (18:1–27)? His hands are weary (17:12), and his schedule of appointments is hectic (18:13).

A key verb used throughout this section is *nāsâ*, "to prove, put to the test." It appears in 15:25 and 16:4 with God as subject and the Israelites as the object of the testing. It is the same verb used to describe God's putting Abraham to the test vis-à-vis Isaac (Gen. 22:1). *Nāsâ* is used similarly in the postlude to the Decalogue, Exodus 20:20 (see also Deut. 8:2, 16; 33:8). Twice the verb is used in this unit with negative overtones (17:2, 7). Here subject and object are reversed. The Israelites are the subject and God is the object, as in Deuteronomy 6:16.

The implications in these two verses of chapter 17 are clear. God is not to be tested. His reliability is not something that needs to be established. A companion to testing

God is murmuring (15:24; 16:2). To be sure, such murmurings are directed immediately at Moses, but to raise a question about God's servant is to raise a question about God (16:7–8; cf. "You have not lied to men but to God," Acts 5:4.) Murmuring is a frame of mind in which one believes that, in difficulties, God is insufficient. The author of Hebrews, referring to the rebellion described in Exodus 17:1–7, suggests that murmuring leads to hardening of the heart, and that leads to forfeiting one's position in God's kingdom (Heb. 3:7–13).

There is here, then, precious little of letting requests be made known unto God with thanksgiving. Nevertheless, God is not piqued. He does respond, not because of the Israelites' murmurings, but in spite of their murmurings.

First, bitter waters become sweet after Moses throws a tree into the water (15:25). This happened in response to prayer by Moses. In the first plague water had become blood. Here brackish water becomes sweet water. In the New Testament water will become wine (John 2:9).

Second, the daily supply of bread and meat came in the form of manna and quail (16:1–36). Both of these foods have been described as typical at one time of the Sinai peninsula. Manna has been explained as a secretion from insects or lice on the branches of tamarisk trees (hardly designed to whet the appetite!). Quail are the smallest member of the pheasant family. The Sinai peninsula is the natural stopping place for these birds when they fly north to Europe from Africa in the spring, and when they return to Africa in the fall.

Most interesting here is God's order not to gather in excess of one day's supply of manna (16:4). The only limitation is that the amount collected be consumable within the day (16:16, 18). None could be left until the next day (16:19). Predictably, some people disobeyed, and had to suffer the embarrassing consequences (16:20). Each day God would furnish a fresh supply of manna for His people. In this way God is teaching them about a relationship of trust, an attitude reflected later in the words of Jesus: "do not be anxious about your life, what you shall eat or what you shall drink . . . do not be anxious about tomorrow" (Matt. 6:25, 34). The Israelites are to trust Him to meet their physical needs one day at a time. Tomorrow is His concern and problem, not theirs.

In addition to the restriction on the amount, there is also a restriction about gathering manna on the Sabbath (16:25–26), for none will be available. Once again, there were those who did not believe Moses meant what he said. He meant what he said! The curious found nothing (16:27).

At the beginning of the narrative God informs Moses (16:5) that the gathering of manna on Fridays would result in the ingathering of a double portion. This is precisely what happened (16:22). But nowhere between verses 5 and 22 is it recorded that Moses relayed this information to the people. Brevard Childs says, delightfully, "God gives Israel, as it were, a surprise party."[1] Indeed, the comment in verse 22b—"and when all the leaders of the congregation came and told Moses"—confirms their happy surprise. Their mouths are opened in astonishment.

Finally, we note Moses' instruction to Aaron to put some manna in a jar and place it "before the testimony." "Testimony" is usually a reference to the tables of the covenant inscribed with the Ten Commandments (see Exod. 31:18; 32:15; 34:29). Or it may refer to the ark into which the "testimony" was placed (see Exod. 25:22; 26:33–34). Exodus 25:16, 21 are the actual command to place the testimony into the ark.

Of course there is no testimony, or ark, or tabernacle, yet in existence in Exodus 16. And yet how significant it is that the reader discovers that before there was any reference to putting God's law in the ark, there is the notice to put God's manna in front of, in, or on the ark. A God

1. *The Book of Exodus: A Critical, Theological Commentary*, Old Testament Library (Philadelphia: Westminster, 1974), p. 290.

who has given us His law? Yes. But first a God who has mercifully and bountifully met our needs and shown Himself faithful and graceful.

The third crisis is a lack of water at Rephidim (17:1–7). The first time there was undrinkable water (15:23). Now it is no water at all. God's solution to this dilemma is unusual. In verse 6 we read that God said to Moses, "I will stand before you there on the rock at Horeb; and you shall strike the rock." And all this is to be done publicly, not privately (v. 6b).

Even to read that God stood before Moses is surprising. To stand before someone else sometimes indicates a state of subordination or servitude (e.g., Gen. 18:8; Deut. 1:38; 10:8; in KJV, I Sam. 16:22). Thus, more than likely, Genesis 18:22, which reads, "but Abraham still stood before the LORD" may once have read, "and the Lord still stood before Abraham." At least there is an indication that the later scribes emended certain passages of Scripture which they felt to be offensive in what they said or implied about God.[2]

God stations Himself on the rock which is to be struck, thus making Himself vulnerable to injury. It is perhaps with this particular imagery in mind that Paul can say that "our fathers . . . all ate the same supernatural food [Exod. 16] and all drank the same supernatural drink [Exod. 17]. For they drank from the supernatural Rock which followed them, and the Rock was Christ" (I Cor. 10:1, 3–4).

Although on this occasion God had saved the Israelites from thirst, and death, the names given to this site recall not God's goodness but the people's faithlessness: Massah

2. Such changes in the text are called *tiqqunē sōfērîm*, "emendations of the scribes." See Christian D. Ginsburg, *Introduction to the Massoretico-Critical Edition of the Hebrew Bible* (reprint ed., New York: Ktav, 1966), pp. 347–363, and pp. 352–353 for Genesis 18:22 in particular.

and Meribah ("proof" and "contention"). Their attitude overshadowed God's act.

Three times in succession God has performed a supernatural act. It is interesting to observe where miracles appear in the Bible. In substantial sections of Scripture there is no hint of miracle at all. The wisdom literature is an obvious example. How many miracles does one read about, for example, in the prophecy of Isaiah or Jeremiah, the historical books of Samuel and Kings, the Pauline Epistles, or the catholic Epistles? Actually there are only three places where one finds a cluster of miracles: during the career of Moses, during the times of Elijah and Elisha, and during the ministry of Jesus and parts of Acts; that is, at the beginning, during the period of greatest temptation, and at the launching of the church. Miracle, yes, but not too much miracle. Too much miracle can be as debilitating as none at all.

The fourth crisis was a surprise invasion against the Israelite camp by the Amalekites (17:8–16). In the first incident at Rephidim it was God who "stood" on the rock. Now Moses will "stand" on the top of the hill (17:8). The slashing rod (17:6) is still in Moses' hand (17:9), but it is his hands, not the rod, that are paramount.

Actually the reference to the raising and lowering of Moses' hands, resulting respectively in either victory or setback, is not explained in terms of purpose or function. Perhaps it is best to say we do not know what Moses was doing. Was it encouragement, as some scholars have suggested? Was it simply raising the rod heavenward, and so invoking divine assistance? The traditional explanation that this is the posture of the intercessor should not be lightly dismissed in light of two factors. One is the references in the Psalter to the raising of hands in prayer, twice as a gesture of adoration (63:4; 134:2), once as a gesture of petition (28:2). The other factor is the consistent picture that emerges of Moses as intercessor par excellence.

Already we have read three times that Moses "cried" to the Lord: 14:15; 15:25; 17:4.

And while Moses is atop the hill with his rod, Joshua is below fighting (17:13). Whatever Moses was doing, it did not eliminate the need to battle with the antagonist. The walls of Jericho will collapse, but not until the Israelites march around them. Jesus can turn the water into wine, but not before the servants fill the jugs with water.

The Amalekite attack is not the last of Israel's problems. On the contrary, all four of the crises described have parallels in Israel's history after she leaves Sinai. The first and third crises, both having to do with water, have their parallel in the incident recorded in Numbers 20:2–13, another Meribah. The second crisis, the need for food, is close to that recorded in Numbers 11:2ff. The fourth crisis is paralleled by a subsequent invasion by the Amalekites (Num. 14:39–45).

There is, however, one major difference between the narratives in Exodus and those recorded in Numbers. In the former the complainers suffer no personal consequences in spite of their attitude. In the latter, with the covenant now behind them, Moses is excluded from entry into Canaan (Num. 20:12); a number of Israelites die because of a God-sent plague (Num. 11:33); the Amalekites, unlike the first time, are victors over the Israelites (Num. 14:45).

The fifth crisis in this unit, if it can be called such, is precipitated by a visit of Moses' father-in-law, Jethro, to the Israelite camp (18:5). The incentive for his visit is rumors that the Lord had brought Israel out of Egypt. Like the queen of Sheba who came to visit Solomon, Jethro must come himself and confirm the veracity of those rumors.

Moses is more than eager to testify (18:8). His testimony elicits praise from Jethro, and either a new commitment or a deeper commitment by Jethro to following Yahweh (depending on how one interprets the phrase "now I know").

All of this sets the context for the overburdened Moses. Jethro's suggestion is that Moses delegate authority, and not try to do everything himself. This is not an easy proposal for administrators to accept, especially if they have a messianic complex about themselves and have the urge to monopolize. Realizing that they were unable to be involved in every issue, the apostles chose to concentrate on preaching and prayer, while the ministry to widows was delegated to seven deacons who met the spiritual qualifications (Acts 6:1–6).

What about Moses? Is he too condescending to take advice? Proverbs 12:15b says that "a wise man listens to advice" and 13:10b says, "with those who take advice is wisdom." That attitude is to be contrasted with that of the "old and foolish king who will no longer take advice" (Eccles. 4:13). Strange, too, it is that the suggestion comes from Jethro, a priest in Midian; it is not whispered into Moses' ear by the angel of the Lord. May the sons of this world ever be wiser than the sons of light (Luke 16:8)?

Happily, Moses accepts approvingly Jethro's idea. The difficult cases he himself will adjudicate. The ordinary cases can be handled by his appointees. The narrative ends by telling us that Jethro said farewell to his son-in-law and returned to Midian. He had come as an enquirer. He now departs contentedly, his curiosity satisfied, his questions answered. He now believes, not because of hearsay evidence, but because he has indeed heard for himself, and knows.

Bibliography

Brueggeman, W. *The Land.* Philadelphia: Fortress, 1977, pp. 28–44.

Coats, G. W. "Moses versus Amalek. Aetiology and Legend in Exodus XVII 8–16." *VTS* 28 (1975): 29–41.

______. *Rebellion in the Wilderness: The Murmuring Motif in the Wilderness Traditions of the Old Testament.* Nashville: Abingdon, 1968.

______. "The Wilderness Itinerary." *CBQ* 34 (1972): 135–152.

Davies, G. I. "The Wilderness Itineraries: A Comparative Study." *TB* 25 (1974): 46–81.

Feliks, J. "Manna." *EncJud* 11 (1971): 883.

______. "Quail." *EncJud* 13 (1971): 1420.

Ferris, P. W. "Manna Narrative of Exodus 16:1–10." *JETS* 18 (1975): 191–199.

Tigay, J. H. "Empirical Basis for the Documentary Hypothesis." *JBL* 94 (1975): 329–342.

Vermès, G. " 'He is the Bread'—Targum Neofiti Exodus 16:15." In *Post-Biblical Jewish Studies.* Leiden: E. J. Brill, 1975, pp. 139–146.

9

Law and Covenant

Exodus 19–24

After three months of traveling the Hebrews reached Mount Sinai, usually associated with Jebel Musa (Arabic, "the mountain of Moses"), which is about 7,500 feet in height. Moses constantly goes up and down the mountain. So, 19:3, "and Moses went up to God"; 19:7, "So Moses came [down]"; 19:9, (implied), "Moses went up"; 19:14, "So Moses went down"; 19:20, "Moses went up"; 19:25, "Moses went down."

The Covenant at Sinai (19)

The first time Moses ascends Sinai, God speaks and Moses listens (vv. 3–6). It is, first of all, a reminder to Israel of God's faithfulness and concern for her. She has not come this far either by coincidence or aggressiveness (v. 4). But from the "what I did . . . I bore . . . and brought you" of verse 4 we pass to the "now . . . if you will obey" of verse 5. We pass from cause to effects, from divine love to human responsibility, and then from effects to results, "you shall be . . ." (v. 5).

1. cause
   "what I did to the Egyptians, . . . I bore you on eagle's wings and brought you to myself"
2. effect
   "if you will obey my voice and keep my covenant"

3. results
   "you shall be my own possession"
   "you shall be a kingdom of priests"
   "you shall be . . . a holy nation." Thus God's people are unique, separated from the world, but only that they may serve as ministers of reconciliation in that world.

Perhaps all too quickly the people responded positively and enthusiastically (v. 8), without taking the time to think about the implications of their response.

The second time (vv. 10–13), there is again only monologue. To verbalize about obedience is one thing. To consecrate and purify oneself is another. Israel's response to God's first word at Sinai was words. Her response to His second word is action: putting on clean clothes, and avoiding physical contact with the mountain at the risk of death. To touch it is as fatal as touching a high-voltage wire. Third, the people temporarily abstain from normal sexual activities (v. 5; cf. the similar injunction of Paul, I Cor. 7:5, and what Eve had said to the snake, "neither shall you touch it, lest you die.")

The people spend the better part of three days (v. 16) preparing to meet God. Nothing is casual or cavalier. There is no place for nonchalance. One does not rush precipitously into the presence of God; rather, it is something for which one prepares diligently and thoroughly. And most importantly, the worshipers must be sanctified or purified (v. 14). Known sins cannot deliberately be transported into the presence of God. Anything that is obnoxious to Him must be purged.

The third time is prefaced by the descent of Yahweh to the peak of Mount Sinai (v. 18). Far from being His domicile, the mountain functions only as Yahweh's temporary abode. His revelation to His people is accompanied by thunder, lightning, a thick cloud, dense smoke, fire, a shaking of the mountain, and trumpet blasts. All of this is hardly intended to encourage the Israelites to press for too much familiarity. It is their *Lord* whom they are about to encounter.

Walther Eichrodt points out how such theophanies are different from pagan counterparts. "In marked contrast to the Canaanite and Babylonian conceptions it is not those natural phenomena which are directly familiar to Man and welcomed by him as beneficent, such as sun and moon, springs and rivers, trees and woods . . . , but the natural forces which break out with startling suddenness to terrify men and to threaten them with destruction."[1]

For a third time Moses ascends to the top of the mountain (v. 20). On this occasion the Lord adds a further restriction. Not even the priests are to approach God (v. 24). Only Aaron may accompany Moses. In anticipation of the tabernacle, the tip of Sinai has become a Holy of Holies—God's holy presence is there. It is forbidden to everyone except Moses and Aaron, who will eventually be the high priest.

The Decalogue (20:1–20)

In all of the dealings between the Israelites and the Egyptians, while the former were in servitude to the latter, Moses' role was primarily that of mediator. God did not speak to Pharaoh, but He did send Moses to speak to Pharaoh. That role continued for Moses into the Passover ("Tell all the congregation of Israel," 12:3), and into the exodus ("Tell the people of Israel," 14:2). At Sinai his function was still to transmit God's word to the people ("These are the words which you shall speak to the children of Israel," 19:6).

In the laws that followed the giving of the Ten Com-

1. *Theology of the Old Testament*, trans. J. Baker, 2 vols. (Philadelphia: Westminster, 1967), vol. 1, p. 16.

mandments (20:21ff.), the mediatorial ministry of Moses is again underscored: "thus shall you say to the people of Israel" (20:22). Similarly, God's word about the tabernacle reaches the people through Moses (25:1; 35:1).

By contrast, in the revelation of the Decalogue, this theme is omitted. Moses joins his peers as listener. God now speaks directly to His people: "And God spoke all these words, saying" (20:1). Is this the Bible's way of informing us that when we read the Decalogue we are face to face with the apogee or the summum bonum of God's will for His followers in terms of lifestyles and moral commitment? Note the sequel to the commandments: "I have talked with you from heaven," not from Sinai (20:22).

When God speaks to the Israelites He addresses them as individuals, not as a group. All of the "you"s in the commandments are singular, not plural. The Hebrew clearly distinguishes between the two. Thus the "You shall not make" of verse 4, *lōʾ taᶜăśeh,* if plural, would be *lōʾ taᶜăśû.*

It is interesting to note that although God alone transmits the Decalogue, He speaks of Himself in verses 2–6 in the first person ("I am the LORD . . . before me . . . I the LORD your God . . . who hate me . . . who love me and keep my commandments"). But in verses 7–17 God speaks of Himself in the third person (for example, "the LORD will not hold him guiltless who takes his name in vain," verse 7, where we might expect "I the Lord will not hold him guiltless who takes my name in vain").

Characteristics of the Decalogue

Eight of the ten commandments are negative prohibitions. Only two are positive: "Remember the sabbath day. . . . Honor your father and mother." This is not surprising in light of the fact that law is essentially restrictive. It functions as a deterrent. It is more proscriptive than it is prescriptive. Behavior in the community is regularized by the outlawing of certain types of activities.

Eight-tenths of the Decalogue are negative apodictic (i.e., categorical) prohibitions, put in the second-person singular. The Hebrew language has two ways of expressing a prohibition: the negative particle *'al* with the jussive form of the verb (reproduced in the Septuagint usually by *mē* with the imperative or aorist subjunctive); the negative particle *lō'* with the imperfect form of the verb (reproduced in the Septuagint usually by *ou* with the future indicative).

John Bright has analyzed the distribution of these two formulations of prohibitions in the Old Testament. As to difference in nuance between the two, he concludes that *'al* with the jussive is the weaker of the two, and is concerned with a specific command for a specific occasion, with no implication for the future. By contrast, *lō'* with the imperfect expresses a categorical prohibition of binding validity for the present and the future.[2]

The first formulation predominates in wisdom literature, where a prohibition is often justified by a motive clause: "do not walk in the way with them . . . for their feet run to evil" (Prov. 1:15–16). The second is clearly the choice in the Pentateuch, especially in sections dealing with legal and cultic matters. Thus, in the four chapters of Exodus occupied with the laws of the covenant—21–23, 34—the first occurs but twice, while the second is used fifty-five times.

It is not incidental that the laws of prohibition in the Decalogue have been consistently couched in the strongest form of negation the Hebrew language had available. The commandments are not open to review and/or revision by any advisory panel, which may freely abandon them if convenience warrants. They have, linguistically, a built-in permanence. Obsolete they are not. Absolute they are.

2. "The Apodictic Prohibition: Some Observations," *JBL* 92 (1973): 185–204.

Purpose of the Decalogue

George E. Mendenhall lists six differences between covenant and law. We are interested here in how he states the difference between the two at the point of purpose. The purpose of covenant is to create a new relationship. The purpose of law is to regulate or perpetuate an existing relationship by orderly means.[3] Similarly, Brevard Childs says, "the law defines the holiness demanded of the covenant people. . . . The measurement of holiness in terms of God's own nature prevents the covenant claim from being given a moralistic interpretation. . . ."[4]

Chapter 19 of Exodus was concerned with the institution of the covenant. Then in chapter 20 and following are the laws. The purpose of the Decalogue is explicitly spelled out in 20:20: "Do not fear; for God has come to prove you, and that the fear of him may be before your eyes, that you may not sin." The verse appears almost to contain a contradiction: "do not fear . . . that the fear of him may be before your eyes."[5]

One type of fear is condemned. Another type of fear is indispensable. Which goes and which remains? That for which there is no permanent place is fear in the sense of terror and trembling. No relationship will be healthy if it is based only on fright. The glory of the Lord that appeared to the shepherds at the birth of Jesus produced in them dread—"they were filled with fear." To calm them the angel had to say, "Be not afraid" (Luke 2:9–10). The angel's "Be not afraid" is the same as Moses' "do not fear."

3. *The Tenth Generation: The Origins of the Biblical Tradition* (Baltimore: John Hopkins Press, 1973), p. 200.

4. *The Book of Exodus: A Critical, Theological Commentary,* Old Testament Library (Philadelphia: Westminster, 1974), p. 383.

5. Hans W. Wolff, in *The Vitality of Old Testament Traditions* (Atlanta: John Knox, 1974), pp. 67–82, has collected and analyzed all the "fear of God" passages in Genesis and Exodus. He translates Exodus 20:20 as "do not fear: for God has come to prove you, and that the fear of him may do its work on you, that you may not sin."

What then is the fear that is encouraged? It is fear in the sense of obedience to God's revealed law. God's purpose for His people in the giving of the Decalogue is "that you may not sin." The language reminds one of I John 2:1, "I am writing this to you so that you may not sin." That is the divine standard. But John's fresh word is that about the divine sympathy: "but if any one does sin, we have an advocate with the Father, Jesus Christ the righteous."

These, then, are God's ten commands. They are law. But is there promise here, too? May the commandments be more than a code imposed from above? Does God provide not only the law, but also the enablement to keep that law? No man is able to live up to this standard in his own power. Augustine's prayer is to the point here: "Command what thou wilt, and perform what thou commandest."

Structure of the Decalogue

The commandments are referred to (in Hebrew) as "ten words" in Deuteronomy 4:13; 10:4; and in Exodus 34:28. Exactly where and how these ten words should be divided and distinguished is still open to question as evidenced by the different enumerations in different religious traditions. In Judaism alone the first commandment is 20:2, "I am the LORD your God, who brought you out of the land of Egypt." In Catholic and Protestant traditions this is considered a prologue to the Decalogue. To continue with Judaism, the word about "no other gods" (v. 3) and no "graven image" (vv. 4–6) is taken as one commandment, and together constitute the second commandment. Commandments three through ten are the same as in most Protestant traditions.

In Roman Catholic and Lutheran traditions verses 3–6 are considered the first commandment. The second commandment (v. 7, the Lord's name), is in Protestant and Jewish tradition the third commandment. The difference of one continues through the ninth (or eighth) commandment (no false witness). What in Protestant and Jewish tradition is the final commandment (v. 17, no coveting) is divided into two distinct commandments (17a, 17b) to form the ninth and tenth commandments in Catholic and Lutheran traditions (nine, "you shall not covet your neighbor's house"; ten, "you shall not covet your neighbor's wife . . ."). In any subsequent reference to a particular commandment we shall follow the numbering system that has generally been used in Protestant traditions.

There is a deuterograph of the Exodus Decalogue in Deuteronomy 5:6–21. Essentially the list is a duplicate, but there are three interesting variations in the wording of commandments four, five, and ten. To the fourth commandment about remembering the Sabbath, Deuteronomy 5:12 reads instead "observe," and adds the motive clause, "as the LORD your God commanded you." In addition, Exodus 20:11 grounds the Sabbath in God's day of rest after the six days of creation. On the other hand, Deuteronomy 5:15 roots the Sabbath in Israel's exodus from Egypt.

The second divergence is in the fifth commandment about parents. Again, Deuteronomy 5:16 adds the phrase "as the LORD your God commanded you," and inserts another phrase not found in Exodus, "that it may go well with you." Third, in the tenth commandment Exodus 20:17 prohibits first the coveting the neighbor's house, and second, the neighbor's wife. Deuteronomy 5:21 reverses the order of these two. It also adds "field" to the list of untouchables.

It is quite obvious that the intent of the first four commandments is different from that of the last six. The first four are vertical in their orientation and have to do with one's relationship to God. The last six are horizontal and deal with man's relationship to his fellow human beings. One wonders if there is any significance in the fact that the commandment about parents is the first in those of a horizontal dimension.[6] There is a shift from creator to procreator. To both one owes his life.

When asked about the greatest commandment (as if they could be arranged in a hierarchy) Jesus quoted Deuteronomy 6:5: "You shall love the Lord your God with all your heart, and with all your soul, and with all your mind" (Matt. 22:36–38). That is a reduction into one sentence of the first four commandments. And although not solicited for further information, He goes on to say: "And a second is like it, You shall love your neighbor as yourself" (Matt. 22:39). That is a reduction into one sentence of the last six commandments. It is interesting that Jesus suggests that love is something that is commanded. Is that not a violation of love? Is not love something voluntarily chosen? By putting love within the context of a demand, or even an ultimatum, Jesus is suggesting that love for God and for one's fellows is centered in the will, not in the emotions.

Following Jesus' word about keeping the commandments in order to enter life, the rich young ruler asked, "which one[s]?" Jesus said nothing about the first four commandments, but drew only from the second category, and even His order of recital was interesting: six, seven, eight, nine, and five! Lack of love for one's brothers cancels out the possibility of love for God, and turns expressions of love for God into a charade (one of the messages of I John).

Exposition of the Decalogue

The first commandment is, "You shall have no other gods before me." Unlike the second commandment, which addresses itself to the "how" of worship, this one speaks to the "who" to worship. Nothing else or nobody else is

6. Umberto Cassuto, *A Commentary on the Book of Exodus* (Jerusalem: Magnes Press, 1976), p. 246.

to exercise an ultimate claim over or demand an ultimate loyalty from God's people. The very fact that this prohibition exists, and even heads the list, assumes that members of the believing community are indeed prone to pay homage to surrogates for God. (This is not a word directed to the Moabites, or to the Philistines, but to those who have embraced a covenantal relationship with God.) Similarly, the establishment of speed limits on our highways is necessitated by the fact—apart from energy conservation—that without any restrictions many drivers would turn roads into Indianapolis 500 speedways.

The commandment to worship no other gods is senseless unless the alternative does indeed exist, is at times attractive, and unless there is proclivity in man compelling him in that direction.

The second commandment is, "You shall not make for yourself a graven image." Old Testament religion is an aniconic religion. To be sure, religious art is permitted—witness the adornments in the tabernacle and temple—but images of God are outlawed. For all the times the patriarchs and Moses spoke "face to face" with God, not once did one of them give us an inkling what they saw, or what He looked like.

Abraham J. Heschel draws a distinction between "real" symbols and "conventional" symbols. Using a national flag as an illustration of a conventional symbol, he suggests that this type of symbol represents a reality, not because it possesses the inherent qualities of the reality it symbolizes, but because of the association, relationship, or convention suggested by it. A real symbol, on the other hand, is a "visible object that represents something invisible, something present representing something absent . . . he who has the image has the god."[7]

7. *Man's Quest for God: Studies in Prayer and Symbolism* (New York: Scribner, 1954), p. 118.

The Bible is not lacking in parodies about idolatry. The latter chapters of Isaiah abound in them. For example, in Isaiah 46:1–2 we read of the Babylonians fleeing Babylon at the invasion of Cyrus. They have placed their gods on the backs of their animals. Why? Are they in danger? Are the people responsible for their gods' safety? If the people do not look after their gods in this time of crisis, who will? And the gods are valuable, made as they were by man. Through this God says to His people, "You do not carry me on your back. I carry you on my back."

To have access to an image of God suggests almost that such a god can be controlled and manipulated. Perhaps we cannot improve on Augustine's definition of idolatry: "Idolatry is worshiping anything that ought to be used, or using anything that is meant to be worshiped."

The third commandment is, "You shall not take the name of the LORD *your God in vain."* Presumably more than profanity or vulgarity, in the modern sense, is proscribed. Also, the frequent statement that the command forbids false swearing or oath-taking in court is true, but not exhaustive of the meaning.

The word *vain* comes from a Hebrew root meaning "to be empty" in the sense of "to be without substance, to be worthless." Any invocation of God's presence, any calling on His name that is simply perfunctory is taking God's name in vain, that is, using the divine name for or in something that lacks vitality, reality, and substance. So Elton Trueblood can say, "The worst blasphemy is not profanity, but lip service."[8]

The fourth commandment is, "Remember the sabbath day, to keep it holy." Childs renders "to keep it holy" as a factitive piel in Hebrew, and translates "to make holy."[9] Those legitimate concerns of the previous six days are to be laid

8. *Foundations for Reconstruction* (Waco, TX: Word Books, 1972), p. 31.
9. *The Book of Exodus*, p. 415.

aside momentarily for what Herman Wouk graphically calls "a retreat into restorative magic."[10] Umberto Cassuto points out the connection between the Sabbath, that is, the seventh day, and the number of living beings who are to observe it—seven: you, your son, your daughter, your manservant, your maidservant, your cattle (even the animals observe the Sabbath!), the sojourner.[11]

Too much should not be made of the different motive clauses in Exodus and Deuteronomy. We have already observed Exodus links the Sabbath with the seventh day of rest after creation, and Deuteronomy connects it with the exodus from Egypt. As B. D. Napier says, "The fundamental sanction of the Sabbath in both statements of commandment is *creation*—in Deuteronomy the creation of a people, in Exodus the creation of the world."[12]

Israel was not alone in her observance of special and sacred days. Not a little has been written about a possible connection between the biblical Sabbath and the Babylonian *shapattu.* Eichrodt writes,

> In Babylonia the 'seventh' days (i. e., the seventh, fourteenth, nineteenth, twenty-first and twenty-eighth of the month) had the character of a *dies nefastus* (Bab. *ûmu limnu*) on which special care had to be taken, the king in particular having to submit to all kinds of precautionary measures (e.g., not to mount his chariot, not to offer sacrifice, etc.). Of a general intermission of work there is no mention whatsoever. Only on the fifteenth day was work suspended in Babylonia; and far from this being due to the joyful, festal character of the day, it was obviously actuated by quite different motives, namely that on this particular day there was no luck to be had, and it was necessary to pacify the gods (whence the name *ûm nuḫ libbi*: 'day of pacifi-

10. *This Is My God* (New York: Doubleday, 1959), p. 60.
11. *Commentary on the Book of Exodus, p. 245.*
12. *The Book of Exodus* (Richmond: John Knox, 1969), p. 82.

cation of the heart') and to appease their anger by a kind of day of penitence and prayer."[13]

The fifth commandment is, "Honor your father and your mother." What the reader of the Bible might have expected is, "obey your father and mother." It is, however, easier to obey than it is to honor. One can hate but obey. One cannot both hate and honor.

The seriousness of the injunction is reinforced by the choice of the verb *honor*. Several times it is used with God as the object (I Sam. 2:30; Ps. 50:23; Prov. 3:9; Isa. 29:13; 43:20, 23). Both God and parents are worthy of honor. The Hebrew word is sometimes translated as "glorify" and describes how God is to be worshiped (Ps. 22:23; 50:15; 86:9, 12; Isa. 24:15).

This is not to say that parents are worthy of worship. Jesus quoted and endorsed the fifth commandment (Matt. 15:4; Mark 7:10; Paul also in Eph. 6:2). But He also said, "He who loves father or mother more than me is not worthy of me" (Matt. 10:37). Parents make feeble gods, if they are one of those "other gods" before Him.

The sixth commandment is, "You shall not kill." Some scholars have translated the verb as "you shall not murder." That is, what is banned is not all forms of killing (such as the death penalty for certain crimes, or involvement in war), but the unnecessary taking of life out of anger or greed. Occasionally the verb describes nonculpable homicide (Num. 35:11; Deut. 4:42; Josh. 20:3, 5), indicated by the addition of some qualifier such as "unintentionally" or "in ignorance or unwittingly." Another illustration of this is Numbers 35:27—the avenger of the blood is not guilty if he kills the manslayer who has wandered outside the limits of the city of refuge.

But these are exceptions. The normal meaning is culp-

13. *Theology of the Old Testament, vol. 1, p. 132.*

able homicide, and the commandment is thus best translated, "you shall not murder," especially in light of the negative particle *lō'*. Cain did this directly. David did it indirectly. God forbids a person from killing another person, and from killing oneself. It is interesting that there is only one clear-cut instance of suicide in the Old Testament, Ahithophel (II Sam. 17:23).

Jesus extended the sixth commandment to include feelings of anger, verbal abuse of another person, or derogatory namecalling (Matt. 5:21–26). His admonition is "make friends quickly with your accuser."

The seventh commandment is, "You shall not commit adultery." If the previous commandment upheld the sanctity of life, and the one before that the sanctity of the home, this commandment upholds the sanctity of marriage. Marriage is not simply a relationship of convenience, nor is it to be tampered with. Infidelity carries with it the most serious of consequences.

Jesus expanded this prohibition to include the ocular as well as the physical (Matt. 5:27–30). Lust is possessive and self-gratifying. Witness David's behavior with Bathsheba. It reduces the other person to a thing. Mutual obligation and commitment are nonexistent.

The eighth commandment is, "You shall not steal." The right of possession is affirmed. The attempt to get something for nothing is condemned. The commandment militates against the philosophy of "what is yours is mine and I'm going to take it away from you."

The antidote for stealing is reflected in Paul's word to the church at Philippi: "And my God will supply every need of yours" (Phil. 4:19), but such a promise covers only needs, not greeds.

The ninth commandment is, "You shall not bear false witness." Probably the original application of this commandment was to the offering of false, misleading testimony in court or at official transactions and exchanges in the marketplace. But a broader and more general interpretation is surely permissible.

The commandment embraces any malicious conversation, intentional or unintentional, that raises a question about the integrity of someone else's character. And character defamation is as ancient as Genesis 3.

Not without reason does James refer to the tongue as an arsonist. Uncontrolled, it becomes incendiary. Unchecked, it becomes the most lethal weapon in destroying the unity in a believing community.

Again we turn to Paul for the opposite of what this commandment forbids. Perhaps it is his word, "count others better than yourselves" (Phil. 2:3). Such an attitude will restrain the temptation to be a false witness.

The tenth commandment is, "You shall not covet." Quite obviously this commandment is different from the preceding nine, or at least the preceding five, in at least two ways. One is the way it appears to prohibit even an inner, subjective attitude, unlike the others which address themselves to specific, visible acts. The second surrounds the means by which one could establish guilt and then prosecute for coveting.

The first nine commandments present no problem here.

One, "You shall have no other gods." Compare Exodus 22:20, "Whoever sacrifices to any god, save to the LORD only, shall be utterly destroyed."

Two, "You shall not make for yourself a graven image." Compare the near-disastrous result after the incident involving the golden calf, Exodus 32.

Three, "You shall not take the name of the LORD your God in vain." Compare the remainder of the verse: "for the LORD will not hold him guiltless."

Four, "Remember the sabbath day, to keep it holy." Compare Exodus 31:15, "the seventh day is a sabbath of solemn rest . . . whoever does any work on the sabbath day shall be put to death."

Five, "Honor your father and your mother." Compare Exodus 21:15, 17, "whoever strikes [or, curses] his father or his mother shall be put to death."

Six, "You shall not kill." Compare Exodus 21:12, "whoever strikes a man so that he dies shall be put to death."

Seven, "You shall not commit adultery." Compare Deuteronomy 22:22, "If a man is found lying with the wife of another man, both of them shall die."

Eight, "You shall not steal." Compare Exodus 22:1–3, "If a man steals an ox . . . he shall pay five oxen for an ox. . . ." See also Exodus 21:16, "Whoever steals a man . . . shall be put to death."

Nine, "You shall not bear false witness." Compare Deuteronomy 19:18–19, "if the witness is a false witness and has accused his brother falsely, then you shall do to him as he had meant to do to his brother."

The pattern is this: in the Decalogue there is a straightforward prohibition, or admonishment, without reference to any penalty for violation. Subsequently we encounter the violation posed as a possibility, and the consequences of such a violation spelled out.

Can the pattern continue into the last commandment: "Thou shalt not covet. . . . If a man covets . . . he shall die [or, be put to death]"? Such a verse would be surprising, but narratives to support the idea are not lacking. This is the story of Eve, of Achan, of Ahab and Jezebel over Naboth's vineyard, of Judas Iscariot.

Some exegetes have suggested that the verb includes actions as well as emotions on the basis of verses such as Deuteronomy 7:25, "you shall not covet the silver or the gold . . . or take it for yourselves," and Micah 2:2, "They covet fields, and seize them. . . ."

One suspects, however, that this explanation is dictated not by exegesis as much as it is by the desire to understand the prohibition in terms amenable to law enforcement. In addition, the two verbs for "covet" in the Deuteronomy Decalogue (Deut. 5:21) are different. The first is the same as that used twice in Exodus 20:17, *ḥāmad*. But the second is *hit'awweh*, "you shall not desire your neighbor's house." And the connotation of this verb, a synonym of *ḥāmad* in Deuteronomy 5:21, concerns emotions, quite apart from any outward act. As Childs says, "the Deuteronomic recension simply make more explicit the subjective side of the prohibition which was already contained in the original command."[14]

Perhaps this is the reason why this particular commandment is placed last. It is the most comprehensive of all the commandments, and includes what is omitted in the rest of the Decalogue. And who will not recognize that behind much killing, adultery, stealing, and lying is covetousness? This is the root of the problem.

I have looked to Paul for some positive reformulations of the prohibitive commandments. Again I may appeal to him, and again the verse is in his Philippian epistle (4:11), "I have learned, in whatever state I am, to be content." This is the difference between being master over or servant of one's desires.

The Book of the Covenant (20:21—23:33)

The title given to this section of Exodus is taken from Exodus 24:7, "Then he took the book of the covenant, and read it in the hearing of the people."

Unlike the Decalogue, which God transmits directly to His people, this section of Exodus finds Moses once again in the ministry of mediation: "Thus you shall say unto the people of Israel" (20:22). He is neither author nor collator, just transmitter. Indeed, it would not be inappropriate to apply here Peter's dictum that "no prophecy ever came by

14. *The Book of Exodus*, p. 427.

the impulse of man, but men moved by the Holy Spirit spoke from God" (II Peter 1:21). The Bible, and these chapters of Exodus especially, goes to great lengths to reinforce the idea that Moses is but conveyor of truth, not originator of truth.

And yet many Christians approach chapters 21–23 of Exodus in the same way as they eat fish. The bones are to be thrown away, and only the meat digested. To press the analogy, the Ten Commandments of chapter 20 are the meat, the "eternal word of God"; the following three chapters are the bones—the unedifying, the unpalatable, the anachronistic, and hence the disposable. That no such hierarchy appears in the biblical text itself is beside the point. It is, for example, difficult to conceive of these three chapters as a gold mine for expository preaching.

Types of Laws in the Book of the Covenant

The laws in this unit are as follows:

1. proscriptions of idols and the law about the altar, 20:22–26
2. the law for male and female slaves, 21:1–11
3. prohibitions against murder, physical and verbal abuse of parents, and kidnaping, all of which elicit the death penalty, 21:12–17
4. laws penalizing those who injure and maim others: a neighbor, a slave, a pregnant woman (violations which do not incur the death penalty), 21:18–26
5. the law about the goring ox that tramples to death a human being, with culpability also attached to a careless owner, 21:28–32
6. the law about the uncovered pit into which an unsuspecting animal tumbles, 21:33–34
7. the law about one animal that is fatally injured by another, with blame to the owner of the killer animal if necessary precautions were shirked, 21:35–36

8. prohibitions against thievery, mandating restitution, 22:1–4
9. the law about destroying the crops of another through illegal grazing of one's own animals or arson, 22:5–6
10. laws pertaining to borrowers and to those who are entrusted with the belongings of others, 22:7–15
11. the law about seduction of a virgin, leading to premarital intercourse, 22:16–17
12. a collection of miscellaneous laws on religious and social matters, such as magic, bestiality, idolatry, mistreating the alien, and usury, 22:18–31
13. justice in the courtroom, both in the witness stand and on the judge's bench, 23:1–9
14. Sabbath laws, 23:10–13
15. a summons to observe the thrice-held festivals on the calendar, 23:14–19
16. epilogue, 23:20–33

While it is vain to look for some significance in the sequence of the laws, perhaps it is not trite to observe that the first law and the last are parallel in subject matter. The code begins and ends with a call to worship, that which brings the devotee directly into the presence of God: worship in the right way—the law about the altar; worship at the right time—the three annual festivals.

If there is no particular pattern in the sequence of the laws there is a distinct pattern in the literary forms in which the laws are couched. Note that the first law (the altar law, 20:22–26) is phrased much like one of the Ten Commandments: "You shall not make gods of silver . . . you shall not go up by steps to my altar." I have previously referred to this type of law as apodictic law.

But beginning with 21:1 and continuing through 22:17, the laws are framed in a conditional way. (The exceptions are the statements in 21:12, 15, 16, 17.) This type of law is usually referred to as casuistic law. That is, instead of making a generalization, a casuistic law addresses itself to a specific situation. Accordingly, most of these laws have first a protasis, a section that deals with the specific situation at question. Normally a violation is described and is introduced by "when" or "supposing that": "when men quarrel," "when a man strikes a slave." Occasionally a legitimate transaction may be involved: "when you buy a Hebrew slave."

The second part of the law is often called the apodosis. Usually this part spells out the consequence of the violation: "When a man strikes his slave . . . and the slave dies [protasis], . . . he shall be punished" (apodosis). Further qualification or extenuating circumstances are often included. The apodosis, if it follows a legitimate transaction, addresses itself to the privileges of any parties involved.

Beginning with 22:18 and continuing to 23:19, there is a return to apodictic law: "You shall not permit a sorceress to live." Thus, the code begins with apodictic law (20:22–26), shifts to casuistic law (21:1—22:17), then returns to apodictic law (22:18—23:19).

One possible conclusion to draw from this is that 21:1—22:17, the casuistic laws, once existed separately from the rest of the code and was only secondarily inserted by a redactor into its present position. Indeed this is the prevailing view of biblical scholarship.

But is not another solution possible? Cyrus H. Gordon has drawn attention to the literary form of ancient Near Eastern literature, including parts of the Bible, an observation that warns against the premature dissecting of the text.[15] Thus, the Book of Job begins and ends in prose, with poetry in between. The Book of Daniel begins and ends in Hebrew, with the middle section in Aramaic. Might not the same literary structure be found in the Book of the

15. *The Ancient Near East* (New York: Norton, 1965), p. 83.

Covenant? The beginning and the end are identical in form. The middle section is different from both its predecessor and successor. (The Decalogue begins with three negative commandments, continues with two positive ones, then concludes with five negative commandments.)

Comparison of Biblical and Nonbiblical Legal Codes

It is not without advantage to compare biblical law to other legal codes composed in those nations that surrounded Israel in the second and first millennium B.C. The most crucial, in order of antiquity, are:

1. Code of Ur-nammu, named after the first king of the third dynasty of Ur (c. 2100–2000 B.C.). This is the first law code known in history (c. 2050 B.C.). It is written in Sumerian, and only portions have survived. This includes a prologue and twenty-nine laws, all of which are casuistic in form.
2. Code of Eshnunna, not a personal name but a place name. It is located near modern Baghdad and flourished between the fall of Ur (2000 B.C.) and the age of Hammurabi (1800–1600 B.C.). The laws, sixty-one in total, are the oldest ones written in Babylonian, and date back to c. 1980 B.C.
3. Code of Lipit-Ishtar, a ruler of the first dynasty of Isin (c. 2000–1900 B.C.), one of the prominent city-states to emerge after the fall of Ur. The code consists of three main parts: a prologue, the laws, and an epilogue. It too is written in Sumerian. Thirty-eight laws, in part or in whole, have survived, and all of these are casuistic in form. They date to c. 1930 B.C.
4. Code of Hammurabi, who was the sixth king of the first dynasty of Babylon, with the years of his reign being 1792–1750 B.C. It is written, as is the code of Eshnunna, in Babylonian and is the most famous of

the extrabiblical law codes. It is structured, as is Lipit-Ishtar, in tripartite fashion: prologue—laws—epilogue. There are 282 casuistic laws in this code.

5. The Hittite laws, which are not precisely datable, although Hittitologist Harry A. Hoffner, Jr. suggests that "it is possible that the first recension of the Hittite laws dates from the reign of Telipinu (1525–1500 B.C.)."[16] The laws are found on two tablets, with 100 laws on each tablet.
6. The Middle Assyrian laws, preserved on clay tablets. The tablets date from the time of the Assyrian king Tiglath-pileser I (1115–1077 B.C.), but the laws may antedate the tablets by as much as three centuries. Some 116 laws are preserved on eleven different tablets, again in casuistic form. To a degree unseen in the previous law codes, penalties for violations often include all forms of bodily mutilation, for example, cutting off the nose or removing a finger.

The existence of such law codes does not mean that they were appealed to by courts or judges in the administration of justice. Never did they assume a normative status. On the contrary, they were all but ignored. The point is well made by two Assyriologists. Says A. Leo Oppenheim, "this code [viz., Hammurabi's Code] . . . does not show any direct relationship to the legal practices of the time. Its contents are rather to be considered in many essential respects a traditional literary expression of the king's social responsibilities and of his awareness between existing and desirable conditions."[17] Or, to quote William W. Hallo, "they [these law codes] made no attempt to provide universal criteria of culpability, nor were they

16. "Hittites," *WBE*, 1, p. 800.

17. *Ancient Mesopotamia: Portrait of a Dead Civilization*, 2d rev. ed. (Chicago: University of Chicago Press, 1977), p. 158.

cited, or even necessarily followed, in the determination of lawsuits. But they were studied in the schools . . . and must have formed part of the education of scribes and judges."[18] Thus, the guides for legal decision are not codes but tradition, public opinion, and even common sense.

An examination of these laws shows in some cases an almost word-for-word correspondence with one of the laws in the covenant code of Exodus, or the laws of Deuteronomy. Other laws are remarkably similar to those of Exodus with changes only in terminology. Childs is able to provide a parallel (or parallels) in pagan law codes to every unit in the covenant code.[19]

The law about female slaves

As an illustration I will use the law in Exodus 21:7–11 about a daughter sold into slavery by her father. The constituent parts are that unlike the male slave, she may not go free after six years; if she is unpleasing to her prospective husband she is to be returned to her family; if she becomes her employer's daughter-in-law she is to be treated as a daughter; if she is married to her employer, a subsequent marriage by the husband to another woman does not diminish the slave's status in any way; violation of any of these last four contingencies by the employer or husband results in the woman's freedom.

Here are the parallels.

Code of Hammurabi, 170, 171: "When a man's first wife bore him children and his female slave also bore him children, if the father during his lifetime has ever said 'my children!' to the children whom the slave bore him . . . after the father dies, the children of the first wife and the children of the slave shall share equally in the goods of the paternal state. . . ." Law 171 deals with the opposite

18. William W. Hallo and William K. Simpson, *The Ancient Near East: A History* (New York: Harcourt Brace Jovanovich, 1972), p. 176.

19. *The Book of Exodus*, pp. 462–463.

situation of the father vis-à-vis the children of his female slave—"if he never said [of them] 'my children!' "—then the slave's offspring are not entitled to part of the paternal estate, but both slave and offspring are manumitted.

Code of Hammurabi, 119: "If an obligation came due against a man and he has accordingly sold his female slave who bore him children, the owner of the female slave may repay the money which the merchant paid out and thus redeem his female slave."

Code of Hammurabi, 146, 147: "A barren wife who provides her husband with a female slave may not sell the slave if the latter mothers a child by the wife's husband before and when the wife does."

Eshnunna, 31: "If a man deprives another man's slave-girl of her virginity, he shall pay one-third of a mina of silver; the slave-girl remains the property of her owner."

Eshnunna, 34: "If a slave-girl of palaces gives her son or her daughter to a palace or temple official for bringing him or her up, the palace may take back the son or the daughter whom she gave."

Hittite Code, 31 (Tablet 1): "If a free man and a slave-girl are lovers and they cohabit, he takes her for his wife, they found a family and have children, but subsequently . . . they break up the family, the man receives the children, but the woman receives one child." Laws 32 and 33 deal respectively with the marriage of a male slave to a free woman and a male slave to a female slave. In both laws, if a marital separation ensues, the consequences are the same as those in law 31.

Lipit-Ishtar, 25, 26: "If a man married a wife and she bore him children, and those children are living, and a slave also bore children for her master, but the father granted freedom to the slave and her children, the children of the slave shall not divide the estate with the children of their former master." Law 26 covers the marriage of a widower to a slave girl with children produced from both the first and second marriages. The children of the first marriage are not negated as heirs.

The law about an ox that gores

One more example of commonality in biblical and non-biblical law codes will suffice. It concerns the law about the goring ox, Exodus 21:28–36. The particulars are that if an ox kills a person it is then killed, but its flesh may not be eaten. No liability is attached to the owner of the ox. If, however, the ox is known to be temperamental, and warnings to the owner have gone unheeded, and if the ox kills a human being, the owner too is executed. If a man's ox falls into an open pit dug by another, the latter must pay restitution to the owner of the deceased animal. If one ox kills an ox belonging to another, there is to be a sharing of the loss. If the owner knew that his ox was prone to goring, and took no precautions, the owner of the goring ox assumes all the damages.

The parallels are:

Code of Hammurabi, 250: "If an ox, when it was walking along the street, gored a man to death, that case is not subject to claim."

Code of Hammurabi, 251: "If a man's ox was a gorer, and his city council made it known to him that it was a gorer, but he did not pad its horns or tie up his ox, and that ox gored to death a member of the aristocracy, he shall give one-half mina of silver."

Eshnunna, 53: "If an ox gores another ox and causes its death, both ox owners shall divide [between themselves] the price of the live ox and also the equivalent of the dead ox."

Eshnunna, 54: "If an ox is known to gore habitually and the authorities have brought the fact to the knowledge of its owner, but he does not have his ox dehorned, and it gores a man and causes his death, then the owner of the ox shall pay two-thirds of a mina of silver."

Differences Between Biblical and Nonbiblical Legal Codes

The point is well taken, then, that many biblical laws have almost precise counterparts in pagan literature. The absence of such parallels, rather than their presence, would raise suspicions about the integrity of the biblical laws. It is fair to say that all societies and cultures outlaw a certain group of practices (murder, hate, or oppression), and encourage the implementation of another group of practices (justice or compassion for the poor). In these areas Israel had no monopoly, and often no word from God beyond that of her neighbors.

This is not, however, to equate all ancient Mediterranean law codes. Even in those areas where similarity may be the greatest, differences between biblical and nonbiblical law are apparent. Consider, for example, the discussion about the various laws about the goring ox. The significant difference is in the much more severe punishment mandated by the passage in Exodus. In the codes of both Hammurabi and Eshnunna the only concern is with the economic compensation of the victim's family: ". . . he shall give one-half mina of silver" (Hammurabi, 251); ". . . the owner of the ox shall pay two-thirds of a mina of silver" (Eshnunna, 54). By contrast, Exodus 21:28 calls for the death of the ox (see Gen. 9:5–6) and abstention from eating its meat. Furthermore, if the owner has callously sloughed off previous warnings about his dangerous animal, and the latter kills someone, the owner dies too (Exod. 21:29), unless the victim's family is willing to settle for the imposition of a steep fine (Exod. 21:30). Note here the high value placed on human life. In taking another's life a fine is no substitute for proper justice.

One observes also a distinct emphasis in the laws dealing with slaves. The particular verses in Exodus are concerned almost exclusively with his or her privileges, or the reparations that fall upon the owner if the slave is in any way abused or mishandled (21:1–11, 20–21, 26–27, 32). Surely it is not without significance that laws on slavery in the covenant code come toward the beginning of that code, while those on this subject in the Code of Hammurabi come at the end (278–282).

Nowhere in the covenant code do punishments take the form of physical mutilation. By contrast, in the first millennium B.C. Middle Assyrian laws, such penalties reach epidemic proportions. But even the Code of Hammurabi legislates for certain offenses the cutting off of half of the hair (127); the removal of the tongue (192), the eye (193), the ear of a slave (205), or the hand (218, 226, 253). Prisoners of war might be treated similarly. Witness Samson at the mercy of the Philistines (Judg. 16:21), the residents of Jabesh-gilead intimidated by Nahash the Ammonite (I Sam. 11:2); the slain Saul and the Philistines (I Sam. 31:9–10); David's troops in Ammonite territory (II Sam. 10:4).

It is true that Scripture does mandate "an eye for an eye, and a tooth for a tooth" (Exod. 21:24–25). This is the famous *lex talionis,* and the parallel in the Code of Hammurabi is 197, "a bone for a bone," and 200, "tooth for a tooth." Both of these laws, however, cover only assaults by one of the aristocracy against a peer.

Primarily because of Jesus' reference to this particular law in Matthew 5:38ff., and a misunderstanding of the intent of that reference, many people have assumed that this is a classic distinction between the spirit of the two testaments. The first teaches retaliation, the second teaches forgiveness. Such a dichotomy could not be further from the truth. Even the Book of the Covenant itself (see Exod. 23:4–5) urges exerting oneself to help one's enemy. What the law in Exodus does teach is the principle of equal justice for all. That is, the penalty must match the crime (an eye or a tooth for an eye or a tooth). The penalty must not be more than the crime merits (thus prohibiting the victimizing of the poor and underprivileged through overpenalization). Nor must the penalty be less than the crime merits (thus prohibiting the rich from escaping the law's demands because of position, contacts, and bargaining money). What Jesus does in the Sermon on the Mount is to elevate one's response to evil perpetrated against one beyond the concern of simple justice to that of voluntarily assisting the person who oppresses one.

We may conclude that the distinctions between biblical and nonbiblical law ought not to be unduly magnified,[20] or minimized. Apart from any specific law, perhaps the most significant thing to be observed, in terms of comparative studies, is the crucial position that God assumes in this section of Exodus. First, God is the author of these laws: "And the LORD said to Moses, 'thus shall you say to the people of Israel' " (Exod. 20:22); "these are the ordinances which you shall set before them" (Exod. 21:1). True, the stela on which Hammurabi's Code is written is topped by a bas-relief showing Hammurabi receiving the commission to write the law code from the sun god, Shamash, the god of justice. And in both the epilogue and prologue appeal is made to the stimulation and authority of Shamash and Marduk. But nowhere in the 282 laws does a god ever speak. The same is true of the other law codes.

By contrast, God not only commissions Moses to speak, but also He Himself speaks in the first person throughout the section, especially in 20:22–26 and 22:20—23:19: "I have talked with you" (20:22); "An altar of earth you shall make for me" (20:24). (The words "me" or "I" appear seven times in the brief section of 20:22–26.) Also, "I will appoint for you a place" (21:13); "I will surely hear their cry" (22:23); "I will kill" (22:24); "I will hear" (22:27); "I

20. Observe the strictures of B. S. Jackson, "Reflections," *JJS* 24 (1973): 8–38.

will not acquit" (23:7); "I have said" (23:13); "I commanded you" (23:15); "Behold, I send" (23:20). Even in the articulation of the laws, Moses, the law mediator, takes a subordinate position to God, the law giver. God does not speak, then disappear, then briefly reappear before the end.

If we wish to underline that Israel, as reflected in these law codes, reached a higher moral sensitivity than did her neighbors, even in the Book of the Covenant some inequities appear still to remain. For all the privileges granted to the slave he is, nevertheless, treated as less than a free man. Murder is a capital offense (Exod. 21:12). If a slave is the victim, the slave owner is "to be punished" (Exod. 21:20). The formula "he shall be put to death" is not used. The *lex talionis,* and its expression of equal justice for all, does not include the slave (Exod. 21:26–27). The male slave may go free after six years (Exod. 21:2). Apparently no such provision was extended to the female slave, except in cases of physical abuse to which she was subjected (Exod. 21:27). For the thrice-held religious festivals only males could make such pilgrimages (Exod. 23:17). Females are excluded.

If the Book of the Covenant rises above the Code of Hammurabi, we must also conclude that the first sermon on the mount anticipates a fuller word from the second Sermon on the Mount.

The Ceremony of Covenant Ratification
(24:1–18)

It is not enough to hear the word of the Lord, to be simply "hearers" but not "doers." Nor is nodding, halfhearted, token obedience acceptable. Perhaps prematurely, the people had said, after first reaching Sinai, "All that the LORD has spoken we will do" (Exod. 19:8). They thought they were prepared to match God's challenge to them, recorded in Exodus 19:5–6, "Now therefore, if you will obey my voice. . . ."

Then follows the divine recitation of the Decalogue and the mediation of the covenant code laws through Moses (Exod. 20–23 and 24:3a, 7), plus their inscripturation (24:4). Unanimously the people affirm their acceptance of and future loyalty to the word of the Lord. And not once, but twice (Exod. 24:3b, 7b)! That the commitment was made in total sincerity is without doubt (as was Peter's, "Lord, I am ready to go with you to prison and to death"). However, as the events of chapter 32 confirm, such a profession of loyalty proved to be short-lived. But at no point does Moses raise a question about the people's integrity. He takes them at their word.

To clinch the covenant agreement Moses builds an altar, and has the appropriate persons offer sacrifices to the Lord (the Hebrew word for "altar" means "place of sacrifice"). Half of the blood from the slain animals is thrown against this altar, and the other half is sprinkled over the people. This particular ritual probably speaks of commitment by both sides to this new relationship. The Lord, here represented by the altar, binds Himself to His people. He will not be faithless. Similarly the people commit themselves. After all, can there be any kind of meaningful relationship if the commitment is not mutual?

With this ceremony behind him, Moses is now free, along with a select group, to ascend the mount. The language is nothing short of astounding: "they saw the God of Israel . . . they beheld God" (Exod. 24: 10–11), and subsequently were treated to a heavenly banquet, "they . . . ate and drank." Not surprisingly, no conversation is recorded.

First, seventy-four men were distinguished from the people (Exod. 24:9). Then Moses is removed from this group (24:12), but only after waiting six days. What then happens brings us back into the milieu of chapter 19. God's glory as a devouring fire envelops the mountain, and Moses too. For Moses, the mountain's peak is his holy of holies, into which he enters, unaccompanied, surely with an accelerated heartbeat.

Bibliography

The Sinai Theophany and the Decalogue

(19:1—20:20)

Althann, R. "A Note on Ex. 19, 12aB–13." *Bibl* 57 (1976): 242–246.

Barclay, W. *The Ten Commandments for Today*. New York: Harper and Row, 1974.

Bright, J. "The Apodictic Prohibition: Some Observations." *JBL* 92 (1973): 185–204.

Cohen, M. B., and Freedman, D. B. "The Dual Accentuation of the Ten Commandments." *1972 and 1973 Proceedings IOMS*. Missoula, MT: Scholars' Press, 1974, pp. 7–19.

Faur, J. "The Biblical Idea of Idolatry." *JQR* 69 (1978): 1–15.

Greeley, A. M. *The Sinai Myth: A New Interpretation of the Ten Commandments*. New York: Doubleday, 1975.

Greenberg, M. "Decalogue." In *EncJud* 5 (1971): 1435–1446.

Haggerty, B. A. *Out of the House of Slavery: On the Meaning of the Ten Commandments*. New York: Paulist Press, 1978.

Mendenhall, G. E. "Covenant." In *Encyclopaedia Britannica* (Macropaedia), vol. 5, 15th edition, pp. 226–230.

Nicholson, E. W. "The Decalogue as the direct address of God." *VT* 27 (1977): 422–433.

Philipps, A. C. *Ancient Israel's Criminal Law: A New Approach to the Decalogue*. Oxford: Basil Blackwell, 1970.

———. "Case of the woodgatherer reconsidered." *VT* 19 (1969): 125–128.

Rad, G. von. *Old Testament Theology*. Translated by D. M. G. Stalker. 2 vols. New York: Harper and Row, 1962, vol. 1, pp. 190–219.

Smith, E. C. "The Ten Commandments in Today's Permissive Society: A Principleist Approach." *SWJT* 20 (1977): 42–58.

Stamm, J. J., and Andrews, M. E. *The Ten Commandments in Recent Research*. Naperville, IL: Alec R. Allenson, 1967.

Trudiger, L. P. "A Much Misunderstood Commandment." *BT* 56 (1971): 501–504.

Tsevat, M. "Basic Meaning of the Biblical Sabbath." *ZAW* 84 (1972): 447–459.

Weinfeld, M. "Bᵉrîth." In *TDOT*, 1, pp. 253–279.

______. "The Origin of the Apodictic Law: An Overlooked Source." *VT* 23 (1973): 63–75.

Williams, J. G. *Ten Words of Freedom: An Introduction to the Faith of Israel.* Philadelphia: Fortress, 1971.

Zimmerli, W. *Old Testament Theology in Outline.* Translated by David E. Green. Atlanta: John Knox, 1977, pp. 115–126; 133–140.

The Book of the Covenant and Covenant Ratification Service (20:21—24:18)

Carmichael, C. M. "A Singular Method of Codification of Law in the *Mishpatim.*" *ZAW* 84 (1972): 19–25.

Clark, W. M. "Law." In *Old Testament Form Criticism.* Edited by John Hayes. San Antonio: Trinity University Press, 1974, pp. 99–139.

Cohn, H. H. "Slavery." in *EncJud* 14 (1971): 1655–1660.

Ellison, H. L. "The Hebrew Slave: A Study in Early Israelite Society." *EQ* 45 (1973): 30–35.

Fensham, F. C. "The Role of the Lord in the legal sections of the Covenant Code." *VT* 26 (1976): 262–274.

Hanson, P. D. "The Theological Significance of Contradiction within the Book of the Covenant," In *Canon and Authority.* Edited by George W. Coats and Burke O. Long. Philadelphia: Fortress, 1977, pp. 110–131.

Haran, M. "Seething a Kid in its Mother's Milk." *JJS* 30 (1979): 23–35.

Huffmon, H. B. "Exodus 23:4–5: A Comparative Study." In *A Light unto My Path: Old Testament Studies in Honor of Jacob M. Myers.* Edited by Howard N. Bream et al. Gettysbury Theological Studies, no. 4. Philadelphia: Temple University Press, 1974, pp. 271–278.

Jackson, B. S. *Essays in Jewish and Comparative Legal History.* Leiden: E. J. Brill, 1975.

______. "Legalism." *JJS* 30 (1979): 1–22.

______. "A Note on Exodus 22, 4 (MT)." *JJS* 27 (1976): 138–141.

______. "The problem of Exod. XXI 22–25 (ius talionis)." *VT* 23 (1973): 273–304.

______. "Reflections on Biblical Criminal Law." *JJS* 24 (1973): 8–38.

______. *Theft in Early Jewish Law*. New York: Oxford University Press, 1972.

Kimbrough, S. T., Jr. "Reconciliation in the Old Testament." *RelLife* 41 (1972): 37–45.

Kline, M. "Lex Talionis and the Human Fetus." *JETS* 20 (1977): 193–201.

Lemeche, N. P. "The Hebrew Slave. Comments on the Slave Law, Ex xxi 2–11." *VT* 25 (1975): 129–144.

______. "Manumission of Slaves—The Fallow Year—The Sabbatical Year—The Jobel Year." *VT* 26 (1976): 38–59.

Loewenstamm, S. E. "Exodus XXI 22–25." *VT* 27 (1977): 352–360.

McKay, J. W. "Exodus XXIII 1–3, 6–8: a decalogue for the administration of justice in the city gate." *VT* 21 (1971): 311–325.

Nicholson, E. W. "The antiquity of the tradition in Exodus XXIV 9–11." *VT* 25 (1975): 69–79.

______. "The interpretation of Exodus XXIV 9–11." *VT* 24 (1974): 77–97.

______. "The origin of the tradition in Exodus XXIV 9–11." *VT* 26 (1976): 148–160.

Patrick, D. "Casuistic Law Governing Primary Rights and Duties." *JBL* 92 (1973): 180–187.

______. "The Covenant Code Source." *VT* 27 (1977): 145–157.

______. "I and Thou in the Covenant Code." *SBL Seminar Papers*, 1978, 1, pp. 71–86.

______. "The Rights of the Underprivileged." *SBL Seminar Papers*, 1975, 1, pp. 1–6.

Paul, S. "Book of the Covenant." In *EncJud* 4 (1971): 1214–1217.

______. "Exod 21, 10 a Threefold Maintenance Clause." *JNES* 28 (1969): 48–53.

______. "Studies in the Book of the Covenant in the Light of Cuneiform and Biblical Law." *SVT* 18 (1970).

Ploeg, J. P. M. Van der. "Slavery in the Old Testament." *SVT* 22 (1972): 72–87.

Sklba, R. J. "Redeemer of Israel (Ex 19–24)." *CBQ* 34 (1972): 1–18.

Smith, R. L. "Covenant and Law in Exodus." *SWJT* 20 (1977): 33–41.

Snaith, N. H. "Exodus 23, 18 and 34, 25." *JTS* 20 (1969): 533–534.

Tate, M. "The Legal Traditions of the Book of Exodus." *RExp* 74 (1977): 483–509.

Uitti, R. W. "Israel's Underprivileged and Gemser's Motive Clause." *SBL Seminar Papers*. 1975, 1, pp. 7–25.

Vannoy, J. R. "The Use of the Word hā'ᵉlōhîm in Exodus 21:6 and 22:7, 9." In *The Law and the Prophets*. In honor of O. T. Allis. Edited by John H. Skilton. Nutley, NJ: Presbyterian and Reformed, 1974, pp. 225–241.

Vriezen, T. C. "The Exegesis of Exodus XXIV, 9–11." *OTS* 17 (1972): 100–133.

Wenham, G. J. "Legal Forms in the Book of the Covenant." *TB* 22 (1971): 95–102.

10

Tabernacle, the Golden Calf, and Covenant Renewal

Exodus 25–40

Quite possibly the last major unit of Exodus (that dealing with the tabernacle) seems anti-climactic, maybe even tedious, for many modern readers of the Old Testament. Apart from some general observations, who might have an abiding interest in these chapters except perhaps an interior decorator or architect? Nevertheless, Scripture has given us an intricate description of the tabernacle, a description that ranges over sixteen chapters, from divine orders to build (25–31), to interruption and delay of implementation because of apostasy (32–34), and to final execution of the divine mandate (35–40).

The Tabernacle (25–31; 35–40)

Most of the concerns of biblical scholarship vis-à-vis the tabernacle have been with historical questions, to the virtual neglect of theological analysis. The late-nineteenth-century formulation of Julius Wellhausen has been revised, but not abandoned. It was his contention that the account in Exodus about the tabernacle is fictional, that indeed no such edifice ever existed during the wilderness period. On the contrary, the story was composed in the late exilic period, using the Solomonic temple as a model.

Historical Analysis

Wellhausen based his conclusions on the following considerations. First, can we believe that the Israelites had available in the desert sufficient quantities of the necessary metals and fabrics? To be sure, verses such as Exodus 12:35–36 (also 3:21, 22; 11:2–3) inform us that the Israelites did not leave Egypt empty-handed. Exodus 38:21–31 summarizes the amounts of gold, silver, and bronze used. Following R. B. Y. Scott on Hebrew weights and their approximate modern equivalents, Brevard Childs calculates 1,900 pounds of gold, 6,437 pounds of silver, and 4,522 pounds of bronze as the respective amounts of precious metals used in the building of the tabernacle—altogether, just less than 13,000 pounds, or six and a half tons, of metal.[1]

As an extension of this, Wellhausen doubted whether the Israelites possessed the necessary skills to work with these metals in the wilderness, to say nothing of engineering and carpentry skills. This is a stronger objection when it is recalled that considerably later Solomon had to import Phoenician craftsmen as construction foremen to build the temple (I Kings 7:13ff.), rather than use indigenous laborers.

Second, Wellhausen observed the virtual silence of Scripture on the role of the tabernacle after the conquest. The references are indeed few, and these are limited primarily to identifying where it was erected in Palestine (Josh. 18:1; 19:51; I Sam. 1:7; 2:22). This paucity of allusions raised suspicions in his mind about the historicity of a tabernacle in the wilderness, if indeed it was as pivotal as Exodus would lead one to believe.

For various reasons modern scholars have divorced themselves from the total skepticism of Wellhausen on this

1. *The Book of Exodus: A Critical, Theological Commentary*, Old Testament Library (Philadelphia: Westminster, 1974), p. 637.

subject. The consensus now is that probably there did exist in the time of Moses some kind of simple tent shrine, reflected in the key paragraph, Exodus 33:7–11. Here the reference is to a much smaller edifice, situated outside—not in the middle—of the camp. The details in Exodus 25–31 and 35–40 are then dismissed as a much later priestly exaggerated tale of an unspectacular tent.

Innumerable suggestions have been made in an attempt either to mesh P's ornate tabernacle and E's simple tent (that is, two mutually exclusive descriptions of the same phenomenon), or to distinguish between the two structures in terms of purpose and provenance. The latter approach is the minority approach. However, the assumption that we are dealing with two different phenomena—and no text in Exodus demands that the two are interchangeable—obviates the need for much hypothetical reconstruction of the history of the tabernacle.[2]

Theological Analysis

About the tabernacle as described in these chapters of Exodus we may make the following observations.

In the tabernacle there are seven pieces of furniture, assuming that the carved cherubim are decorative extensions of the mercy seat. Can the number of furniture pieces be fortuitous?

The articles of clothing to be worn by those officiating in the tabernacle number eight, four of which are worn by the high priest alone (the ephod, 28:6–12; the breastpiece of judgment, 28:15–30; the ephod's robe, 28:31–35; a turban, 28:36–38), and four more which are worn by all the priests (a coat, girdle, cap, and linen breeches, 28:40–42). The only part of the human body not covered is the feet, indicating perhaps that the priests performed their tasks

2. See C. L. Feinberg, "Tabernacle," *ZPEB*, 5, p. 582.

Figure 5

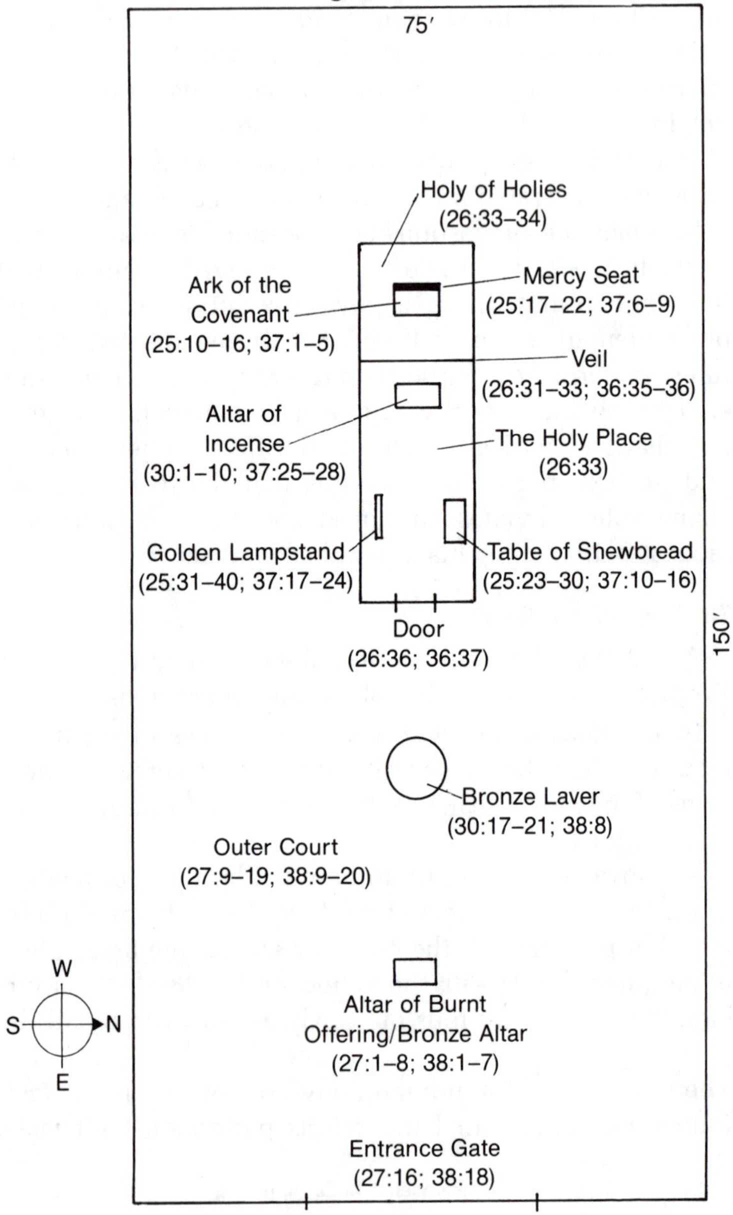

75′
Holy of Holies
(26:33–34)
Ark of the
Covenant
(25:10–16; 37:1–5)
Mercy Seat
(25:17–22; 37:6–9)
Veil
(26:31–33; 36:35–36)
Altar of
Incense
(30:1–10; 37:25–28)
The Holy Place
(26:33)
Golden Lampstand
(25:31–40; 37:17–24)
Table of Shewbread
(25:23–30; 37:10–16)
Door
(26:36; 36:37)
150′
Bronze Laver
(30:17–21; 38:8)
Outer Court
(27:9–19; 38:9–20)
W
S
N
E
Altar of Burnt
Offering/Bronze Altar
(27:1–8; 38:1–7)
Entrance Gate
(27:16; 38:18)

barefooted (compare God's command to Moses and Joshua to remove their shoes in His presence, Exod. 3:5; Josh. 5:15).

God does not delegate the responsibility for designing the tabernacle to any building or advisory committee. He alone is architect. The tabernacle, no less than the Decalogue, is rooted in divine revelation. Therefore, one is not surprised to encounter the frequently repeated phrase "he [or, they] did [or put] . . . as the Lord had commanded Moses" in the closing chapters of Exodus. It appears ten times in chapter 39 (vv. 1, 5, 7, 21, 26, 29, 31, 32, 42, 43) and eight times in chapter 40 (vv. 16, 19, 21, 23, 25, 27, 29, 32). It also appears twice in chapter 36 (vv. 1, 5). God's commands are thus for execution and implementation, not for consideration and discussion.

The materials necessary for the tabernacle and the priestly vestments are to come from the freewill offerings of the people. No one is taxed or assigned dues or apportionments. The giving is voluntary (25:1–7, especially v. 2). The response to Moses' appeal was overwhelming. Unlike most clergymen, who often beg and cajole for monies, Moses had to have the people restrained from further giving. A magnanimous spirit on the part of the congregation indeed (36:2–7)!

The description of the furniture of the tabernacle starts with the pieces at the center and works outward, but not consistently so. And in the sections dealing with the actual construction, the order of completion is different from the order of instruction. See Table 7.

In the left-hand column what is most intriguing is the separation by two chapters (28–29) of the command to build the incense altar (30:1–10) from the previous commands about the furniture. Responding to scholars who would view this particular paragraph as a later interpolation, Menahem Haran remarks, "No doubt the literary form in which P has come down to us does not satisfy the requirements of classical taste . . . but such phenomena

Table 7

	Instruction		Completion		
Holy of Holies	ark	25:10–16	ark	37:1–5	**Holy of Holies**
	mercy seat	25:17–22	mercy seat	37:6–9	
The Holy Place	table of shewbread	25:23–30	table of shewbread	37:10–16	**The Holy Place**
	lampstand	25:31–40	lampstand	37:17–24	
Outer Court	bronze altar	27:1–8	altar of incense	37:25–28	
The Holy Place	altar of incense	30:1–10	bronze altar	38:1–7	**Outer Court**
Outer Court	laver	30:17–21	laver	38:8	

. . . cannot be taken as an argument for splitting up the sources into different strata."[3]

The text of Exodus itself should caution us against reading too much of symbolic interpretation into the tabernacle. To detect in each piece of furniture, in each fabric, in each curtain ring, in each color, some hidden meaning is more speculative than it is exegetical.

Similarly, modern attempts to assert the superiority of the tent or tabernacle over the later temple seem to be open to the same charge. Thus Walter Brueggemann says that "the old tradition of 'tent' asserts a claim of mobility and freedom for God. The 'house' tradition . . . stresses the abiding presence of Yahweh to Israel. . . . Now the notion of presence is primary and God's freedom is severely constricted."[4] I respond by asking, does the Old Testament clearly delineate such a tension? Is such friction the transparent witness of Scripture?

There is symbolism in the portrayal of the tabernacle. The symmetrical dimensions bear this out. The length of the court is twice that of the width. The Holy Place is

3. *Temples and Temple Service in Ancient Israel* (Oxford: Clarendon Press, 1978), pp. 228–229.

4. "Trajectories in OT Literature," *JBL* 98 (1979), pp. 169–170.

twice the size of the Holy of Holies. The latter was a cube of ten cubits.

The choice of metals is indicative of greater degrees of sanctity. The more crucial the object, the more expensive it is. The term "pure gold" is applied only to the furniture of the tabernacle proper: the ark (25:11); the mercy seat (25:17); the table of shewbread (25:24); the lampstand (25:31, 36, 38, 39); the altar of incense (30:3). By contrast the altar and the laver in the court are made of bronze or copper (27:2, 4, 6; 30:17). Ordinary gold was used for the moldings, the rings and the poles (the latter used for carrying objects such as the ark), the table of shewbread, and the incense altar. In the case of the ark, these poles were never to be pulled out of the rings (25:15). Silver was limited to objects such as the base of a pillar near the veil (26:32) or rods joining the pillars around the edge of the court (27:10).

The same gradation applies to fabrics. The most crucial piece of fabric is the veil, separating the Holy Place from the Holy of Holies. Primarily it is made of blue, purple and crimson wools, along with fine linen (26:31). The tabernacle curtains are just the opposite: primarily a fine linen product, along with the blue, purple, and crimson wool (26:1). Last are the curtains of goat's hair (26:7).

Parallels Between the Passages about Creation and the Tabernacle

In the earlier discussion of Joseph's story in Genesis I attempted to show some parallels between the beginning and end of the Book of Genesis. Some scholars have suggested parallels between the beginning of Genesis and the end of Exodus, or more specifically, between creation and tabernacle. Thus, P. J. Kearney relates the seven divine speeches in chapters 25–31 (25:1; 30:11; 30:17; 30:22; 30:34; 31:1; 31:12) to the seven days of creation, noting parallels between each day, and each corresponding divine speech in Exodus about the tabernacle.[5] Some of these parallels appear forced, while others appear to have validity, especially those involving days six and seven, and speeches six and seven. Exodus 25–31 is creation. Exodus 32–33 is the fall. Exodus 34–40 is the restoration.

Somewhat differently, Joseph Blenkinsopp has united the two by isolating vital parallel phrases in both the creation and tabernacle sections.[6] Following Blenkinsopp's argument, it is convenient to structure the passages as I have done in Figure 6.

Further, binding the two together is the reference to "the Spirit of God" in both the creation of the world and the creation of the tabernacle (Gen. 1:2; Exod. 31:3; 35:31). It should not escape us that the first individual who was filled with God's Spirit is not a patriarch, a lawgiver, a prophet, or a judge, but a craftsman, Bezalel, foreman of the tabernacle project.

Parallels Between Mount Sinai and the Tabernacle

Apart from the relationship of the tabernacle to creation, what, if any, is the relationship of tabernacle to Sinai? First, the tabernacle perpetuates Mount Sinai. At the conclusion of the revelation at Sinai we read that "The glory of the Lord settled on Mount Sinai, and the cloud covered it six days" (24:16). When the tabernacle was finished, "the cloud covered the tent of the meeting, and the glory of the Lord filled the tabernacle" (40:34). God's presence, once on Sinai, is now over the tabernacle.

5. P. J. Kearney, "Creation and Liturgy: The P Redaction of Ex 25–40," *ZAW* 89 (1977): 375–387.

6. "The Structure of P," *Bibl* 38 (1976), p. 280; *Prophecy and Canon: A Contribution to the Study of Jewish Origins* (Notre Dame, IN: University of Notre Dame Press, 1977), p. 62.

Figure 6

And God saw everything that he had made and behold, it was very good. [Gen. 1:31]	And Moses saw all the work, and behold, they had done it; as the LORD had commanded, so had they done it. [Exod. 39:43]
Thus the heavens and the earth were finished....[Gen. 2:1]	Thus all the work of the tabernacle of the tent of meeting was finished....[Exod. 39:32]
God finished his work which he had done....[Gen. 2:2]	So Moses finished the work. [Exod. 40:33]
So God blessed the seventh day. ...[Gen. 2:3]	And Moses blessed them. [Exod. 39:43]

Second, the tabernacle intensifies Mount Sinai. At the peak of Mount Sinai, Moses "entered the cloud" (24:18). But when the same divine glory enshrouded the tabernacle, Moses "was not able to enter the tent of meeting" (40:35). At Sinai the divine presence is penetrable. At the tabernacle the divine presence is initially impenetrable.

Third, the tabernacle completes Mount Sinai. Sinai is a marriage, the start of a new relationship. Now the partners must start to live together. In Sinai God has said, "I have chosen you." In the tabernacle God has said, "I will dwell among the people of Israel, and will be their God" (29:43–46). Of course, it is precisely this fact that gives the tabernacle its sanctity. It is not the gold, or expensive fabrics, or the presence of the Levites. The tabernacle is holy only because it is the dwelling place of a holy God. If He leaves, all sanctity leaves too.

The tabernacle is the place where God and man can be closest to each other. Here God meets with His people (29:42–43). As such, the tabernacle "is the principal bridgehead in the OT to the doctrine of the Incarnation."[7] God, who once dwelt among His people in an edifice, now dwells among us in Jesus Christ (John 1:14, "the Word . . . [tabernacled] among us"; Col. 1:19, "For in him all the fulness of God was pleased to dwell").

For the author of Hebrews the tabernacle or tent is a prefigurement of the heavenly tent. The latter is greater and more perfect. It is not made with hands (Heb. 9:11). Its officiating high priest is Jesus Christ. The point then of the New Testament use of the tabernacle is twofold: the dwelling of God in Jesus Christ in the incarnation, and the dwelling of God in heaven. In both the believer is brought into proximity with his God.

The Golden Calf and Covenant Renewal
(32–34)

Exodus 32 relates how, in the absence of Moses, the Israelites and Aaron built a golden calf at the foot of Sinai, an act of flagrant apostasy. These are the same people who had said recently, not once but twice, "All the words which the LORD has spoken we will do" (24:3, 7). Converts and committed believers had become casualties, almost overnight. An affirmation of obedience was forgotten.

Clearly Aaron emerges as the villain in the story. As far back as the pre-exodus days the Lord had said to Moses of Aaron: "Is there not Aaron . . . I know he can speak well . . . he shall be a mouth for you" (4:14, 16); "Aaron your brother shall be your prophet" (7:1). This proved to be no understatement! Aaron talked so well and so convincingly that he became the leader in soliciting materials

7. G. Henton Davies, "Tabernacle," *IDB*, 4, p. 506.

for the idolatrous calf (32:2–3), and in the actual construction (32:4). And all this coated with religious praxis (32:5–6)! The setting is perfect for a prophet to intrude and say, "Has the LORD as great delight in burnt offerings and sacrifices, as in obeying the voice of the LORD?" (I Sam. 15:22).

To make matters worse, when confronted by his younger brother, Aaron is prepared to place all the blame on the people at large: "you know the people, that they are set on evil" (32:22). He is also audacious enough to gloss over his own participation in this fiasco: "they gave it [the gold] to me, and I threw it into the fire, and there came out this calf" (32:24)! Some scholars are not prepared to say that Aaron was not telling the truth, but that indeed the story presupposes that the calf emerged from the flame self-produced (see the articles by S. E. Loewenstamm, cited in the bibliography). This can hardly be the case, and besides, such an interpretation badly misses one of the points of the chapter, to contrast the faithful Moses with the conniving Aaron.

If Aaron is villain, then Moses is hero. He is first intercessor. In language almost without equal for boldness in the Old or New Testament, he urges God not to carry through on His intentions to wipe out His people (32:12). And to Moses' pleadings God accedes: "and the LORD repented of the evil which he thought to do to his people" (32:14). Said Pascal, "God instituted prayer to lend His creatures the dignity of causality." Yehezkel Kaufmann remarks that Moses does not "avert God's wrath from Israel by rousing them to repentance; he intercedes on their behalf, invoking God's promise to the patriarchs, and the glory of his name."[8] Such intercession is carried to the extent that Moses risks his own relationship with God:

8. *The Religion of Israel,* trans. Moshe Greenberg (Chicago: University of Chicago Press, 1960), pp. 284–285.

"If not, blot me, I pray thee, out of the book which thou hast written" (cf. the Pauline language of Rom. 9:3).

But Moses is more than intercessor. There is no concession made to the people. In a fit of rage, not unlike Jesus in the temple, he casts the divinely made and inscribed tablets to the ground upon observing this scenario. After the calf is ground to powder, it is mixed with water, and the people are made to drink (32:20).

Still, it is for the people's redemption and reclamation that Moses is ultimately concerned (32:30). In the presence of the people and Aaron he is critic, fulminator, and antagonist. In the presence of God he is mediator, intercessor, and protagonist.

Far from obliterating His people, God commands Moses to lead the congregation on, but God will supply a surrogate for His presence (32:34; 33:1–5). God's refusal to be in the midst of His people is reinforced by the reference to the tent "outside the camp" to which Moses goes alone (33:7–11). God has become aloof.

If God is not finished with Israel, Moses is not finished with God. The intercessions of Moses, begun in chapter 32, continue into chapter 33. Moses wants God to "show me now thy ways" (v. 13); "show me thy glory" (v. 18).

It is hard to miss the glaring contrast between "I will not go up among you" (33:3) and "my presence will go with you" (33:14). Childs has caught the implication in Moses' request: "God has said: 'My presence will go with you.' Moses replies: 'If thy presence will not go, then do not make us leave this place.' The effect is to minimize the partial concession in order to press for the full request. Indeed, what Moses is really after comes out clearly in his repetition of the phrase 'I and thy people'. God's response had continued to attach itself to Moses himself. Moses shakes it off and demands that the response include the people."[9]

9. *The Book of Exodus*, p. 595.

To both of Moses' requests there is an answer. To the first, "show me thy ways," the answer is, "My presence will go with you." To the second, "show me thy glory," the answer is, "I will make all my goodness pass before you [i.e., a visual revelation], and will proclaim before you my name" (i.e., a conceptual revelation). The promise is then dropped and picked up in 34:6, "The LORD passed before him, and proclaimed, 'The LORD, the LORD, a God merciful and gracious. . . .' " What follows is a description of God's character, often referred to in Jewish tradition as the "thirteen attributes of God," a list reflected in passages such as Numbers 14:18; Nehemiah 9:17, 31; Psalms 86:15; 103:8; 145:8; Jeremiah 32:18; Joel 2:13; Jonah 4:2; and Nahum 1:3. God is seen in what He does, and how He acts.

Before God Himself had stood on the rock at Horeb (17:6). Now it is Moses' turn to stand in a cleft of the rock and catch a fleeting glimpse of God's back (33:23).

By chapter 34 we are prepared for covenant renewal. The language is reminiscent of Exodus 19—"Be ready in the morning. . . . No man shall come up with you . . . let no flocks or herds feed before that mountain. . . . The Lord descended in the cloud" (34:2–5).

Moses is still concerned about his congregation—"go in the midst of us . . . pardon our iniquity and our sin and take us for thy inheritance" (34:9). There is no boastfulness here, nor is Moses attempting to exonerate himself. He identifies fully with his people.

Verses 10–26 are God's words to all Israel. First, God commands intolerance toward all pagan forms of worship (vv. 11–16). There is to be no yoking with unbelievers. Then follows in verses 17–26 a selective sample of laws from both the Decalogue (34:17, 21) and from the book of the covenant (34:23, 26). These particular prohibitions or admonitions fall into one of two general categories: the prohibition of apostasy and the cultic calendar. These are precisely the areas in which Israel trespassed in building the golden calf—erecting a forbidden idol, followed by a religious festival.

Fittingly, the chapter concludes with Moses' descent from Sinai, his face aglow, a fact that becomes readily apparent to everyone except Moses (34:29–30). Childs remarks, "the biblical story is concerned that the divine glow on Moses' face should not be understood as a type of metamorphosis. Moses did not himself become a deity. He was unaware of any transformation. The whole point of the story emphasizes that his was only a reflection of God's glory."[10] Indeed, this is the point of Psalm 8—man is made a little less than God, and is crowned with glory and honor. Man is a reflection of God, but never an equal.

Bibliography

The Tabernacle (25–31, 35–40)

Abrahams, I. "Tabernacle." In *EncJud* 15 (1971): 679–688.

Blenkinsopp, J. *Prophecy and Canon: A Contribution to the Study of Jewish Origins.* Notre Dame, IN: University of Notre Dame Press, 1977, pp. 54–79.

______. "The Structure of P." *Bibl* 38 (1976): 275–292.

Eichrodt, W. *Theology of the Old Testament.* Translated by J. Baker. 2 vols. Philadelphia: Westminster, 1967, vol. 1, pp. 102–114.

Feinberg, C. "Tabernacle." In *ZPEB*, 5, pp. 572–583.

Glueck, N. "Incense Altars." In *Translating and Understanding the Old Testament: Essays in Honor of Herbert G. May.* Edited by Harry T. Frank and William L. Reed. Nashville: Abingdon, 1970, pp. 325–329.

Gutmann, J. "The History of the Ark." *ZAW* 83 (1971): 22–30.

Haran, M. "Priestly Vestments." In *EncJud* 13 (1971): 1063–1069.

______. "Shewbread." In *EncJud* 14 (1971): 1394–1396.

______. *Temples and Temple Service in Ancient Israel.* Oxford: Clarendon Press, 1978.

Kearney, P. J. "Creation and Liturgy: The P Redaction of Ex 25–40." *ZAW* 89 (1977): 375–387.

10. *Ibid.*, p. 619.

Lewis, J. "The Ark and the Tent." *RExp* 74 (1977): 28–44.

Lipinski, E. "Urim and Thummīm." *VT* 20 (1970): 495.

McEvenue, S. E. "The Style of a Building Instruction." *Semitics* 4 (1974): 1–9.

Motyer, J. A. "The God Who Is Sufficient: The Indwelling God (Exodus 25:1—40:38)." *The Keswick Week 1974,* pp. 111–121.

Woudstra M. H. "The Tabernacle in Biblical-Theological Perspective." In *New Perspectives on the Old Testament.* Edited by J. Barton Payne. Waco, TX: Word Books, 1970, pp. 88–103.

The Golden Calf and Covenant Renewal

(32–34)

Bailey, L. R. "The Golden Calf." *HUCA* 42 (1971): 97–115.

Coats, G. W. "The King's Loyal Opposition: Obedience and Authority in Exodus 32–34." In *Canon and Authority.* Edited by George W. Coats and Burke O. Long. Philadelphia: Fortress, 1977, pp. 91–109.

Dunn, J. D. G. "2 Corinthians III:17; the Lord is the Spirit." *JTS* 21 (1970): 309–320.

Fensham, F. C. "New Light from Ugaritica V on Ex 32, 17." *JNWSL* 2 (1972): 86–87.

Halpern, B. "Levitic Participation in the Reform Cult of Jereboam I." *JBL* 95 (1976): 31–42.

Hanson, A. "John 1:14–18 and Exodus 34." *NTS* 23 (1976): 90–101.

Honeycutt, R. L., Jr. "Aaron, the Priesthood, and the Golden Calf." *RExp* 74 (1977): 523–535.

Hooker, M. D. "Johannine Prologue and the Messianic Secret." *NTS* 21 (1974): 40–58.

Loewenstamm, S. E. "The Making and Destruction of the Golden Calf." *Bibl* 48 (1967): 481–490.

———. "The Making and Destruction of the Golden Calf—A Rejoinder." *Bibl* 56 (1975): 330–343.

Oswalt, J. "The Golden Calves and the Egyptian Concept of Deity." *EQ* 45 (1973): 13–20.

Perdue, L. G. "The Making and Destruction of the Golden Calf—A Reply." *Bibl* 54 (1973): 237–246.

Part THREE

Leviticus

11

The Sacrificial System

Leviticus 1–7

Leviticus divides naturally into five units:

1. laws about sacrifice, 1–7
2. laws about priestly ordination, 8–10
3. laws about physical and moral impurities, 11–16
4. laws about physical and moral holiness, 17–26
5. laws about vows, 27

Norman L. Geisler has suggested that Leviticus be understood as a two-part book: the way to the Holy One (chaps. 1–10), that way being by sacrifice and priesthood; the way to holiness (chaps. 11–27), that way involving both sanitation and sanctification.[1]

Leviticus underscores that the material found in its chapters is divinely-revealed content. No hint is given that any institution described is incorporated from another religious system. Nor is there any indication that the substance of the book is the product of a committee on liturgy that imposes on the community its recommended means of worshiping God.

The revelatory nature of the material in Leviticus is underlined by the fact that twenty of the twenty-seven chapters begin with the formula, "the Lord said unto Moses." The exceptions are chapters 2, 3, 5, 7, 9, 10, and 26. And some of these simply continue the emphasis of

1. *A Popular Survey of the Old Testament* (Grand Rapids: Baker, 1977), p. 66.

the preceding chapter (hence the absence of the formula), or else contain this formula in the body of the chapter instead of at the beginning.

Leviticus is addressed to the members of a believing community. The covenant is in the past, and the marriage relationship is well under way. Exodus ended by devoting a good bit of attention to *where* God is to be worshiped—in the tabernacle. Leviticus extends the theme to include *how* God is to be worshiped. In Exodus the emphasis is on locality. In Leviticus the emphasis is on attitude and proper relationships.

More than any other Old Testament book, at least in terms of prominent vocabulary, Leviticus summons Israel to a holy life. Precisely what is involved in the holy life will surface as we make our way through the book. But for starters, we note that the word *holy* occurs in this book of the Bible more often than in any other. Strong's *Exhaustive Concordance*, based on the KJV, lists ninety uses of "holy" in Leviticus, and fifty of these occur in chapters 19–27. Strong also cites seventeen uses of the verb *to sanctify*, and again a majority of these are in chapters 19–27 (i.e., 14 of 17). If we concentrate exclusively on the Hebrew root *q-d-š*, we discover, using Mandelkern's concordance, that some form of this root, in adjectival, nominal, or verbal structure, appears 150 times in Leviticus (about 20 percent of all occurrences in the Old Testament).

And lest it be thought that Leviticus addresses itself to the holiness demanded exclusively, or even primarily, of the priest, we need to observe that just the opposite is the situation. Precious little in this book is directed exclusively at the clergy (these exceptions are chapters 8–10, 16 partially, and 21:1—22:16). The remainder is addressed to all the people. So Leviticus is describing a holiness that applies to everyone, not just a holiness for the religious hierarchy; a holiness within the reach of all, out of the reach of none.

Description of the Sacrifices

The first seven chapters are devoted to a description of the sacrifices ordained by God that bear on the perpetuation of man's relationship with God. Worship without sacrifice is inconceivable. Wherever sin has driven a wedge between God and man, both sacrifice (the outer act) and penitence (the inner attitude) become incumbent on the sinner.

There are five sacrifices:

1. the whole burnt offering—chapter 1, called in Hebrew the *ᶜôlāh*, "that which goes up," and in the LXX, "holocaust"
2. the cereal offering—chapter 2, involving here exclusively cereal products
3. the peace offering—chapter 3, perhaps a covenant meal
4. the sin offering—chapters 4—5:13, a sacrifice of repentance for sins
5. the guilt offering—chapters 5:14—6:7, also a sacrifice of repentance for sins, but additionally underscoring the need of restitution; thus, a special kind of sin offering

Immediately one can distinguish between points 1–3 and 4–5. The first three climax, in their respective narration, with the impact that such a sacrifice has on God. Such a sacrifice, when offered, becomes "a pleasing odor to the LORD" (10 references):

1. 1:9, 13, 17 (whole burnt)
2. 2:2, 9, 12; 6:15, 21 (cereal)
3. 3:5, 16 (peace)

In connection with the last two sacrifices the phrase appears only in 4:31.

By contrast, a unique phrase occurs repeatedly in the narration of the last two sacrifices: he or they "shall be forgiven" (9 references):

4. 4:20, 26, 31, 35; 5:10, 13
5. 5:16, 18; 6:7

The first three sacrifices move to their climax in indicating their result on God. To Him it is a pleasing odor. The last two sacrifices move to their climax in indicating their result on the one who gives the offering. He is forgiven.

There is a second difference between the two categories of sacrifices. None of the first three sacrifices is identified with either an occasion that prompts the sacrifice or a particular violation that elicits it. They are to be spontaneous acts, sacrifices offered to God in praise and thanksgiving. To be sure, one reads in 1:4 that the burnt offering is "to make atonement" for the individual. We also need to observe that the phrase "it shall be accepted for him" is unique, occuring in neither 4 nor 5, and the significant phrase—"he shall be forgiven"—is absent here.

By contrast, the latter two sacrifices are identified with a specific occasion: "If any one sins unwittingly in any of the things which the LORD has commanded not to be done" (4:2). This sacrifice covers the inadvertent violation of God's prohibitive laws. The guilt offering also addresses itself to inadvertent violations, not in the area of the prohibitive laws, but in the area of "any of the holy things of the LORD" (5:15). The first would cover sins of commission and the second sins of omission. Quite clearly then, the latter two sacrifices, unlike the first three, are expiatory or propitiatory in nature. Explicitly, sin and its forgiveness are the issues.

From this distinction there emerges in the biblical narration a third difference between the two categories of sacrifices. This distinction involves the use of the blood. In the first three sacrifices (really only in the whole burnt offering and the peace offering), the blood of the sacrificed animal is thrown by the priests against the outer altar, the bronze altar (1:5, 11, 15; 3:2, 8, 13). The same procedure is followed in the sin offering of one of the rulers or tribal chieftains (4:25), and in the sin offering of one of the common people (4:30, 34).

However, in the case of the sin offering of either the priest or the whole congregation the picture is changed. In these two situations the blood is brought by the priest into the tent of meeting. Some of the blood is then sprinkled seven times before the veil that separates the Holy Place from the Holy of Holies. Some is put on the horns of the altar of incense (i.e., the inner altar). The remainder is poured at the base of the outer, brazen altar (4:5–7, 16–18). This is the Bible's way of saying that the greater the offender, the greater the offense. In addition, Leviticus 6:30 specifically prohibits the eating of the flesh of the sin offering if the animal's blood has been brought into the tent of meeting. Here incineration, not consumption, is the mandate. (In anticipation of the discussion about the Day of Atonement—chapter 16—let it be briefly noted that on that day the blood of the sacrifical victim is brought into the Holy of Holies—16:14–15—a procedure not permitted in any of the sacrificial rituals of Leviticus 1–7.)

Thus far we have observed three significant differences between sacrifices that may be termed voluntary and those that may be termed propitiatory or expiatory. Another relationship in these sacrifices needs to be emphasized. This has to do with the connection between 1:1—6:7, the sacrificial system, and 6:8—7:38, supplementary instructions on the sacrifices.

Two things need to be observed. First, 1:1—6:7 spells out primarily the responsibilities of the ones who give the offerings. Thus one reads in 1:2, "Speak to the people of

Israel." On the other hand, 6:8—7:38 deals with the responsibilities of the officiants. Thus the opening statement of 6:9 is, "Command Aaron and his sons." One section addresses the laity. The other section addresses the clergy. A shirking of responsibility by either renders the sacrifice void.

Instructions about the Sacrifices

The second observation deals with the order of the sacrifices in both sections. See Table 8.

Table 8

1:1—6:7	6:8—7:38
whole burnt	whole burnt
cereal	cereal
peace	sin
sin	guilt
guilt	peace

A. Rainey has called the first grouping a didactic order, a kind of pedagogical classification in which the offerings are grouped according to their logical or conceptual association. The second grouping he terms an administrative order, the order in which the administrative details of the sacrifices were entered in the record books of the temple.[2] G. J. Wenham suggests that the first grouping is governed by theological motivations. The food offerings precede those offerings which deal with the forgiveness of sin. The second grouping is arranged in order of frequency, from the regular daily sacrifices to those that were optional.[3]

Nowhere does Leviticus 1–7 arrange these offerings in

2. "The Order of Sacrifices in Old Testament Ritual Texts," *Bibl* 51 (1970), pp. 486–487.

3. *The Book of Leviticus*, New International Commentary of the Old Testament series (Grand Rapids: Eerdmans, 1979), pp. 118–119.

any hierarchy. There is no indication in the biblical text itself that we are progressing from the less important to the more important or vice versa, any more than a hierarchy is suggested by Paul in the New Testament in his listing of the gifts or fruits of the Spirit. To designate some of these sacrifices as the pith and marrow of biblical thought, while assigning others to only marginal significance, is unwarranted.

I believe Rainey has correctly discerned a third order in the sacrifices. This he calls the procedural order.[4] To illustrate, in the ceremony of the ordination of the priests (Lev. 8), the sin offering *precedes* the burnt offering—an order different from anything in Leviticus 1–7—which is then followed by the wave (peace) offering (8:14–17; 8:18–21; 8:22ff.). The next chapter covers the commencement of Aaron's high-priesthood. Again the order is interesting. To make atonement for himself Aaron offered first a sin offering, then a burnt offering (9:8–11; 9:12–14). The order of the people's offerings were sin (9:15); burnt (9:16); cereal (9:17); peace (9:18–21).

The order is brought out strikingly in the case of the Nazirite. From the perspective of what he is to bring to the Lord the order is a burnt offering, a sin offering, and a peace offering (Num. 6:14–15), But the order in which they are presented to the Lord by the priest is sin offering, burnt offering, and peace offering (Num. 6:16–17). In Hezekiah's cleansing of the temple, sin offerings come first (II Chron. 29:20–24), then burnt offerings (29:25–30), then other sacrifices (29:31–35). Consistently the sin offering has priority of place. The point is that sin has to be dealt with first. To talk about consecration and fellowship with God while ignoring unconfessed sin is a priori impossible and not permissible.

4. "The Order of Sacrifices," pp. 494–498.

Common Elements among the Sacrifices

The majority of the sacrifices here prescribed in Leviticus have several common denominators.

The Worshiper Brings a Gift

The worshiper never comes into the presence of God empty-handed. The sentiment expressed in the hymn ("nothing in my hand I bring") would find little echo in Leviticus. A worshiper comes either with his gifts or with God's Gift.

The Meaning of the Gift

The gift that is brought is frequently described as a *qorban*, usually translated as "offering." It is used at least once to describe each of the five sacrifices except the guilt offering. Leviticus and Numbers have a monopoly on this word. It appears 38 times in Numbers, 39 times in Leviticus (31 of which are in chapters 1–7), and only twice more in the Old Testament. A more literal translation of the word than "offering" would be "a thing brought near." (The word appears also in Mark 7:11.) The sacrifices are thus concerned with the issue of how one can live in nearness to God. Leviticus is answering the question, "Can there be proximity and propinquity between God and man?"

The Description of the Gift

The offering overwhelmingly is a domesticated animal—a bull, a goat, or a sheep. Occasionally grains are offered. The offering of grains rather than the offering of animals seems to depend on the range of one's financial resources. Yet it is that which is most costly, most valuable, that is given to God. And that is not all! The animal that is offered is to be without blemish.

The same Hebrew word used to describe the sacrificial

animal (*tāmîm*) can describe Noah (Gen. 6:9), Abraham (Gen. 17:1), Job (Job 12:4), or any worshiper hoping to enter God's presence (Ps. 15:2). The word then encompasses both physical purity and moral purity. The Old Testament itself seems to shift its emphasis, in terms of sacrifice, from the sacrifical animal without physical impurities (Leviticus) to the sacrificial servant—person without moral impurities. This certainly is the message of Isaiah 53, the servant who bears our griefs, who was wounded for our transgressions and iniquities, yet who opened not his mouth. The scene for the New Testament message could not be more beautifully and ideologically prepared (see I Peter 1:19).

It is well known that the prophets inveighed against the abuse of sacrifices. Their ire was raised whenever they saw the people of God simultaneously faithful in their observance of ritual but faithless in their lifestyles. Sacrifice must never be used as a smokescreen for ethical depravity. Outward conformity must be matched by inner holiness. To support this, one thinks of passages such as Isaiah 1:11–17; Hosea 6:6; Amos 5:21–24; and Micah 6:6–8, voices from the eighth and early seventh centuries B.C. Later in the seventh and into the sixth centuries B.C. the emphasis is found again in Jeremiah, 6:20, or his famous temple sermon, 7:1–15. Such sentiments are reflected even in the Psalter (cf. Ps. 51:16–17).

Perhaps the clearest analogy to the theme of unblemished sacrificial victim is in the message of the post-exilic Malachi. Not only are the people's offerings *incomplete* ("you are robbing me," 3:8) and their lives *impure* ("You have wearied the LORD," 2:17), but also their sacrifices to God are *imperfect* ("the priests despise my name," 1:6). The animals presented are lame, blind, or sick, in such poor condition that the people would not dare to give them to their earthly leader (1:8b).

It is not particularly distant from this stress on the purity of the victim to the teaching of Paul when he says we are "to present [our] bodies as a living sacrifice [not dead or alive, but dead *and* alive!], holy and acceptable to God" (Rom. 12:1). And Paul inserts that we are able to do this only "by the mercies of God."

The Gift Depends on One's Resources

In most of the sacrifices, that which is to be presented is graded according to the donor's ability and resources. For example, the burnt offering may be a bull (1:3–5), a sheep or goat (1:10), or a bird (1:14). No exorbitant demands are placed on those whose means are meager. The widow's two mites are as acceptable as the gifts of the wealthy philanthropist. Jacob Milgrom has suggested that the cereal offering, the one sacrifice in which animals do not play a part, eventually became the poor man's burnt offering.

In the sacrifices of expiation similar gradations appear, but there they are in the spectrum of more serious perpetrator to less crucial perpetrator. Thus, in the sin offering, the priest or the whole congregation brings a young bull (4:3, 14). The ruler presents a male goat (4:23); one of the common people brings a female goat (4:28), a female lamb (4:32), or birds (5:7). Nowhere is there any indication that God desires to deprive His followers. We are to give as has been given to us.

The Donor Participates in the Ritual

The person who brings an offering is actively involved in the ritual, and is not a passive spectator. He presents the sacrifical victim, and as he does, he lays his hands on the animal's head (1:4; 3:2, 8, 13; 4:4, 15, 24, 29, 33). The absence of such a procedure in the cereal offering is dictated by at least two facts. First, how would it be possible for one to both present and then place his hands on flour or grain? Second, the procedure is limited to blood offerings, and hence not applicable to the cereal offering.

But what purpose is served by the imposition of hands? Leviticus 1–7 does not attempt to answer this question. It merely states the procedure and avoids a rationale. Elsewhere the laying on of hands is connected with either the transmission of blessing (Gen. 48:13–14), or of curse and judgment (Lev. 24:14). Numbers 8:9–10 is perhaps the closest parallel. Moses is "to present" (the root is *q-r-b*, the same as in Lev. 1–7) the Levites to the congregation, who in turn lay their hands on the Levites. The latter are substitutes for the congregation's first-born: "For they are wholly given to me from among the people of Israel, instead of all that open the womb. . . . I have taken the Levites instead of all the first-born" (Num. 8:16, 18).

If indeed this is a parallel then the laying on of hands on the animal signifies that the animal is a substitute. Can we assume, then, that involved in this is the transference of sin from the worshiper to the sacrificial victim? Not necessarily. In the Day of Atonement ritual, the laying on of Aaron's hands on the live goat does signify the transference of sins: "Aaron shall lay both his hands upon the head of the live goat . . . and he shall put them [i.e., sins, iniquities, and transgressions] on the head of the goat" (Lev. 16:21). However, this goat is not then offered to God as a sacrifice, with its flesh to be either burnt or eaten. Instead it is sent to the wilderness.

The Worshiper's Responsibilities

After the animal is brought to the place of worship, the worshiper, not the priest, kills the animal (by slitting its throat?). The Hebrew word that is used for "kill" is *š-ḥ-ṭ*. Its use is normally restricted to ritual killing and appears eighty-four times in the Old Testament, thirty-six of which are in Leviticus. For Roland de Vaux, the significance of this killing (and subsequent burning) is that it makes the offering useless, except for consumption, and therefore the offering is an irrevocable gift, given to God, and therefore withdrawn from profane use.[5]

In addition to slaying the victim the worshiper was responsible for skinning and dissecting the animal, and washing the entrails (1:6–9, 12–13).

The Priest's Responsibilities

The sacrificial victim's blood is drained and then scattered around or on either the outer or inner altar, depending on which sacrifice is involved. This is specifically a priestly duty (e.g., 1:5, 11, 15; 3:2, 8, 13; 4:5–7).

Interestingly, Leviticus 1–7 nowhere points out the significance of this act, or the role of the blood in the ritual. The rite is simply described, without commentary or theological analysis. Such an answer is provided by Leviticus 17:11: "For the life of the flesh is in the blood; and I have given it for you upon the altar to make atonement for your souls; for it is the blood that makes atonement, by reason of the life."

Some of the problems inherent in this crucial verse become evident just by comparing widely different translations that have been proposed by competent Hebraists.

> For the life of the flesh is in the blood, and I have assigned it to you to serve as expiation for your lives on the altar; for the blood may expiate according to the value of life.[6]

> The life-essence of flesh is in the blood and I for my part have on your behalf designated it (to be put) on the altar to serve as compository payment, for it is the blood which serves as compository payment for the life (taken).[7]

5. *Ancient Israel*, vol. 2, *Religious Institutions* (New York: McGraw-Hill, 1965), p. 452.

6. B. A. Levine, *In the Presence of the Lord: A Study of Cult and Some Cultic Terms in Ancient Israel* (Leiden: E. J. Brill, 1974), p. 68.

7. H. C. Brichto, "On Slaughter and Sacrifice, Blood and Atonement," *HUCA* 47 (1976), pp. 23, 28.

> For the life of the flesh is the blood, and it is I who have assigned it to you upon the altar to expiate for your lives, for it is the blood, as life, that expiates.[8]

> For the life of the flesh is in the blood; and I have given it for you upon the altar to make atonement for your souls; for it is the blood that makes atonement, by reason of the life (that is in it).[9]

Perhaps it is debatable whether Leviticus 17:11 may serve as *the* basis for a substitutionary theory of sacrifice. Why, for example, does Leviticus 1–7 omit any reference to a substitutionary rationale? Why do we not find a 17:11 in chapters 1–7? What is the relationship of 17:11 to its immediate context, namely verses 1–16, a paragraph dealing with restrictions upon the slaughter of animals? And what is to be made of the fact that these verses deal with the peace offering (17:5), the one sacrifice that has nothing to do with atonement and forgiveness of sin?

Perhaps the heavy emphasis on the role of blood in Leviticus 1–7 highlights not the idea of substitution per se, but the simple idea that sacrifice involves death.

The Sacrifice and Its Meaning

After the animal is offered, killed, quartered, and cleaned, and its blood is drained, either all or selected parts of the victim are placed on the altar and burned (1:9, 13, 17, 3:5, 11, 16; 4:10, 19, 26, 31, 35). The same holds true for the cereal offering (2:2, 9, 16). Consistently the Hebrew text uses the verb *q-ṭ-r* to describe the burning on the altar.

To describe the burning of animal flesh "outside the camp" the Hebrew uses the more usual word for "burn-

8. Jacob Milgrom, "A Prolegomenon to Leviticus 17:11," *JBL* 90 (1971), p. 156; "Kipper," *EncJud* 10 (1971), p. 1041.

9. A. Rainey, "Sacrifice," in *EncJud* 14 (1971), p. 600.

ing," *ś-r-p* (cf. *seraphim*, "the burning ones"): 4:12, 21; 8:17; 9:11. This verb is limited in Leviticus to the sin offering of the high priest or the whole community. It connotes the rapaciousness with which fire consumes, and perhaps is best translated as "incinerate," and so contrasts with *q-ṭ-r*, a slower, more gradual, and controlled burning.

It is not unexpected that those sacrifices burned on the altar by the priest are described as a "pleasing odor to the LORD." What shall we do with a phrase like this? Were the sacrifices food for God, a source of nutrition? Have we here vestiges of myth? To my mind, Yehezkel Kaufmann has provided the best explanation. Calling such phrases "petrified linguistic survivals," he quotes identical phrases or ideas in the writing of the prophets, and then adds,

> That the classical prophets felt free to use these phrases is the best testimony to their innocence. Had the people at large believed that sacrifice was food for the deity, the prophets and legislators—who surely did not hold this view—would hardly have used such expressions which could only have lent support to what they must consider a gross error. Indeed they would have combated this notion.[10]

In the light of the sacrifices as a pleasing odor to God one can more fully understand Paul's handling in Ephesians 5:2 of Christ's death: "And walk in love, as Christ loved us and gave himself up for us, a fragrant offering and sacrifice to God."

Disposing of the Sacrificial Victim

Various procedures were followed in the disposition of the sacrificial victim. In the burnt offering the entire ani-

10. *The Religion of Israel*, trans. Moshe Greenberg (Chicago: University of Chicago Press, 1960), p. 111.

mal was consumed (1:9, 13), except for the hide, which went to the priest (7:8). Some of the cereal offering was given to the priest for food (2:3, 10; 6:16, 18). In the sin offering some of the animal was burned on the altar by the priest. This included the choice entrails and the suet over and on the entrails (4:8–10). In the case of the sin offering of the priest and the congregation, the carcass and the remaining entrails were burned outside the camp as refuse (4:11, 12, 21), but not in the case of the laity's sin offering. Additionally we are informed that the priest could not eat the flesh of the sin offering brought by himself or the congregation (6:30). Again we see the principle illustrated: the greater the offender, the greater the offense.

The peace offering is unique. It is the one sacrifice that has multiple ways of disposition of the meat. Part is consumed on the altar (3:3–5). Part is given to the priests (7:31–35). The third element is the most radical departure. The person who gave the offering also ate part of the sacrificial victim (7:15–21). This is the only sacrifice in which that permission is granted. It is for this reason that warnings about "eating blood" come in the context of the peace offering (3:17; 7:26, 27; 17:10, 12, 14). In eating the meat, the worshiper must be certain that all the blood has been drained.

The Forgiveness of Sin

I have stated that the last two sacrifices—sin and guilt—deal exclusively with the forgiveness of sin. Yet there is a qualification made. These two sacrifices are aimed to forgive sins committed "unwittingly," "in ignorance," or "inadvertently." The phrase is applied to all four levels of the sin offering: 4:2, 13, 22, 27 (but not in 5:1–13), as well as to the guilt offering, 5:14, 18.

Two implications have often been drawn from this contingency. One is the statement that in the Old Testament sacrificial system there is provision only for accidental sins, not for those perpetrated deliberately. Furthermore, Numbers 15:27–31 explicitly states that there is the provision of atonement for the one who sins inadvertently, but then adds, "but the person who does anything with a high hand . . . reviles the Lord, and that person shall be cut off from among his people . . . his iniquity shall be upon him."

As an extension of this observation, many Christian interpreters of Leviticus have concluded, secondly, that it is precisely here that the superiority of Christ's sacrifice emerges, for in His death there is atonement—provision for all sins, those done accidentally and those done deliberately. While this idea is inviting, one might suspect that such conclusions rest on faulty exegesis. Even the contention that there is no sacrificial provision in Leviticus for deliberate sin is seriously open to question, as I shall attempt to show shortly.

But first, what, may we ask, is the intent of the qualification about inadvertent sin? Why does Leviticus make such a distinction? Can this be the Old Testament's way of saying that sin is disastrous, an affront to God, and not a chance for Him to display His capabilities? The Old Testament is as vehement in its repudiation of the antinomian spirit as is the New Testament. The Old Testament believer, no less than the New Testament believer, can affirm that "where sin increased, grace abounded all the more" (Rom. 5:20). But that beautiful truth must not be perverted into a license for sinning.

To return to Leviticus 1–7, is there anything in the sacrificial system that militates against the idea of no forgiveness for deliberate sins? The clue is found in an examination of the guilt offering (5:14—6:7), introduced also by the qualifying comment, "If any one commits a breach of faith and sins inadvertently. . . ." (5:14). The analysis of this particular sacrifice has been skillfully done by Jacob Milgrom, and here I am basically following his argument.[11]

The common denominator for this sacrifice is that it covers those cases in which the sin committed results in another party suffering some kind of loss of what is rightfully his. The wronged or deprived party may be God Himself (the point of the two cases given in 5:14–16 and 5:17–19) or some other human being (6:1ff.). For this reason restitution, plus 20 percent, is at the heart of this sacrifice (see 5:16; 6:5).

An examination of the particular situations covered in 6:1–7 (sins against another person) shows that these cannot possibly be sins done inadvertently. For example, refusing to return something that an acquaintance has placed in one's safekeeping, or stealing from him, or lying about something that was lost by another and found by oneself can hardly be called inadvertent sins! Yet these are precisely the areas covered in 6:1–7. And to compound the problem of the sinner, he issues a false statement, (or as 6:3, 5 state it, "swearing falsely") to establish his innocence or to cover up his otherwise blatant sin.

To solve the dilemma—how can deliberate sins be forgiven?—we may turn to a variant of Leviticus 5:14—6:7, and that is Numbers 5:6–8. What is novel and crucial in the passage in Numbers is that confession is essential in the case of a deliberate sin. It must succeed conviction and precede restitution (Num. 5:7). Thus the sin moves into the category of inadvertent sins and may be expiated.

To quote Milgrom, "A more correct understanding of this priestly postulate [i.e., that only involuntary wrongdoers are eligible for sacrificial atonement] would be that sacrificial atonement is barred to the unrepentant sinner"[12]

11. *Cult and Conscience: The ASHAM and the Priestly Doctrine of Repentance* (Leiden: E. J. Brill, 1976), especially pp. 84ff.

12. *Ibid.*, pp. 109–110.

or, "It is not the deliberate sinner who is excluded from sacrificial expiation but the unrepentant sinner."[13]

To say this is to echo exactly what is said by Hebrews. Compare the language of Hebrews 6:4, 6, "For it is impossible to restore again to repentance . . . if they then commit apostasy, since they crucify the Son of God. . . ." Or this, "if we sin deliberately after receiving the knowledge of the truth, there no longer remains a sacrifice for sins" (Heb. 10:26). It is the absence of confession and contrition that bars the way of the backslider into restored, redemptive fellowship with Christ.

Bibliography

Commentaries

Childs, B. *Introduction to the Old Testament As Scripture*. Philadelphia: Fortress, 1979, pp. 180–189.

Clements, R. E. "Leviticus." In *Broadman Bible Commentary*. Nashville: Broadman, 1970, vol. 2, pp. 1–74.

Heinemann, J. "Profile of a Midrash; The Art of Composition in Leviticus Rabba." *JAAR* 39 (1971): 141–150.

Hummel, H. *The Word Becoming Flesh*. St. Louis: Concordia, 1979, pp. 79–86.

Kidner, F. D. "Leviticus—Deuteronomy." *Scripture Union Bible Study Books*. Grand Rapids: Eerdmans. 1971.

Kinlaw, D. "Leviticus." In *Beacon Bible Commentary*. Kansas City, MO: Beacon Hill Press, 1969, vol. 1, 317–395.

Milgrom, J. "The Book of Leviticus." In *The Interpreter's One-Volume Commentary on the Bible*. Nashville: Abingdon, 1971, pp. 66–84.

______. "Leviticus." In *IDBSuppl*, pp. 541–545.

______. "Leviticus, Book of." In *EncJud* 11 (1971): 138–147.

Noth, M. *Leviticus: A Commentary*. Revised translation. Old Testament Library. Philadelphia: Westminster, 1977.

Porter, J. R. *Leviticus*. Cambridge Bible Commentary on the NEB. Cambridge: At the University Press, 1976.

13. *Ibid*., p. 124.

Wenham, G. J. *The Book of Leviticus*. The New International Commentary on the Old Testament series. Grand Rapids: Eerdmans, 1979.

Leviticus 1–7

Abba, R. "The Origin and Significance of Hebrew Sacrifice." *BTB* 7 (1977): 123–138.

Brichto, H. C. "On Slaughter and Sacrifice, Blood and Atonement." *HUCA* 47 (1976): 19–56.

Collins, J. J. "The Meaning of Sacrifice. A Contrast of Methods." *BRes* 22 (1977): 19–37.

Davies, D. "An Interpretation of Sacrifice in Leviticus." *ZAW* 89 (1977): 387–398.

Eichrodt, W. *Theology of the Old Testament*. Translated by J. Baker. 2 vols. Philadelphia: Westminster, 1967, vol. 1, pp. 141–172.

Freeman, H. E. "The Problem of the Efficacy of the Old Testament Sacrifices." *GJ* 3 (1963): 21–28.

Gray, G. B. *Sacrifice in the Old Testament: Its Theory and Practice*. Prolegomenon by B. A. Levine. 1925; reprint ed. New York: Ktav, 1970.

Kaufmann, Y. *The Religion of Israel*. Translated by Moshe Greenberg. Chicago: University of Chicago Press, 1960, pp. 110–115.

Kickasola, J. "Leviticus and Trine Communion." *ATB* 10 (Spring 1977): 3–58.

Landman, L. "The Guilt Offering of the Defiled Nazirite." *JQR* 60 (1970): 345–352.

Levine, B. A. *In the Presence of the Lord: A Study of Cult and Some Cultic Terms in Ancient Israel*. Leiden: E. J. Brill, 1974.

McCarthy, D. J. "The Symbolism of Blood and Sacrifice." *JBL* 88 (1969): 166–176.

———. "Further Notes on the Symbolism of Blood and Sacrifice." *JBL* 92 (1973) : 205–210.

Milgrom J. "The Alleged Wave-Offering In Israel and in the Ancient Near East." *IEJ* 22 (1972): 33–38.

———. "Atonement in the OT." In *IDBSuppl*, pp. 78–82.

———. "The Compass of Biblical Sancta." *JQR* 65 (1975): 205–216.

———. *Cult and Conscience: The ASHAM and the Priestly Doctrine of Repentance*. Leiden: E. J. Brill, 1976.

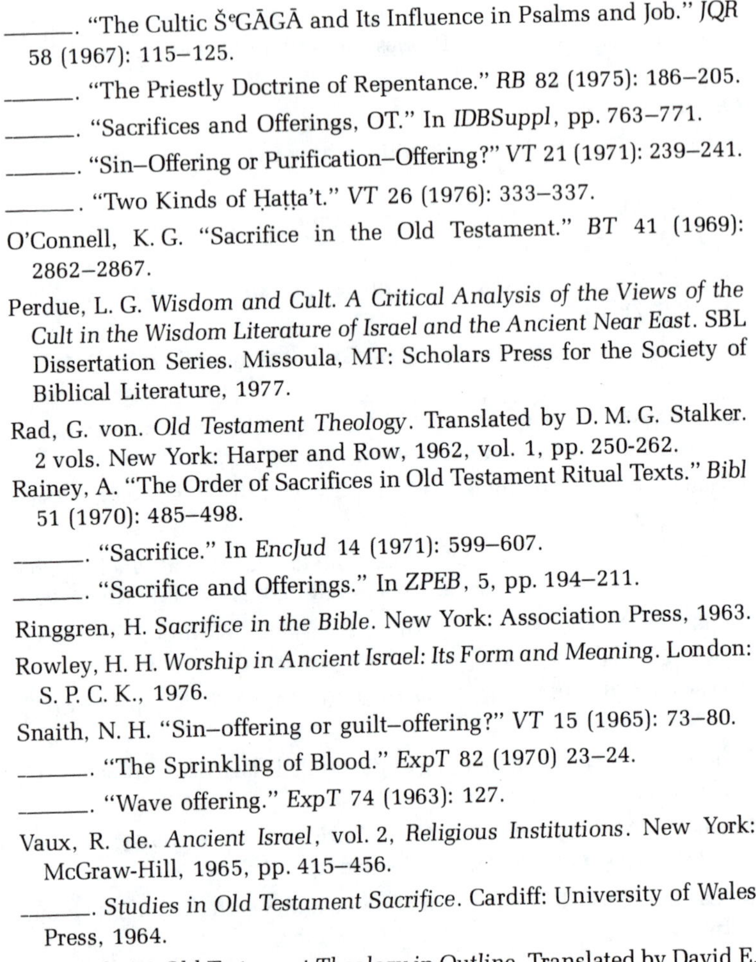

______. "The Cultic Š^{e}GĀGĀ and Its Influence in Psalms and Job." *JQR* 58 (1967): 115–125.

______. "The Priestly Doctrine of Repentance." *RB* 82 (1975): 186–205.

______. "Sacrifices and Offerings, OT." In *IDBSuppl*, pp. 763–771.

______. "Sin–Offering or Purification–Offering?" *VT* 21 (1971): 239–241.

______. "Two Kinds of Ḥaṭṭa't." *VT* 26 (1976): 333–337.

O'Connell, K. G. "Sacrifice in the Old Testament." *BT* 41 (1969): 2862–2867.

Perdue, L. G. *Wisdom and Cult. A Critical Analysis of the Views of the Cult in the Wisdom Literature of Israel and the Ancient Near East*. SBL Dissertation Series. Missoula, MT: Scholars Press for the Society of Biblical Literature, 1977.

Rad, G. von. *Old Testament Theology*. Translated by D. M. G. Stalker. 2 vols. New York: Harper and Row, 1962, vol. 1, pp. 250-262.

Rainey, A. "The Order of Sacrifices in Old Testament Ritual Texts." *Bibl* 51 (1970): 485–498.

______. "Sacrifice." In *EncJud* 14 (1971): 599–607.

______. "Sacrifice and Offerings." In *ZPEB*, 5, pp. 194–211.

Ringgren, H. *Sacrifice in the Bible*. New York: Association Press, 1963.

Rowley, H. H. *Worship in Ancient Israel: Its Form and Meaning*. London: S. P. C. K., 1976.

Snaith, N. H. "Sin–offering or guilt–offering?" *VT* 15 (1965): 73–80.

______. "The Sprinkling of Blood." *ExpT* 82 (1970) 23–24.

______. "Wave offering." *ExpT* 74 (1963): 127.

Vaux, R. de. *Ancient Israel*, vol. 2, *Religious Institutions*. New York: McGraw-Hill, 1965, pp. 415–456.

______. *Studies in Old Testament Sacrifice*. Cardiff: University of Wales Press, 1964.

Zimmerli, W. *Old Testament Theology in Outline*. Translated by David E. Green. Atlanta: John Knox, 1977, pp. 148–155.

12

Priestly Ordination

Leviticus 8–10

I have already suggested that Leviticus 6:8—7:38 is not only a supplement to the information given in 1:1—6:7, but also specifically is instructions to the priests concerning their obligations in the sacrificial ceremonies. What is it, however, that qualifies the priest to perform his sacerdotal functions?

Ordination of the Priests (8)

The means is consecration, involving first anointment (8:10–13), then the offering of sacrifices, specifically the sin, burnt, and peace or ordination offerings, in that order (8:14–35). The instructions for this installation ceremony are to be found in Exodus 29. The ceremony is implemented in Leviticus 8.

There is a literary comparison to the tabernacle sections of Exodus. Exodus 25–31 give the instructions for the tabernacle. Chapters 35–40 narrate their implementation. The movement from instructions to implementation in both instances is clear: the tabernacle—Exodus 25–31 and Exodus 35–40; the priesthood—Exodus 28–29 and Leviticus 8. Similarly, the implementation section climaxes both times with the same phraseology, "he did . . . as the Lord commanded." We have already noted the proliferation of this phrase in Exodus 39 and 40 especially. To this add

Leviticus 8:4, 5, 9, 13, 17, 21, 29, 34, 36. There is also a contrast in both sections between the right and wrong way of doing something—how to worship God (Exod. 25–31) and how not to worship God (Exod. 32); how to officiate properly (Lev. 8–9) and how to officiate improperly (Lev. 10:1–2, 16–20).

The Hebrew words for "consecration" or "ordination" and "ordain" are closely related. The word for "consecration" is *millû'îm*, "a filling," translated in the Septuagint as "completion" or "perfection." The verb "to ordain" is rendered by a Hebrew expression, "to fill the hands," *millē' yād*.

The ordination offering is discussed in 8:22–35, with the parallel in Exodus 29:19–34. Several things are especially noteworthy. First, not only in this chapter, but in the next two as well, Moses is supervisor and Aaron is subordinate.[1] Jacob Milgrom thus comments, "strikingly, the superiority of prophet over priest is insisted upon by the priestly document."[2]

A second interesting fact is that again there is a more extensive use of the blood than there is in the peace offering of Leviticus 3. The blood of the ram is daubed on the tip of the priest's right ear, the thumb on his right hand, and the large toe on his right foot. Why these parts of the anatomy? Was the priest one who was to be especially sensitive to the Lord, thus able to *hear* God's word? Was the priest indeed the one who needed clean *hands* to enter the presence of God, as the psalmist suggested (24:4)? Was the priest the one who, par excellence, *stood* in God's holy place (Ps. 24:3) and must *walk* blamelessly (Ps. 15:2)?

The expression for "ordain" appears in 8:33. The verse

1. G. J. Wenham, *The Book of Leviticus*, New International Commentary of the Old Testament series (Grand Rapids: Eerdmans, 1979), p. 132.

2. "Leviticus," *IDBSuppl*, p. 542; "Leviticus, Book of," *EncJud* 11 (1971), p. 142.

may be read: "and you shall not go out from the door of the tent of meeting for seven days, until the day of the filling of the days of your filling, for within seven days he will fill your hands." The same expression for priestly ordination appears in Exodus 28:41; 29:9, 33, 35; 32:29; Leviticus 16:32; 21:10; Numbers 3:3; Judges 17:5, 12; I Kings 13:33.

To become a priest then meant to have one's hands filled. But what can be the meaning of such a passage? Does it refer to a salary the priest was to receive; is he given the right to a part of the revenues and offerings brought to the sanctuary?[3] This inference is made on the basis of cuneiform texts from Mari that deal with the distribution of booty. For example, slaves taken as booty from a conquered city "fill the hand" (*mil qati*) of the conquerors.

Perhaps it is impossible to discover precisely the antecedents of the Hebrew phrase. May it be that the filled hands of the priest symbolize the fact that his life was to be filled with nothing except holy things? Priesthood is a preoccupation, not a pastime. Like Jesus, the priests must be about their Father's business. It is interesting to speculate on the meaning of Leviticus 9:17, "and he presented the cereal offering and filled his hand (*way*^{e}*mallē' kappô*) from it, and burned it upon the altar." Does this mean he took a fistful (as in Lev. 2:2, "and he shall take from it a handful" [*w*^{e}*qāmaṣ miššām m*^{e}*lō' qumṣô*]), or does it mean he celebrated his first sacrifice?

The Hebrew verb "to fill" is used in nonclerical contexts where the emphasis again is on total consecration to God's work. About Caleb Moses says, "he has wholly followed the Lord" (Deut. 1:36). The Hebrew reads, literally, "he

3. Roland de Vaux, *Ancient Israel*, vol. 2, *Religious Institutions* (New York: McGraw-Hill, 1965), pp. 346, 347; Aelred Cody, *A History of Old Testament Priesthood* (Rome: Pontifical Biblical Institute, 1969), pp. 153–154.

completely filled [himself] after the Lord." The phrase is used again for Caleb's level of devotion in Numbers 32:11–12 and Joshua 14:8, 9, 14.

The ordination of the priests is to be a public ceremony (8:3–4). But before either Aaron and his sons are anointed (vv. 10–13), or any sacrifices are offered (vv. 14–35), it is important that Aaron be outfitted in the proper priestly regalia (vv. 5–9). Two of the puzzling pieces are what are called the Urim and the Thummim (v. 8). Whatever they are, they are mentioned again in Exodus 28:30; Numbers 27:21; Deuteronomy 33:8; I Samuel 14:41; 28:6; Ezra 2:63; Nehemiah 7:65. The consensus is that these were two flat pieces, stones perhaps, sacred lots by which the priest could receive guidance from God. The word *Urim* is related to the Hebrew verb meaning "to curse" (thus a no from God?), and *Thummim* is related to the Hebrew verb meaning "to be perfect, blameless" (thus a yes from God?).

Some scholars have contended that the Urim and Thummim are unique to Israel and Old Testament practice.[4] Others have suggested an approximate counterpart in pagan religions.[5] Whether we are dealing here with adoption, adaption, or innovation, Walther Eichrodt has made an acute comment. He says,

> It is a significant indication of the spirit of the Yahweh religion that it should never have absorbed into its system any but this, the simplest technical device for inquiring the will of God. Because of this the control of the priest over the divine decisions, which is bound up with the development of a science of divination incomprehensible to the layman, was prevented for all time.[6]

4. Yehezkel Kaufmann, *The Religion of Israel*, trans. Moshe Greenberg (Chicago: University of Chicago Press, 1960), p. 89.

5. E. Lipinski, "Ūrim and Tummīm," *VT* 20 (1970), p. 496.

6. *Theology of the Old Testament*, trans. J. Baker, 2 vols. (Philadelphia: Westminster, 1967), vol. 1, p. 114.

The Commencement of Priestly Ministry
(9)

Chapter 8 has described the consecration and ordination of Aaron and his sons. Now that that is behind him Aaron is ready for the first offering on behalf of the congregation. But that will have to wait until the last half of chapter 9. Verses 1–14 are for Aaron himself. Only in verses 15–21 does he become celebrant.

Leviticus 9 seems to stress that the priest's ministry to others is useless unless his own relationship to God is above reproach. The chapter is also reminding the priest that although he is the occupant of a holy office, and holds holy orders, he is still an imperfect human being, one who needs constantly to be purified.

That there has been a sin and burnt offering at Aaron's consecration is good, but not sufficient (8:14–21). The whole process must be repeated before the recently ordained clergyman can become mediator. Again, he must offer the sin offering for himself (9:8–11), then the burnt offering (9:12–14).

Perhaps to make the situation even more dramatic, Moses tells Aaron to take a *calf* for his sin offering, and a *ram* for his burnt offering (9:2, 8). A calf? The last calf Aaron had seen was the golden calf he fashioned at the foot of Mount Sinai (Exod. 32)! And a ram? Was this not the substitute that God supplied for Abraham in place of Isaac (Gen. 22:13)? The calf—a reminder of recent disobedience; the ram—a reminder of distant obedience.

Only after Aaron's own needs are met is he able to become to the congregation all that he is meant to be. He oversees the presentation to God of four congregational sacrificial offerings: sin, burnt, cereal, and peace (9:15–21). The chapter observes at least three times that the offering of sacrifices brings the presence of God near. Note the repetition of "for today the LORD will appear to you" or "and the glory of the LORD will appear to you" in verses 4, 6, 23. The first two are promises—"will appear." The last one is fulfillment—"appeared."

The order of events, then, in chapter 9 is a mandate from Moses; priestly sacrifices; congregational sacrifices; the appearance of the glory of God; worship in praise and prostration—"and when all the people saw it, they shouted, and fell on their faces" (v. 24). The glory of God, manifested in all its awe, makes a congregation fall prostrate in worship. The same happens in the life of an individual. Witness Ezekiel (Ezek. 1:28; 3:23), Daniel (Dan. 8:17), Paul (Acts 9:4), John (Rev. 1:17).

Correct and Incorrect Procedures (10)

Chapter 9 has ended with an emphasis on worship. What a jolt it is then to move into chapter 10 whose emphasis, at least at the beginning, is divine judgment. Two of Aaron's sons, Nadab and Abihu, offered "strange fire" to the Lord, and for this trespass paid with their lives. To lose two sons, both of whom are ordained clergymen, is blow enough. In addition, Aaron and his two surviving sons must abstain from any public demonstration of grief or mourning over these deceased relatives (10:6).

What precisely was the nature of the sin, a sin so enormous as to merit death? A specific answer to that question escapes us. From the times of the rabbinical writings to the present a host of suggestions have been offered. Leviticus Rabbah, a homiletical commentary written in the fifth century A.D. in Palestine, tries to answer the question. Were Nadab and Abihu drunk? Did they enter the sanctuary without washing their hands? Were they schemers and opportunists who said, "when will those two old men [Moses and Aaron] die so that we shall exercise control over the community?"

Perhaps the error was in some incorrect ritual procedure. This is the view adopted by much of modern scholarship. Thus, J. C. H. Laughlin suggests the sin was making incense with fire taken from a source other than the fire on the altar.[7]

G. Robinson goes a step further. On the basis of passages in Scripture that prohibit kindling a fire on the Sabbath (Exod. 35:2–3; Num. 15:32–36), a sin meriting the death penalty, and passages that refer to the use of fire in the worship of false gods (e.g., Jer. 44:15–23) he concludes, "this may suggest that the crime in question has to do with apostasy, with idolatrous worship."[8]

The point to the narrative is that the priest follows orders. Disobedience and departure from the divinely revealed way have catastrophic repercussions.

But not all trouble is past. Soon Moses finds himself in an altercation with Aaron over his two surviving sons, Eleazer and Ithamar (vv. 16–20). Between these two scenes is the note that Aaron is to *teach* the people of Israel all the statutes of the Lord (v. 11). The irony is hard to miss. He is failing with his own family and is unable to teach them!

The two sons stumble over the sin offering brought to them by the people. In such a case the sacrifice is to be eaten by the priests (6:26, 29). This they refused to do (10:17). But why should such an omission lead to a heated argument? I believe Milgrom has correctly assessed the point:

> When the P code prescribed that every *ḥaṭṭā't* except that brought for severe sins should be eaten by the priests, it took a giant step towards eviscerating the magical and demonic elements from Israelite ritual. For it must be

7. "The 'Strange Fire' of Nadab and Abihu," *JBL* 95 (1976), p. 561; also Menahem Haran, *Temples and Temple-Service in Ancient Israel* (Oxford: Clarendon Press, 1978), pp. 183, 232.

8. "The prohibition of strange fire in ancient Israel," *VT* 28 (1978), pp. 308ff.

assumed in keeping with the evidence from the ancient Near East, that ritual detergents were always destroyed after they were used lest their potent remains be exploited for purposes of black magic. By requiring that the *ḥaṭṭā't* be eaten, Israel gave birth to a new and radical idea: the sanctuary is purged not by any inherent power of the ritual but only by the will of God. Thus, when Aaron and his sons burned an ordinary *ḥaṭṭā't*, instead of eating it, they engendered the suspicion that they were afraid to eat it, possibly opening the flood-gates to a reincursion of magical practices and beliefs.[9]

Bibliography

Cody, A. *A History of Old Testament Priesthood*. Rome: Pontifical Biblical Institute, 1969.

Haran, M. "Priests and Priesthood." *EncJud* 13 (1971): 1069–1086.

______. *Temples and Temple-Service in Ancient Israel*. Oxford: Clarendon Press, 1978, pp. 165–174.

Laughlin, J. C. H. "The 'Strange Fire' of Nadab and Abihu." *JBL* 95 (1976): 559–565.

Lipinski, E. "Ūrim and Tummīm." *VT* 20 (1970): 495–496.

Milgrom, J. "Two kinds of *ḥaṭṭā't*." *VT* 26 (1976): 333–337.

Robinson, G. "The prohibition of strange fire in ancient Israel." *VT* 28 (1978): 301–317.

Sabourin, L. *Priesthood. A Comparative Study*. Leiden: E. J. Brill, 1973.

Vaux, R. de. *Ancient Israel*, vol. 2, *Religious Institutions*. New York: McGraw-Hill, 1965, pp. 345–357.

9. "Two kinds of *ḥaṭṭā't*," *VT* 26 (1976), p. 337.

13

Clean and Unclean

Leviticus 11–15

In the midst of chapter 10 we were informed that one of the functions of the priest is "to *distinguish* between the holy and the common, and between the unclean and the clean, and . . . to *teach* . . . all the statutes which the Lord has spoken" (10:10–11, italics mine). The priest, then, is both celebrant and educator, both liturgist and instructor.

Even here the subordinate role of Aaron to Moses is clear. The distinctions between holy and clean and common and unclean that follow in these three chapters are not Aaron's ideas. Nor were the distinctions hammered out in committee by the priestly triumvirate of Aaron, Eleazar, and Ithamar. They are to teach what the Lord has spoken to Moses (10:11). The chapter beginnings are either, "the LORD said to Moses and Aaron" (11 and 13) or, "the LORD said to Moses" (12 and 14). Moses may be addressed alone. Aaron is spoken to only with Moses.

Clean and Unclean Animals (11)

The entire eleventh chapter is consumed with one issue: the Israelites' diet—what they may eat and that from which they must refrain. Five areas are examined in Table 9.

It is immediately clear that nowhere are any fruits or vegetables listed as unacceptable food—only certain types of meat. God's first dietary directive to man supplies the reason: "Behold, I have given you every plant yielding

Table 9

Ref.		Ref.		Ref.		Ref.		Ref.	
1–8	land animals	9–12	fish	13–23	birds & winged insects	24–40	uncleanness transmitted by contact with dead or unclean animals	41–44	swarming things
1–3	permitted	9	permitted	13–19	outlawed birds	24–28	to a person via non-edible land animals	41–44	outlawed
4–8	outlawed	10–12	outlawed	20, 23	outlawed winged insects	29–38	to a nonhuman entity via “swarming things”		
						39–40	to a person via edible land animals		
								45–47	conclusion
								45	rationale for abstinence
								46–47	summarizing statement

seed which is upon the face of all the earth, and every tree with seed in its fruit; you shall have them for food" (Gen. 1:29). The same holds true for creatures inhabiting land and air (Gen. 1:30).

Only after the flood does man change from herbivorous to carnivorous (see Gen. 9:3–5). Only after the serpent is cursed does an apron of fig leaves (Gen. 3:7) give way to a covering of skins (Gen. 3:21).

A number of suggestions have been made in an attempt to justify the list of clean and unclean animals, suggestions that, by and large, are not in the biblical text itself. At least four rationales have been offered repeatedly. One is the ethical explanation. This approach is reflected in the quote from Aristeas, a first-century B.C. Egyptian Jew: "The dietary laws are ethical, since abstention from the consumption of blood tames man's instinct for violence by instilling in him a horror of bloodshed." It is interesting to observe that Noah, at God's command, took aboard the ark both clean and unclean animals (Gen. 7:2). The unclean animals are also objects of God's mercy.

A second is the aesthetic. Animals whose very appearance is repulsive are unlikely to find themselves on the dinner table.

A third reason is the theological. Animals associated with pagan religions were taboo for Israel, just as, for example, were pagan mourning customs.

Perhaps the most frequently cited rationale is hygienic. As more likely carriers of disease, some animals are automatically eliminated. Maimonides, the twelfth-century Jewish philosopher and theologian, illustrates this emphasis: "These ordinances seek to train us in the mastery of our appetite. . . . All the food which the Torah has forbidden us to eat have some bad and damaging effect on the body" (*Guide to the Perplexed* 3:48).

More recently a novel suggestion has been put forward by anthropologist Mary Douglas. She first appeals to the morphological criteria listed in Leviticus 11 itself. Mammals that part the hoof and chew the cud are permitted. Aquatic creatures must have fins and scales. Says Douglas, "it [the dietary code] rejects creatures which are anomalous, whether in living between two spheres, or having defining features of members of another sphere, or lacking defining features."[1] The clean species must have all the necessary criteria of its class.[2] It is not difficult to project the criteria of anomaly from the animal to the human. If God rejects the animal which lacks the crucial and distinguishing characteristics of its species, how much more will He reject one who tries to live in two worlds, the anomalous believer.

It is no accident that every time food regulations appear in the Pentateuch the word *holy* is not far away. Exodus 22:31 reads, "You shall be men consecrated to me; therefore you shall not eat any flesh that is torn by beasts in the field; you shall cast it to the dogs." See also Leviticus 20:25–26 and Deuteronomy 14:21. The best example is in the chapter we are discussing, especially verse 44: "consecrate yourselves . . . be holy . . . I am holy." Jacob Milgrom rightly says, "Relatively few individual statutes of the Bible are coupled with the demand for holiness. And none of these have the demand with the same staccato emphasis and repetition as do the food prohibitions."[3]

That this was no trivial matter to the Jew is evidenced by Ezekiel's own testimony (Ezek. 4:14). Daniel, although invited to sit at a king's table and eat a meal suitable for royalty, chooses to follow the dietary restrictions (Dan. 1:8). Peter, now a follower of Jesus, and filled with the Holy Spirit at Pentecost, was never able to extricate himself from the prohibitions of Leviticus 11 (Acts 10:14). If

1. *Implicit Meanings: Essays in Anthropology* (Boston: Routledge and Kegan, 1975), p. 266.
2. *Ibid*., p. 284.
3. "The Biblical Diet Laws as an Ethical System," *Intr* 17 (1963), pp. 291–292.

this had not been just a vision, one can only wonder how gingerly he would sink his teeth into one of these pieces of meat for his first bite!

Uncleanness from Childbirth (12)

This chapter deals with the procedures mandated for a mother after the delivery of a child. First she must remain in seclusion for a week (v. 2); after the child's circumcision she remains in seclusion for another month (v. 4). Her first trip out of the home is to go to church (v. 6). Feminists who decry the patriarchal imbalance of much of the Old Testament cite the fact that in the case of the birth of a girl, the mother's length of seclusion is doubled (one week to two weeks, thirty-three days to sixty-six days).

It is only *after*, not before or during, these forty to eighty days of purification have passed that the mother brings a burnt offering and a sin offering to the Lord. Does the bringing of such offerings imply that sex is sinful, and procreation is a trespass requiring expiation? Hardly. If this is the case, then Leviticus 12 would refute everything else Scripture teaches on this subject.

We note that in connection with both male and female bodily discharges both the burnt and sin offering are required (Lev. 15:13–15, 29–30). Defilement during a Nazirite vow requires these two sacrifices also (Num. 6:10–11). It would be rather ridiculous and far-fetched to link any of these occasions with sin in the life of the person involved. It would be much more correct to describe these offerings as purification rituals. It is the postnatal flow of blood that is the cause of the uncleanness.

To be sure, much of this type of ritual is unknown in a modern Christian church, or in the maternity section of a hospital. But Dennis F. Kinlaw correctly says, "In a society like ours where much of the danger of childbirth has been removed by modern medicine and the mystery removed by biological knowledge, who is to say that some customs are not needed to restore the element of gracious mystery and sacredness to such events?”[4]

Leprosy (13–14)

Two full chapters of Leviticus are given to a description of leprosy, its diagnosis (chap. 13), and the cleansing of the leper (chap. 14). We can safely assume that the word *leprosy* is a generic term, and covers a number of skin diseases, most of which would be noncontagious. (For examinations of the Hebrew word for “leprosy,” see the bibliographical entries for R. K. Harrison, E. V. Hulse, J. Sawyer, and J. Wilkinson.) That the disease in question can affect both clothing and buildings seems to imply a range of meanings that would cover even rot, fungus, and mildew.

Table 10 outlines the areas covered in this section of Leviticus.

Quite predictably the priestly sections of Scripture address themselves to the issue of purity, that is, cleanness

Table 10 Leprosy

Reference		**Reference**	
13:1–59	diagnosis	14:1–57	cleansing and further diagnosis
1–28, 38–39	skin	1–32	ritual for rehabilitation
		33–53	diagnosis of leprosy in houses
24–37	hair		
40–44	scalp		
45–46	quarantine		
47–59	deteriorating garments		
		54–57	summarizing statement

4. “Laws Concerning Uncleanness,” *Beacon Bible Commentary* (Kansas City, MO: Beacon Hill Press, 1969), vol. 1, p. 355.

and uncleanness. The Hebrew word for "clean" occurs more than 200 times in the Old Testament. Ninety-three of these occurrences (i.e., 43.7 percent of the total), are in Leviticus and Numbers. The word for "unclean" appears more than 280 times in the Old Testament. One hundred and eighty-two of these occurrences (i.e., 64.3 percent of the total), are in Leviticus and Numbers.[5]

There is a threefold ritual in which the leper must involve himself to remove his "uncleanness" if he is to be reintroduced to the community. There is a ceremony for the first day (14:2–8). It is important to observe that the purpose of this ritual is not to cleanse the disease, but is a witness to the fact that the disease is already healed. This is the plain intent of 14:3, "if the leprous disease is healed. . . ." The ritual then is symbolic and religious, not therapeutic. Nor does the priest ever function as healer or physician. If anything, he is an ecclesiastical public health official.[6]

There is also a second ceremony for the seventh day (14:9), and a third ceremony for the eighth day (14:10–32), with the focus here on the offering of the appropriate sacrifices. Again, as in Leviticus 1–7, there are revisions in the sacrificial requirements if the leper is poor.

It would be wide of the mark to say that the Old Testament considers leprous diseases to be the result of sin. (To be sure, stories like that narrated about Miriam show leprosy to be one manifestation of divine judgment, Numbers 12.) As in the case of the woman after the birth of her child, a period of absence from the community is mandated for those with blemishes on their bodies. The offering of sacrifices allows readmittance into community activities. Ostracism is replaced by fellowship.

5. See the charts in Jacob Neusner, *The Idea of Purity in Ancient Judaism* (Leiden: E. J. Brill, 1973), p. 26.

6. Jacob Milgrom, "Leprosy," *EncJud* 11 (1971), p. 35.

It is extremely difficult, if not impossible, to make a case for the fact that leprosy is a "type" of sin in the Bible. Leviticus is saying that leprosy is like sin, but is not itself sin, or a sign of sin. It is like sin in that it bars man from cultic fellowship with God. Of course, leprosy—like sin—is insidious, progressive, pervasive, benumbing, and loathsome. Why allegorists have made the analogy appears obvious.

Not a few of Christ's miracles involved lepers. Interestingly, the blind are healed, the crippled are healed, but the lepers are "cleansed" (*katharidzō*). In other contexts this same Greek verb takes on a very distinct moral nuance: Acts 15:9; II Corinthians 7:1; Ephesians 5:26; James 4:8; I John 1:7, 9.

Uncleanness and Bodily Discharges (15)

Specifically emissions from the genital area of the body are the concern in this section of Leviticus.

1. abnormal emissions of men (15:1–15)
2. normal emissions of men (15:16–18)
3. normal emissions of women (15:19–24)
4. abnormal emissions of women (15:25–33)

Note that for the emissions discussed in (2) and (3) bathing is sufficient to remove the impurity (15:18, 21). In the case of (1) and (4) the offering of sacrifices is required (15:14–15, 29–30).

The explanation for this type of legislation is found in 15:31, "Thus you shall keep the people of Israel separate from their uncleanness, lest they die in their uncleanness by defiling my tabernacle that is in their midst." Responding to this rationale, Jacob Neusner says, "Here in a single sentence is the complete priestly ideology of purity. All matters of purity attain importance because of the cult. No other occasion for attaining or preserving purity is considered."[7]

The area covered here finds further reflection in Christ's healing of the woman with the issue of blood (Mark 5:25–34). She wanted to touch his garments. But what made the difference was not Jesus' garments, so much as the woman's faith. Jesus did not say, "My garments have made you well." Nor did He even say, "I have made you well." What He said was, "Your faith has made you well." Not superstition, but the exercise of faith.

By way of summary, almost all the categories of clean or unclean, spelled out in Leviticus 11–15, fall into the area of the nonmoral. With the exception of the dietary code, all of the applications of the purity laws address themselves to events in one's life which are normal or unavoidable: childbirth, contraction of diseases, and bodily emissions.

We have seen, in the discussion of leprosy, that the New Testament uses the same Greek word to describe cleansing from leprosy as it does to describe cleansing from sin. That is, purity is both a physical and a moral matter.

This is not, however, an innovation with the New Testament. Strikingly the Old Testament has already extended the idea of purity beyond the cult to include the concept of moral blamelessness. For example, David's prayer on one occasion was, "Purge me . . . and I shall be clean . . . create in me a clean heart . . ." (Ps. 51:7, 10). God promises to cleanse the iniquities of restored Israel (Ezek. 36:33). Consistently, then, the Old Testament's emphasis on moral cleansing takes its vocabulary directly from ritual language. What is the force of this adaptation? In my judgment Geerhardus Vos has made the most astute observation. He says, in explaining the parallels, "God teaches people to feel about sin as they are accustomed to feel

7. *The Idea of Purity*, p. 20.

about an ignominious and uncomfortable exclusion from the ritual service."[8] Moral uncleanness, no less than physical uncleanness, erects a barrier between God and man. The divine remedy is nothing short of cleansing.

Bibliography

Albright, W. F. *Yahweh and the Gods of Canaan: An Historical Analysis of Two Contrasting Faiths*. New York: Doubleday, 1968, pp. 175–182.

Brin, G. "Firstling of Unclean Animals." *JQR* 68 (1977): 1–15.

Douglas, M. "Deciphering a Meal." *Daedalus* 101 (1972): 61–81, esp. pp. 70–80.

______. *Implicit Meanings: Essays in Anthropology*. Boston: Routledge and Kegan, 1975.

______. *Purity and Danger. An Analysis of Concepts of Pollution and Taboo*. Boston: Routledge and Kegan, 1966.

Harrison, R. K. "Leprosy." In *IDB*, 3, pp. 111–113.

Hoenig, S. "Qumran rules of impurities." *RQu* 6 (1969): 559–567.

Hulse, E. V. "Nature of Biblical Leprosy and the Use of Alternative Medical Terms in Modern Translations of the Bible." *PEQ* 107 (1975): 87–105.

Jocz, J. "Clean." In *ZPEB*, 1, pp. 884–887.

Milgrom, J. "The Biblical Diet Laws as an Ethical System." *Intr* 17 (1963): 228–301.

______. "Leprosy." *EncJud* 11 (1971): 33–36.

______. "Sin–offering or Purification–offering?" *VT* 21 (1971): 237–239.

Neusner, J. *The Idea of Purity in Ancient Judaism*, with a critique and a commentary by Mary Douglas. Leiden: E. J. Brill, 1973, esp. chapter 1, "The Biblical Legacy."

______. "The Jewish–Christian Argument in Fourth Century Iran: Aphrahat on Circumcision, the Sabbath, and the Dietary Laws." *JES* 7 (1970): 282–298.

Otwell, J. H. *And Sarah Laughed: The Status of Woman in the Old Testament*. Philadelphia: Westminster, 1977, esp. chapter 9, "Women in the Cult."

8. *Notes on Biblical Theology* (Grand Rapids: Eerdmans, 1948), p. 182.

Rabinowicz, H. "Dietary Laws." *EncJud* 6 (1971): 26–46.

Rad. G. von. *Old Testament Theology*. Translated by D. M. G. Stalker. 2 vols. New York: Harper and Row, 1962, vol. 1, 272–279.

Sawyer, J. "A note on the etymology of ṣāraᶜat." *VT* 26 (1976): 241–245.

Toombs, L. "Clean and Unclean." *IDB* 1, pp. 641–648.

Wilkinson, J. "Leprosy and Leviticus. The Problem of Description and Identification." *SJT* 30 (1977): 153–170.

———. "Leprosy and Leviticus. A Problem of Semantics and Translation." *SJT* 31 (1978): 153–166.

14

The Day of Atonement

Leviticus 16

One full chapter in Leviticus is given to a description of the Day of Atonement. Leviticus 23:26–32—part of a sacred calendar—is a further reference to this particular day, called there "a day of [the] atonement[s]," *yôm (hak)kippûrîm*. In rabbinic literature it is simply called "the day" or "the great day" (see the tractate in the Mishnah, "Yoma"). The New Testament is similarly brief in the title it uses—"the fast": ". . . because the fast had already gone by. . . ." (Acts 27:9).

Critics' Views about the Day of Atonement

The preoccupation of most commentaries is the literary dissection of chapter 16. Two conclusions about the chapter's integrity enjoy all but universal acceptance among the critics. One conclusion is that the Day of Atonement, as such, never existed in the period of Moses. That is to say, where it stands now is a blatant anachronism, equivalent to the claim of a day honoring Martin Luther King, Jr. in the time of Lincoln. More than likely, say the critics, the Day of Atonement emerged only relatively late in Israel's history—not only post-exilic, but even after the time of Ezra and Nehemiah!

This particular interpretation is based primarily on the

argument from silence.[1] No pre-exilic text—nothing in the historical books or in the prophetic corpus—mentions the day. Therefore, it did not exist then. One should, however, use the argument from silence hesitatingly, and the interested reader should refer, for this particular case, to the comments of Yehezkel Kaufmann[2] and Jacob Milgrom.[3]

The second widely accepted theory is that Leviticus 16 is a heterogeneous unit, divisible into multiple literary strands. Martin Noth's comment is illustrative:

> It is evident at the first glance that the chapter is in its present form the result of a probably fairly long previous history that has left its traces in a strange lack of continuity and unity about the whole. The material is indeed so complicated that all attempts hitherto at factual and literary analysis have not led to at all convincing results. But the fact itself, that the chapter came into being through an elaborate process of growth, is generally recognized and accepted.[4]

Reasons advanced for this idea include the appearance of doublets or repetitions. Thus we read in verse 6, "And Aaron shall offer the bull as a sin offering for himself and shall make atonement for himself and for his house." This is repeated in verse 11. Does the repetition argue indubitably for dual traditions? Cannot verses 6–10 be considered a general outline of the events? Verses 11–28 would then be a close-up, detailed account of those same events.

A second reason for discerning mixed sources in this chapter is the conclusion, verses 29–34, which appears to

1. Roland de Vaux, *Ancient Israel*, vol. 2, *Religious Institutions* (New York: McGraw-Hill, 1965), pp. 509–510.

2. *The Religion of Israel*, trans. Moshe Greenberg (Chicago: University of Chicago Press, 1960), p. 210, n. 17.

3. "Atonement, Day of," in *IDBSuppl*, p. 83.

4. *Leviticus: A Commentary*, Old Testament Library, revised translation (Philadelphia: Westminster, 1977), p. 117.

be a later appendix. Together with other information in these verses, the reader is informed that the Day of Atonement is to be observed annually on the tenth day of the seventh month, that is, Tishri (v. 29). Usually the date or day for observing the rituals comes at the beginning of a section. Here it is at the end. The conclusion? The author of this appendix is different, at least from the author who described the festivals in Leviticus 23. (Could one argue, to cite a New Testament illustration, that because Paul's prayers appear at the beginning or by the middle of his epistles, that the prayer recorded in I Thessalonians 5:23–24 must therefore be non-Pauline? Order or placement seem to have little to do with authenticity.)

Aspects of Atonement

Perhaps it is not an accident that the phrase "Day of Atonement" reads, literally, in the Hebrew, "day of atonements." Atonement covers three areas in this chapter: the high priest himself; the sanctuary; the people.

Through the use of repetition, at least of key phrases, Leviticus 16 emphasizes some crucial ideas. Before anything redemptive can happen the high priest must deal with his own sins. "And Aaron shall offer . . . a sin offering for himself . . . make atonement for himself . . . a sin offering for himself . . . make atonement for himself . . . a sin offering for himself . . . has made atonement for himself . . . make atonement for himself" (vv. 6, 11, 17, 24). Thus the phrase "for himself," used seven times, underscores the absolute necessity that the ranking clergyman first rectify his own errors. That a high priest could be above this requirement would be unthinkable, and heresy.

Hebrews 9 tells us that Jesus broke the pattern. He entered once, not annually, into the holy place, and with His own blood, not that of an animal (Heb. 9:11–14).

It is interesting to observe that not only people, but

inanimate objects as well, need atonement on this day. Compare the following: "he shall make atonement for the holy place" (v. 16); "he shall go out to the altar . . . and make atonement for it" (v. 18); "cleanse it and hallow it" (v. 19); "And when he has made an end of atoning for the holy place, and the tent of meeting and the altar" (v. 20); "he shall make atonement for the sanctuary . . . for the tent of meeting, for the altar" (v. 33).

In a very real sense, then, judgment does begin at God's house. The temple does need to be cleansed, which Jesus did. Is the Old Testament suggesting here that sin is almost substantival, something that creeps into God's presence because of the sins of God's people, and locks itself around the holy vessels in the sanctuary?

The use of the Hebrew verb *kipper*, "to expiate, make atonement," is itself interesting. Semitists widely disagree among themselves on the nuances implicit in the verb. A moderate suggestion is that the verb means "to rub." Something can be either rubbed off (e.g., sin is wiped off or purged), or rubbed on (e.g., sin is covered). It is significant that the Targum of Leviticus from Qumran (second century B.C.?), in which several verses from Leviticus 16 are all that have survived, translates the Hebrew word *kappōret* ("mercy seat, propitiatory") with the Aramaic word *ksy'*, meaning "cover, lid."[5]

What we are particularly interested in here is how the Hebrew language handles an object after this verb. A person is seldom, especially in liturgical literature, the direct object of the verb *kipper*. In Leviticus at least, the subject of this verb is the priest, never God. If the object is a person, the noun is preceded by some preposition, "for," "on behalf of," "with respect to." The person is not the object

5. See J. A. Fitzmyer, "The Targum of Leviticus from Qumran Cave 4," *Maarav* 1 (1978), pp. 15–17; *JBL* 99 (1980), pp. 17–18.

of the rites of expiation—blood is not poured or daubed on him—but he is the beneficiary of those rites of expiation.

By contrast, inanimate objects may be direct objects of the verb *kipper* with no intervening preposition. Leviticus 16:33 illustrates the difference between the two: "he shall make atonement for the sanctuary, and . . . for the tent of meeting and for the altar [*kipper* plus direct object, indicated by the untranslated particle *'et*], and . . . for the priests and for all the people of the assembly" (*kipper* plus the preposition *ᶜal* before "priests" and "all the people").

B. A. Levine speculates that Leviticus, and related literature, avoided the construction of the verb *kipper* plus a direct object—if a person—to negate the association that it is the rites themselves that are automatically effective.[6] The acts are prerequisite, but not causational. They are only means to an end. God Himself gives forgiveness and grants atonement.

Use of the Blood

In our examination of Leviticus 1–7 we observed the frequent references to blood in the sacrifices of expiation. The one distinguishing fact about Leviticus 16 is that on the Day of Atonement, and only on that day, the blood is carried into the Holy of Holies, the innermost sanctuary of the tabernacle. The biblical phrases are "within the veil . . . on the front of . . . and before the mercy seat" (vv. 12–15). An examination of Figure 7 clarifies the procedures mentioned in these verses.

One wonders why on this particular day the blood is carried into the tabernacle's most hallowed precinct. Perhaps the answer lies in a strategic word that occurs in this chapter, "transgressions," in verses 16 and 21. Gerhard

6. *In the Presence of the Lord: A Study of Cult and Some Cultic Terms in Ancient Israel* (Leiden: E. J. Brill, 1974), p. 66.

Figure 7

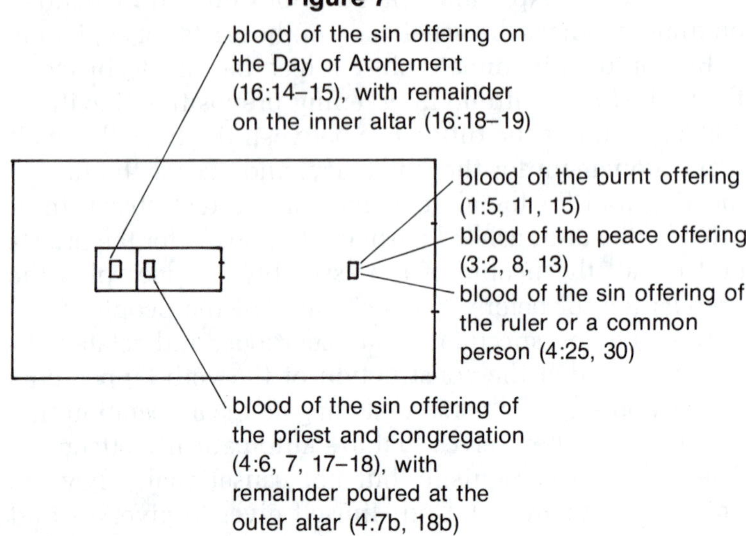

von Rad observes that of the eighty-six occurrences of this word in the Old Testament only two are in that sizable section of Scripture designated by the critics as P.[7] Those two are Leviticus 16:16, 21. They appear nowhere else in Leviticus. The word is taken from the language of politics and international relationships. As such the word conveys the idea of revolt or rebellion. Von Rad goes on to say that "it [i.e., *pesha*[c]] is unquestionably the gravest word for sin, especially on the lips of the prophets."[8]

This kind of sin is precisely the opposite of sin committed inadvertently. For this reason, on the Day of Atonement, given to deal with sin in its most gross manifestation, the blood is carried as close to the presence of God as possible. Neither the outer brazen altar nor the inner incense altar will suffice here as the main receptacle for the blood.

7. *Old Testament Theology*, trans. D. M. G. Stalker, 2 vols. (New York: Harper and Row, 1962), vol. 1, p. 263, n. 177.

8. *Ibid.*, p. 263, n. 177.

The Scapegoat

The presentation of the blood of the slain sin offering is one-half of the ceremony of the Day of Atonement. The second half is again unique to this particular occasion. One of the goats for the congregation's sin offering is to be kept alive (vv. 5, 10, 20). Unlike the procedures described in chapters 1–7, in this ritual it is Aaron, not the worshiper, who lays his hands on the head of the goat (v. 21). The officiating priest then "confesses" Israel's sins and transgressions. Again, this is a departure from Leviticus 5:5, where it is the worshiper himself who "confesses" his sin. The goat then "bears" the iniquities to the wilderness. (The reader should know that the idea of "to bear or carry" and "to forgive" is covered by the same verb in Hebrew.) This idea of carrying sin away is the antecedent for Isaiah's song about the suffering servant who "has borne our griefs" (Isa. 53:4) and who "bore the sin of many" (Isa. 53:12); or John the Baptist's exclamation: "Behold, the Lamb of God, who takes away the sin of the world" (John 1:29). The typological significance of this event is expounded in Hebrews 6:19–20; 9:7–14.

The problem of interpretation can be focused by comparing the translations of the RSV and KJV in the following verses:

verse 8 and Aaron shall cast upon the two goats, one lot for the LORD and the other lot for Azazel (RSV)

. . . and the other lot for the scapegoat (KJV)

verse 10 but the goat on which the lot fell for Azazel shall be presented alive before the LORD . . . that it may be sent away into the wilderness to Azazel (RSV)

But the goat, on which the lot fell to be the scapegoat, shall be presented alive before the LORD . . . to let him go for a scapegoat into the wilderness (KJV)

The difference between the two versions is obvious. For the RSV the Hebrew word *ᶜăzā'zēl* is the name of an individual (or place?) to whom the live goat is sent. For the KJV the Hebrew word refers to the live goat itself.

The translation of the RSV carries the day among the scholars. For this reason the prevailing interpretation is that Azazel is a supernatural power, probably demonic, whose haunt is the wilderness. The idea is that the most efficient way to get rid of evil is by banishing it to its original source.

Further support for this idea is usually located in two places. First, appeal is made to a few other verses in the Old Testament that suggest a belief that the wilderness was inhabited by demons. Leviticus 17:7 refers to the offering of sacrifices to "satyrs" (*'śeᶜîrîm*) in the open field. The most frequently quoted passage is Isaiah 34:14, in which the prophet says, in speaking of God's destruction of Edom, that the land will turn into a wilderness filled with wild animals and birds. Among the creatures mentioned here are the satyr (as in Lev. 17:7), and lilith (RSV, "the night hag"), the female night-demon famous, or infamous, in incantations. There is a third reference to the satyrs, as objects of worship, in II Chronicles 11:15. The idea of the wilderness as the haunt of the unclean spirit also surfaces in Matthew 12:43.

The second area of support for the equation of Azazel with a demonic force is found in apocryphal literature. In I Enoch Azazel is identified as the leader of the angels who, as recorded in Genesis 6, wanted the daughters of men. Eventually Azazel is bound by Raphael, and cast into a dark wilderness.

Are we then dealing with a vestige of myth that never was censored from Israel's religious history? Can we believe that a major part of such a critical event—whenever it arose—included dispatching an animal to a demon's den?

G. J. Wenham quotes J. H. Hertz on this, an observation I believe to be pungent. "The offering of sacrifices to 'satyrs' is spoken of as a heinous crime in the very next chapter (17:7); homage to a demon of the wilderness cannot, therefore, be associated with the holiest of the Temple-rites in the chapter immediately preceding."[9] Could Scripture affirm in one chapter the activity of Baal in the storm, then in an adjacent chapter have the Shema?

Where, then, does the KJV obtain its translation "scapegoat"? First, the Hebrew word *ᶜăzā'zēl* is made up of two Semitic words, the Hebrew word for "goat" and the Aramaic verb "to go." Hence, Azazel is the goat which goes, the scapegoat. Second, this is the way the word was understood by many of the ancient versions, particularly the Septuagint and the Vulgate.

As Kaufmann says, Azazel, if he is the destination of the goat, plays no active role. "Unless the sin is expelled the deadly wrath of YHWH may be aroused, but no harm will come from Azazel. . . . The value of the rite does not lie in exorcising a dangerous demonic power, but in fulfilling a commandment of God."[10] (Levine's criticism of Kaufmann's interpretation of Azazel centers mostly around the translation of Leviticus 16:10, and advocates a much greater magical objective than Kaufmann observes in the ritual.)[11]

The Role of the People

It should be obvious that the congregation has played only a minimal role in the ceremonies. Aaron selects the two male goats. Aaron places his hands on the live goat.

9. *The Book of Leviticus*, New International Commentary of the Old Testament series (Grand Rapids: Eerdmans, 1979), p. 234.

10. *The Religion of Israel*, p. 114.

11. *In the Presence of the Lord*, pp. 79–83.

The other goat Aaron kills as a sin offering for the people. Aaron alone enters the sanctuary.

What of the people? Are they passive and uninvolved? Hardly. The point of verses 29 and 31 is that the Day of Atonement is to function as a Sabbath. Not only are the people to abstain from work, but also they are "to afflict themselves." This certainly does not mean self-laceration or self-flagellation. It means that the Day of Atonement, for the layman, is to be a national day of prayer, fasting, and repentance. See also Leviticus 23:27–32 for the idea of "afflicting" oneself on the Day of Atonement.

The ceremonies in the tabernacle are appropriate and God-ordained, but they become effective only if accompanied by genuine contrition in the community of believers. The Bible nowhere accepts the idea that its rituals are *ex opere operato*.

Bibliography

Aḥiṭuv, S. "Azazel." *EncJud* 6 (1971): 111–119.

Eichrodt, W. *Theology of the Old Testament*. Translated by J. Baker. 2 vols. Philadelphia: Westminster, 1967, vol. 1, pp. 130–131.

Fearghail, F. "Sir 50:5–21: Yom Kippur or the Daily Whole Offering?" *Bibl* 59 (1978): 301–316.

Feinberg, C. "Atonement, Day of." In *ZPEB*, 1, 413–416.

Fitzmyer, J. A. "The Targum of Leviticus from Qumran Cave 4." *Maarav* 1 (1978): 5–23.

Kaufmann, Y. *The Religion of Israel*. Translated by Moshe Greenberg. Chicago: University of Chicago Press, 1960, pp. 114–115.

Kraus, H. J. *Worship in Israel*. Richmond: John Knox, 1966, pp. 68–70.

Levine, B. A. *In the Presence of the Lord: A Study of Cult and Some Cultic Terms in Ancient Israel*. Leiden: E. J. Brill, 1974, "Sacrifices of Expiation," pp. 55ff.

Lyonnet, S., and Sabourin, L. *Sin, Redemption, and Sacrifice. A Biblical and Patristical Study*. Rome: Biblical Institute Press, 1970, esp. pp. 61–184.

Milgrom, J. "Atonement, Day of." In *IDBSuppl*, pp. 82–83.

Rad, G. von. *Old Testament Theology*. Translated by D. M. G. Stalker. 2 vols. New York: Harper and Row, 1962, vol. 1, pp. 262–272.

Vaux, R. de. *Ancient Israel*, vol. 2, *Religious Institutions*. New York: McGraw-Hill, 1965, pp. 507–510.

15

A Holiness Manifesto

Leviticus 17–27

The critical view is that these last chapters of Leviticus, excluding chapter 27, once existed as an independent legal code, and only later were grafted into P, much as the Book of the Covenant is considered an insertion into the text of Exodus.

This "discovery" was made in the late nineteenth century by the German scholar August Klostermann, and to this unit of Leviticus he gave the title *Heiligkeitsgesetz*, that is, Holiness Code. (Today the symbol *H* is often all that is used to designate this source.)

Regardless of how one feels about the critical assessment of these last chapters of Leviticus, the observation is certainly valid that the reader finds an explicit emphasis on holiness as a motivation for conduct and lifestyle. I have already alluded to the fact that the Hebrew root *q-d-š* occurs 150 times in Leviticus (as a verb, noun, or adjective). The breakdown is interesting. See Table 11.

It is self-evident that there is a much greater use of *q-d-š-* related words in the last eleven chapters of Leviticus than there is in the first sixteen. And within this unit (in descending order), chapter 27, 22, 21, and 23 employ the root most often (sixty-six of eighty-five times). Neither of the first two chapters in this pericope—17 and 18—uses the root.

Several times in Leviticus the people of God receive a call to holiness in the form of a divine ultimatum. For

Table 11

Chap. Num.	Occurrence	Total
1–16	65	
17–27	85	150
17	0	
18	0	
19	5	
20	7	
21	13	
22	19	
23	12	
24	3	
25	2	
26	2	
27	22	85

example, 11:44–45, "consecrate yourselves therefore and be holy, for I am holy"; 19:2, "you shall be holy, for I the LORD your God am holy"; 20:7, "consecrate yourselves, therefore, and be holy; for I am the LORD you God"; 20:26, "You shall be holy to me, for I the LORD am holy." That these verses are not time-conditioned or eclipsed by a fuller revelation is documented by Peter's freedom to place these verses, without change, in the context of his Christian message to a community of believers (see I Peter 1:15–16).

In the four instances cited in the preceding paragraph we observe that each summons to holiness has attached to it a motivational clause—"for I am the LORD your God," or, "for I the LORD am holy." It is no accident that these commands are always given by the Lord Himself, speaking directly in the first person. Never in Leviticus does Moses or Aaron say, "you shall be holy for He is holy." God Himself establishes the standard. And Peter quotes God, not Moses!

Of course, the phrase "you shall be holy as God is holy" does not mean "you shall be as holy as God is holy." The idiom is known elsewhere in Scripture, for example, "You, therefore, must be perfect, as your heavenly Father is perfect" (Matt. 5:48). Such comparisons abound in I John: "if we walk in the light, as he is in the light" (1:7); "he who says he abides in him ought to walk in the same way in which he walked" (2:6); "And every one who thus hopes in him purifies himself as he is pure" (3:3); "He who does right is righteous, as he is righteous (3:7); "we should believe . . . love . . . just as he has commanded us" (3:23).

Certainly Leviticus is claiming that God alone is holy intrinsically. He is the origin and the source of all that is holy. In addition, affirms Leviticus, God not only delivers the people from captivity, and grants them a new land; but He also desires to produce in them a pattern of living that is worthy of the follower of a holy God. If Exodus covered the area of salvation and deliverance, it also laid the foundations for the sanctification (see Exod. 19:6; 22:31), now accentuated in these chapters of Leviticus. What specifically is involved in this holy life will emerge as we make our way through this unit.

Eating Meat, But with a Caution (17)

Appropriately, this section of Leviticus, dealing with practical holiness, begins with some legislation about diet. Although no form of the Hebrew root *q-d-š* occurs in this particular chapter, we have already observed in other scriptural contexts (see the discussion of Leviticus 11) the sanctity which is attached to one's choice of edible foods.

As Menahem Haran has observed, the laws in this section of Leviticus are concerned with the everyday affairs of the community and/or the individual.[1] Ritual matters and explanations are minimal. Leviticus 17 illustrates this. How is the believer to eat meat (a luxury item anyway?), and where is he to bring his sacrifices?

Two principal restrictions are given. First, no domestic,

1. "Holiness Code," *EncJud* 8 (1971), p. 821.

sacrificial animals are to be slaughtered outside the sanctuary (vv. 3–4). Much has been made of the contrast between these two verses and Deuteronomy 12:15, "you may slaughter and eat flesh within any of your towns," and similar sentiments in Deuteronomy 12:21, "you may eat within your towns." What Leviticus prohibits Deuteronomy allows.

The critical view that places P after D is faced here with an oddity, or at least a priestly rule that could be labeled as patent nonsense. In effect, the law would ban eating of meat for the majority of Israel. It would be tantamount to saying that only in Saint Peter's Basilica could a mass be celebrated. What, then, about Catholics not living in Rome?

G. J. Wenham says, correctly, "This law [i.e., Lev. 17:3ff.] could be effective . . . when everyone lived close to the sanctuary as during the wilderness wanderings. After the settlement it was no longer feasible to insist that all slaughtering be restricted to the tabernacle. It would have compelled those who lived a long way from the sanctuary to become vegetarians."[2]

In the wilderness, God was teaching His people that His tabernacle was a special place, unique and set apart from every other edifice in the camp. It was the heart of that organism. Sacrifices could not be offered casually, indifferently, or at any place the worshiper deemed appropriate or convenient. Only one house was God's house. See further the interesting comments by Yehezkel Kaufmann.[3]

The second restriction placed on the slaughter of animals was that before consumption, the blood had to be drained. The prohibition is against eating, not drinking, blood. This rule has already been sounded in Leviticus (3:17; 7:26; cf. Deut. 12:16, 23).

2. *The Book of Leviticus*, New International Commentary of the Old Testament series (Grand Rapids: Eerdmans, 1979), p. 243.

3. *The Religion of Israel*, trans. Moshe Greenberg (Chicago: University of Chicago Press, 1960), pp. 180–182.

It is a moot question whether Leviticus 19:26 speaks to the same issue: "you shall not eat any flesh with blood in it." This is, however, quite a free translation. The Hebrew says simply, "you shall not eat over the blood." The same expression appears in I Samuel 14:32–33 and Ezekiel 33:25. Perhaps this refers to a pagan rite in which blood was offered to underground deities,[4] or pouring sacrificial blood on the ground instead of on the altar.

Sexual Purity (18–20)

Chapter 18 is replete with the phrase "you shall not." Chapter 19 is equally filled with the phrase "you shall." Thus, the idea of holiness is formulated both negatively and positively. Chapter 20 contains the penalties for the infringement of any of the illicit relationships covered in chapter 18 (sexual) and 19 (magical). These penalties include death by man, or by God if the community defaults, for worship of Molech (20:2–5) or death by God for engaging in prohibited magical practices (20:6), for illicit sexual unions the penalty may be death by man (20:10–16, "they shall be put to death"), death by God (20:17–19, "they shall be cut off"), or childlessness (20:20–21, "they shall die childless").

Once again the emphasis is that Israel's conduct is to be morally above that of her pagan neighbors (18:3). Israel does not look to Egypt or Canaan for her sexual standards. The unbelievers do not establish the moral criteria by which the believers live in community.

Something of the understanding and approach to sexual matters in nonbiblical religions can be gleaned from this comment by Cyrus H. Gordon: "the modern student must not make the mistake of thinking that the ancient easterner had any difficulty in reconciling the notion of divinity

4. Jacob Milgrom, "Blood," *EncJud* 4 (1971), pp. 1115–1116.

with carryings on that included chicanery, bribery, indecent exposure for a laugh, and homosexual buffoonery."[5] And if this describes life at the divine level, can life at the human level be far behind, especially if people portray their gods as resembling themselves?

It would be wrong to conclude that these prohibitions are basically reactions against practices of Israel's geographical neighbors. Addressing himself to the subject of homosexuality, John Oswalt observes, "the rationale behind that ethic [of Lev. 18 and 20] is not simply a reaction to a life style that happens not to be Hebrew. . . . Rather these activities are prohibited because they grow out of and lead to a world view that is radically opposed to that of the Bible. . . . they represent one common outlook on sex and the world, that is, the denial of boundaries."[6]

Most of chapter 18 is devoted to a listing of incestuous relationships (vv. 6–18), but other sexual offenses are also included (vv. 19–23): intercourse with a woman during her menstrual period (v. 19); adultery (v. 20); giving children to the temple, perhaps for training as male or female prostitutes (v. 21); homosexuality (v. 22); bestiality (v. 23).

We note that at least two of the prohibited relationships in verses 6–18 were not always prohibited. Leviticus 18:9 states: "You shall not uncover the nakedness of your sister." Yet Abraham was married to Sarah, his half-sister (Gen. 20:12, and II Sam. 13:13[?]—"he will not withhold me from you"). Leviticus 18:18 says, "you shall not take a woman as a rival wife to her sister, uncovering her nakedness while her sister is yet alive." Yet this is precisely what Jacob did (Gen. 29:16–30). This is indirect

5. *The Common Background of Greek and Hebrew Civilizations* (New York: Norton, 1965), p. 125.

6. "The Old Testament and Homosexuality," in *What You Should Know About Homosexuality*, ed. Charles W. Keysor (Grand Rapids: Zondervan, 1979), pp. 59–60. See pages 17–77 for the complete discussion.

proof of the antiquity of the patriarchal traditions. What was once legal now became illegal.[7]

Leviticus moves without fanfare from its apodictic pronouncements against illicit sex (chap. 18) to equally apodictic pronouncements about positive holiness (chap. 19). Basically chapter 19 is a collection of ethical and ritual laws, many of which conclude with the phrase, "I am the LORD." This phrase is used thirteen times in this chapter (as opposed to five times in chap. 18). The repeated use of this phrase underscores the fact that these laws are rooted in God and in His holy character. They are not a product of some assembly or theological clique.

Holiness is defined in this chapter in terms of social holiness. That is to say, the demonstration of holiness will emerge most clearly in one's relationships. Little in this chapter is private and monastic. Holiness covers relationships to parents (v. 3), to children (v. 29), to God (vv. 4–8, 26–28, 30–31), to the poor and the stranger (vv. 9–10, 15, 33–34), to women (vv. 20–22), to one's neighbor or brother (vv. 11–18, 35–36), to the aged (v. 32), to animals (v. 19), and to the soil (vv. 19, 23–25).

Each section denotes a different response from the holy life: obedience to parents and God; respect for the elderly; meeting the physical needs of the poor; telling the truth; rising above the temptations of injustice.

The most memorable verse in this chapter is verse 18b, "you shall love your neighbor as yourself." This is quoted nine times in the New Testament (Matt. 5:43; 19:19; 22:39; Mark 12:31, 33; Luke 10:27; Rom. 13:9, Gal. 5:14; James 2:8). The sentiment is also contained in verses such as I John 4:20, "If any one says, 'I love God,' and hates his brother, he is a liar."

But, according to Leviticus 19, it is not enough to love one's neighbor as himself. One must also love the stranger

7. Again, see Kaufmann, *The Religion of Israel*, pp. 318–319.

or sojourner as himself (vv. 33–34). The outsider is not to be kept psychologically on the outside.

Priestly Purity (21–22)

It is the priest as human being, as citizen, who is discussed in these two chapters. The following items are highlighted: restrictions on the number of people for whom the priest may mourn, and the categories of women from which he may not choose a prospective bride (21:1–9); these restrictions are even more stringent for the high priest (21:10–15); physical blemishes prohibit a priest from officiating (21:16–24); the priest may not eat any of the sacrificial food whenever he is unclean—as spelled out in chapters 13–15 (22:1–9); who in the priest's family has a right to eat priestly food (22:10–16); blemished animals are unacceptable for sacrifice (22:17–30).

The common denominator in all these regulations is that God has "sanctified" the priest (21:8, 15, 23; 22:9, 16, 32). Therefore he is to be "holy." By and large these are unique standards imposed only on Israel's clergymen. Certainly in any age God's summons to holiness must be exemplified unquestionably in the life of those who "bear the vessels of the Lord." If they do not set and implement the standard, how shall the congregation ever exemplify the holy life?

Again we note that, for the priest too, holiness does not become a reality when he withdraws himself from society. Holiness has to do with one's relationship to his family, his wife, his household employees, and his own physical appearance.

Holy Festivals (23)

People may be holy. Priests may be holy. Buildings and particular sites may be holy. This section adds to that list certain holy days and festivals on the calendar. The list includes the Sabbath (v. 3); Passover and unleavened bread (vv. 4–8); First fruits, that is, the dues, sacrifices, and rites of Passover and unleavened bread (vv. 9–14); Feast of Weeks or Pentecost (vv. 15–22); Feast of Trumpets (vv. 23–24); Day of Atonement (vv. 26–32); Feast of Tabernacles (vv. 33–44).

These holy days are to be happy days. Often these two ideas are kept worlds apart. One can be holy, but not at the same time happy, or vice versa. The people of God are "to rejoice before the LORD" (v. 40).

On the majority of these days normal manual labor is suspended (vv. 3, 7, 8, 21, 25, 28, 30, 31, 35, 36). It is a time for families to be together. It is a time to be generous in assisting the poor (v. 22).

To say that all days are holy will probably evolve into the concept that no days are holy. Something of the significance of these festivals to Judaism can be seen in the post-exilic prophets. For seventy years God's people had been in captivity. They had not celebrated Passover, Pentecost, or Tabernacles for three-quarters of a century. Imagine a Christian who is denied the privilege of celebrating Christmas, Good Friday, or Easter for this length of time! Then the Lord sent two interesting prophets to the community, whose names were symbolic of their messages. One was Zechariah, "the Lord has remembered." Has He? Can we be sure He hasn't forgotten us? The second prophet was Haggai, "my feasts." Fancy having a new pastor named Reverend Feasts, when you haven't celebrated one of your feasts in seventy years! Both names speak of promise, and divine faithfulness.

The Holy Place and the Holy Name
(24)

Two areas are discussed with regard to the tabernacle. The first is the necessity of using pure oil for the lighting of the tabernacle (vv. 1–4). The second is that the shewbread, consisting of twelve wheat loaves (for the twelve tribes), set in two rows of six, be replaced every Sabbath (vv. 5–9).

Then comes a story of a man who cursed the Name (vv. 10–16), an infraction mandating the death penalty, a penalty enforced by the community, and not by one hooded executioner (vv. 14, 16).

The chapter concludes with a catena of laws. What is of special interest here is the resurfacing of the *lex talionis* for maiming (vv. 19–20; Exod. 21:23–24), and its extension to apply both to the sojourner and the native (v. 22). Jacob Milgrom says, "That *lex talionis* . . . was extended to the stranger is one of the great moral achievements of P's legislation. Not only is every distinction eradicated between the powerful and the helpless but even between the Israelite and the non-Israelite."[8] Holiness that is authentic overcomes parochialisms and provincialisms that are so much a part of unholy life.

The Sabbatical and Jubilee Years (25)

Two strategic years are discussed in this chapter: the sabbatical year (vv. 1–7), that is, each seventh year; and the jubilee year (vv. 8–55), that is, every fiftieth year.

The emphasis on the sabbatical year is that the land is to lie fallow every seventh year. Other emphases are stated elsewhere in Scripture. Exodus 23:10–11 says the sabbatical year is for the sake of the poor. Deuteronomy 15:1–11 says this year is for debtors, and the remission of their debts.

The name *jubilee* is an anglicized transliteration of the

8. "Lev. 17–26, The Holiness Source," *EncJud* 11 (1971), p. 146.

Hebrew word *yôbēl* (v. 10). As in the sabbatical year, land must lie fallow (vv. 11–12). Landed property is returned to its original owner (vv. 25–55), without compensation. Land ownership is to be equalized every fifty years. The theological basis for this is found in verse 23: "for the land is mine." He is the Lord of land and of economics.

I am to be my brother's redeemer if, for some reason or other, understandable or nonunderstandable, he becomes poor (vv. 25ff.; vv. 35ff.; vv. 47ff.). There is a ban on the taking of interest for room or board by a creditor (vv. 35–38). Nor is the debtor to be treated as a slave (vv. 39–46) if he was forced to enslave himself.

Ronald J. Sider points out tellingly: "It is surely more than coincidental that the trumpet blast announcing the Jubilee sounded forth on the day of atonement (Lev. 25:9)! Reconciliation with God is the precondition for reconciliation with brothers and sisters. Conversely, genuine reconciliation with God leads inevitably to a transformation of all other relationships."[9] Once again, genuine holiness spills over into one's relationship with others, in this case especially the poor, the indebted, or the enslaved.

The Two Ways (26)

The two ways are the lifestyle that brings the blessing of God (vv. 3–13) or the lifestyle that brings the wrath of God (vv. 14–46). Blessings are threefold: sufficient rains for the harvest (v. 4); peace in the land (v. 6); most of all, the presence of God (v. 11). The wrath of God includes circumstances ranging from disease and sickness (v. 16) to war (vv. 23–39), whose by-products are plague, famine, and cannibalism.

9. *Rich Christians in an Age of Hunger: A Biblical Study* (Downers Grove, IL: Inter-Varsity, 1977), p. 89.

Religious Vows (27)

It would be more accurate to say that this chapter deals with the retraction of, not the making of, religious vows. Is there room in Old Testament faith for legitimate desanctification? This chapter answers yes, in certain instances.

1. Persons may be redeemed (vv. 1–8)
2. Only impure animals may be redeemed (vv. 9–13), but not pure animals that are offerable
3. Houses may be redeemed (vv. 14–15)
4. Land may be redeemed (vv. 16–25)
5. Only unclean firstlings may be redeemed (vv. 26–27)
6. No "devoted thing" (man, animal, land) may be redeemed (vv. 28–29)
7. The tithe from crops may be redeemed, but the animal tithe may not (vv. 30–33), for it is offerable as in number 2

In each case, if one desires to reclaim what he has given to God the penalty is 20 percent more than the value of the item (vv. 13, 15, 19, 27, 31). This has to be the Bible's way of saying that the taking of a vow, giving something or somebody to God, is—like marriage—"not to be entered into lightly or unadvisedly."

Chapter 26 has articulated God's vows to people. How appropriate it is that Leviticus follows this with a chapter about people's vows to God. At the heart of religion and holiness is promise and commitment: His to me; mine to Him.

Bibliography

The Holiness Code

Eichrodt, W. *The Theology of the Old Testament*. Translated by J. Baker. 2 vols. Philadelphia: Westminster, 1967, vol. 1, "The Holiness of God," pp. 270–282.

Eissfeldt, O. "The Holiness Code." In *The Old Testament, an Introduction*. New York: Harper and Row, 1965, pp. 233–239.

Haran, M. "Holiness Code." *EndJud* 8 (1971): 820–825.

Milgrom, J. "Lev. 17–26, The Holiness Source." *EncJud* 11 (1971): 143–147.

______. "Leviticus." In *IDBSuppl*, pp. 543–545.

______. "Sanctification." In *IDBSuppl*, pp. 782–784.

Chapter 17

Brichto, H. C. "On Slaughter and Sacrifice, Blood and Atonement." *HUCA* 47 (1976): 22–36.

Milgrom, J. "A Prolegomenon to Lev. 17:11." *JBL* 90 (1971): 149–156.

Snaith, N. H. "The meaning of *ś[ec]îrîm*." *VT* 24 (1974): 115–118.

______. "The verbs *Zābaḥ* and *Šāḥaṭ*." *VT* 25 (1975): 242–246.

Chapters 18–20

Bigger, S. "The Family Laws of Leviticus 18 in their Setting." *JBL* 98 (1979): 187–203.

Derrett, J. "Love thy neighbor as a man like thyself." *ExpT* 83 (1971): 55.

Hoffner, H. A., Jr., "Incest, Sodomy and Bestiality in the Ancient Near East." In *Orient and Occident. Essays presented to Cyrus H. Gordon on the occasion of his sixty–fifth birthday*. Edited by Harry A. Hoffner, Jr. Neukirchen-Vluyn: Neukirchener Verlag, 1973, pp. 81–90.

Horton, F. L. "Form and Structure in Laws Relating to Women: Lev. 18:6–18." *SBL Seminar Papers*, 1973, pp. 20–23.

Kaiser, W. C., Jr. "Leviticus 18:5 and Paul: Do This and You Shall Live (Eternally?)." *JETS* 14 (1971): 19–28.

McKeating, H. "Sanctions Against Adultery in Ancient Israelite Society, with some Reflections on Methodology in the Study of Old Testament Ethics." *JSOT* 11 (1979): 52–72.

Milgrom, J. "The Betrothed Slave–girl, Lev. 19, 20–22." *ZAW* 89 (1977): 43–49.

______. "Blood." *EncJud* 4 (1971): 1115–1116.

______. *Cult and Conscience: The ASHAM and the Priestly Doctrine of Repentance*. Leiden: E. J. Brill, 1976, pp. 129–137.

Muraoka, T. "A Syntactic Problem in Lev XIX, 18b." *JSS* 23 (1978): 291–297.

Chapters 21–22

See also the bibliography at the beginning of chapter 12.

Levine, B. A. "Priests." In *IDBSuppl*, pp. 687–690.

Milgrom, J. *Cult and Conscience: The ASHAM and the Priestly Doctrine of Repentance*. Leiden: E. J. Brill, 1976, pp. 63–66.

Wenham, G. J. "*Bᵉtûlāh* 'a girl of marriageable age.' " *VT* 22 (1972): 326–348, esp. pp. 336–340.

Chapter 23

Eichrodt, W. *The Theology of the Old Testament*. 2 vols. Philadelphia: Westminster, 1967, vol. 1, pp. 119–133.

Kaufmann, Y. *The Religion of Israel*, Translated by Moshe Greenberg. Chicago: University of Chicago Press, 1960, pp. 115–121, 305–309.

Kraus, H. J. *Worship in Israel*. Richmond: John Knox, 1966, pp. 32–35.

Chapter 24

Mittwoch, H. "Story of the Blasphemer Seen in Wider Context." *VT* 15 (1965): 386–389.

Weingreen, J. "The Case of the Blasphemer (Leviticus XXIV, 10ff.)." *VT* 22 (1972): 118–123.

Chapter 25

Brueggemann, W. *The Land*. Philadelphia: Fortress, 1977.

Gamoran, H. "The Biblical Law against Loans on Interest." *JNES* 30 (1971): 127–134.

Joenig, S. "Sabbatical Years and the Year of Jubilee." *JQR* 59 (1969): 222–236.

Lemeche, N. "Manumission of Slaves—the Fallow Year—the Sabbatical Year—the Jobel Year." *VT* 26 (1976): 38–59.

Maloney, R. "Usury and Restrictions on Interest-Taking in the Ancient Near East." *CBQ* 36 (1974): 1–20.

North, R. *Sociology of the Biblical Jubilee*. Rome: Pontifical Biblical Institute, 1954.

Sider, R. J. *Rich Christians in an Age of Hunger: A Biblical Study*. Downers Grove, IL: Inter-Varsity, 1977, pp. 88–92.

Vaux, R. de. *Ancient Israel*, vol. 1, *Social Institutions*. New York: McGraw-Hill, 1965, pp. 173–177.

Westbrook, R. "Jubilee Laws." *ILR* 6 (1971): 209–226.

______. "Redemption of Land." *ILR* 6 (1971): 367–375.

Westphal, M. "Sing jubilee." *The Other Side* 14 (March 1978): 29–35.

Ziskind, J. "Petrus Cannaeus on Theocracy, Jubilee, and the Latifundia." *JQR* 68 (1977/78): 235–254.

Zimmerli, W. *The Old Testament and the World*. Translated by John J. Scullion. Atlanta: John Knox, 1976, pp. 75–77.

Chapter 27

Gehman, H. S. "The Oath in the Old Testament: its Vocabulary, Idiom, and Syntax: its Semantics and Theology in the Massoretic Text and the Septuagint." In *Grace upon Grace*. Edited by James I. Cook. Grand Rapids: Eerdmans, 1975, pp. 51–63.

Milgrom, J. *Cult and Conscience: The ASHAM and the Priestly Doctrine of Repentance*. Leiden: E. J. Brill, 1976, pp. 44–63.

Wenham, G. J. "Leviticus 27, 2–8 and the Price of Slaves." *ZAW* 90 (1978): 264–265.

Part FOUR

Numbers

16

Preparations for Departure from Sinai

Numbers 1:1—10:10

It is almost a consensus that the Book of Numbers leaves much to be desired, and much that is puzzling in the presentation of its material. Thus, B. A. Levine says that it "is the least coherent of all the Torah books."[1] R. C. Dentan's statement is similar: "Since the book has no real unity and was not composed in accordance with any logical, predetermined plan, whatever outline may be imposed on it will have to be recognized as largely subjective and arbitrary."[2]

Dissenters from this evaluation are few, but among these is Brevard Childs. His thesis is that all the materials in Numbers—the cultic, legal, and narrative, even the statistical information—revolve around the overarching theme of holiness. So he states, "In spite of its diversity of subject matter and complex literary development the book of Numbers maintains a unified sacerdotal interpretation of God's will for his people which is set forth in a sharp contrast between the holy and the profane."[3] I am more inclined to accept the evaluation of Childs than of those

1. "Numbers, Book of," in *IDBSuppl*, p. 634.

2. "Numbers, Book of," in *IDB*, 3, p. 567.

3. *Introduction to the Old Testament As Scripture* (Philadelphia: Fortress, 1979), p. 199.

who view Numbers as a random collection of J/E and P materials.

Perhaps it is best to begin by observing the divisions within the book, based on geographical and chronological notations.

1:1—10:10 Preparation for departure from Sinai
1:1—"The LORD spoke to Moses in the wilderness of Sinai . . . on the first day of the second month, in the second year after they had come out of the land of Egypt"

10:11—20:21 Departure from Sinai and arrival at Kadesh
10:11—"In the second year, in the second month, on the twentieth day of the month, the cloud was taken up from over the tabernacle of the testimony"

20:22—36:13 Journey from Kadesh to Moab
20:22—"And they journeyed from Kadesh"

Table 12 lists the chronology of each section.

It should be noted that not all commentators agree on precisely where the second section ends and the third section begins. Both Martin Noth and Dentan conclude the second section at 20:13. G. B. Gray (*A Critical And Exegetical Commentary on Numbers*, 1903) ends the second section at 21:9. The New Oxford Annotated Bible (RSV, 1973), in editorial notes, terminates the second section at 21:13. F. L. Moriarty suggests 22:1 as the conclusion to the unit.

Table 12

Duration	Reference	Cross-reference
20 days	1:1—10:10	Num. 1:1; 10:11
38 years	10:11—20:21	Num. 33:38 (date of Aaron's death)
6 months	20:22—36:13	Num. 33:38; Deut. 1:3

I have labeled the first unit in Numbers as "preparation for departure from Sinai." It covers 1:1—10:10. Geographically the Israelites have not moved from Mount Sinai. What are the preparations for departure?

Census and Tribal Arrangement (1–2)

For pure excitement and dramatic effect on the reader, the material presented in the first two chapters of Numbers does not measure up to that impact created by the clashing thunder and smoke that engulfed Sinai, followed by the revelation of God's will. Have we gone from the miraculous to the mundane, from the terrific to the trite?

In these two chapters, Moses is told by God to take a census of the congregation of Israel (1:1–3). He is assigned a representative from each tribe, except that of Levi, to assist in the census taking (1:4–16). The census is taken (1:17–46). The Levites are exempted from this particular census (1:47–54). An area is assigned to each of the tribes on the east, south, west, or north side of the tent of meeting, an area of residence that is to be maintained, whether one is encamped or on the march (2:1–34).

There are, however, a few things here that merit our attention. The census is to include all males from twenty years and older, "all in Israel who are able to go forth to war" (1:3). Israel is being sent forth as a sheep among wolves. Military activity, either for preservation or conquest, will be inevitable. The previous encounter with the Amalekites (Exod. 17:8–16) is a harbinger of experiences ahead.

One notes here that the initiative for taking the census is from God. Moses does not suddenly feel the need to increase the number of military personnel. The reader fails to detect in Moses any attitude similar to that ascribed by Joab to David and his census taking: "but why does my lord the king delight in this thing?" (II Sam. 24:3, with an added word evidenced by the parallel, I Chron. 21:3).

Previously I mentioned the theme of holiness in Numbers. It is in the last paragraph of chapter 1 (vv. 47–54) that this particular theme emerges. To be sure, we are informed that the Levite is not to be numbered in the census involving the laic tribes. Are they left out completely? Numbers 1:50–51 assigns three duties to the Levites: transporting the tabernacle, dismantling it, and reassembling it. But then follows this awesome note: "And if any one else comes near, he shall be put to death" (1:51b). To trespass on another's responsibilities brings death.

Yet there is more. Two verses later we read, "the Levites shall encamp around the tabernacle of the testimony, that there may be no wrath upon the congregation of the people of Israel; and the Levites shall keep charge of [or, shall do guard duty] the tabernacle of the testimony" (1:53). The Levites are sacerdotal guards who must strike down an intruder who attempts to violate a prohibition with regard to tabernacle service. If he is not stopped the whole community falls under God's judgment.

Thus Israel must not be nonchalant in meeting her enemy ahead (vv. 1–46). But neither must she be careless or indifferent in her worship of God (vv. 47–54). An enemy can wipe her out, but so can God's wrath! She must avoid at all costs the attitude that says, "I'll do it my way."

Two Levitical Censuses (3–4)

Most of the content in these two chapters is devoted to a description of the numbers and duties of the Levites. But even before the reader encounters the results of the first census he is greeted with a reminder of Aaron's two sons, Nadab and Abihu, who "died before the LORD when they offered unholy fire before the LORD . . . they had no children" (3:4). There is a right way to worship the Lord, an infraction of which brings disastrous consequences both for the layman (1:51) and for the clergy (3:4).

But that is not all. Two more times in chapter 3 the ominous threat of execution for trespass in the worship of God is highlighted: "if any one else comes near, he shall be put to death" (vv. 10, 38). Jacob Milgrom has shown convincingly that the translation "come near" or "approach" is not what the text is prohibiting.[4] Instead, the word can only mean "to exceed one's privileges" or "to usurp the responsibilities of another." The Israelites were to know what they must do and must not do, and were not to confuse the two. Otherwise, they must accept the consequences!

Why two Levitical censuses (3:14–39; 4:1–49)? Actually the two are quite distinct from each other. A clue in discerning the distinction is found in 3:15, "Number the sons of Levi . . . every male from a month old and upward." By contrast, the second census includes those "from thirty years old up to fifty years old" (4:3). So then, the first census starts with those in infancy and is open-ended. The second is limited to those falling within the twenty years from thirty to fifty.

Might we assume, then, that the Levites included in the first census are being earmarked for a service that will be lifelong? Thus, there is no age restriction. On the other hand, the second census includes Levites who are to be inducted into a ministry for which there is a time restriction, the twenty years after adolescence and young manhood, and before the beginning of advanced age.

The text itself affirms the reason for the limitation of service in chapter 4. Here it is physical labor that is being described. Specifically it involves assembling, disman-

4. *Studies in Levitical Terminology, 1: The Encroacher and the Levite, the Term ʿAboda*. University of California Publications in Near Eastern Studies, vol. 14 (Berkeley: University of California Press, 1970), pp. 17–18.

tling and carrying the tabernacle. It is not wide of the mark to translate the word "service" (Num. 4:3, 4, 23, 24, 27, 30, 31, 33, 35, 39, 43, 47) as "strenuous physical labor." For that reason a retirement age is prescribed—fifty. And a starting age is prescribed—thirty.

The responsibilities are threefold and divided among the sons of Levi. The responsibilities for the Kohathites are spelled out in 4:4–20. They have the special distinction of carrying "the holy things" of the tabernacle (vv. 15, 19). For that reason two extra items are added. In the first place, the chapter says that the actual work of dismantling these most sacred parts of the tabernacle is the responsibility of Aaron and his sons, not the Kohathites at all (vv. 5–14)! The Kohathites are transporters, not dismantlers.

Second, to give the injunction force, it is noted that the Kohathites will die (vv. 15, 18, 20) should they overstep their boundaries. At least so far, Numbers seldom has missed the opportunity to inject, in the midst of statistical reports and work assignments, the somber note about the consequences of disobedience. God in His holiness will have it no other way.

The second group of Levites is the Gershonites (vv. 21–28). Their work primarily is carrying the tabernacle curtains, or at least standing guard by the wagons on which the curtains are carried. Absent here is any note, as with the Kohathites, that they operate under priestly directive, or that usurpation is a capital offense.

The third group of Levites is the Merarites (vv. 29–33). Like the Gershonites, they stand guard over a portion of the tabernacle carried in wagons. This time the material is the wooden frames and pillars.

One can see that the Kohathites have the greatest privilege. They also have the greatest responsibilities. To whom much is given, of the same much is required. Those who climb highest may fall farthest.

Keeping the Camp Holy (5)

Numbers began by devoting two chapters to the laity in Israel (1–2). Two chapters were given to the clergy, the Levites (3–4). Now there is a return, for two more chapters, to the laity (5–6).

The first four chapters have underscored the sanctity of the tabernacle, either in place assignment or in role assignment. It is God's dwelling place, and all is to be observed and implemented as He has spoken. It is not without significance that these first four chapters all end on the same note: "thus did the people [or, Moses] according to the word of the LORD, as the LORD commanded" (1:54; 2:34; 3:51; 4:49).

Having thus delineated this idea, it is very natural for the text to follow these directives with various ordinances that will help to make the camp holy. The first four chapters have been positive: this is where you station yourself; this is what you are supposed to do. By contrast, chapter 5 is negative in its emphasis. It deals with putting out of the camp those who defile it, or detract from its sacred character. Thus, the leper is banned (Lev. 13:46). To be sure he is not executed, put to death like a Kohathite, but he is exiled from the community.

Only with the knowledge of a stipulation like this is one able to appreciate fully Jesus' actions in "touching" the leper (Mark 1:41). Were the disciples present to observe this it is not difficult to believe they protested: Lord, you've just contaminated yourself. Could it be possible that, to prove the point, contrariwise, Jesus immediately pressed his hand flat on the flesh of one of his disciples, probably Peter?

If certain types of physical impurities defile God's camp (5:1–4), what then of deliberate sin and its baleful effects? To this question 5:5–10 speaks. Wherever sin surfaces in the community it must be openly acknowledged by the perpetrator. For to sin against another child of God is to sin against God Himself. Therefore oral confession is indispensable—"he shall confess his sin"—as is full restitution plus 20 percent more than the value of what was taken or stolen. All of this precedes the atonement ritual performed by the priest.

There is also a new note added in this paragraph. If the victim of the crime is deceased and has no relatives this does not cancel obligations of restitution. Far from it. Now the monies are to be turned over to the priest and the sanctuary (vv. 8–10). Once again the note is sounded. God's camp is to be a holy place, a pure place. Neither Levitical nor lay deviations from the divine plan will be tolerated. Unclean people must be excluded. Sin against a neighbor must be articulated by the perpetrator, and repented of, thus paving the way for full restitution with both the offended party and with God.

The third paragraph in the chapter (vv. 11–31) continues the theme of the maintenance of holiness among God's people. Here the issue is alleged adultery by the wife. The husband suspects her infidelity, but there were no witnesses, nor was the wife apprehended in an embarrassing situation.

The previous paragraph had discussed actual sin between two people. This paragraph discusses potential sin between mate and mate. How interesting it is that even possible sin must be investigated. If the suspicion turns out to be nothing but that, so be it. But if disturbing and aberrant factors are uncovered they must be dealt with.

The modern reader of Scripture may come away from such a story with second thoughts about its legitimacy. Why, for example, is there a trial only for the suspected wife? What if the woman suspects her husband of unfaithfulness? Does she have any options open to her? Then again, does such a procedure give the husband the right to force his wife through an ordeal any time and every time he entertains illusions about possible escapades by his wife? Must she imbibe this unpalatable "mixed drink" just to satisfy his curiosity?

The following observations may be made. First, we may safely assume that the husband resorts to this trial procedure only if and only when he is unable to repress and eradicate his suspicions. Nagging doubts will not go away. Therefore something must be done. It is unlikely that an insanely jealous and very insecure husband would be allowed to continually test his wife.

Second, it is inaccurate to call the procedure to which the wife is subjected a trial by ordeal. The accused adulteress is not told to plunge her hand into hot water, nor must she walk barefoot on spikes, nor is she thrown into water over her head. Such are the tests used in trial by ordeal. There the danger is very real. Here it is only hypothetical. (And what after all is the meaning of the penalty, "the water . . . shall cause bitter pain, and her body shall swell, and her thigh fall away"? Is this physical atrophy, sterility, or something else?) Another reason that negates the idea of a trial by ordeal is that in such a trial the party on trial is assumed guilty unless proven innocent. As both H. C. Brichto and J. Sasson have observed, this ritual is just the opposite.[5] It judges on the innocence, not the guilt, of the accused.

A third observation grows out of the preceding paragraph. Far from dehumanizing the woman by making her accountable to every whim of a capricious husband, the procedure urges just the opposite. Says Brichto, after observing the often disadvantaged place of women in the Old Testament, "the ritual . . . is a ploy in her favor—it proposes that the husband 'put up or shut up.' "[6] If he is

5. Brichto, "The Case of the Śōṭā and a Reconsideration of Biblical Law," *HUCA* 46 (1975), p. 66; Sasson, "Numbers 5 and the 'Waters of Judgement,' " *BZ* 16 (1972), p. 251.

6. "The Case of the Śōṭā," p. 67.

suspicious of his wife's integrity then let him be brave enough to initiate a scheme that will establish the situation one way or another. If he is not brave enough to move from imagination to implementation, then let him drop the charges and stop the insinuations.

The Nazirite (6)

Except for verses 21–27, which feature the Aaronic benediction, this entire chapter is given over to a description of the Nazirite. We are accustomed to this office because of those auspicious individuals in Scripture who were Nazirites. This list would include such notables as Samson, Samuel, and John the Baptist (Luke 1:15). These three were all leaders in their respective periods. Samson and Samuel were both outstanding military chieftains or prophets leading Israel's armies against the Philistines. In their activities they resemble more a West Point graduate than they do a member of a monastic community.

Yet in Numbers 6 none of these positive elements emerges. The chapter is more concerned to describe what the Nazirite may not do than what he is to do. I suggest that this is in keeping with the emphasis seen so far in Numbers vis-à-vis God's demands for holiness. His laws are not to be sidestepped.

Three restrictions are placed on the Nazirite. First, he is to abstain from wine, strong drink, vinegar, grapes, and grape juice. Second, he is not to cut his hair. Third, he is to avoid contact with anybody deceased, including members of his own family. So the Nazirite is to be disciplined in his appetites, distinctive in his appearance, discreet in his associations.

Should a Nazirite contaminate himself through accidental contact with a corpse, atonement proceedings become mandatory (vv. 9–12). Even at the completion of the Nazirite vow the individual brings a burnt offering, a sin offering, and a peace offering. The offerings are then presented to the Lord in this order: sin offering, burnt offering, peace offering (vv. 13–20).

Chapter 5 began with a note regarding the presence of the unclean in the camp of God. They are to be quarantined, both male and female (5:3). The chapter continued with the emphasis, "When a man or a woman commits any of the sins. . . ." The remainder of that chapter dealt with husband-wife relationships. In the same way the Nazirite office is open to "either a man or a woman." Neither sex has a monopoly on this position.

That such an office was available to women becomes even more startling when one realizes that the proscriptions for the Nazirite parallel most closely those for the high priest, as opposed to the lower echelons of the priesthood. For example, the Nazirite may not contaminate himself by contact with the deceased in his own family (Num. 6:7). This is true also for the high priest (Lev. 21:11), but not for the ordinary priests (Lev. 21:1–4). The Nazirite is to abstain from intoxicants (Num. 6:4). This is true also for Aaron and his sons when they "go into the tent of meeting" (Lev. 10:9). Parallel to the injunction against cutting the hair is an injunction regarding the hair directed toward the high priest (Lev. 10:6; 21:10) and the anointing of his head with oil (Lev. 21:10; Exod. 29:7). No one is barred from Nazirite ministry on the basis of sex, as is the case in the Levitical and priestly ministry for which only males are eligible.

Perhaps the last paragraph, the Aaronic benediction in verses 21–27, is to be connected with the information about the Nazirite by the notation that the Nazirite is to be "holy to the LORD" (v. 8). This is true of the priests too. They are "to be holy to their God" (Lev. 21:6–7). Also, the section about Nazirites is introduced by "Say to the people of Israel" (v. 2). To Aaron and his sons Moses is to say, "Thus you shall bless the people of Israel" (v. 23).

It is important that we observe that it is not Aaron who blesses. He is transmitter, not author. It is the Lord, and only the Lord (note the threefold use of the tetragrammaton in the blessing) who blesses. The Lord's work is to "bless and keep" His people. The first verb is familiar enough to readers of the Bible. The meaning of the second verb—"keep"—is not equally well known. This verb is used about 450 times in the Bible and, according to Paul Riemann, "nowhere is there a single instance where a man's keeping another man is an expressed covenant norm or even a recognized social obligation."[7] The Lord, and the Lord alone, is the keeper.

He also "makes his face to shine" and "lifts up his countenance" upon His people. One wonders here if perhaps what is involved in this blessing is the deliberate use of court imagery. God as king graciously grants His subjects an audience with royalty. He is not aloof. The phrase *to lift up one's face* is used elsewhere in Scripture with a definite connotation. Thus, Job 42:8–9, ". . . my servant Job shall pray for you; for him will I accept. . . . The LORD accepted Job" (KJV). In both instances "to accept" is literally "to lift up the face." For God to "lift up his face" on His people is for Him to accept them, to raise the features of His face into a smile. By contrast, "to drop one's face" is "to frown" (see Gen. 4:6; Jer. 3:12).

Perhaps Numbers 1–6 has been describing a cause-to-effect movement. When there is obedience and a commitment to holy living (1:1—6:21) the result is the presence of a blessing God (6:22–27).

"Offerings Before the LORD" (7:1—10:10)

The information that follows in chapter 7 antedates the information in 1–6 by one month. The year, month, and

7. "Am I My Brother's Keeper?" *Intr* 24 (1970), p. 483.

day on which Moses finished setting up the tabernacle (Num. 7:1) was the second year, *first* month, and first day (see Exod. 40:17). Numbers 1 is dated a month later than this: the second year, *second* month, and first day.

Chapter 7 is the longest chapter in the Pentateuch. It is concerned with the offerings from the tribal leaders for the Lord. Verses 12–88 identify the tribal leader and the offering brought for the tabernacle. The list starts with Judah and ends with Naphtali. In every instance the individual is to bring not only commodities (a silver plate or a golden dish) but also various animals for the following offerings: cereal, burnt, sin, and peace, always in that order. Worship is more than handing God a gratuity. It is fellowship through sacrifice.

The part of chapter 7 about offerings (vv. 12–88) is preceded once again by a note not lacking in gravity or a reminder of God's holiness (vv. 1–11). The princes are to present wagons for the transportation of tabernacle equipment (vv. 1–8). The exception is for the "holy things" of the tabernacle that are to be carried on the shoulders of the Kohathites (v. 9). Numbers 4:1–15 had informed us that the Kohathites must not dismantle the "holy things." That is left to the priests. But neither must the "holy things" be piled on wagons. Human porterage is necessary.

The chapter concludes (v. 89) with the observation that God spoke with Moses from the Holy of Holies. The text simply says, "he [Moses] heard the voice." It does not say he saw the Lord. God's communion with Moses is aural, not visual. He is heard, not seen.

Chapter 8 deals with the consecration of the Levites, a chapter much like Leviticus 8, that covers the ordination of the Aaronic priests. The description of the actual consecration service (vv. 5–22) is preceded by a brief paragraph (vv. 1–4) noting the responsibility of the Aaronic priests for the lighting of the lamps in the tabernacle (see Exod. 25:31–40; 27:20–21; Lev. 24:2–4). Thus for a second time Numbers has placed a prelude directed at the priests before information for the Levites (see 4:5–15a, priests; 4:15b–49, Levites).

Almost exclusively the consecration rite of the Levites is a purification ceremony. The Levites need "cleansing" (vv. 6–7 [2 times], 15, 21). They must "purify themselves" (v. 21). A burnt offering and a sin offering are mandated (v. 12). Much like the sacrificial animal, the Levite is a substitute for the first-born, and as such receives the laying on of hands (vv. 10, 11, 16, 18). Their function is to avert divine wrath from consuming Israel (v. 19). This they do by turning back any encroacher (see also 1:53 and 18:5).

Milgrom has explained the rationale for the emphasis on atonement in Levitic consecration. "I submit that 'service' in Num. ch. 8 means removal labor in all cases. . . . This view alone can explain the need for purificatory rites accompanying the induction service of the Levites. For guard duty performed around and at a distance from the Tabernacle contact with sancta is entailed; removal operations, on the other hand, being the sole Levitic function for the direct handling of sancta would require purificatory aspergings and sacrifice."[8]

To review the material in Numbers from the perspective of the addressee, we have the following: chapters 1–2, laymen; 3–4, clergy; 5–6:21, laymen; 6:22–27, clergy; 7:1–89, laymen; 8, clergy.

Chapter 9:1–14 brings us back to the laity and particularly to the subject of the postponed passover. In certain instances the passover may be observed one month later, that is, the second month instead of the first month (vv. 3, 5, 11). What are the legitimate reasons for postponement of passover observance? Two situations are listed. If one is on a long-distance journey, or if one is unclean through contact with a corpse (v. 10), delay becomes mandatory.

8. *Studies in Levitical Terminology*, 1, p. 74, n. 271.

Refusal to observe passover in the first month for any other reason than those two results in the culprit being "cut off" from his people. Once again a note of warning, caution, and somberness has been sounded. Delay if you are unclean to be in His presence. Otherwise, do not try to sidestep your responsibilities to Him in worship.

The conclusion to chapter 9 is much like that of chapter 6. There the emphasis was on the divine presence which blesses. It is His face that shines. Here the emphasis (vv. 15–23) is on the divine presence that guides. It is the hovering cloud that indicates encampment. It is the ascending cloud that indicates the Israelites were to move forward.

The section concludes (10:1–10) with a reference to two silver trumpets. These instruments were to be blown at certain feasts, at the beginning of the year, for summoning the congregation, or breaking camp. Verses 5–7 emphasize that the trumpets sound an alarm, something like a military siren. The trumpets are thus more for emergencies than they are for worship or concerts. Musical instruments have an almost negligible role in the ministry of the priests.[9]

Bibliography

Commentaries and Monographs

Caine, I. "Numbers, Book Of." *EncJud* 12 (1971): 1249–1254.

Childs, B. *Introduction to the Old Testament As Scripture*. Philadelphia: Fortress, 1979, pp. 190–201.

Dentan, R. C. "Numbers, Book Of." In *IDB*, 3, pp. 567–571.

Levine, B. A. "Numbers, Book Of." In *IDBSuppl*, pp. 631–635.

Milgrom, J. *Studies in Levitical Terminology, 1: The Encroacher and the Levite, The Term ᶜAboda*. University of California Publications in

9. Yehezkel Kaufmann, *The Religion of Israel*, trans. Moshe Greenberg (Chicago: University of Chicago Press, 1960), p. 11, n. 304.

Near Eastern Studies, vol. 14. Berkeley: University of California Press, 1970.

Moriarty, F. L. "Numbers." In *The Jerome Biblical Commentary*. Englewood Cliffs, NJ: Prentice-Hall, 1968, vol. 1, pp. 86–100.

Noth, M. *Numbers: A Commentary*. Old Testament Library. Translated by James D. Martin. Philadelphia: Westminster, 1969.

Oswalt, J. "Numbers, Book of." In *ZPEB*, 4, pp. 461–469.

Snaith, N. H. *Leviticus and Numbers*. The Century Bible. London: Nelson, 1967, pp. 179ff.

Sturdy, J. *Numbers*. Cambridge Bible Commentary. Cambridge: Cambridge University Press, 1976.

Chapters 1–2

Archer, G. L. *A Survey of Old Testament Introduction*. Chicago: Moody, 1973, pp. 234–238.

Mayes, A. D. H. *Israel in the Period of the Judges*. Naperville, IL: Alec R. Allenson, 1974, pp. 16–34.

Mendenhall, G. E. "The Census Lists of Numbers 1 and 26." *JBL* 77 (1958): 52–66.

Milgrom, J. "Priestly Terminology and the Political and Social Structure of Pre-Monarchic Israel." *JQR* 69 (1978): 65–81, esp. 79–81.

Sasson, J. "A Genealogical 'Convention' in Biblical Chronography?" *ZAW* 90 (1978): 171–185.

Vaux, R. de. *The Early History of Israel*. Philadelphia: Westminster, 1978, pp. 724–727.

Wenham, J. W. "Large Numbers in the Old Testament." *TB* 18 (1967): 19–53, esp. pp. 24–39.

Chapters 3–4

Abba, R. "Priests and Levites." In *IDB*, 3, pp. 876–889.

Cody, A. *A History of Old Testament Priesthood*. Rome: Pontifical Biblical Institute, 1969, pp. 29–38.

Milgrom, J. *Studies in Levitical Terminology, 1: The Encroacher and the Levite, the Term ᶜAboda*. University of California Publications in Near Eastern Studies, vol. 14. Berkeley: University of California Press, 1970. See "References," p. 102.

Vaux, R. de. *Ancient Israel*, vol. 2, *Religious Institutions*. New York: McGraw-Hill, 1965, pp. 358–371.

Chapter 5

vv. 5–10

Milgrom, J. *Cult and Conscience: The ASHAM and the Priestly Doctrine of Repentance*. Leiden: E. J. Brill, 1974, pp. 104–106.

vv. 11–31

Brichto, H. C. "The Case of the *Śōṭā* and a Reconsideration of Biblical Law." *HUCA* 46 (1975): 55–70.

Fishbane, M. "Accusations of Adultery: A Study of Law and Scribal Practice in Numbers 5:11–31." *HUCA* 45 (1974): 25–45.

Frymer, T. S. "Ordeal, judicial." In *IDBSuppl*, pp. 638–640.

Phillips, A. C. *Ancient Israel's Criminal Law. A New Approach to the Decalogue*. Oxford: Basil Blackwell, 1970, pp. 118–121.

Sasson, J. "Numbers 5 and the 'Waters of Judgement.' " *BZ* 16 (1972): 249–251.

Ward, E. F. de. "Superstition and Judgment." *ZAW* 89 (1977): 1–19, esp. pp. 13–14.

Chapter 6

vv. 1–21

Eichrodt, W. *Theology of the Old Testament*. Translated by J. Baker. 2 vols. Philadelphia: Westminster, 1967, vol. 2, pp. 303–306.

Milgrom, J. *Cult and Conscience: The ASHAM and the Priestly Doctrine of Repentance*. Leiden: E. J. Brill, 1974, pp. 66–70.

———. "Nazirite." *EncJud* 12 (1971): 907–909.

Rainey, A. "The Order of Sacrifices in Old Testament Ritual Texts." *Bibl* 51 (1970): 485–498, esp. pp. 494, 495.

Vaux, R. de. *Ancient Israel*, vol. 2, *Religious Institutions*. New York: McGraw–Hill, 1965, pp. 466–67.

vv. 22–27

Brichto, H. C. "Priestly Blessing." *EncJud* 13 (1971): 1060–1061.

Miller, P. D. "The Blessing God. An Interpretation of Numbers 6:22–27." *Intr* 29 (1975): 240–251.

Westermann, C. *Blessing in the Bible and the Life of the Church*. Overtures to Biblical Theology series. Edited by Walter Brueggeman and

John R. Donahue. Translated by Keith R. Crim. Philadelphia: Fortress, 1978, pp. 42–45.

Chapters 7–8

See bibliography for chapters 1–4.

17

From Sinai to Kadesh

Numbers 10:11—20:21

The Israelites have heard much from both God and Moses since reaching Sinai. Instructions, rules, and exhortations have been abundant. But now is the time to break camp and move on. Sinai is no more God's goal for His people, geographically, than was the Mount of Transfiguration for Peter, James, and John. It should, however, nerve His people for the future by giving them a deeper exposure of Himself.

From Marching to Murmuring
(10:11—12:16)

Frank M. Cross has observed the proliferation of the phrase "and the children of Israel journeyed from . . ." in Exodus and Numbers, and compares it with the phrase "these are the generations of . . ." that appears ten times in Genesis.[1] Seven of these "and they journeyed from . . ." phrases are in Exodus: 12:37; 13:20; 14:2; 15:22; 16:1; 17:1; 19:2.

The remaining five phrases are in Numbers: 10:12; 20:1; 20:22; 21:10; 22:1. But the departure from Sinai is unique. Israel will take with her from there memories that she cannot forget. The scene in 10:1–35 is dramatic, pulsating.

1. *Caananite Myth and Hebrew Epic: Essays in the History of the Religion of Israel* (Cambridge, MA: Harvard University Press, 1973), pp. 308–317.

Flags are flying. God's presence is distinctly manifest. Conquest is on everybody's mind.

One is hardly prepared for the rude shock, then, that meets him in chapters 11 and 12. Far from there being a mood of optimism and gallantry, there is instead the ugly spectacle of divisiveness, complaints, depression, bewilderment, and divine judgment as the appropriate response.

Three different scenes are presented in this debacle. First, there is a general complaining about "misfortunes." God responds with a consuming fire on the fringes of the camp. Only the intercessory prayers of Moses terminate the punishment (11:1–3). Second, not satisfied with a one-dish menu—manna—the people cry to God for diverse food (11:4–34). Third, Miriam challenges both the sagacity of Moses in the choice of a wife and the credibility of his unique relationship to God (12).

The immediate purpose of these events is to contrast the God who is present in His camp to bless (chaps. 1–10) with the God who is present in His camp to judge whenever a group or an individual attempts to shatter the brotherhood in the community (chaps. 11–12). Thus, a fire consumes (11:1); a plague breaks out (11:33); an accuser of the brethren becomes leprous (12:10).

The role of Moses in each episode is interesting. In the first he is successful intercessor. He raises no question, offers no rebukes. The craving of the "rabble" for meat is another matter, however. If "Moses prayed" in 11:2, he is "displeased" in 11:10. Moses assumes that the people's complaining and memories of the food in Egypt is an indictment against him. He is distraught and wants no more responsibility for this ungrateful, unresponsive parish. Even death is preferable to further ministry (v. 15). Murmuring is contagious. Moses is lowering himself to the level of his congregation, adopting its mentality.

God's response to Moses (vv. 16ff.) is one of both respite and rebuke. Respite is provided in that Moses no longer needs to function alone. God will provide him with seventy elders who will share the burden of leadership. But it is also a word of rebuke. If Moses wants to leave, that is allowed. But first let him choose any seventy of the congregation. God will then put on them "the Spirit" that he has put on Moses. Moses is not indispensable. But the presence of God's Spirit is. Only the gift of the divine Spirit on him can explain Moses' abilities.

This all transpired in the tent of meeting (vv. 16b, 24). But the Spirit is not confined to a cubicle. It also rests on two—Eldad and Medad—in the camp (v. 26). But orthodox Joshua wants that to cease (v. 28). Rigidity dies hard. This attitude is reflected in John: "Master, we saw a man casting out demons in your name, and we forbade him, because he does not follow with us" (Luke 9:49).

God did honor the people's urge for seasoned dishes. Unlike Exodus 16, however, there is a price to be paid. At the very moment they are enjoying these succulent morsels a plague is unleashed (v. 33). In the commentary of Psalm 106:15, "he gave them what they asked, but sent a wasting disease among them." God acquiesces, but He does not acquit.

The third incident is in chapter 12. If in chapter 11 Moses was indirectly challenged, here the attack is frontal. The first innuendo is leveled against the propriety of his choice of a spouse. He has married a "Cushite" woman (12:1). The charge seems to come more from Miriam than from Aaron. For 12:1 says, literally, "and she spoke, Miriam, and Aaron, against Moses." The verb is third-person, feminine, singular—not plural. (The same construction is found in Judges 5:1, "then she sang, Deborah, and Barak.")

Perhaps this is the reason why Miriam becomes leprous, although Aaron is also implicated in the plural, "why then were you not afraid to speak against my servant Moses?" Cross points out that if the term "Cushite" implies blackness, or an Ethiopian—as it does usually in the Bible—

the story renders "the whitened skin of Miriam a singularly fit punishment for her objections to the Cushite wife."[2]

On the other hand, Numbers 12:1 may simply be saying that Moses' wife was from the tribe of Cushan, an area parallel to that of Midian in Habakkuk 3:7, "the tents of Cushan . . . the curtains of the land of Midian." This would then accord perfectly with Exodus 2:21—that Moses married Zipporah, a Midianite.

Interestingly, Aaron can ask mercy only from Moses (vv. 11–12). It is Moses who again intercedes (v. 13). We are, thus, brought back to the Moses of 11:1–3, a Moses whose prayers result in the mitigation, but not the cancellation, of the divine sentence. There is no word of remonstration against either Miriam or Aaron. He adopts a policy of silence toward his detractors.

Not only is Moses' relationship to a unique wife questioned, but so is his unique relationship to God—"has the LORD indeed spoken only through Moses?" Is he the only vehicle of revelation? Does he have a monopoly on God's pronouncements? Is Moses God's vicar on earth, a kind of papal figure? God's answer is simple—yes (see vv. 6–8).

As Brevard Childs has pointed out, these stories, and those that follow, perpetuate the theme of 1:1—10:11, that is, the absolute necessity for holiness among God's people.[3] The sacred character of the community is impugned when the fabric of that community is torn by dissension and nitpicking. It compels God to move from blessing to judgment.

All too often critical studies have been preoccupied with the attempt to detect two different stories—now untidily combined—in both chapters 11 (the quail and the elders) and 12 (Moses' wife, and his relationship to God). See, for

2. *Ibid*., p. 204.

3. *Introduction to the Old Testament As Scripture* (Philadelphia: Fortress, 1979), p. 198.

example, the studies of George W. Coats, heavily influenced as they are by Martin Noth, the scholar who emphasizes the history of traditions. To be applauded is the intensive study of David Jobling which goes beyond the genetic approach to Scripture—what is the prehistory of the text?—and deals with the final form of the text.

In such a study the commonality of theme in these two chapters becomes transparent. In each narrative there is a main program: God is giving to Israel the promised land of Canaan. Then there is a counterprogram, instigated by the people against the march, by the rabble against the food, by Moses against his role, by Miriam and Aaron against Moses. Finally there is a counter-counterprogram from God, the purpose of which is to restore unity. The instigators are punished. God's will is one people, one food, and one leader.[4]

Shall We Go Up Or Shall We Not?
(13:1—14:15)

These two chapters of Numbers discuss the dispatching of spies from Kadesh to Canaan to determine the advisability of attacking Canaan, the reports brought back, and the repercussions. We should note that the original plan is God's: "The LORD said to Moses, send men to spy out the land of Canaan." One might think that God could have supplied the information about Canaan directly, and thus save all the time and bother of this adventure. But the people must do the searching and the investigation.

The modern Bible critics agree unanimously that these two chapters represent a weaving together of two stories. There is the original event, traceable to J/E. Subsequently this story was reworked and supplemented by another narrative, this one from P.

4. "A Structural Analysis of Numbers 11 and 12," *SBL Seminar Papers*, 1977, pp. 180ff.

The criterion for supposing the heterogeneity of the text here is the presence of indubitable doublets that are mutually exclusive. Thus, the spies survey only the area of the Negeb, 13:22 (J/E). Or did they survey the whole land of Canaan, "to Rehob, near the entrance of Hamath," 13:21 (P)? Is it only Caleb who protests the negative report, 13:30 (J/E), or is it both Caleb and Joshua, 14:6 (P)? Is only Caleb to enter the Promised Land, 14:24 (J/E), or is it Caleb and Joshua, 14:30 (J/E, or a gloss on J/E?)?

The critical reconstruction (with minor variations) is approximately as follows:

13:1–7a	P	13:25–26	P	14:5–10	P
13:7b–20	J/E	13:27–31	J/E	14:11–25	J/E
13:21	P	14:1–3	P	14:26–38	P
13:22–24	J/E	14:4	J/E	14:39–45	J/E

It is to be debated, however, that the contradictory doublets are indeed that. But before we address that issue it will bid us well to recall C. S. Lewis's caveat about the whole area of biblical criticism. In *Christian Reflections*, he observes that reviewers of his own works, whenever they attempted to answer questions about why Lewis wrote this, what influenced him, what his purpose was in writing—areas not always specifically addressed or annotated by the author—they were invariably wrong.[5] Still, to the uninformed reader of the review, these comments might be so convincing as to be accepted as entirely truthful.

Turning specifically to the issue of "reconstructing" how an ancient book was written, Lewis says:

> The superiority in judgement and diligence which you are going to attribute to the Bible critics will have to be almost super human if it is to offset the fact that they are every-

5. (Grand Rapids: Eerdmans, 1967), pp. 159ff.

> where faced with customs, language, race-characteristics, class-characteristics, a religious background, habits of composition, and basic assumptions, which no scholarship will ever enable any man now alive to know as surely and intimately and instinctively as the reviewer can know mine. And for that very same reason, remember, the Biblical critics can never be crudely proved wrong. St Mark is dead. When they meet St Peter there will be more pressing matters to discuss.[6]

In the case of Numbers 13–14 it seems possible that one story has been laid over an earlier one. Doublets, if they be that, could be a giveaway for such an arrangement. The next step would then be to isolate the two stories from each other (as we have done above, following the consensus). That is as far as older biblical criticism went. More recent trends have been to treat suggestively the implications of this editorial process.[7]

Logic impels us to ask if Numbers 13–14 is indeed laced with contradictions. Are there other explanations that are equally viable? The twelve spies would not likely travel as a group. Clandestine operations necessitate separation. How much would the phrase "Negeb" mean to Hebrew spies who had known only two places in their lives, Egypt and part of the Sinai peninsula? Might "Negeb" be a designation for Canaan in the sense of *pars pro toto*?

The opposition of Caleb on the first day, and the opposition of Caleb and Joshua on the second day, is understandable. In chapter 13 the opposition is from the spies, but in chapter 14 that spirit of morbidity has engulfed all the congregation. A. MacRae observes about chapter 13, "It would be more effective for Caleb to do this, since Joshua

6. *Ibid.*, p. 161.

7. That is, for example, the approach of Sean E. McEvenue in *The Narrative Style of the Priestly Writer* (Rome: Biblical Institute Press, 1971). See especially pp. 117ff.

was so closely associated with Moses that he would not be so readily accepted as an independent witness."[8]

The salvation of Caleb stands over against the perdition of the unbelieving spies (14:24). The salvation of Caleb and Joshua stands in stark contrast with that of the "wicked congregation" (14:27, 30).

Should we try to wring from these "contradictions" all that is possible or implicit? What then would we do with this: "not one shall come into the land where I swore that I would make you dwell, except Caleb . . . and Joshua" (14:30)? How far do we press the "*not one* . . . except Caleb and Joshua" (italics mine)? Are Moses and Aaron condemned too by this incident? Certainly not.

What is to be said about the two chapters in their final form—be they homogeneous or composite? In the first place, it should be obvious that they perpetuate the point of the narratives of chapters 11 and 12. There the sin of unbelief wreaked havoc on God's camp: death by fire, plague, leprosy. Similarly, in these two chapters the results of the sin of unbelief are disastrous: immediate death (14:37), premature death and exclusion from the land of promise (14:22–23, 29–30), defeat (14:45). The Israelites have an even record against the Amalekites—a pre-Sinai victory (Exod. 17:8–14) and a post-Sinai defeat.

Again, the two chapters abound in inner contrasts. Chapter 13 focuses on the negative response of the spies; chapter 14 on the negative response of the whole congregation. The report of the spies is defeatist and pessimistic; that of Caleb is positive (13:25–33). The fruit in the land is huge (13:23, 24, 27b), but its occupants are bigger still (13:28, 31, 33). The people debate about returning to Egypt (14:1–5) or fighting to possess Canaan (14:6–9). God threatens to destroy these people (14:11–12); Moses pleads

8. "Numbers," in the *New Bible Commentary*, revised edition (Grand Rapids: Eerdmans, 1970) p. 179.

with Him not to (14:13–19). "All the people of Israel murmured against Moses and Aaron" (14:2); God asks, "How long shall this wicked congregation murmur against me?" (14:27). Caleb and Joshua will enter Canaan; none of their peers will (14:28–30). The children of the faithless spies will enter Canaan (14:31), but they also must suffer for their fathers' faithlessness (14:33). The unbelievers wanted to stone Moses, Aaron, Caleb, and Joshua (14:10); Moses seeks his antagonists' forgiveness and pardon (14:19). God metes out immediate chastisement (14:37), and promises delayed chastisement (14:29, 32, 34).

We have become accustomed, thus far in our Pentateuchal studies, to those situations that called for the death penalty where there was a violation of the accepted norms of behavior. The list has included murder, idolatry, sexual aberrations, and illicit physical contact with sancta. The implementation of justice is directed toward individual trespassers of covenant regulations.

But here the whole congregation is indicted for faithlessness, and not just selected individuals in the larger group. Only a few survive unscathed, like Noah in an earlier generation.

And as surely as Noah had to tolerate the minority opinion of his day, so did Caleb and Joshua. The respective faith of each in the integrity of the promise of God gives Noah victory over sarcasm and Caleb and Joshua victory over hostility. The taunters and the incredulous, on the other hand, are denied the ark and the land.

Further Revolts Against Moses (15–18)

Chapter 15 breaks sharply into the narrative of Numbers, having no immediate observable relationship to what follows and what precedes. It is a unit given completely to cultic matters, and is sandwiched between incidents of murmuring against Moses (13–14; 16–18). As a comparable example, imagine an elaborate disquisition on the preparation of wine for the Eucharist by Luther squeezed in between his descriptions of his altercations with the leadership of the Roman Catholic Church.

To dismiss the placement of the chapter as a pointless insertion and intrusion is unwarranted, however. Five issues are broached in the chapter: additional information about the first three sacrifices spelled out in Leviticus—whole burnt, cereal, and peace (vv. 1–16); an offering of first fruits (vv. 17–21); supplementary and repeated information about the sin offering, revolving around the theme of sins of ignorance or inadvertence (vv. 22–31); an instance of the death penalty for violation of the Sabbath, specifically gathering sticks (vv. 32–36); wearing of tassels on one's clothing (vv. 37–41). The importance of this ornament in latter Judaism can be gauged by the two references to the custom in Matthew 9:20, "the fringe of his garment," and Matthew 23:5, "they make . . . their fringes long."

The chapter seems to be related to its immediate context in several possible ways. Conceivably it serves as a pause in the drama,[9] but why is such a pause needed and what is accomplished thereby? Is the law of (general) association at work here? Chapter 14 dealt with the sin of congregation. Chapter 15 (vv. 22–26) provides, via the sin offering, atonement for the whole congregation.

May the law of contrast be also evident here? At the end of chapter 14, Israel is unable to attack Canaan and thus has to abort plans to penetrate Canaan from the south (vv. 39–45). At the beginning of chapter 15 we read, "When you come into the land you are to inhabit." Judgment yes, but that is not God's goal, or ultimate word.

The first three sacrifices of the Levitical code, addressed in 15:1–16, are not the expiatory sacrifices, but those that

9. I. Caine, "Numbers, Book of," *EncJud* 12 (1971), p. 1250.

are voluntary, spontaneous, given to God in gratitude and praise. One will find precious little of gratitude and praise in Numbers 13, 14, and 16!

The whole issue of inadvertent sin, both of the congregation (15:22–26) and of the individual (15:27–29), contrasts vividly with the sin of "a high hand" (15:30). The scenario described in 13–14 and 16 is the latter type. For these there are no sacrificial provisions. Only the intercessory prayers of Moses save the perpetrators (14:13–19; 16:22), and even then not completely.

God's purpose for the tassels on the clothing is a way for God to communicate to Israel that they are to be holy to their God, not a moralistic holiness, but a holiness that is rooted in obedience (15:40). If holy living is God's moral goal for His people, the chapters surrounding this summons have displayed the exact antinomy of that lifestyle.

With the beginning of chapter 16 we find more criticism of Moses. Thus far opposition to him has come from the congregation (chap. 11), his family (chap. 12), and the spies (chap. 13). We now add to that list clerical opposition (chap. 16).

The instigator is Korah, a Levite of the Kohathite branch. Joined by two laymen, Dathan and Abiram, plus 250 prominent men of the congregation, Korah attacks Moses (16:3). Has Moses a monopoly on sanctity, asks Korah?

The criticism is strong. But is it legitimate or a falsification? Restraining any impulse to defend himself, Moses is willing to leave the matter to God's adjudication (vv. 5–7). As in the contest with Elijah and the prophets of Baal at Carmel (I Kings 18), the Lord will distinguish between truth and error, between prophet and prevaricator. As at Carmel the confrontation was between one and the many. So then Moses says, "Hear now, you sons of Levi" (16:8). He does not say, "Hear now, Korah." Korah is simply spokesman for the larger group.

The motivation behind Korah's protest is discovered in

16:8–10. Why be content with being a parish priest when a bishopric is a possibility?

God is not quite as patient as Moses is! He wants to solve the impasse in blitzkrieg fashion (v. 21). Moses and Aaron, however, make intercession for the transgressor (v. 22). Let any punishment necessary be limited to the culprit instead of something pervasive. And that is precisely what happened (vv. 31–33). Korah and his kin were swallowed up by the earth.

The sin of Korah is twofold. It consists of an attitude of defiance plus the actual performance of duties not apportioned to him. The earth's swallowing of Korah and his accomplices is "to be a reminder to the people of Israel, so that no one who is not a priest, who is not of the descendants of Aaron, should draw near to burn incense before the LORD" (v. 40). Once again Numbers has underscored the fact that God has assigned different responsibilities to different groups. The trouble starts when one group says, "I have *not* learned in whatsoever state I am to be content."

The seriousness of this arrangement is enforced by the phrase in 18:3, "They [the tribe of Levi] . . . shall not come near to the vessels of the sanctuary or to the altar, lest they, and you [Aaron and the priests], die." (See also 18:7.) That particular ultimatum we have already found in Numbers 1:51; 3:10; 3:38; 4:20. One will look in vain here for any concept of the priesthood of all believers. Authority has been established. Boundaries have been set. Ministries have been defined. Activities have been regulated.

One of the characteristics of murmuring is that it is so contagious. Having already faced one tête-à-tête, Moses must now endure another one. Surprisingly, Moses is blamed for something God has done—"You have killed the people of the LORD" (v. 41). If Moses' intercession saved the people earlier (v. 22), here it saves them from chaos (vv. 46–48). Once again Moses placates God, even when Moses has been the butt of the vilification! Here Moses is imitating his wife, whose quick action earlier saved him from divine wrath (Exod. 4:25).

Chapter 17 relates in several ways to what preceded. Through the incident of Aaron's budding rod the attempt is made to establish Aaron's position of preeminence. In both chapters 16 and 17 the theme of divine selection is sounded. The key word is "choose." In one case it is the acceptance of an incense offering (16:7) and in the other the acceptance of a rod (17:5). The decision is left to God. God's clear response on the second issue should stifle further murmuring.

What is the emotional response by the people to the aperture in the earth, the demise of Korah, the plague, and the divine attestation placed on Aaron? They are shocked, dumfounded, filled with terror, and are about as eager to approach the sanctuary as was Daniel to walk into the lion's den. Why precipitate one's death (17:12–13)?

I suggest that the purpose of chapter 18 is to show God's response to this outbreak of chagrin and phobia. After all, can there be genuine corporate worship if God's house is perceived as a trap which lures the unsuspecting to their deaths? In what follows, the line of argument I pursue is heavily indebted to Jacob Milgrom.[10]

The purpose of 18:1–7 (and for that matter, vv. 21–23) is to alleviate the people's concern. Here we are informed that the priests "shall bear iniquity in connection with the sanctuary and your priesthood" (18:1). Later we are told that the "Levites shall do the service of the tent of meeting, and they shall bear their iniquity" (18:23). The purpose is stated in 18:5, "that there be wrath no more upon the people of Israel."

There are problems in the interpretation of the key

10. *Studies in Levitical Terminology, 1: The Encroacher and the Levite, the Term ᶜAboda*. University of California Publications in Near Eastern Studies, vol. 14. Berkeley: University of California Press, 1970, pp. 18ff.

phrase of 18:23, "they shall bear their iniquity." What is the identification of "they" and "their"? Is it, "and they [the Israelites] shall bear their [own] iniquity"? Hardly. Is it, "and they [the Levites] shall bear their [own] iniquity"? Possibly. Or is it, "and they [the Levites] shall bear their [the Israelites'] iniquity"? That is, one party bears the guilt of a second party. If that is the case, Numbers 18, especially verses 21–23, is saying that the Levites are vicariously culpable for the sins of the laity. Milgrom says, after defending the third interpretation,

> Whereas the doctrine of collective responsibility is a cornerstone of P's theology for all sins against God, within the sanctuary there is an attempt to limit its destructive impact to the clergy alone. Herein lies the magnitude of the solace offered the panicky Israelites: henceforth, this cardinal doctrine of collective responsibility shall be compromised for their sakes so that they may worship at the sanctuary without fear.[11]

Two Types of Impurity (19:1—20:21)

Chapter 19 is concerned with one type of impurity—ritual impurity contacted by touching something deceased (vv. 11–13, 16), or by being in proximity to something deceased (v. 14). The theme of death had been prominent in the previous unit (chaps. 16–18), the victims including Korah and his co-insurrectionists (16:35) and the 14,700 plague casualties (16:49). Moses stands between the dead and the living (16:48). There is a fear of death (17:12–13), and the possibility of death for encroachment (18:3, 7, 22) or improprieties in tithing (18:32).

For the person who is contaminated by contact with a corpse there is provided the possibility of cleansing. The

11. *Ibid.*, pp. 32–33.

ritual involves the sprinkling of the blood of a red heifer which is slaughtered outside the camp. The ashes of the incinerated heifer are mixed with water and sprinkled on the unclean person on the third and seventh days after the contamination (19:17–19).

This is not the first time in Numbers we have met with contamination through contact with a corpse. Numbers 5:2–3 say explicitly that "one that is unclean through contact with the dead" is to be put out of the camp. But no such directive is given for the exactly similar situation discussed in Numbers 19. Why? Must we resort to source criticism? Or may the "discrepancy" be explained by the fact that Numbers 5 deals with the camp in the wilderness, the immediate situation, whereas Numbers 19 is concerned with the future only: "And it shall be a perpetual statute for them" (19:21), that is, when Israel is settled in Palestine?[12]

If that is the case then there is a perceptible pattern in this part of Numbers. Present history, usually disastrous, is followed by a chapter regarding a future time for which God has made redemptive provision. Thus, chapters 11–14 deal with divine judgment in the present; chapter 15 includes cultic regulations for the future (15:15, 21, 23) underlining God's grace to cover man's sin. Again, chapters 16–18 are concerned with divine judgment in the present; chapter 19 sets forth cultic regulations for the future, again underlining God's power to cleanse man from uncleanness.

The second type of impurity, although not called such, centers on the complaint about the absence of water (cf. Exod. 17:1–7). The imbroglio is ringed by the report of the death of Miriam (20:1) and the death of Aaron (20:22–29).

Interestingly the people suffer no consequences, as they

12. Jacob Milgrom, "Studies in the Temple Scroll," *JBL* 97 (1978), p. 516.

did in Numbers 11. But Moses does! He is to be excluded from the land of promise because "you did not believe in me, to sanctify me in the eyes of the people of Israel" (20:12). When the people were in trouble, Moses interceded for them. But who will pray for Moses? Does he have a mediator? If nothing else, the story illustrates the principle: to whom much is given much is required. One might apply Amos's "You only have I known of all the families of the earth; therefore I will punish you" (3:2) to Moses. This could be paraphrased, "You alone have I chosen among the people as leader; therefore I will punish you."

Bibliography

Chapter 10:11–36

Coats, G. W. "Wilderness Itinerary." *CBQ* 34 (1972): 135–152.

Leiman, S. Z. "The Inverted '*Nuns*' at Numbers 10:35–36 and the Book of Eldad and Medad." *JBL* 93 (1974): 348–355.

Levine, B. A. "More on the Inverted *Nuns* of Num. 10:35–36." *JBL* 95 (1976): 122–124.

Chapters 11–12

Butler, T. C. "An anti-Moses Tradition." *JSOT* 12 (1979): 9–15.

Coats, G. W. *Rebellion in the Wilderness: The Murmuring Motif in the Wilderness Traditions of the Old Testament*. Nashville: Abingdon, 1968, pp. 96–115, 124–127, 261–264.

DeVries, S. J. "The Time Word *maḥar* as a Key to Tradition Development." *ZAW* 87 (1975): 65–79, esp. 73–77.

Jobling, D. "A Structural Analysis of Numbers 11 and 12." *SBL Seminar Papers*, 1977, pp. 171–204.

______. *The Sense of Biblical Narrative: Three Structural Analyses in the Old Testament*. JSOT Supplement Series, vol. 7. Sheffield: Department of Biblical Studies, University of Sheffield, 1978.

Kselman, J. S. "Notes on Numbers 12:6–8." *VT* 26 (1976): 500–505.

Neve, L. *The Spirit of God in the Old Testament*. Tokyo: Seibunsha, 1972.

Chapters 13–14

Brin, G. "The Formula 'From . . . and Onward/Upward' (*m . . . whl' h wm*ᶜ*lh*)." *JBL* 99 (1980): 161–171.

Coats, G. W. *Rebellion in the Wilderness: The Murmuring Motif in the Wilderness Traditions of the Old Testament*. Nashville: Abingdon, 1968, pp. 137–156.

Flanagan, J. W. "History, Religion, and Ideology, The Caleb Tradition." *Horizons* 3 (1976): 175–185.

McEvenue, S. E. "A Source–Critical Problem in Nm 14, 26–38." *Bibl* 50 (1969): 453–465.

———. *The Narrative Style of the Priestly Writer*. Rome: Biblical Institute Press, 1971, pp. 90–144.

Ovadiah, A. "The Relief of the Spies from Carthage." *IEJ* 24 (1974): 210–214.

Sakenfeld, K. D. "The Problem of Divine Forgiveness in Numbers 14." *CBQ* 37 (1975): 317–330.

Vaux, R. de. *The Early History of Israel*. Philadelphia: Westminster, 1978, pp. 523–526.

Chapter 15

Fox, M. V. "The Sign of Covenant Circumcision in the Light of Priestly *'ôt* Etiologies." *RB* 81 (1974): 481–523.

Robinson, G. "The Prohibition of Strange Fire in Ancient Israel. A New Look at the Case of Gathering Wood and Kindling Fire on the Sabbath." *VT* 28 (1978): 301–317, esp. 313–317.

Toeg, A. "A Halakhic Midrash in Num XV, 22–31." *Tarbiz* 43 (1973/74): 1–20, English summary, pp. 1–2.

Chapters 16–18

Coats, G. W. *Rebellion in the Wilderness: The Murmuring Motif in the Wilderness Traditions of the Old Testament*. Nashville: Abingdon, 1968, pp. 156–184.

Hanson, H. E. "Num. XVI, 30 and the Meaning of Bārā'." *VT* 22 (1972): 353–359.

Milgrom, J. *Studies in Levitical Terminology, 1: The Encroacher and the Levite, the Term* ᶜ*Aboda*. University of California Publications in Near Eastern Studies, vol. 14. Berkeley: University of California Press, 1970, pp. 18–35.

Snaith, N. H. "Notes on Numbers 18:9." *VT* 23 (1973): 373–375.

Chapter 19

Etkin, W. "The Mystery of the Red Heifer: a Scientific Midrash." *Jud* 28 (1979): 353–356.

Wold, D. J. "The Kareth Penalty in P: Rationale and Cases." *SBL Seminar Papers*, 1, 1979, pp. 1–45.

Chapter 20:1–21

Coats, G. W. "Conquest Traditions in the Wilderness Theme." *JBL* 95 (1976): 177–190.

18

From Kadesh to Moab

Numbers 20:22—36:13

This unit opens with a narration of Aaron's death (20:22–29), an event that is recalled in 33:38–39 and Deuteronomy 32:50. Moses has already lost one member of his family, his sister Miriam (20:1). Again the story is reflective of a theme so prevalent in Numbers—sin cannot go unchecked. In collusion with Moses, Aaron did not "believe" in God (20:12) but rather "rebelled" against His command (20:24)—both of these verbs are second-person, masculine plural.

Surprisingly, perhaps, it is Moses who is informed of Aaron's imminent death. Moses is to "take" Aaron and his son Eleazar up to Mount Hor, and transfer Aaron's high-priestly clothing to Eleazar. The scene is certainly reminiscent of Abraham and Isaac at Beer-sheba (Gen. 22). Abraham is to "take" Isaac—who does not know about the mission's purpose—to Mount Moriah. A fully cooperative, nonquerying Abraham parallels a fully cooperative, nonquerying Moses. Both are prepared to say a final good-by to a close relative.

Moses knew only too well the reason for Aaron's demise. But there is no indication that Moses felt constrained to make a public disclosure of the reason, nor did he capitalize on the opportunity to turn a funeral into an evangelistic opportunity, replete with warnings and exhortations.

Some Early Opposition (20:22—21:35)

Three conflicts are presented in chapter 21. The first is a battle with some Canaanites in the Negeb area. Israel is delivered from subjugation after they "vowed a vow" to the Lord (21:2), a theme which will shortly occupy the entire chapter of Numbers 30. Once more the Israelites complain of no food or water (21:4–9). Also, the Israelites encounter opposition on the way to Moab from Sihon, king of the Amorites (21:10–32) and Og, king of Bashan (21:33–35). Israel must not only fight to get *into* the Promised Land. She must also fight to get *to* the Promised Land.

The second conflict adds some interesting new developments. This time God does not send water or food. Before Moses can do or say anything, God sends "fiery serpents." The Hebrew word for "serpent" is the same as that for the serpent of Genesis 3, "bronze one[s]." The Hebrew word for "fiery" is the word *seraph*, the term that is used to describe the angelic creatures in the temple in Isaiah's vision (Isa. 6:2).

Faced with the prospect of death through snakebite, the people confess, "We have sinned," and then ask for a suspension of the plague. The language is a reminder of earlier language in Exodus. The Pharaoh says, "Entreat the LORD to take away the frogs" (Exod. 8:8). Here the Israelites say, "pray to the LORD, that he take away the serpents from us" (21:7).

God's response to the people's request is interesting. Moses does pray, but God does not take away the serpents. He provides a cure, a fiery serpent which is to be raised on a pole. The presence of this elevated serpent does not guarantee immunity from attack. Its presence does become therapeutic, however, when an individual, if bitten, looks at it.

One can easily see how the New Testament is able to draw a parallel to this event: "And as Moses lifted up the serpent in the wilderness, so must the Son of man be lifted up, that whoever believes in him may have eternal life" (John 3:14–15).

God did not get rid of the serpents. He also had not (yet!) abolished the presence of sin. But He had provided relief from the problem, a relief that is like the problem, yet different from the problem. The New Testament equivalent of the Old Testament "to look" is "to believe." Here they are synonymous terms. Faith, then, is "the gaze of the soul upon a saving God."[1]

In this particular incident perhaps the wrong prayer has been prayed. Instead of asking, "Take away the serpents from us," the people should have prayed, or at least gone on to pray, "take away from us the attitudes that do not glorify and honor your name." Respite, not reformation, is their concern.

Verses 10–20 of chapter 21 provide an itinerary of Israel's further trek through the wilderness. The journey itself is uneventful, but is noteworthy by virtue of the two poetic sections in the unit, one a quote from a lost book identified as "the Book of the Wars of the LORD" (vv. 14–15)—an evidence of real rather than hypothetical sources behind the Pentateuch—and the other, which we may call, for convenience, "the Song of the Well" (vv. 17–18).

The remainder of the chapter describes Israel's confrontation with Sihon of the Amorites and Og of Bashan, with much greater detail for the battle with Sihon than for that with Og. The former is treated in twelve verses, the latter in three.

The people of God have no interest in the territory of Sihon. Rather, their sights are set on something else, a better land "whose builder and maker is God." To that end, the Israelites desire only to pass through (is this theme

1. A. W. Tozer, *The Pursuit of God* (Harrisburg, PA: Christian Publications, 1948), p. 89.

similar to that of *Pilgrim's Progress?*) to a greater destination. That simple courtesy Sihon refused to grant. He who will lose his life will save it; he who will save his life will lose it. An easy enough yes and there would have been no storm. Instead there is a recalcitrant no and Sihon sees his cities, especially Heshbon, pass from his control into the control of Israel. Jesus, much later, found Himself in a similar situation. He wanted passage through a Samaritan village. The request was denied. The Samaritans acted as Sihon had. But instead of routing the Samaritans Jesus rebuked those who wanted precisely that to happen (Luke 9:51–56). Rather than pressing the issue Jesus took an alternate route, as Moses had done earlier with the Edomites (Num. 20:21; Luke 9:56). Circumvention is most of the time preferable to confrontation.

And perhaps Israel would have done the same with Sihon and the Amorites had not Sihon rushed into action his military forces (21:23). Israel had no choice but to respond militarily, and this she did quite well.

The event is sealed and justified by the recitation of a poem, verses 27–30, the contents of which deal at least in part with Sihon's former capture of Heshbon from the Moabites (see v. 29). But now Sihon has surrendered his gains. To be sure, there are extremely difficult problems in translating the poem. For instance, who recites this poem (v. 27)? The KJV has "they that speak in proverbs." The RSV has "the ballad singers." Or could the Hebrew *mōšᵉlîm* be translated as "taunters"? Then again, verse 30, a key verse, is puzzling, as indicated by divergencies in both the ancient and modern versions of the Bible. Is verse 30 a further description of Sihon's victory over Moab, or a description of Israel's victory over Sihon?

At least the whole story, and the poem in particular, says that gains can become losses, new frontiers can be forfeited. Stubbornness may be nothing more than stupidity.

There are two other accounts of the battle against Sihon in Scripture. One is Deuteronomy 2:26–37, and the other is Judges 11:19–26. In attempting to relate these three narrations, biblical scholars have drawn one of two conclusions. Numbers is the original account. That found in Deuteronomy 2 and Judges 11 is derived from the account in Numbers (J. R. Bartlett, Roland de Vaux). The other conclusion is that the account in Deuteronomy is the oldest of the three, and Numbers 21:21–31 is a later adaptation of that (John Van Seters).

Van Seters is concerned not only to make the Numbers story post-Deuteronomic, but also to make the whole episode fictional! In part he bases his conclusions on the differences between the accounts in Numbers and Deuteronomy.

Indeed there are differences. One significant difference is that "Then Israel sent messengers to Sihon" (Num. 21:21); "so I [i.e., Moses] sent messengers . . . to Sihon" (Deut. 2:26). Was it Moses who sent the couriers to Sihon or was it the people? As an extension of this we note that Moses is mentioned nowhere in Numbers 21:21–31. He assumes no role in the narrative.

Unlike the account in Numbers, the account in Deuteronomy 2 is replete with references to divine activity. Note these phrases unique to Deuteronomy: "I have given into your hand Sihon . . . contend with him in battle" (v. 24); "This day I will begin to put the dread and fear of you upon the peoples . . ." (v. 25); "for the LORD your God hardened his spirit" (v. 30); "And the LORD said to me, 'Behold, I have begun to give Sihon and his land over to you' " (v. 31); "And the LORD our God gave him over to us" (v. 33); "the LORD our God gave all into our hands" (v. 36).

What implications may be drawn from these differences? Van Seters is prepared to say that Numbers, "if anything, secularizes the other accounts."[2] But is there not another reason for deemphasizing the role of Moses and the activity of God in Numbers, a reason that does justice to the larger context?

The story about Sihon is not particularly removed from the incident at the rock, in which Moses is informed by God that his activity is unacceptable. He is to be barred from entering into the land of promise (20:12). Aaron was already denied entrance (20:29), and is dead. The silence about Moses' role in Numbers 21:21ff. may be a reflection of the incident in 20:12; Moses will, therefore, have only a minimal role to play in the acquisition of land.[3]

I also find myself nonplussed by Van Seters's statement that these accounts "have a highly ideological character which makes these episodes historically untrustworthy."[4] On what possible basis can we say that the ideological is nonhistorical and the nonideological is historical? The logic of that escapes me.

Balaam the Diviner (22–24)

This particular section of Numbers is among the best known of the whole book. Israel's reputation precedes her, causing panic in Balak, Moab's head of state. Earlier in Numbers it was Israel who was afraid of the people (13:33). Now it is Israel who has become, figuratively, the "Anakim" and the "Nephilim." The Moabites are the grasshoppers.

Israel, in her distress, yearned for a return to Egypt. But where can the Moabites go? Where is their security? Military resistance is a risky option. A person inundated in

2. "The Conquest of Sihon's Kingdom: A Literary Examination," *JBL* 91 (1972), p. 196.

3. George W. Coats, "Conquest Traditions in the Wilderness Theme," *JBL* 95 (1976), pp. 189–190.

4. "Conquest of Sihon's Kingdom," p. 197.

fear can only speak in hyperboles. For Balak Israel is so many as to "cover the face of the earth" (22:5).

In such a crisis perhaps one's trump card is magic. To that end, Balak sends an urgent message to Balaam, who lives a considerable distance from Moab—at Pethor, south of Carchemish on the Euphrates.

Balaam's job, should he decide to accept, is simple enough. He is to pronounce a curse on the Israelites that will immobilize them, making them especially vulnerable to defeat by Balak. To make the offer as tempting as possible Balak throws in an almost irresistible honorarium (22:7, 17). Behind this approach is the idea that religious power can be purchased—that it is a commodity, a marketable item. Simon the magician thought there was a monetary price on the power of the Spirit in one's life as if it were an item on a menu (Acts 8:18–19).

Balaam eventually accepts Balak's offer, and goes to Moab on the back of a donkey to await Balak's palm leaves and hosannas. The episode about Balaam's donkey seems humorous to everybody except Balaam. Only the physical manifestation of the angel of the Lord restrains Balaam from precipitous action against his beast of burden. Confronted by the divine, Balaam can only fall on his face (22:31) as Joshua was later to do before the angel of the Lord (Josh. 5:14). Balaam also says, "I have sinned," a confession that parallels the people's confession in the preceding chapter, "We have sinned" (21:7).

The rest of the story involves Balak and Balaam together, with the latter delivering orally four oracles: 23:7–10; 23:18–24; 24:3–9; 24:14–24. These four messages are called "discourse[s]." The Hebrew word for this is *māshāl*, and it may provide another connecting link with the previous unit in Numbers, the song sung by the *mōšᵉlîm* (21:27).

What Balak hears from Balaam is precisely the opposite of what he was hoping he would hear. These were words of blessing, not curse; benediction, not malediction. No one was more surprised than Balaam himself. There is no indication that he was being duplicitous with Balak, and that all along he intended to bless Israel. There are two equally miraculous events in this story, and both have to do with talking. One is for God to make Balaam's donkey talk. The other is to make Balaam a speaker of blessing rather than a spewer of blasphemy on Israel. Two tongues are divinely touched.

Addressing himself to Balaam's speech (with the approval of the Lord), Gerhard von Rad says,

> God lets the magician go on his way. He does not bar the road before him; He does not strike him down in His wrath; He will merely direct the word that Balaam is to utter. Here our story gives expression to something that is very important in the faith of the Old Testament; God does not guide history and the destiny of men by continually opposing men in the projects that they have taken in hand. On the contrary, he lets them act. To all appearance, they are acting simply according to His plan.[5]

Balaam is not an Israelite. More than likely he is not a monotheist, at least by upbringing and tradition. His vocation is a vice in Israel. True, the Lord does guide those who do not know Him, as in the case of Cyrus of Persia (Isa. 45:4b). But Balaam knows the Lord, or knows of Him. God speaks to him (22:9, 12, 20). He speaks of the Lord as "my God" (22:18). He recognizes the angel of the Lord (22:31). The Lord meets with Balaam (23:16), and "put[s] a word in his mouth" (23:5, 16). Balaam even shows some spiritual metamorphosis as he gradually sloughs off the old pagan techniques of which he is master (24:1). The Spirit of God rests upon him (24:2).

Some interpreters, religiously pluralistic, have seized this as one of the more significant points in the story as

5. *Moses* (New York: Association Press, 1960), pp. 72–73.

far as contemporary value and application are concerned: here the unbeliever, the man of another religion (or no religion) speaks the truth of God. Thus A. E. Zannoni, under his discussion of the story's "implications for the Church," says, "It is not unknown in our times that secular institutions have 'preached the gospel' while the church, the new Israel, has remained thunderously silent."[6] George W. Coats, in his concluding remarks about "Balaam the Saint," hints at the same point.[7]

But before we cite the story as a score for pluralism and tolerance and a blow against confessionalism and dogmatism, let us observe that Balaam makes no reference to any other gods. He knows only the Yahweh of Israel. What he says about Israel does not (necessarily) represent his own opinions on the subject. He probably loathes the Israelites, an attitude witnessed by his active role in the Israelite apostasy at Baal-peor (Num. 25, and especially 31:16). Also, we need to be reminded of Yehezkel Kaufmann's observation that while Scripture tells us of individual non-Israelites who knew God intimately, it also says that outside of Israel no nation knows Him.[8]

What is the relationship of this story to the larger context of Numbers? Two items seem apparent. In the first place, Moses is once again conspicuously absent in these three chapters. He is not a part of the drama at all. We have observed this in chapter 21 in the incident involving Sihon and Heshbon, and there related it to God's sentence of condemnation on Moses. His inconsequential role continues into the story of Balak and Balaam. Of course, in this particular story all of Israel, and not just Moses, is uninvolved. Presumably they are not aware of any of the machinations of Balak and Balaam.

6. "Balaam: International Seer/wizard Prophet," *StLukeJ* 22 (1978), p. 18.

7. "Balaam: Sinner or Saint?" *BRes* 17 (1972), p. 29.

8. *The Religion of Israel*, trans. Moshe Greenberg (Chicago: University of Chicago Press, 1960), p. 294.

This latter point raises the question of how Moses is privy to the content of Balaam's oracles if he is not geographically involved. The critics can be expected to dismiss the question as ludicrous, on the grounds that the whole story is from the ninth to eighth century B.C., the Yahwist and the Elohist. The four oracles would antedate the narrative framework by a century or two (if one follows the conclusion of W. F. Albright's linguistic analysis of Balaam's oracles).

On the other hand, could not a case be made for the fact that when Balaam was apprehended for his involvement in the Baal-peor debacle, part of his defense was to retell his oracles to Moses?[9] That he had blessed Israel and spoke of her future prosperity, maybe even a Messiah (24:17?), would be in his favor, so he may have thought.

Returning to the relationship of the story to Numbers, we may note another connection. Ad nauseam Numbers has related (and will relate) stories in which Israel's existence is threatened. But why? Consistently the reason for potential demise has been internal. Israel has been her own worst enemy. She may destroy herself.

Israel need not fear, says this story, the incantations of an international wizard. This is not where the potential hazard is. But begin to do some deep soul-searching when a critical spirit, faultfinding, and backbiting emerge. They are to the threats of a Balaam as cancer is to an upset stomach.

Baal-peor (25)

The Israelites have now reached Shittim, east of the Jordan and almost directly across the river from Jericho. Numbers 31:16 informs us that Balaam devised the scheme

9. C. G. Seerveld, *Balaam's Apocalyptic Prophecies: A Study in Reading Scripture* (Toronto: Wedge Publishing Foundation, 1980), p. 73, n. 10.

to get the Israelites involved in sexual debauchery with "the daughters of Moab." He is as eminently successful in this as he was unsuccessful in his attempts to place a curse on Israel. Where the potency of spell fails, the potency of seduction succeeds. Where the indirect approach fails, the frontal attack takes over.

The Israelites, again reflecting their insensitivity to matters moral and spiritual, are only too happy to become involved with the daughters of Moab (possibly virgins, on the basis that in biblical Hebrew the term *daughters of* followed by a place name may designate unmarried women; see Gen. 36:2; II Sam. 1:20, 24; Isa. 3:16.)[10] Thus an unholy alliance is created between the sons of God and the daughters of men (Gen. 6:1–4).

God's first response is anger against Israel. (In the story about Balaam and Balak, God's anger was kindled against Balaam [22:22]; Balaam's anger against his donkey [22:27]; Balak's anger against Balaam [24:10].) Divine anger leads eventually to the outbreak of a plague (v. 9), but the narrative indicates that the repercussions might have been significantly reduced had the divine mandate been followed. Scholars are sometimes bothered by the fact that the Lord's directive to "Take all the chiefs of the people, and hang them in the sun before the LORD" (v. 4) is ignored by Moses. He orders the judges to kill those who have "yoked themselves to Baal of Peor [god of fire]" (v. 5). In other words, what Moses orders has nothing at all to do with what God has ordered.

It is possible to suggest some disarray in the text, although the critics assign both verses 4 and 5 to the non-P materials in Numbers. Taking the text as it stands, I suggest there are no gaps here in the logical development of the story. Precisely because Moses did not implement

10. See also George E. Mendenhall, *The Tenth Generation: The Origins of the Biblical Traditions* (Baltimore: John Hopkins Press, 1973), p. 111.

the word of the Lord many who might have been spared (v. 4b) were not (v. 9). If that is the case, then we have another illustration of Moses attempting to improve on God's plan, or at least revise it (see Num. 20:10–12). Both times the consequences are tragic.

Why, may we ask, does the Lord specify the "chiefs of the people" should be impaled? Two possibilities suggest themselves. This may be an example of vicarious punishment in which the innocent suffer for the guilty, here the innocent being those with social power who did not restrain those under their authority; that is, the sins of the children being visited upon the fathers.[11] Or it may be that the "chiefs of the people" were indeed the ringleaders, one of whom is identified as Zimri, the Simeonite (v. 14). More than likely the daughters of Moab would try to entice the leaders. Also, the woman in the story, Cozbi, is identified as a member of a prominent Midianite family (v. 15).

More than half of the chapter, verses 6–15, is given to the act of unfaithfulness of one Israelite, Zimri, and the intuitive response to that apostasy by one Israelite, Phinehas, grandson of Aaron. (The source critics are unable to agree among themselves whether this part of the chapter is from P.) Here the focus is on the individual trespasser, not the people; and on the individual vindicator, not Moses and the judges.

Zimri's crime was to bring a Midianite woman into "the inner room" (v. 8), presumably for intercourse. The word in Hebrew for "inner room" is used only here in the Old Testament. De Vaux translates this word as "pavilion, tent, or alcove," and suggests it may have been used for sacred prostitution.[12] The whole affair took place in the sight of Moses and the people who "were weeping at the door of

11. *Ibid.*, p. 114.
12. *The Early History of Israel* (Philadelphia: Westminster, 1978), p. 569.

the tent of meeting." This may imply that the act was perpetrated near Israel's sanctuary.

If that is the case, Phinehas's leap into action becomes quite comprehensible. Three times (3:10, 38; 18:7) Numbers has said that one of the responsibilities of the priesthood was "to put to death any unauthorized person who comes near" the sacred things of the tabernacle. This passage would then serve as an illustration of that principle in operation.[13]

This section of the chapter also serves to contrast the amendment-oriented Moses and the action-oriented Phinehas. Earlier it was Moses who made atonement on Israel's behalf (see, for example, Exod. 32:30), or Moses who urged Aaron to make atonement on behalf of the congregation (Num. 16:46–48), thus arresting the divine plague. Moses is not involved here at all. It is Phinehas who makes atonement for Israel (v. 13).

It is hard not to take the Lord's speech to Moses as a rebuke: "Phinehas . . . has turned back my wrath from the people of Israel. . . ."

A Second Census and Questions about Inheritance (26–27)

On the heels of an act of apostasy (chap. 25) comes an extended census, a second one akin to that described in chapter 1. Those registered in this census include those who came out of Egypt (v. 4b), but who were twenty and older, the minimum age for inclusion in the first census. The immediate purpose of this survey is to provide statistical data for alloting the land after it has been conquered (vv. 52–56). That in itself is interesting, since there is formidable opposition ahead.

13. Jacob Milgrom, *Studies in Levitical Terminology, 1: The Encroacher and the Levite, the Term ʿAboda*, University of California Publications in Near Eastern Studies, vol. 14 (Berkeley: University of California Press, 1970), pp. 48–49.

God's look to the future is different from that of the spies. The spies say, "We are unable to take the land"; God says, "You *will* take the land." To that end, Israel can confidently begin preparations, and sense nothing premature in that. For a comparable situation, imagine a presidential candidate choosing his running mate and the members of his cabinet even before the primaries have begun.

The results of the census create one problem, however. There is one family, in which Zelophehad, the father, is deceased; there are no sons, only five daughters (27:1). The problem is that women do not inherit property (see Deut. 21:15–17). Are they then to be totally without patrimony? It is true that the three daughters of Job received an inheritance (Job 42:15), but the situation is different, for there the father is still alive.

Perhaps the subordinate role of women is emphasized here even by the Hebrew construction that is used. We read that the daughters of Zelophehad "drew near" *(qārab)*, and "stood before" *(lipnê)* Moses and the priest (27:1–2). Joshua 17:4 simply says that the daughters "came before" *(qārab lipnê)* Eleazar. There is one other instance in Numbers where a person "came before" *(qārab lipnê)* Moses. That is the time when those who were unclean through contact with a corpse approached him. In both instances there is proximity, but not contact. Both the contaminated and the daughters of Zelophehad are to keep their distance.

What is the solution to an apparent conundrum? God's word is simple and direct. A new law is initiated. Inheritance may pass not only to sons, but also, where circumstances dictate, to daughters (v. 8), to brothers of the deceased (v. 9), to uncles of the deceased (v. 10), or to the nearest living relative (v. 11).

And this law is to become binding for future generations, rather than being a temporary measure (v. 11b). Note again the prospect of a guaranteed future. The census of chapter 26 anticipates occupation of the land of Palestine. The juridical innovation of chapter 27 likewise looks into the future with optimism.

The second half of the chapter deals with the commissioning of Joshua to succeed Moses (27:12–23). Its position at this point in Numbers is quite natural. The census detailed the second generation. The daughters of Zelophehad are the successors to their father. Moses too needs an heir, not biologically but functionally. The first generation will become casualties in the wilderness because of their sins. God has raised up a second generation to set foot on the land of promise. Similarly, the first leader will join the first generation outside of that land. Joshua is a new leader for a new generation.

The appointment of Joshua also serves as a guarantee, as did the census and the incident of Zelophehad's daughters, of where God is taking His people. Natural qualifications do not commend Joshua for the job. He is supernaturally prepared, for in him is the Spirit (v. 18).

It is worthy of note that Moses makes the suggestion to God about a successor (v. 16). His magnanimous spirit shows through in his concern that Israel not "be as sheep which have no shepherd" (v. 17). To the end, and even under divine judgment, his spirit remains pastoral. Might an indication of Moses' zeal be evidenced by the Lord's instruction to Moses to lay "your hand"—singular—upon Joshua (v. 18), to which Moses responded by laying "his hands"—plural—on Joshua (v. 23)?

A Religious Calendar and Vows (28–30)

The first two chapters of this unit describe *ad seriatim* the various offerings Israel is to give the Lord. In all, eight different occasions are highlighted. I shall list them in the left-hand column of Table 13, with their parallels from one of the other cultic calendars in the Pentateuch (Exod.

23:10–19; 34:18–24; Lev. 23:1–44; Deut. 16:1–17). See Table 13.

Israel's offerings to the Lord are to be in the form of animals, fine flour, oil, and wine. Numbers 28–29 provide us with an exact number of each, or quantity of each, that is to be given for the specific occasion. The sacrifices of animals are listed in Table 14.

The number of animals offered as whole burnt offerings outnumbers those offered as sin offerings in approximately a 40:1 ratio. In our studies of Leviticus we saw that the whole burnt offering, unlike the sin offering, is not primarily expiatory in purpose. Rather, it is an expression of praise and gratitude. This, then, earmarks the outstanding characteristic of Hebrew worship.

It is also interesting to observe that for the feast of tabernacles alone there is a specific number, and a decreasing number, of animals specified for each day. This one feast accounts for approximately 60 percent of the total of young bulls, 40 percent of the total of rams, and 36 percent of the total of goats.

Once again, as we have observed in the immediately preceding chapters, Numbers establishes policies for Israel to follow once she is settled in Palestine. The land will be divided (chap. 26), Joshua will be leader (chap. 27), and Israel's life will be permeated by worship (chap. 28–29).

It is of some interest that the thrice-noted "three times in the year shall all your males appear before the LORD God" in these calendars (Exod. 23:17; 34:23; Deut. 16:16) does *not* appear in Numbers 28–29 in its discussion of unleavened bread, Pentecost, and tabernacles. "Women's rights" have already been discussed in Numbers 27:1–11.

It is somewhat unexpected, therefore, to read in chapter 30, the last part of this unit, that a father may overrule an unmarried daughter's vows to the Lord (vv. 3–5). Similarly a husband may nullify the religious vows of his wife (vv. 6–8). The exception to this is the widow or the divor-

Table 13 Cultic Calendars

Numbers 28–29		Exodus 23:10–19	Exodus 34:18–26	Leviticus 23:1–44	Deuteronomy 16:1–17
1. 28:3–8	daily offering	(29:38–42)			
2. 28:9–10	Sabbath offering	12*	21*	1–3*	
3. 28:11–15	offering at first of month				
4. 28:16–25	offering at Passover and unleavened bread	15	18–20, 25	5–8	1–8
5. 28:26–31	offering at Pentecost (weeks/first fruits)	16a	22a, 26	15–22	9–12
6. 29:1–6	offering at new year			23–25	
7. 29:7–11	offering on Day of Atonement			26–32	
8. 29:12–38	offering at tabernacles	16b	22b	33–36, 39–43	13–15

*No offering is prescribed. The Sabbath observance is enjoined.

Table 14*

Occasion	Frequency per year	Type of offering: Whole Burnt — Young Bulls	Whole Burnt — Rams	Whole Burnt — Male Lambs	Sin — Goats
1. Daily					
morning	365			1	
evening	365			1	
2. Sabbath	52			2	
3. First of month	12	2	1	7	1
4. Unleavened bread	7	2	1	7	1
5. Pentecost	1	2	1	7	1
6. New Year's	1	1	1	7	1
7. Day of Atonement	1	1	1	7	1
8. Tabernacles	1				
Day one		13	2	14	1
Day two		12	2	14	1
Day three		11	2	14	1
Day four		10	2	14	1
Day five		9	2	14	1
Day six		8	2	14	1
Day seven		7	2	14	1
Day eight		1	1	7	1
Annual totals		113	37	1,093	30

*Table is based on the work of Anson Rainey, "The Order of Sacrifices in Old Testament Ritual Texts," *Biblica* (1970): 492–493. Used by permission. I have changed the totals for the columns regarding rams and male lambs.

cée (v. 9), but only if the vow was made after the divorce or the husband's decease (vv. 10ff.).

There is one thing in the woman's favor. The husband or father must respond negatively, if he chooses to do so, on the very day he hears about his wife's or daughter's vow (vv. 5, 8, 12, 14). To delay a response to some time later means that the man becomes vicariously culpable: "he shall bear her iniquity" (v. 15).

Concluding Events in Moab (31–36)

I will briefly note the last events covered in Numbers. The first item is God's command to conduct a holy war against Midian (chap. 31), as retaliation for the latter's seduction of Israel into acts of harlotry and idolatry. The reason is that the Lord's "vengeance" may be displayed against Midian (31:2–3). "Vengeance" does not mean revenge or pique, but rather the legitimate expression of divine authority when that authority is challenged.[14] Two major concerns dominate this chapter. One is the concern for the ritual purity of the soldiers (vv. 19–24, 50), a concentrated theme in different contexts in Numbers. A second concern is that a percentage of the spoil taken in war is to go to both the sanctuary and the Levites (vv. 25–54), with the soldiery contributing .2 percent of their share, and the rest 2 percent of their share.

The second subunit is chapter 32. Various territories east of the Jordan are alloted to Reuben, Gad, and half of the tribe of Manasseh, with the proviso that they assist the other tribes in the conquest of Canaan. If Canaan is to be taken, all of God's people must participate. There is no room for spectators, only for soldiers.

The third subunit is chapter 33, a stage-by-stage description (at least vv. 1–49) of Israel's itinerary from Egypt to the plains of Moab. This is one chapter whose orientation is principally toward the past, and as such, it is surrounded by materials whose orientation is principally toward the future. True, the chapter is narrated without commentary or homiletical addenda, but the facts speak for themselves. The God who guided will guide. But this must not encourage complacency in the people; thus the concluding exhortation in verses 50–56.

The fourth subunit is chapter 34. It describes the boundaries of the Promised Land (vv. 1–15), and identifies the individuals who are to oversee the division of the land among the tribes (vv. 16–29). This is all rather irrelevant

14. See Mendenhall's discussion of this concept in *The Tenth Generation*, chapter 3, and especially p. 99 for Numbers 31:2–3.

for Moses. He will play no part in this. His successor has already been selected. Yet it is he who transmits the divine instructions. He is still leader!

The fifth subunit is chapter 35. Once in Canaan the Israelites are to set up forty-eight Levitical cities (vv. 1–8), and six cities of refuge (vv. 9–15) to which the manslayer may flee to escape blood revenge (vv. 16–34; see also Exod. 21:13). Once again, the ultimate concern voiced here is that of purity and holiness. If God's regulations on the taking of life are not enforced the land will be polluted (v. 33) and defiled (v. 34).

The last subunit is chapter 36 which deals with potential problems when the family inheritance goes not to an heir but to an heiress. What if she marries outside her tribe (v. 3)? As in chapter 27 (giving their father's inheritance to the daughters of Zelophehad), a new law is formulated to meet this contingency. Tribal intermarriage is to be denied to a woman if she is an heiress (vv. 6–8). Subsequently, the daughters of Zelophehad are held up as paragons of obedience (vv. 10–12), a refreshing change from many of the lackluster and sorry models we have encountered thus far, and on this positive note Numbers concludes.

Bibliography

Chapters 20:22—21:35

Bartlett, J. R. "Conquest of Sihon's Kingdom: A Literary Re-examination." *JBL* 97 (1978): 347–351.

______. "Historical Reference of Numbers XXI: 27–30." *PEQ* 101 (1969): 94–100.

______. "Sihon and Og of the Amorites." *VT* 20 (1970): 257–277.

Borass, R. S. "Of Serpents and Gods." *Dialog* 17 (1978): 273–279.

Christensen, D. L. "Num 21:14–15 and the Book of the Wars of Yahweh." *CBQ* 36 (1974): 359–360.

Coats, G. W. "Conquest Traditions in the Wilderness Theme." *JBL* 95 (1976): 177–190.

———. *Rebellion in the Wilderness: The Murmuring Motif in the Wilderness Traditions of the Old Testament*. Nashville: Abingdon, 1968, pp. 115–124.

Culley, R. C. *Studies in the Structure of Hebrew Narrative. Semeia* Supplements. Philadelphia: Fortress, 1976, pp. 102–104.

Fretheim, T. E. "Life In The Wilderness." *Dialog* 17 (1978): 266–272.

Gunn, D. M. " 'Battle Report'; Oral or Scribal Convention?" *JBL* 93 (1974): 513–518.

Joines, K. R. *Serpent Symbolism in the Old Testament: A Linguistic, Archaeological, and Literary Study*. Haddonfield, NJ: Haddonfield House, 1974.

Van Seters, J. "The Conquest of Sihon's Kingdom: A Literary Examination." *JBL* 91 (1972): 182–197.

———. "Once Again—The Conquest of Sihon's Kingdom." *JBL* 99 (1980): 117–119.

———. "Oral Patterns or Literary Conventions in Biblical Narrative." *Semeia* 5 (1976): 139–154.

Vaux, R. de. *The Early History of Israel*. Philadelphia: Westminster, 1978, pp. 551–567.

Yohanan, A. "Nothing Early and Nothing Late: Re–writing Israel's Conquest." *BA* 39 (1976): 55–76, esp. pp. 71–73.

Chapters 22–24

Albright, W. F. "The Oracles of Balaam." *JBL* 63 (1944): 207–233.

———. "Balaam." *EncJud* 4 (1971): 121–123.

Coats, G. W. "Balaam: Sinner or Saint?" *BRes* 17 (1972): 21–29.

Craigie, P. C. "The Conquest and Early Hebrew Poetry." *TB* 20 (1969): 76–94.

Hoftijzer, J. "Prophet Balaam in a 6th Century Aramaic Inscription." *BA* 39 (1976): 11–17.

Kaufmann, Y. *The Religion of Israel*. Translated by Moshe Greenberg. Chicago: University of Chicago Press, 1960, pp. 84–91.

Long, B. O. "Two Question and Answer Schemata in the Prophets." *JBL* 90 (1971): 129–139.

Lust, J. "Balaam, An Ammonite." *ETL* 54 (1978): 60–61.

Rad, G. von. *Moses*. New York: Association Press, 1960, pp. 71–80.

Seerveld, C. G. *Balaam's Apocalyptic Prophecies: A Study in Reading Scripture*. Toronto: Wedge Publishing Foundation, 1980.

Smick, E. B. "A Study of the Structure of the Third Balaam Oracle." In *The Law and the Prophets*. In honor of O. T. Allis. Edited by John H. Skilton. Nutley, NJ: Presbyterian and Reformed, 1974, pp. 242–252.

Tosato, A. "The Literary Structure of the First Two Poems of Balaam." *VT* 29 (1979): 98–106.

Westermann, C. *Blessing in the Bible and the Life of the Church*. Overtures to Biblical Theology series. Edited by Walter Brueggemann and John R. Donahue. Translated by Keith R. Crim. Philadelphia: Fortress, 1978, pp. 49–53.

Wifall, W. R. "Asshur and Eber, or Asher and Ḥeber? A Commentary on the last Balaam oracle, Num 24:21–24." *ZAW* 82 (1970): 110–114.

Zannoni, A. E. "Balaam: International Seer/wizard Prophet." *StLukeJ* 22 (1978): 5–19.

Chapter 25

Mendenhall, G. E. *The Tenth Generation: The Origins of the Biblical Tradition*. Baltimore: John Hopkins Press, 1973, pp. 105–121.

Reif, S. C. "What Enraged Phinehas? A Study of Numbers 25:8." *JBL* 90 (1971): 200–206.

Stern, E. "Phinehas." *EncJud* 13 (1971): 465–467.

Van Unnik, W. C. "Josephus' Account of the Story of Israel's Sin with Alien Women in the Country of Midian." In *Travels in the World of the Old Testament: Studies presented to professor M. A. Beek on the occasion of his 65th birthday*. Edited by M. S. H. G. Heerma van Voss, P. H. J. Houwink ten Cate, and N. A. van Uchelen. Assen: Van Gorcum, 1974, pp. 241–261.

Vaux, R. de. *The Early History of Israel*. Philadelphia: Westminster, 1978, pp. 568–570.

Chapters 26–27

Coats, G. W. "Legendary Motifs in the Moses Death Reports." *CBQ* 39 (1977): 34–44.

Snaith, N. H. "The Daughters of Zelophehad." *VT* 16 (1966): 124–127.

Chapters 28–30

Fisher, L. R. "Literary Genres in the Ugaritic Texts." In *Ras Shamra Parallels*. Edited by L. R. Fisher, Rome: Pontifical Biblical Institute, 1975, vol. 2, pp. 131–152.

———. "New Ritual Calendar from Ugarit." *HTR* 63 (1970): 485–501.

Kraus, H. J. *Worship in Israel*. Richmond: John Knox, 1966, pp. 35ff.

Chapters 31–36

Chapter 32

Vaux, R. de. *Ancient Israel*, vol. 2, *Religious Institutions*. New York: McGraw-Hill, 1965, pp. 366–367.

Chapter 33

Davies, G. I. "The Wilderness Itineraries. A Comparative Study." *TB* 25 (1974): 46–81.

———. *The Way of the Wilderness. A Geographical Study of the Wilderness Itineraries in the Old Testament*. Cambridge: Cambridge University Press, 1979.

Chapter 35

Greenberg, M. "Avenger of Blood." In *IDB* 1, p. 321.

———. "City of Refuge." In *IDB* 1, pp. 638–639.

———. "Idealism and Practicality in Numbers 35:4–5 and Ezekiel 48." *JAOS* 88 (1968): 59–66.

———. "Levitical Cities." *EncJud* 11 (1971): 136–138.

Vaux, R. de. *Ancient Israel*, vol. 2, *Religious Institutions*. New York: McGraw-Hill, 1965, pp. 366–367.

Part FIVE

Deuteronomy

19

Remember the Past

Deuteronomy 1:1—4:40

Qoheleth was certainly accurate when he said, "of making many books there is no end" (Eccles. 12:12). Had Qoheleth had access only to studies about Deuteronomy, he would not have had to revise or retract his statement. Compared with work that has been done, for example, on Leviticus or Numbers, the research on Deuteronomy has been enormous.

Analyses of Deuteronomy

In relationship to the rest of the Pentateuch, Deuteronomy is considered something of an oddity. For one thing, so the suggestion goes, its theology and the themes it sounds are distinctly different from its Pentateuchal neighbors. The kerygma of the Deuteronomist is, therefore, to be seen as a part of the theology of the Pentateuch, but is not to be considered as representative of the whole. It becomes understandable, then, why one encounters articles about themes in Genesis through Numbers adjacent to those about themes in Deuteronomy and Deuteronomic literature. Or perhaps the reader will encounter preaching and proclamation commentaries on only Genesis through Numbers in one volume.

The Documentary Hypothesis

Part of the reason for considering Deuteronomy apart from the rest of the Pentateuch is due to several points of the documentary hypothesis. One of the basic tenets of this theory is that the hypothetical sources J, E, and P are to be found in an amalgamated fashion throughout Genesis to Numbers. But nothing of D has intruded into these four biblical books. Conversely, nothing of J, E, and P has made its way into the text of Deuteronomy.

This latter point in no way suggests that the Book of Deuteronomy is viewed as a homogeneous unit by the critical exegetes. Quite the contrary. In only two areas of Deuteronomic studies is there anything that approaches unanimity. One of these "assured results" is that Deuteronomy is not the work of Moses, although "Mosaic elements" may surface here and there. Scholars conclude this, in spite of the fact that Deuteronomy, of all the books of the Pentateuch, claims most adamantly to be the work of Moses; for example, "and Moses wrote this law" (31:9).[1] The Pentateuch is replete with instances of Moses speaking, but references to scribal activities are minimal.

Let it be observed that defenders of partial, substantial, or ultimate Mosaic authorship are not lacking. These writers include Protestant conservative scholars such as P. C. Craigie, R. K. Harrison, K. A. Kitchen, M. Kline, G. T. Manley, S. J. Schultz, and J. A. Thompson, all of whom are referred to in the bibliography. They are joined by Jewish writers such as J. H. Hertz and more recently M. H. Segal.[2] Along similar lines, Max Margolis suggested that Josiah's "Book of the Law," to be fully intelligible, must have included not only Deuteronomy but also Exodus through Numbers, a legitimate observation that is counter to the trend of twentieth-century scholarship about Deu-

1. See also Moshe Weinfeld, "Deuteronomy," *EncJud* 5 (1971), p. 1574.

2. Hertz, "Deuteronomy: Its Antiquity and Mosaic Authorship," in *Journal of the Transactions of the Victoria Institute*, 72 (1940): 88–103; Segal, "The Composition of the Pentateuch—A Fresh Examination," in *Scripta Hierosolymitana* 8 (1961): 68–114, especially 110–112.

teronomy.[3] Substantially the same point is made by Cyrus H. Gordon.[4]

The second area of consensus, one that is related to the question of authorship, is the heterogeneous nature of the book. That is, Deuteronomy grew by stages and underwent editorial revisions until it reached the final form in which it is now preserved in our Bibles. A corollary of this has been the attempt to identify, if possible, what precisely constituted "Ur-deuteronomy," the original nucleus to which the additions were appended. Those who have addressed themselves to this issue have usually settled on chapters 5–26 and 28 as the kernel. Few authors have attempted to deal with the significance of the "final form" of Deuteronomy—how the parts relate to each other and to the whole—but perhaps the writings of Brevard Childs and Robert Polzin (see the bibliography) are reflective of a new trend in studies of Deuteronomy, be that through canonical criticism (Childs) or structural analysis (Polzin).

Modern surveys of studies in the history of Scripture usually identify the early-nineteenth-century scholar W. M. L. De Wette as the forerunner of current analyses. His work on Deuteronomy, the exact conclusions of which are accepted by hardly any scholar today, paved the way for a host of biblical specialists to follow. And the issue is far from settled. It is fashionable for a writer to say, after he has outlined "the current issues," that no final conclusion has been reached. As far as Deuteronomy is concerned, it is difficult to perceive that there will ever be a final conclusion on matters of date, authorship, and provenance.

De Wette's analysis of Deuteronomy was as follows. Deuteronomy was written *after* the reforms of the Judean

3. *Hebrew Scriptures in the Making* (Philadelphia: Jewish Publication Society, 1922), pp. 102ff.

4. *The Ancient Near East* (New York: Norton, 1965), p. 150, and *The Common Background of Greek and Hebrew Civilizations* (New York: Norton, 1965), p. 293.

king Josiah (late seventh century B.C.). Some individuals, sympathetic to the Josianic reforms (for example, cult centralization), penned Deuteronomy—using Moses as an alias and the plains of Moab as the fictional setting—and conveniently placed it in the temple ruins. There it was discovered by those repairing the temple and subsequently "baptized" and "justified" the agenda of Josiah. For after all, was not Josiah implementing Moses' words and laws, standards that had been dormant for centuries?

This theory spawned the famous phrase that Deuteronomy essentially is "a pious fraud." According to this theory, it is pious in the sense that it attempted to provide historical precedent for religious reform. It is fraudulent in the sense that the whole book was artificially produced, akin to Hitler's chaplains writing a book—using an apostolic name—that reeked with anti-Jewish rhetoric and then placing it in one of the confessional booths of Notre Dame before the invasion of France.

More recent critics have attempted to soften De Wette's view. Whether they have softened that view, or simply revised it, is in my opinion debatable. For instance, for the last several years Moshe Weinfeld has insisted, in various publications, that Deuteronomy—contra P—reflects a trend toward humanism and secularization. By this he does "not refer to an atheistic trend or to any opposition to religion or religious institutions, but to a general tendency to free religious institutions and ways of thinking from strict adherence to the rules of taboo, etc., and thus to give them a more secular appearance."[5] Nevertheless, De Wette's "pious" Deuteronomy has become Weinfeld's "humanistic" Deuteronomy.

It would be unfair to modern scholars to suggest they have maintained De Wette's hypothesis. In their views, by

5. Weinfeld's own redefinition and defense of his position in *IEJ* 23 (1973), p. 230.

and large, the only thing counterfeit about Deuteronomy is the contention that the historical recitations, hymns, and laws were spoken and reduced to writing by Moses in the plains of Moab after thirty-eight years in the wilderness, sometime in the thirteenth century B.C. Granting the spurious nature of this alone, the critics were willing to grant authenticity to Deuteronomy.

Julius Wellhausen (*Prolegomena to the History of Israel*, 1885), as much as anyone, gave Deuteronomy a new anchor. His exposition of documentary sources in the Pentateuch was to become definitive and classical. The foundation of Wellhausen's theory, on which every other tenet might be constructed, was the intrinsic connection of Deuteronomy and Josiah's reform, a connection that led to Wellhausen's conclusion that Deuteronomy (chaps. 12–26 anyway) was written just prior to the reforms, that is, around 622 B.C.

So important for his overall source theory did Wellhausen consider the dating of Deuteronomy that he labeled it "the fulcrum" of his literary reconstruction of the Pentateuch. The year 622 B.C. became for Wellhausen what the Ḥijrah of A.D. 622 became for Muslims, the first fixed date in Islamic history. As for the Muslim, for whom everything is either ante-Ḥijrah or post-Ḥijrah, so for Wellhausen, scripturally speaking, everything is either ante-Deuteronomy or post-Deuteronomy.

It is safe to say that nearly all higher-critical scholars accept Wellhausen's dating of Deuteronomy in the seventh century B.C. The departure from classical Wellhausianism would be the suggestion that some parts of Deuteronomy antedate the seventh century B.C., and were later added to Ur-deuteronomy. (A further departure is reflected by those scholars who, on exegetical grounds, would reverse Wellhausen's view and date P *before* D, not after D, as did Wellhausen. See, for example, the writings of Yehezkel Kaufmann and his student Weinfeld.)

Although, as I have said, a majority of scholars place Deuteronomy's composition in the seventh century B.C., the routes they have followed in reaching that conclusion have been varied and sundry.

To begin with, there are commentators who think that Deuteronomy had its origin in the northern Israelite community, and not in Judah at all. This is the interpretation of the celebrated nestor of studies in Deuteronomy, the late Gerhard von Rad. His basic observation was that Deuteronomy is more sermonic than it is anything else. Even the laws, and the way they were promulgated, would be more appropriate in the pulpit than in the courtroom. Who would be the most likely group of homileticians who could blend historical recitation and exhortation? In von Rad's view it was the northern Levites. It was they who brought these traditions with them to southern Judah after Israel's demise at the hands of the Assyrians in 721 B.C. In cooperation with some concerned layman, seventh-century Levites, living in Judah, "produced" Deuteronomy in the hopes of providing a stimulus for religious revival.

Very close to von Rad's view is that of E. W. Nicholson. He too posits the origin of Deuteronomy in the north, but with this difference. The authors of Deuteronomy are not the Levites but representatives of the northern prophetic groups who also fled to the south after the Assyrian takeover in the north. As for an actual time for composition, Nicholson suggests the reign of Manasseh, the grandfather of Josiah. The idea behind this suggestion is that reform movements, as reflected in Deuteronomy, are spawned on the heels of periods of debauchery and immorality, eras in which there are not even traces of religious zeal. The reign of Manasseh meets that qualification nicely. Thus, out of the murkiness emerges either a Levitical or prophetical Martin Luther.

On the other side of the coin are those scholars who fully agree with the dating of Deuteronomy to the seventh century. Their distinction, however, is their emphatic point that Deuteronomy originated in the south, not in the north. It is Judean, not Israelite.

Most prolific in their writings have been the German Jesuit Norbert Lohfink, and the Jewish scholar Weinfeld, both of whom see the language of Deuteronomy as having more affinities with court language and wisdom language than with any other. Hence, the Judean or Jerusalemic background of the book.

For Lohfink, Deuteronomy, which was composed in several stages, functioned first as an underground text, a voice of protest against a growing Assyrian hegemony over Judah that went back at least as far as Hezekiah's father Ahaz. For it was Ahaz who gave the order to build an Assyrian-like altar for the Jerusalem temple (II Kings 16:10–16). The reaction of Judah to this upheaval was culture shock.[6] Deuteronomy represents part of this reaction. Only under Josiah did Deuteronomy begin to assume the status of official law. It also legitimated the independence movement of Josiah (a return to De Wette?).

Weinfeld produced a most original and provocative treatment of Deuteronomy with *Deuteronomy and the Deuteronomic School*.[7] His position is that Deuteronomy was written by sages and scribes who were connected with the royal house of Judah from the time of Hezekiah to that of Josiah. For further evidence to buttress his position, Weinfeld claimed that the composition of Deuteronomy was influenced by the literary model of seventh-century B.C. Assyrian state treaties, particularly the treaty between Esarhaddon, king of Assyria (680–669 B.C.), and his eastern vassals. Who, then, in Judah would be more informed about such models than the narrow circle of scribes within the court?

6. "Culture Shock and Theology," *BTB* 7 (1977), pp. 12–21.
7. (Oxford: Clarendon Press, 1972).

One of Weinfeld's key observations was born out of his comparison between the legal sections of Deuteronomy and the counterparts in the rest of the Pentateuch. For example, observing that Deuteronomy permits profane slaughter—"you may slaughter and eat flesh within any of your towns" (12:15, 21), unlike Leviticus 17:1–9, which legislates that animals for food be sacrificed at the sanctuary—he concluded that Deuteronomy is reflective of a seventh-century trend to secularization and demythologization.

It appears that Weinfeld's treatment of Deuteronomy is suspect on three grounds. In the first place, a good case can be made for the fact that the literary structure of Deuteronomy parallels more closely the second-millennium B.C. covenants than it does the first-millennium B.C. covenants. To illustrate, the later covenantal forms, unlike the earlier ones, lack a historical prologue and a listing of promised blessings (to match the threatened curses). Deuteronomy possesses both of these phenomena.

A second criticism challenges the wisdom influence on Deuteronomy which Weinfeld claims to have seen. Why, for example, if the hand of the scribes and sages is so evident in Deuteronomy, is there no legislation covering their activities, as there is for the king, prophet, and judge? Why would they omit themselves? Again, if Deuteronomy is the work of the sapientialists, how did they usurp the authority to write Torah literature, and was this control retained in the second temple period, or did it revert to the priests?[8]

Third, are the differences between the laws of Deuteronomy and the counterparts to be explained as a movement toward secularization? Scholars embracing the traditional interpretation of Deuteronomy would explain the

8. See further the insights at this point in the review by A. Rofé in *ChrNIsr* 24 (1974), pp. 204–209.

differences as necessitated by a change from a wilderness and nomadic milieu to that of a territorial and sedentary milieu. That is, the differences are to be explained chronologically, not sociologically, as Weinfeld has done.

But even apart from this contention it can be demonstrated that Deuteronomy moves in precisely the opposite direction from secularization. For example, Deuteronomy reminds Israel that she already *is* holy (7:6; 14:2, 21). By contrast, Leviticus lays holiness before Israel as a goal, "You shall be holy" (Lev. 19:2). Again, it is in Deuteronomy alone that the priest functions beyond the temple area. He accompanies the troops into battle as a chaplain (20:1–4). He sits on a supreme tribunal to hear cases of homicide and assault (17:8–13), and thus assumes a new judicial role not specified for him elsewhere.[9]

Having briefly examined some current ideas about Deuteronomy's place of origin, authorship, and raison d'être, we see that there is anything but a consensus. It is unlikely that a monograph will ever appear that will silence all contrary views. For some this is the genius of biblical scholarship. It is a scientific discipline in which one can speak only about the current state of knowledge. For others, such a smorgasbord of opinions reduces biblical scholarship to an exercise in novelty. Concerning Deuteronomy, there are really only two options on the issues—either the classical position, or some form of De Wette *redivivus*.

The Traditional View

On what grounds does the classical position rest? To begin with, there is the claim of Deuteronomy itself, such as, "These are the words that Moses spoke to all Israel beyond the Jordan" (1:1); "Moses undertook to explain

9. See further the rebuttal by Jacob Milgrom, *IEJ* 23 (1973): 156–161, and the counter-rebuttal by Weinfeld, *IEJ* 23 (1973): 230–233.

this law saying" (1:5); or, "And Moses wrote this law" (31:9). Such statements must either be accepted as authentic or dismissed as spurious.

The New Testament also pairs Deuteronomy and Moses. Jesus refers to Moses' law on divorce (Matt. 19:8 and Deut. 24:1–4). Paul speaks of the muzzled ox in the "law of Moses" (I Cor. 9:9 and Deut. 25:4). The anonymous author of Hebrews mentions the "law of Moses" about the testimony of witnesses at a trial (Heb. 10:28 and Deut. 17:2–6). These Mosaic references agree with the Talmudic witness (*Baba Bathra* 14b–15a) about Deuteronomy.

What is to be done with such references? For the higher critics they are meaningless and irrelevant. These references are dismissed immediately for, so goes the argument, Jesus—and the others—are not making a historical judgment, but rather are making a concession to the traditional beliefs of the time. We would be led to believe, then, that either Jesus knew Deuteronomy was Josianic, but chose not to raise this ancillary issue lest it lead Him and His audience away from the subject at hand, or nineteenth- and twentieth-century biblical scholarship has made Jesus look silly, a child of His times, whenever He cited historical sources. Another reason that the witness of post-Old Testament literature must be ignored is that if such a witness is valid it means that a substantial percentage of the modern work done on Deuteronomy would be discredited, and multiple theories would have to be laid to rest.

Third, many evangelical writers, especially Kline and Kitchen, have made a strong case for the fact that the literary structure of Deuteronomy resembles most closely that of second-millennium B.C. political treaties between suzerain and vassal. These are from Hittite archives, and the structural items include title or preamble (equivalent to Deut. 1:1–5); historical prologue (Deut. 1:6—4:49); stipulations, both general (Deut. 5–11) and specific (Deut. 12–26); blessings for obedience and curses for disobedience (Deut. 27–28); deposit of the text in a place accessible to the vassal (Deut. 31:26), and periodic public reading (Deut. 31:9–13); the presence of witnesses for ratification (Deut. 30:19; 31:19, 26).

Not all writers are predisposed, however, to say this settles the issue. For Weinfeld, as we have seen, the parallels with first-millennium B.C. treaties are more inviting. George E. Mendenhall, the first to point out the identical sequence in nonbiblical and biblical treaties, has not suggested, thereby, that Deuteronomy is essentially a Mosaic piece of work. Reflective of how tenaciously some refuse to surrender a late date for Deuteronomy is the quote in Craigie from K. Baltzer: "it remains however, a striking and historically unexplained fact that the Old Testament resembles most closely the highly developed formulary of the Hittite treaty."[10]

W. F. Albright has observed, with documentation, that in the seventh century B.C. there was throughout the Middle East a nostalgic turn to the past.[11] Judah was no exception, as reflected in a Josianic Deuteronomy that recalled the golden days of Moses. For that reason, Albright has no problem dating "late" books such as Job and Proverbs that are filled with linguistic parallels to Canaanite literature produced six to nine hundred years earlier. If indeed there was a revival of Canaanite literature during the seventh century, then to be consistent we would have to maintain that there was a revival of Hittite treaty forms at the same time.

A fourth pillar in the evangelical position is an alternate

10. *The Book of Deuteronomy*, New International Commentary of the Old Testament series (Grand Rapids: Eerdmans, 1976), p. 26, n. 23.

11. *From the Stone Age to Christianity: Monotheism and the Historical Process*, second edition (New York: Doubleday, 1957), pp. 314ff.

explanation to the laws of Exodus 21–23 that appear again in Deuteronomy 12–26. I shall discuss some of these later, but such amplifications, as found in Deuteronomy, are necessitated by the shift from Israel in the wilderness to Israel now about to be settled permanently in Canaan. This is at least as plausible as the explanation that the laws in Deuteronomy are adaptations to the monarchic period.

Fifth, one may challenge the contention that one of the main themes in Deuteronomy is centralization of worship, and thus a product of the time of Hezekiah and Josiah.[12] Rather, Deuteronomy's main theme is an opposition to idolatry, a sin on which no chronological period has a monopoly. Does it not seem probable that if Deuteronomy wanted to reinforce the point of centralization, that somewhere "the place which the LORD your God will choose" (Deut. 12:5) would be identified as Jerusalem? In fact, Jerusalem is *never* mentioned in the book. Does this absence mean that Deuteronomy was reduced to writing before Jerusalem assumed prominence, or does Deuteronomy reflect the northern provenance of Proto-Deuteronomy, or does the absence of the name lend "a certain timelessness to a theology of place"?[13]

Lastly, a word may be said about the common ideas in Deuteronomy and the prophets Hosea and Isaiah, especially the former. Weinfeld devotes a whole appendix to affinities between Deuteronomy and Hosea.[14] When A resembles B, did B take his material from A or vice versa? Or did both have access to the same tradition? Ostensibly any of the three could be cogently argued, but certain factors suggest that Deuteronomy was the source from

12. G. T. Manley, *The Book of the Law: Studies in the Date of Deuteronomy* (Grand Rapids: Eerdmans, 1957), pp. 122–136.

13. John F. X. Sheehan, *Let the People Cry Amen!* (New York: Paulist Press, 1977), p. 61.

14. Weinfeld, *Deuteronomy and the Deuteronomic School*, pp. 366–370.

which Hosea the northern prophet drew his emphases and even phraseology.[15]

The Deuteronomic History

Biblical scholars recognize the late Martin Noth for his seminal studies of the Deuteronomic history. This particular term, as used by Noth and others, designates the books of Joshua, Judges, I and II Samuel, I and II Kings, and limited parts of Deuteronomy, specifically chapters 1–4 and perhaps 29 and 30. It is suggested that these are a theological treatise, written most likely by one person, around the time of the exile, about 550 B.C. Its purpose is to explain to those dispersed from their land why the exile happened. And the explanation offered is informed by the religious emphases of Ur-deuteronomy (chaps. 5–26, 28).

Specifically, Noth suggested that the Deuteronomist produced his work in order to inform both the exiled Judeans and the motley group left in Judah (those who had escaped either execution or deportation) that what had happened in 587 B.C. had happened because of their disobedience to God and His covenantal demands. What had just transpired was the manifestation of covenant curse on covenant disobedience. After all, was not this the negative side of Ur-deuteronomy's theology: obedience leads to blessing, disobedience leads to curse?

As far as Noth interpreted the evidence, he failed to see any hope in the narration of this large portion of Scripture he labeled the Deuteronomic history. As such, the Deuteronomist represents the quintessence of morbidity. His role would be akin to that of a rabbi in the 1940s and

15. See Manley, *The Book of the Law*, pp. 143–145, and F. R. McCurley, Jr., "The Home of Deuteronomy Revisited: A Methodological Analysis of the Northern Theory" in *A Light unto My Path: Old Testament Studies in Honor of Jacob M. Myers*. Edited by Howard N. Bream et al. Gettysburg Theological Studies, no. 4 (Philadelphia: Temple University Press, 1974), pp. 298–302.

1950s fulminating against European Jewry who survived the genocidal pogroms of the Third Reich. What had happened to European Jewry had happened because they had been unfaithful to God. No word of hope is offered, only unmitigated gloom.

More recent studies of the Deuteronomic history have attempted to salvage some positive emphases within that history. All is not gloom or hopelessness. In the midst of the Deuteronomist's articulation of history he reminds his audience that God is good, He can be trusted even by a landless people (Walter Brueggemann); and He summons the bewildered and the exiled to repent and return to Him (Hans W. Wolff).

It must be admitted that the whole idea of a Deuteronomic history, as reconstructed by Noth et al., is plausible and possible. It is not as easy to say that the reconstruction is probable. For one thing, we are reminded by D. N. Freedman that "in the last analysis, however, it must be admitted that DH is not a given part of the Hebrew Bible as we have it; this caution must be kept in mind throughout."[16]

Equally reasonable as the theory of an exilic composition is the idea of a thirteenth-century B.C. Deuteronomy—which the book specifically underlines. This is followed by Joshua, the events described therein being reduced to writing any time between the death of the one after whom the book is named and the days of the early monarchy. The whole book would serve as an impressive illustration of the blessings of God that come on the heels of the life of commitment and God-honoring living. There is no generation that does not need to hear that, and be reminded of that, be they newcomers, old, or the dispossessed.

By contrast the Book of Judges would make clear to these relative newcomers, or pioneers, the consequences

16. "Deuteronomic History, the," in *IBDSuppl*, p. 226.

of the attempt to evade the will of God. And so we could continue through Kings.

Finally, we may question the validity of the concept of a peculiar Deuteronomic theology that applies to only one part of the Old Testament, in contradistinction to other Old Testament theologies; and even granting the legitimacy of a distinctive Deuteronomic theology, why must such be only an exilic phenomenon? In terms of the first point, we need to note that probably all of the Old Testament is Deuteronomic. Is, for example, Chronicles diametrically different from Samuel and Kings in the theology it espouses when it deals with covenantal matters? Are not the patriarchal narratives informed by a Deuteronomic substratum?

As far as the second point is concerned, it is sufficient to say that Israel had no monopoly on Deuteronomism. Sentiments very close to some of those expressed in Deuteronomy can be found in Near Eastern literature in hymns, prayers, and wisdom texts that date from the third millennium to the first millennium B.C. This literature comes from Egypt, Mesopotamia, Asia Minor, and Canaan. To illustrate, writing about "the good life" in Mesopotamia, cuneiformist Thorkild Jacobsen can say, "the way of obedience, of service and worship is the way to achieve protection; and it is also the way to earthly success, to the highest values in Mesopotamian life: health and long life, honoured standing in the community, many sons, wealth."[17] Why must we assume that Israel produced a theological construct parallel to that of her neighbors, but a millennium or two later?

The Book of Deuteronomy plays a large role, a programmatic role, in all discussions of Deuteronomistic history. As far as the opening three or four chapters of Deuteronomy are concerned, it was Noth's contention that they

17. *Before Philosophy* (reprint ed. Baltimore: Penguin Books, 1964), p. 220.

were written not by the author of Deuteronomy, but by the author of the Deuteronomic history. As such, Deuteronomy 1–4 must be identified as "deuteronomistic." Deuteronomy 5ff. must be identified as "deuteronomic."

One of Noth's principal reasons for such a cleavage was that there are "two introductions" (chaps. 1–4 and chaps. 5–11) to Deuteronomy. A doublet in a biblical book, especially at the beginning, is always suspect. (Note how the first two chapters of Genesis have been scissored.)

In the last century Wellhausen, then the doyen of biblical studies, had suggested that chapters 1–4 and 5–11 were parallels, each from different editions of the book. Noth has suggested they are not parallels, but rather that chapters 5–11 are the real introduction to Deuteronomy. This has by and large been embraced by contemporary Old Testament scholars (although I am not aware of any commentary on Deuteronomy that starts with chapter 5).

Noth's attempt to divorce chapters 1–4 from 5–11 has three immediate effects. First, if the divorce is granted, then it becomes all but impossible and even extraneous to relate chapters 1–4 to the rest of Deuteronomy. It is placed where it is for convenience, but beyond that it plays only a minimal role for understanding the shape of Deuteronomy, being the orphan that it is.

Second, the removal of chapters 1–4 from the whole destroys the literary structure of Deuteronomy, which fits in toto almost perfectly the form of the second-millennium B.C. covenants. To wrench chapters 1–4 from their setting is to strip away the preamble (1:1–5) and the historical prologue with exhortations (1:6—4:40). In essence, then, Noth has taken a literary unit that structurally is usual and conforms to all Near Eastern analogues, and artificially has disunited it.

Third, this reconstruction, if valid, vitiates the book's own witness about its organization. The first thirty chapters represent three distinct speeches of Moses, each introduced by a distinct formula: "These are the words that Moses spoke to all Israel," 1:1 (and 1:5) for chapters 1:6—4:40; "And Moses summoned all Israel and said to them," 5:1 for chapters 5–28; "And Moses summoned all Israel and said to them," 29:2 for chapters 29–30 (or perhaps through 31:6). The rest of the book represents a collection of Moses' discourses, which are mostly poetic (chaps. 32–33), plus the description of several concluding events of Moses' life (31:7–29; 34:1–12).

Moses' First Speech (1:1—4:40)

The first speech of Moses, then, constitutes the first four chapters of Deuteronomy. Clearly it has two divisions within it: chapters 1–3, which are a historical review of Israel's odyssey beginning with her departure from Sinai, followed by her wilderness wanderings; and chapter 4, which is primarily an exhortation. So the orientation of chapters 1–3 is the past, framed in the indicative mood. The emphasis is on recollection. The orientation of chapter 4 is the present and the future, framed in the imperative mood, "give heed . . . do . . . go in . . . take possession." In chapters 1–3 Moses is panoramist; in chapter 4 he is preacher. The narrator becomes exhorter; the historian is also analyst.

We should observe that these words of Moses are addressed to "all Israel" (1:1). The significance of this phrase is underscored not only by its proliferation in Deuteronomy (fourteen times, eleven of which are in the framework sections), but also by the fact that the same phrase appears only two times in the rest of the Pentateuch, Exodus 18:25 and Numbers 16:34.[18] There is no one

18. J. W. Flanagan, "The deuteronomic meaning of the phrase *kol yíśrā'ēl*," *StRel* 6 (1976–77), p. 162.

who does not need to hear this divine word and then respond appropriately.

Reminiscence

In this speech, Moses recalled seven events:

1. 1:9–18 Moses' burdens are reduced by the appointment of judges who will function as assistants (cf. Exod. 18:13ff. and Num. 11:10ff.)
2. 1:19–46 The story of the spies sent out to gather data about the land of Canaan (cf. Num. 13 and 14)
3. 2:1–8a Israel's passage around the territory of Edom (cf. Num. 20:14–21)
4. 2:8b–25 Israel's passage through the territory of Moab (cf. Num. 21:4–20)
5. 2:26–37 Israel's victory over Sihon of Heshbon (cf. Num. 21:21–32)
6. 3:1–22 Israel's victory over Og of Bashan (cf. Num. 21:33–35) and the distribution of tribal territories east of the Jordan (cf. Num. 32)
7. 3:23–29 Moses' request to enter Canaan and the denial of permission (cf. Num. 27:12–14, although they are different incidents)

We note that the first and last items in the list deal with provisions that concern only the Israelites. In both instances, Moses' burdens will be lifted. Assistants will lighten his load. Not going beyond Pisgah will put the burden on someone else, namely, Joshua. Every other event deals with Israel's international relationships, either potential (3) or real (4–6).

It should be immediately observable that Moses' recall of the past is not merely repetitive. It is also interpretive. New insights are inserted. Earlier incidents may even be ignored. A quick look at the seven events of Deuteronomy 1–3 bears this out.

First, to be sure, Deuteronomy 1:9–18 is a blend of two earlier biblical events, one pre-Sinai (Exod. 18:13ff., and the only pre-Sinai event in this pericope; see especially Deut. 1:13–17), and one post-Sinai (Deut. 1:9–12; Num. 11:14–17). That being the case, we observe there is no hint in Deuteronomy about the role of Jethro, whose idea it was that Moses reduce his workload and parcel out the responsibilities, nor is there any reference to the Lord's word to Moses to choose seventy elders. In Numbers it is God who is the object of Moses' "I am not able to carry all this people alone" (Num. 11:14). In Deuteronomy it is the people who are the object of Moses' "At that time I said to you, 'I am not able to bear you' " (Deut. 1:9).

Second, the account about sending the spies, and their report, is substantially the same as that of Numbers 13–14. But the narration in Deuteronomy includes the intriguing observation that "The LORD was angry with me [i.e., Moses] also on your account, and said, 'You also shall not go in there' " (Deut. 1:37), a point that is reiterated in 3:26 and 4:21. Missing from Deuteronomy is Moses' great prayer of intercession that is recorded in Numbers 14:13–19.

Third, before Moses reached Edom he sent an advance group to the Edomites to obtain permission for passage. That permission was denied, and thus Israel was forced to circumvent Edom (Num. 20:14–21). Deuteronomy does not record the activities of an advance party or the denial of permission. What is novel here is God's command to make no militaristic moves against Edom, and also God's reference to the fact that He has apportioned the Edomites land, too (Deut. 2:5).

Fourth, the Lord gives a similar word to Israel about Moab, as recorded in Deuteronomy. Avoid military confrontation, for the Moabites too hold their land by right of Yahweh's allotment (Deut. 2:9). One can only wonder what was the effect psychologically on the Israelites on hearing that other nations besides themselves received their land from Israel's God. (Amos 9:7 suggests that the God of Israel not only brought Israel out of Egypt, but also directed other nations' exoduses as well.) Did such ideas inflate Israel or did they deflate Israel? One suspects the latter.

Fifth, in Israel's encounter with Sihon of Heshbon, Deuteronomy explains Sihon's refusal to grant Israel passage as due to the Lord hardening his heart (Deut. 2:30). He gave to Edomites, Moabites, and Ammonites land, but to Sihon He gave a hardened heart and spirit.

Sixth, the victory over Og of Bashan occupies eleven verses in Deuteronomy as compared with three verses in Numbers.

Seventh, in this last event we have a further notation about Moses the vicarious sufferer (Deut. 3:26, restatement of 1:37). And though he was afflicted, yet opened he not his mouth. Or did he? We need to take a second look at whether Deuteronomy and Numbers are as far apart in their respective explanations of why Moses was excluded from the land of promise as many of the commentators suggest. Does Numbers attach personal responsibility to Moses—"you did not believe in me" (20:12); "you rebelled against my word" (27:14)—while Deuteronomy exonerates Moses and pictures him as the one who, although innocent, has placed on him the penalty for the sins of others?

Are not the three passages in Deuteronomy (1:37; 3:26; 4:21) simply saying that Israel was Moses' stumbling block? Indeed it was precisely on account of their constant bickering and complaining that Moses was driven to his tantrum, and thus the divine condemnation. Note that 3:26, God's sentence of exclusion, is followed by the command to transfer authority to Joshua (3:28), precisely the sequence in Numbers 27:12–14, the sentence of exclusion, and verses 15–23, the transfer of authority to Joshua.

Exhortation

We have already observed the shift in chapter 4 to exhortation, and away from the exclusively historical reminiscences of chapters 1–3. But even within chapter 4 there is still some historical recital, evidenced by the reference to the incident at Baal-peor (v. 3; cf. Num. 25), and God's self-revelation at Sinai (vv. 9–14; cf. Exod. 19–20). This movement from recollection to appeal is further underscored by the frequent use of direct discourse in chapters 1–3 and indirect discourse in chapter 4.[19] Observe these times in the first three chapters when Moses quotes God directly: 1:6–8, 35–36, 37b–40, 42; 2:3–7, 9, 13, 18–19, 24–25, 31; 3:2, 26–28. In the following passages he quotes himself directly: 1:9–13, 16–17, 20–21, 29–31; 2:27–29; 3:18–22, 24–25. In the following passages he quotes the people directly: 1:14, 22, 25b, 27–28, 41a. By contrast, in chapter 4 Moses quotes God directly only in verse 10, and never quotes himself or the people in a past reference.

Moses' particular concern in this chapter is that the Israelites, once in Canaan, will find the temptation of idolatry irresistible (vv. 15–19, 23, 25). It is particularly interesting that when Moses lists the forms of graven images prohibited (vv. 16–19) his sequence is exactly the opposite of the creation sequence of Genesis 1—2:4a: male and female, beast and animal, bird, creeping things, fish, sun, moon, and stars, all the host of heaven.[20] For Israel to abandon her Lord and to engage in idolatry would so reverse His will for their lives. It would be a reversal equal to the undoing, the *bouleversement*, of God's creation.

Moses is also urging the Israelites not only to learn from prehistory and history, but also from *his* personal experience. Moses wants Israel to live (v. 1) although he him-

19. Robert Polzin, *Moses and the Deuteronomist: A Literary Study of the Deuteronomic History* (New York: Seabury, 1980), pp. 39–40.

20. Michael A. Fishbane, "Varia Deuteronomica," *ZAW* 84 (1972), p. 349.

self must die (v. 22). A fourth stimulus to obedience is the character of God. He is jealous, a devouring fire (v. 24).

A final basis for Moses' appeal for obedience is the threat of exile. The Lord who drove out nations before Israel (v. 38) will drive out Israel herself (v. 27). It is an accepted axiom of critical biblical studies that all references in Scripture to an exile of Israel presuppose that the writer of such passage lived after the Babylonian devastation of Judah and Jerusalem in 587 B.C. Gerhard von Rad's comment is illustrative: "it [4:25ff.] gives a clue for dating the whole, since this preacher knows already of the exile of 587."[21]

But this conclusion surely avoids the simple fact that Israel, except for a brief period of glory during David's time, lived perpetually under the shadow of neighbors much mightier than she, and hence, exile or loss of independence was always a possibility (witness the testimony of Judges!). Additionally, this hypothesis completely skirts the evidence from the second and first millennia B.C., in which we read of the capture of a place, followed by the deportation of its citizenry.[22] Must everything and anything predictive or prophetic in the Old Testament be reduced to a *vaticinium ex eventu*?

Threat, however, is never the ultimate word. Indeed God is jealous, a devouring fire (v. 24). There is no other besides Him (v. 35). He is heard, but not seen (v. 12). But He is also "merciful" and never "will fail you . . . or forget . . ." (v. 31). The conclusion to this great summons of Moses is a promise about "the land which the LORD your God gives you for ever" (v. 40).

And because He is merciful even the apostate and the

21. *Deuteronomy: A Commentary*, Old Testament Library (Philadelphia: Westminster, 1966), p. 50.

22. See the evidence collected by Kenneth A. Kitchen, "Ancient Orient, 'Deuteronomism,' and the Old Testament," in *New Perspectives on the Old Testament*, edited by J. Barton Payne (Waco, TX: Word Books, 1970), pp. 4–7.

exiled may "return" (v. 30) to Him. If the door to the reestablishment of communion with God is closed, it is man who insists on that, not God.

Bibliography

Commentaries and Monographs

Blenkinsopp, J. *Deuteronomy. The Book of the Covenant. A Scripture Discussion Outline*. London, 1968.

———. "Deuteronomy." In *The Jerome Biblical Commentary*. Englewood Cliffs, NJ: Prentice-Hall, 1969, part 1, pp. 101–122.

Carmichael, C. M. *The Laws of Deuteronomy*. Ithaca: Cornell University Press, 1974.

Childs, B. "Deuteronomy." In *Introduction to the Old Testament As Scripture*. Philadelphia: Fortress, 1979, pp. 202–225.

Clements, R. E. *God's Chosen People: A Theological Interpretation of the Book of Deuteronomy*. Valley Forge: Judson, 1969.

Craigie, P. C. *The Book of Deuteronomy*. New International Commentary of the Old Testament series. Grand Rapids: Eerdmans, 1976.

Cunliffe–Jones, H. *Deuteronomy*. Torch Bible Paperbacks. London: SCM Press, 1951.

Finkelstein, L. *Sifre on Deuteronomy*. New York: Ktav, 1969.

Harrison, R. K. *Introduction to the Old Testament*. Grand Rapids: Eerdmans, 1969, pp. 635–662.

Kaufmann, Y. *The Religion of Israel*. Translated by Moshe Greenberg. Chicago: University of Chicago Press, 1960, pp. 172–211.

Kitchen, K. A. *The Bible in Its World*. Downers Grove, IL: Inter-Varsity, 1979, pp. 79–85.

Kline, M. *Treaty of the Great King: The Covenant Structure of Deuteronomy*. Grand Rapids: Eerdmans, 1963.

Lohfink, N. "Deuteronomy." In *IDBSuppl*, pp. 229–232.

Manley, G. T. *The Book of the Law: Studies in the Date of Deuteronomy*. Grand Rapids: Eerdmans, 1957.

McCarthy, D. J. *Treaty and Covenant*. Second edition. Rome: Pontifical Biblical Institute, 1978.

Moran, W. L. "Deuteronomy." In *A New Catholic Commentary on Holy Scripture*. Camden, NJ: Thomas Nelson and Sons, 1969, pp. 256–276.

Nicholson, E. W. *Deuteronomy and Tradition*. Philadelphia: Fortress, 1967.

Phillips, A. C. *Deuteronomy*. Cambridge Bible Commentary. Cambridge: At the University Press, 1973.

Polzin, R. *Moses and the Deuteronomist: A Literary Study of the Deuteronomic History*. New York: Seabury, 1980.

Rad, G. von. *Deuteronomy: A Commentary*. Old Testament Library. Philadelphia: Westminster, 1966.

______. *Studies in Deuteronomy*. London: SCM Press, 1953.

______. "Deuteronomy." In *Old Testament Theology*. Translated by D. H. G. Stalker. 2 vols. New York: Harper and Row, 1962, vol. 1, pp. 219–231.

Schultz, S. J. *Deuteronomy*. Everyman's Bible Commentary series. Chicago: Moody, 1971.

Thompson, J. A. *Deuteronomy: An Introduction and Commentary*. Tyndale Old Testament Commentary. Downers Grove, IL: Inter-Varsity, 1978.

Weinfeld, M. "Deuteronomy." In *EncJud* 5 (1971): 1573–1583.

______. *Deuteronomy and the Deuteronomic School*. Oxford: Clarendon Press, 1972.

Wijngaards, J. N. M. *The Dramatization of Salvific History in the Deuteronomic School*. Leiden: E. J. Brill, 1969.

Wright, G. E. "Deuteronomy: Introduction." In *Interpreter's Bible*, vol. 2. Nashville: Abingdon, 1953, pp. 311–331.

Deuteronomy 1:1—4:40

Brueggemann, W. "The Kerygma of the Deuteronomistic Historian. Gospel for Exiles." *Intr* 22 (1968): 387–402.

Cazelles, H. "Passages in the singular within discourse in the plural of Dt 1–4." *CBQ* 24 (1967): 207–219.

Davies, G. I. "The Significance of Deut. 1:2 for the location of Mt. Horeb." *PEQ* 111 (1979): 87–101.

Fishbane, M. "Varia Deuteronomica." *ZAW* 84 (1972): 349–352.

Freedman, D. N. "Deuteronomic History, The." In *IDBSuppl*, pp. 226–228.

Kitchen, K. A. "Ancient Orient, 'Deuteronomism,' and the Old Testament." In *New Perspectives on the Old Testament*. Edited by J. Barton Payne. Waco, TX: Word Books, 1970, pp. 1–24.

Lilley, J. P. U. "By the river-side." *VT* 28 (1978): 165–171.

Lindars, B. "Torah in Deuteronomy." In *Words and Meanings: Essays presented to David Winton Thomas on his retirement from the Regius Professorship of Hebrew in the University of Cambridge*. Edited by Peter R. Ackroyd and Barnabas Lindars. London: Cambridge University Press, 1968, pp. 117–136.

McKenzie, J. L. "The Historical Prologue of Deuteronomy." In *Fourth World Congress of Jewish Studies*, papers, vol. 1., pp. 95–101.

Noth, M. *The Deuteronomic History*. Journal for the Study of the Old Testament, Supplement Series, n. 15. Ann Arbor, MI: Eisenbrauns, 1980. English translation of the German original published in 1943.

Polzin, R. *Moses and the Deuteronomist: A Literary Study of the Deuteronomic History*. New York: Seabury, 1980, pp. 25–43.

Sumner, W. A. "Israel's Encounters with Edom, Moab, Ammon, Sihon and Og according to the Deuteronomist." *VT* 18 (1968): 216–228.

Vaux, R. de. *The Early History of Israel*. Philadelphia: Westminster, 1978, pp. 555–560.

Wolff, H. W. "The Kerygma of the Deuteronomic Historical Work." In *The Vitality of Old Testament Traditions*. Atlanta: John Knox, 1974, pp. 83–100.

See also the bibliographical entries for J. R. Barlett and J. Van Seters at Numbers 20:22—21:36.

20

Be Careful in the Future

Deuteronomy 4:41—11:32

This unit begins with a brief paragraph (4:41–43) about the three cities of refuge that Moses established east of the Jordan. Here is the second reference in the third person, to Moses in Deuteronomy, the first being 1:1, 5. We instinctively ask why this particular notation is placed here. Is it an awkward addition inserted by a later editor, with no discernible relationship to its immediate context? Perhaps. On the other hand, throughout the preceding chapters and in chapter 4 Moses has been expatiating on God's law and statutes. If observed and implemented they lead to life. The faithful adherent of God's laws will not die. His days will be prolonged. This paragraph, too, deals with death and life, life for the one who takes another's life unintentionally. Is God's word and revelation a city of refuge itself? To leave it is to make oneself a target.

We shall see later in the discussion of the laws of chapters 12–26 that apparently unrelated laws are conjoined simply because of a key word in each, or a phrase similar to both, or an ultimately common theme in both. Not only does 4:41–43 serve as a transition between the first and second speeches of Moses, but it also highlights the theme of life, a theme underscored in the immediately preceding and succeeding chapters of Deuteronomy.

The Theme of Oneness (5–6)

Moses' second address starts with 5:1, a summons to "all Israel" to listen, not to the advice or reflections of a sage, but to the recitation of God's standards. Two things are of interest here. First is Moses' reminder to his audience that at Horeb (i.e., Sinai) the Lord made a covenant "with us . . . Not with our fathers" (5:2–3). Moses is addressing people who were either infants at that time, or were born after the event. Also, he clearly refers in 4:31 to "the covenant with your fathers which he swore to them."

Thus we are confronted with a paradox—"covenant with your fathers" (4:31) and "Not with our fathers" (5:3). Precisely here is a clue to how this material in Deuteronomy functions. To be sure, God did make a covenant with that first generation. He is not about to make another covenant with the next generation. What Moses is appealing for is that his contemporaries fully appropriate that earlier covenant for themselves. God's word to the first generation is to be appropriated by the next generation. Nowhere does Moses even hint that God needs to do something more, or that His work is unfinished. He has done everything necessary to make possible the obedience of every generation.

The second thing of interest in this chapter is the second reading of the Ten Commandments. (The first version is found in Exodus 20:1–17.) There are indeed differences, some major, some minor, between Deuteronomy's version of the Decalogue and the version in Exodus. Most of these we have discussed in the section about Exodus. Here, however, we need to ask what specific role is played by the repetition of the Decalogue at this point in Deuteronomy. Thus far we have encountered the recalling of history. Now we encounter the recalling of Sinaitic law.

Is this repetition Moses' way of reminding his audience that God's law is immutable and eternal? He does not issue revised versions about His will on idolatry, murder, theft, and coveting. To be sure, there is adaptation in some particulars to new circumstances. There are amendments to the constitution. But the eternality of the Decalogue is firmly set. To erase the prohibition against coveting or disrespect to one's parents is no more possible than to strike the phrase *all men are created equal* from the Declaration of Independence.

Thus, for this new generation the simple recitation of that old law is sufficient. But that old law must become *my* law, the standard and authority by which I shall measure my life and my lifestyle. The issue then is making past history present history. There are many generations, but only one law.

Of course this is precisely what happens when Christians observe the sacraments, or the Israelites observed the Old Testament sacraments such as Passover. To observe the sacrament is to re-enact previous history in such a way that it has a bearing on my history. When a person relives the Passover he experiences an exodus because he re-enacts this history, not simply because he says, "yes, God did deliver the people back there." To observe communion means to relive and re-enact the death of Christ, and is the appropriation of that death for me.

Following the recital of the Decalogue, Moses reminds the people of tremors which they experienced when God did speak (5:23–27), and how they were only too happy to select Moses to stand in the breach between themselves and God. To this arrangement God consented (5:28–29).

The immediate function of these verses is to emphasize Moses' unique mediatorial position. He alone stands between God and Israel. His credentials are both congregational appointment and divine approval. As such, this position confers on him the role of teacher and invests his announcements with authority.

The repetition of the Decalogue had impressed on Israel the idea of one divine law. The theme of oneness is then continued into the last half of chapter 5. Not only is there *one law*. There is also only *one mediator*.

This elevation of Moses to preeminence is indicated further by the relationship between Moses' use of "our God" and "your God" (in direct discourse) in his first and second speeches. Table 15 indicates this distinction.

It can be seen that Moses' use of "our God," used frequently in chapters 1–4, becomes almost nonexistent in the next twenty-four chapters. By contrast, in the second speech Moses' "your God" is used copiously, almost exclusively. Observing this psychological shift, Robert Polzin says, "Moses at chapter 5 leaves off speaking to his audience as a fellow Israelite, and henceforth (apart from 5:2 and 6:4) speaks only from the viewpoint of his role as teacher."[1]

Chapter 6 is best known for its celebrated verse 4: "Hear, O Israel: the LORD our God is one LORD," frequently referred to as the *Shema* (a transliteration of the Hebrew imperative, *hear!*). There are indeed translation problems with even this basic verse, as a look at the commentaries will

Table 15

"our God"			"your God"		
Chapter	**Verse**	**Frequency**	**Chapter**	**Verse**	**Frequency**
(1–4) 1	6, 19, 20, 25	4	(1–4) 1	10, 21, 26, 30, 31, 32	6
2	29, 33, 36, 37	4	2	7(twice), 30	3
3	3	1	3	18, 20, 21, 22	4
4	7	1	4	2, 3, 4, 10, 19, 21, 23(twice), 24, 25, 29, 30, 31, 34, 40	15
Total		10			28
(5–28) 5	2	1	(5–28)		approx. 250
6	4	1			
Total		2			±250

1. *Moses and the Deuteronomist: A Literary Study of the Deuteronomic History* (New York: Seabury, 1980), p. 49.

show. But regardless of which translation one prefers, the verse remains a *locus classicus* for the biblical doctrine of monotheism.

So again the idea of oneness, sounded in chapter 5, is perpetuated in chapter 6. The progression is *one law, one mediator*, and now *one Lord*.

Why must there be at this point a reference to one God? For one thing, much of chapter 6 is an elaboration of the first commandment, or a spelling out of the implications of 5:6–10—6:5, "you shall love the LORD your God" and 5:10, "thousands of those who love me"; 6:12, "who brought you out of the land of Egypt" and 5:6, "who brought you out of the land of Egypt, out of the house of bondage"; 6:14, "You shall not go after other gods" and 5:7, "you shall have no other gods"; 6:15, "the LORD your God . . . is a jealous God" and 5:9, "I the LORD your God am a jealous God"; 6:17, "You shall diligently keep the commandments of the LORD" and 5:10, "who . . . keep my commandments."

When discussing the concept of one law I made the observation that the duplication of the Decalogue served to make the point of one law to transcend and serve as a grand depositum for every succeeding generation. One wonders, as an extension of that, if the intent of 6:4 is more than simply to affirm belief in one God versus many gods, monotheism versus polytheism, one Yahweh versus a plurality of Baals.

I suspect that the Old Testament's (and Deuteronomy's in particular) concept of monotheism is not to be understood ontologically, but historically. That is, the emphasis is not with one being or more than one being, but whether this being acts in a way that is consistent. If, in facing the same situation he does one thing one time, and in facing that same situation another time he does something else, then we have two gods. A god who is inconsistent is historically polytheistic. This point is beautifully illustrated by Paul in Romans 3:21–31, the aim of which is to show that all men—Jew and Gentile—are justified through faith. Inserted into this theological argument is the statement "since God is one" (3:30). If in facing the Gentiles God does one thing, and if in facing the Jews He does another, then we have two gods. But He does not do that. The problem is the same for both Jew and Gentile. And so is God's solution. He is one.

Moses in 6:4 lifts monotheism and the nature of God beyond arithmetic and numbers and places it in the realm of ethics, a God who is always consistent with Himself and with us. And that is true for any generation that chooses to follow Him. For this reason Moses is able to add to his monotheistic statement the exhortation to "love the LORD your God with all your heart, and with all your soul, and with all your might" (6:5).

There seems to be no logical relationship between 6:4, "God is one," and 6:5, "love the LORD your God," if monotheism is limited to the concept of the one and the many. If, however, Moses is saying that as God's law is the same from generation to generation, so God Himself is the same from generation to generation, then that means He is not fickle, capricious, or unpredictable. He can be loved enthusiastically because He is lovable, and consistent.

Love for God, if it is genuine, inevitably entails obedience to the word of God. One cannot love Him with all his heart but be lukewarm toward His word. Thus, Moses follows the injunction to love God with the injunction to put His word "upon your heart" (6:6). One is to consider it so indispensable that he is to pass it on to the next generation at all costs (6:7a), and let that word become a conversation piece to him, something almost approaching a preoccupation (6:7b). To place the word on the hands (6:8) and on the doorposts of the house (6:9) is desirable, but only after it has been placed in the heart. External performance must not be a substitute for inner reality.

Moses consistently reminds his people that their appropriate response to God—love, fear, obey—is indeed just that, a response. They were delivered from Egypt by grace. They were preserved in the wilderness by grace. They will receive the land of promise by grace. Chapter 6 illustrates the proper perspective. Verses 1–9 and 12–19 emphasize human responsibility; verses 10–11 and 20–23 emphasize divine grace, especially the gratuitous gift of land.

A Call to Remembrance (7–11)

If Israel needs a proper relationship to her God (chap. 6), it is also incumbent on her that she have a proper relationship to those among whom she will live (chap. 7), something of a dwarf surrounded by giants. His counsel is clear: do not fraternize with your neighbors (7:1–5). His second counsel is equally clear: do not live in fear of them (7:17–26).

The reason for such advice is twofold. What Israel has in her favor is not impressive size—"you were the fewest of all peoples" (7:7)—but a life of holiness that mandates separation from everything impure (7:6). But even more importantly, Israel is the object of God's love, and the recipient of the divine promise that the nations are God's problem, not Israel's (7:8–9, 20–24). Indeed Israel does need, as 6:6 had urged, to put God's word in her heart. For if she tries to put her own word in her heart—"If you say in your heart" (7:17)—the result is fright, anxiety, and consternation.

So Israel needs to know who the Lord is, and the power of His word (chap. 6). She needs to know who the enemy is and where she is to draw the line (chap. 7). Israel also needs to make sure she knows who she is, and who she is not (chap. 8).

Perhaps in this eighth chapter Moses is suggesting that Israel need not fear her enemies as much as she need fear herself. She may become a more lethal weapon than any group of Hittites or Canaanites. To that end 8:2 is a call to Israel to remember what the Lord had done to *her* in the wilderness, in contrast to 7:18 which is a call to remember what the Lord did to *Pharaoh*. He humbled him, but He also humbled Israel, as the incident in Exodus 16 illustrates.

In a sense God is taking a risk in sending His children into a garden of Eden (8:7–10). The contrast between the wilderness and the resources of this land could not be drawn more strongly. For once a person has succeeded it becomes fatally easy to forget help received along the way. So few know how to handle affluence.

Gerhard von Rad observes that phrases such as "My power and the might of my hand" (8:17) sound very much like Lucifer's language in Isaiah 14:12–14 and Ezekiel 28:2–10.[2] If he was cast down for his arrogance and presumption, Israel will be cast out for hers if she capitulates to that temptation. The way to avoid such a humiliation is to remember the Lord who brought her out of bondage (8:14), who led her through the wilderness (8:15), who fed her in the wilderness (8:16), who has given her power (8:18).

Almost everything in 9:1—10:11 recalls the incident of the golden calf (Exod. 32). Chronologically this event precedes just about every historical event alluded to in Moses' first address, yet it is placed in his second address. In 5:22ff. we observed how Deuteronomy had given special attention to Moses' ministry of mediation. He stands between God and Israel. This particular story returns to that motif and provides another illustration of the critical contribution of Moses to Israel's well-being. The key to Israel's continued existence is neither her power (8:17) nor

2. *Deuteronomy: A Commentary*, Old Testament Library (Philadelphia: Westminster, 1966), p. 73.

her righteousness (9:4). The keys are a gracious God and a gifted Moses.

A quick look at 9:1—10:11 reveals that it is more a free retelling of Exodus 32–34 than it is an exact retelling. To illustrate, were we to arrange the two accounts in parallel columns, the following differences (among others) would emerge. Exodus 32 records Moses' first intercessory prayer before he descends the mountain (Exod. 32:11–14). Deuteronomy records his first prayer after he descends the mountain (9:18–20), and includes the notice of a special prayer for Aaron (9:20).

Also, before Deuteronomy records Moses' second intercessory prayer (9:25–29, and much like Exod. 32:11–14), it inserts three other incidents of aberrant living on the part of Israel: Taberah, Massah, and Kibroth-hattaavah. Finally, in the reestablishment of the covenant (10:1ff. and Exod. 34) Moses not only receives orders to cut out two new tables of stone, but he also is told to make an ark of wood in which the tables will be deposited. This latter bit of information was not recorded in Exodus.

What is accomplished by Moses' recalling the event of the golden calf and the renewed covenant (Exod. 32–34)? I suggest that it sets into even more bold relief the contrast between Moses and Israel. For one thing, chapter 9 falls into an *ABAB* pattern: the disobedience of the people (9:7–17); the intercession of Moses (9:18–21); the disobedience of the people (9:22–24); the intercession of Moses (9:25–29).

The "insertion" of 9:22–24 is anything but haphazard. In 9:22 Moses refers to Israel's past disobedience at Taberah (Num. 11:1–3), Massah (Exod. 17:1–7), and Kibroth-hattaavah (Num. 11:31–34). Chronologically, the order should be Massah, Taberah, and Kibroth-hattaavah. The prayers of Moses saved them at Taberah (Num. 11:2), and thus fittingly is first in the list. At Kibroth-hattaavah the people died of plague. Perhaps there will be another Kibroth-hattaavah, as 9:25 suggests: "because the LORD had said he would destroy you." Unless Moses prays! Interestingly, Moses does not repeat his words to God as recorded in Exodus 32—"repent" (32:12) and "blot me . . . out of thy book" (32:32). The omissions may be insignificant. But again, it is not too difficult to imagine Moses, upon reflection, saying to himself: did I really order God to repent? Was I really audacious enough to put my own relationship to Him in jeopardy?

What is added to the whole by the new bit of information about the wooden ark, of which mention is made in Deuteronomy only here and in chapter 31 (for the possible implications of this, see the article by T. E. Fretheim that is cited in the bibliography)? Commentators such as von Rad have made much of the fact that the ark in Deuteronomy functions only as the receptacle of the tablets of law, and not as the place of divine residence or divine glory. The implication drawn about this shift from aura to commonality for the ark is that Deuteronomy has indeed undergone a process of demythologization. One can question, however, whether the role of the ark in Deuteronomy has been demoted to something less significant. To meet God in His word is no less spectacular than to meet Him in a cloud, or sitting between cherubim.

By adding information about the ark here (material omitted from Exodus 34) Moses emphasizes that the covenant is secure, inaccessible, permanent, and available only as Moses will give teaching from it and about it.[3] Once again, the arrangement or introduction of new material serves to reinforce the unique, mediatorial ministry of Moses and the unchanging God who has issued an unchanging covenant—"and there they are" (10:5).

3. B. Peckham, "The Composition of Deuteronomy 9:1—10:11," in *Word and Spirit*, Essays in Honor of David Michael Stanley, S. J. (Willowdale, Ontario: Regis College Press, 1975), p. 51.

The remainder of chapter 10 through 11:32 is a concluding, hortatorical section built primarily around a series of exhortations followed by a motivation for obeying that exhortation (for example: exhortation, 10:12–13; motivation, 10:14–15; exhortation, 10:16; motivation, 10:17–18).

Of special interest here is Moses' concern that the people "Circumcise therefore the foreskin of their heart" (10:16). Thus, even as early as Deuteronomy the point is made that true circumcision is of the heart, not simply an incision into the external flesh. This particular exhortation chimes with Moses' restatement in 11:18–21 of 6:6–8. The law must be put on one's heart first, then on the hands, the eyes, the gates, and the doorposts. One wonders if, when Jeremiah spoke of the new covenant, one feature of which was the divine writing of the law on the heart (Jer. 31:33), he was not deliberately using a bit of irony. For after all, much of the new covenant is old, unless one has strayed so far from its precepts that even the old sounds as if it is new.

Chapter 11:26–32 serves as a transition between the preaching of 5–11 and the list of laws that begins in chapter 12. As W. L. Moran has observed, the three items listed here are in inverse order to their actual treatment in the subsequent chapters: blessings and curse (11:26–28 and chap. 28); the ceremony at Shechem, between Ebal and Gerizim (11:29–31 and chap. 27); and the laws of the Lord (11:32 and chaps. 12–26).[4] Now the stage is set for the announcement of the laws of Deuteronomy.

Bibliography

Childs, B. *Introduction to the Old Testament As Scripture*. Philadelphia: Fortress, 1979, pp. 215–217.

4. "Deuteronomy," in *A New Catholic Commentary on Holy Scripture* (Camden, NJ: Thomas Nelson and Sons, 1969), p. 267.

Crump, W. "Dt. 7: A Covenant Sermon." *RestQ* 17 (1974): 222–235.

Fretheim, T. E. "The Ark in Deuteronomy." *CBQ* 30 (1968): 1–14.

Gammie, J. G. "The Theology of Retribution in the Book of Deuteronomy." *CBQ* 32 (1970): 1–12.

Horowitz, H. L. "The Sh'ma Reconsidered." *Jud* 24 (1975): 476–481.

Ishida, T. "The Structure and Historical Implications of the Lists of Pre-Israelite Nations." *Bibl* 60 (1979): 461–490.

McBride, S. D. "The Yoke of the Kingdom, An Exposition of Deuteronomy 6:4–5." *Intr* 27 (1973): 273–306.

McKay, J. W. "Man's love for God in Deuteronomy and the father/teacher-son/pupil relationship." *VT* 22 (1972): 426–435.

Moran, W. L. "Conclusion of the Decalogue, Ex. 20:17—Dt. 5:21." *CBQ* 29 (1967): 543–554.

Peacock, H. F. "Dt. 7, 10." *BTrans* 27 (1976): 244.

Peckham, B. "The Composition of Deuteronomy 9:1—10:11." In *Word and Spirit*. Essays in Honor of David Michael Stanley, S. J. Edited by Joseph Plevnik. Willowdale, Ontario: Regis College Press, 1975, pp. 3–59.

Polzin, R. *Moses and the Deuteronomist: A Literary Study of the Deuteronomic History*. New York: Seabury, 1980, pp. 43ff.

Walsh, M. F. "Shema Yisrael: Reflections on Deuteronomy 6:4–9." *BT* 90 (April 1977): 1220–1225.

Willis, J. T. "Man Does Not Live By Bread Alone, (Dt. 8:3 and Mt. 4:4)." *RestQ* 16 (1973): 141–149.

Willoughby, B. E. "A Heartfelt Love: An Exegesis of Deuteronomy 6:4–19." *RestQ* 20 (1977): 73–87.

21

The Laws of Deuteronomy

Deuteronomy 12–26

The next fifteen chapters of Deuteronomy represent a long series of laws, some of which are duplicates from other legal sections of the Pentateuch, some of which are adaptations of other Pentateuchal laws, and some of which are novel. As far back as 1:5 we read, "Moses undertook to explain this law"; however, what follows is not law, but four chapters of historical review followed by an exhortation.

A phrase similar to that of 1:5 is repeated in 4:44, "This is the law which Moses set before the children of Israel," but once again, what follows through chapter 11 is an amalgamation of historical reminiscences and appeals for obedience. (To be sure, the Sinaitic Decalogue is repeated in chapter 5.) What this historical background accomplishes is to provide a foundation on which the laws themselves may be superimposed. The God who speaks a word of law (12–26) does so only after He has spoken a word of grace (1–11). The divine standards are not placed in a vacuum but are set against the bountiful resources of a gracious God. Additionally Israel is to obey these laws not in order to become holy; rather, she is to obey them because she is holy. The observance of law is a by-product of holiness, not a means of attaining holiness.

A perpetually vexing problem for interpreters has been

the mostly futile attempts to decipher some significant order in the arrangement of the laws. Laws that seemingly have nothing to do with each other are placed in sequence. This phenomenon is particularly true in the last few chapters of this unit.

Earlier scholarship dismissed the issue as unsolvable. All that could be said of chapters 12–26 is that they were "without form and void," one massive *tōhû wābōhû*. The haphazardness of the Deuteronomic corpus was attributed to endless editorial activity. Subsequently, scholars began to see form, where before only formlessness was apparent. But even here the attempt ended with mixed results.

For example, Gerhard von Rad divided the unit as follows: 12:1—16:17, cultic laws; 16:18—18:22, laws concerning officials (judge, king, priest, prophet); 19:1—21:9, laws for criminal cases; 21:10—22:30, regulations concerning families. Von Rad then put chapters 23–26 aside, for they had no demonstrable unity, no common theme to tie them together.[1]

Similarly, the editor who, along with Moshe Weinfeld, contributed the article on Deuteronomy to the *Encyclopaedia Judaica*, suggested the following outline: 12:1—16:17, ceremonial laws (agreeing with von Rad); 16:18—18:22, civil laws (again agreeing with von Rad); 19:1–21, criminal laws. But in this outline the cut-off point is chapter 20, for in chapters 20–26 there is no discernible order.[2]

The philosopher and conservative, Norman L. Geisler, has proposed this outline: 12:1—16:17, ceremonial duties (agreeing with the other two suggested outlines); 16:18—20:20, civil duties; social duties to one's family (chap. 21), to one's friends (chap. 22), to the whole fraternity of Israel and strangers (chap. 23–25).[3] The latter part of the outline

1. *Old Testament Theology*, trans. D. M. G. Stalker, 2 vols. (New York: Harper and Row, 1962), vol. 1, p. 226, n. 86.

2. "Deuteronomy," *EncJud* 5 (1971), p. 1573.

3. *Popular Survey of the Old Testament* (Grand Rapids: Baker, 1977), p. 79.

is especially forced. For instance, if the point of chapter 22 is social duties to one's friends, what does this have to do with the law of a woman dressing like a man (22:5), or the law about the bird's nest with the mother bird and her young ones inside (22:6–7)?

Two recent studies have appeared that either plow new grounds of exploration or resurrect and refine long-abandoned ideas. Calum M. Carmichael believes the laws of Deuteronomy are "the work of one hand and demonstrate a remarkable system of order and presentation."[4] His proposal is to see within this unit a series of laws in which the arrangement proceeds on the same principle of arrangement as that in the Covenant Code (Exod. 21:2—23:19). As such, Carmichael detects in Deuteronomy 12–26 a series of Edomite laws, Egyptian laws, "rest" laws, and so forth.

Few scholars now consider the problem solved as a result of Carmichael's studies. Interestingly, his proposal of the organizing principles within the legal corpus of Deuteronomy has been dismissed as much too arbitrary and fanciful. (To be sure, his thesis is quite ingenious at times, but does this element dismiss his work from serious consideration, and is his thesis more fanciful than any others?)

A much more trenchant criticism of Carmichael than that of fanciful ingenuity is the observation that he still views chapters 12–26 as a group of unrelated segments, with no unity to the whole.

Most recently S. Kaufmann has suggested that the arrangement of the laws is linked to the sequence of the Ten Commandments as listed in Deuteronomy 5. Kaufmann says, "The thesis presented here is that the Law of Deuteronomy (chaps. 12–26) is a highly structured com-

4. *The Laws of Deuteronomy* (Ithaca: Cornell University Press, 1974), p. 67.

position whose major topical units are arranged according to the order of the laws in the Decalogue";[5] "it is a unified masterpiece of jurisprudential literature created by a single author . . . an expanded Decalogue."[6]

I admit my preference for Kaufmann's analysis. Indeed some of the relationships seem stronger than others. Perhaps at times a proposed relationship between laws themselves and how the unit relates to a particular commandment may be forced.

But Kaufmann's thesis does "unify" chapters 12–26, and connects these specific laws to the Sinaitic Decalogue sounded in chapter 5, thus suggesting even a larger degree of homogeneity for this second speech of Moses (5–26).

Worship in the Right Way (12)

Perhaps more has been written about this particular chapter than any other in the legal corpus of Deuteronomy. The reason for this is the often-made statement that the classical theme of Deuteronomy—centralization of worship—is most clearly articulated in this chapter. Indeed, the phrase "the place which the LORD will choose" appears six times: 12:5, 11, 14, 18, 21, 26 (plus three times in chap. 14, one time in chap. 15, six times in chap. 16, two times in chap. 17, one time in chap. 18, 26, and 31, for a total of twenty-one times).

Added to this prominent phrase is the extended phrase "to put his name there" (12:5, 21 and 14:24) or "to make his name dwell there" (12:11, and five more times in Deuteronomy).

Much has been made of the emphasis on both the "cult-centralization" and "name theology" of Deuteronomy. Those who hold tenaciously to the dominance of central-

5. "The Structure of the Deuteronomic Law," *Maarav* 1 (1979), pp. 108–109.
6. *Ibid.*, p. 147.

ization in Deuteronomy feel, of course, that the place where God puts His name is Jerusalem. A proposal has been made that Josiah used religious reform as a cover for his real motives in supporting this centralization reform. For part of the reform is, "thither you shall bring your burnt offerings and your sacrifices, your tithes" (12:6). In the words of W. G. Claburn, "How does an ambitious king get his hands on the largest possible proportion of the peasantry's agricultural surplus? By reforming the fiscal system so that he brings into the capital a larger proportion of the taxes already being assessed."[7] Thus, in one sweep Claburn is able to portray Josiah as a racketeer and a charlatan, a characterization not borne out by the material in Kings and Chronicles. I cite this as an illustration of the possibilities of exegetical imagination if centralization is made the theme of Deuteronomy. Even von Rad points out that "there are, after all, a large number of ordinances which neither mention the demand for centralization nor even seem to be at all aware of it."[8]

The name theology of Deuteronomy—"he will put his name there"—is intriguing. It is His name, not He Himself, that is there. Is this an attempt on the part of Deuteronomy to moderate more explicit references elsewhere in Scripture to the effect that God Himself dwells in the tabernacle or temple? Von Rad's comment is again illustrative: "The idea must therefore be understood as a protest against popular conceptions of the actual presence of Yahweh at the sanctuary."[9] Weinfeld seconds the interpretation and utilizes the name theology as an additional indication of the demythologization process at work in Deuteronomy. Essentially the emphasis on name theology is a polemic

7. "The Fiscal Basis of Josiah's Reforms," *JBL* 92 (1973), p. 15.

8. *Deuteronomy: A Commentary*, Old Testament Library (Philadelphia: Westminster, 1966), p. 89.

9. *Ibid.*, p. 90.

against corporeal conceptions of God, according to this analysis.[10]

Or is it? The phrase "to put one's name," or a variation of it, is not unique to Scripture. G. J. Wenham observes that in cuneiform literature the expression has at least three nuances: the phrase is used as an affirmation of ownership, the equivalent of taking possession; the phrase is used in texts describing conquests and is associated with the erection of victory monuments: the phrase may be used in inscribing a name on the foundation stones of sanctuaries.[11]

Any one of these three is applicable to Deuteronomy. The place where God is to be worshiped is His possession. Is the shift from something as God's dwelling place to something as God's possession really a move away from the anthropomorphic? And what could be more suitable than for God to put His own signature on the place of worship? For He is "a cornerstone chosen and precious, and he who believes in him will not be put to shame" (I Peter 2:6).

Finally, if Deuteronomy attempts to establish that it is only God's name and not God Himself that dwells in the place of worship, what are we to do with phrases such as "the LORD your God walks in the midst of your camp" (23:14); "he shall dwell . . . in your midst" (23:16); "your males shall appear before the LORD your God" (16:16); "you shall set it down before the LORD your God" (26:10)? God's name does not walk in the camp; God's name does not dwell in the midst; one does not appear before the name of the Lord or present his offering before the name of the Lord.

Chapter 12 is a series of contrasts. First, there is the

10. *Deuteronomy and the Deuteronomic School* (Oxford: Clarendon Press, 1972), pp. 193ff.

11. "Deuteronomy and the Central Sanctuary," *TB* 22 (1971), p. 113.

contrast between "here" (v. 8) and "there" (v. 7). Once in the land there will be changes with no longer "every man doing whatever is right in his own eyes" (v. 8b). Second, there is a contrast between "their gods" (v. 2) and "your God" (v. 4); "their name" (v. 3) and "his name" (v. 5); and between all the "places" of false worship (vv. 2–3) and "the place" the Lord will choose.

This second contrast seems to suggest that the real issue in this chapter is not one sanctuary versus many sanctuaries but pure worship versus false worship. To that end the chapter both begins (vv. 2–4) and ends (vv. 29–31) with notes about pagan icons and religious practices. And in Israel's worship there is to be neither. Israel's religious observances are to be characterized by rejoicing (vv. 7, 12, 18), ostensibly because it has nothing of the macabre in it.

And in the midst of a chapter given over to concerns about worship—and what more appropriate subject with which to begin the legal corpus?—there is also a substantial discussion of observances at home, verses 15–28. For example, "you may . . . eat flesh . . . as much as you desire" (vv. 15, 21). And even the verb used for "killing" is *zābaḥ*, a verb used 129 times in Scripture and used almost exclusively for sacrificial slaughter.[12] Can we imply from this that even eating together in one's home with one's family and enjoying the physical blessings of God is also a sacrament? For even here God has a directive to give. In worship, eliminate the false gods. In eating, eliminate the blood (vv. 16, 23). Knock the false altars and pillars to the ground, and pour the blood on the ground.

The Temptation of Idolatry (13)

In this chapter the concern of Moses is still with purity of worship. In chapter 12 the emphasis was on idolatry;

12. Jacob Milgrom, "Profane Slaughter and a Formulaic Key to the Composition of Deuteronomy," *HUCA* 47 (1976), p. 1.

here the emphasis is on the idolater. In the case of the former Israel is to demolish all places and relics associated with idolatry. But what if the temptation is not from one of the silent Asherim or cult images, but instead is from a vocal prophet (13:1–5), a family member (13:6–11), or evangelistic rabblerousers (13:12–18)? In each instance Israel's response is to be quick and decisive—"he shall be put to death" (vv. 5, 9–10, 15–17). Even a whole community may be the object of a holy war if it allows itself to be swayed. There is no indication that subsequent repentance is an option that alleviates the recrimination.

In each of the three paragraphs a different reason is given that makes the temptation all the more enticing. In verses 1–5 the impressive thing is that the temptation is accompanied by a sign or a wonder. Might Jesus have had this passage in mind when he spoke of forthcoming false Christs and false prophets who would show great signs and wonders that appear so authentic as to befuddle even the elect (Matt. 24:24)?

In the second paragraph (vv. 6–11) it is the source of the temptation that is powerful to resist. Indeed a man's foes may be of his own household, or inner circle of friends or relatives to whom one may have to say: "get thee behind me, Satan." Chapter 12 has highlighted the home as a place of worship, rejoicing, and festivity. Chapter 13 presents the other side of the role of the home. It may be a place of temptation, a stumbling block rather than a steppingstone.

The third possibility that makes the temptation to idolatry so alluring is statistics (vv. 12–18). The masses have adopted the heretical teachings of the "base fellows." Can they all be wrong? Can a whole community be swayed? Can there be mass apostasy? Yes. But mass sinning must inevitably lead to mass repercussions, if indeed all the facts and allegations have been thoroughly checked ("you shall inquire and make search and ask diligently," v. 14), and found to be true.

Holiness and Stewardship (14)

The movement in chapter 14 is from cause to effect. The cause is "You are the sons of the LORD your God" (v. 1a); the effect is how you respond to death (v. 1b), your eating patterns (vv. 3–21), and what you do with your possessions (vv. 22–29).

In one-half of a verse (1b) the Mosiac law prohibits a pagan mourning custom, self-laceration or the shaving of a bare spot on the forehead. Might the insertion of this prohibition here be related to the notes of the previous chapter regarding putting to death or putting to the sword those who inspire or embrace idolatry? Especially in the case of the enticing relative the extra warning is given that "your eye shall not pity him."

The chapter is still concerned with the idea that Israel is to be distinctive, different in many ways from her neighbors. In chapter 12 the temptation is from idolatrous objects that are quite visible. In chapter 13 the temptation takes the form of verbal encouragement from an apostate. There are, however, in this chapter no enticers encouraging the Israelites to shave their foreheads or eat forbidden foods. Israel is to get rid of the pillars (12:3) of the Canaanites, but she is not to get rid of the pelicans (14:17).

The concern of this chapter then is that Israel not only shun the blatantly wicked things (chaps. 12–13), but also the apparently more innocent and innocuous things: showing respect for the dead via a particular gesture, or avoiding certain kinds of meats. It is of no little significance that the section on clean animals is introduced with this phrase: "You shall not eat any abominable thing" (14:3). The Hebrew word for "abominable thing" is *tôᶜēbâ*, which most often in Deuteronomy is used in reference to Canaanite practices, where the translation is usually "an abomination." By contrast, the parallel chapter in Leviticus (chap. 11) about food laws uses the Hebrew word *sheqeṣ* for "abomination," and not the word used here. Thus Deuteronomy 14 deliberately uses a word that elsewhere in the book primarily designates acts of perversion by the Canaanites. Presumably the list of permitted and prohibited animals for food has something to do with that lifestyle, but beyond that we are unable to go.

The last half of the chapter is concerned with tithing—the annual tithe (vv. 22–27), and the triennial tithe (vv. 28–29). The concern is still with food, except the emphasis has moved from meat to seed and grains. There is also a shift from the negative (do not worship that, or do not eat that) to the positive (tithe).

The tithe is in the form of produce, but under certain conditions (a far distance to travel) the tithe could be converted into money which would be easier to carry (v. 25). The pilgrim is even given a traveling allowance: "you shall eat the tithe" (v. 23) and you shall "spend your money for whatever you desire" (v. 26).

Sacred and festive celebrations must not become a time for only oneself and family. It is to be a time for opening the doors and inviting to one's table the penny-scraping Levite and the indigent sojourner, the fatherless, and the widow. For getting rid of the wrong type of company God brings blessing (13:17–18). For welcoming the right type of company God brings blessing (14:29b).

The Personae Miserabiles (15)

Three items are discussed in this chapter: the sabbatical year, verses 1–11; guidelines for owners of slaves, verses 12–18; and the sacrifice of firstlings, verses 19–23, a law whose current positioning in the corpus might at first sight seem out of place and somewhat intrusive.

Chapter 14:22 had spoken of what Israel is to do with her possessions "year by year." Chapter 14:28 mentioned what she is to do with her possessions "every three years."

This emphasis on time is continued into chapter 15, "At the end of every seven years" (15:1). And then there follows a commentary on observance of the sabbatical year.

This particular year was initially described in Exodus 23:10–11. There the emphasis was on allowing the land to lie fallow for the sake of the poor and the animals. A second emphasis is found in Leviticus 25:1–7. The land, or rotating portions thereof, is to lie fallow every seventh year. It is to be a rest for the land which "I [the Lord] give" (Lev. 25:2). The crop that grows by itself will provide the necessary food both for the family and the indigent (Lev. 25:6).

This chapter in Deuteronomy adds yet another factor. In the sabbatical year there is to be a remission of debts (15:2). Presumably this particular directive would be applicable only to a number of people, for, after all, in any given society what is the ratio between creditors and population? The additional stipulation about debt cancellation also envisions more clearly a people who are now about to move into a more complex, highly-developed society in which economics will play a larger role than heretofore. This will include the accumulation of equity, financial security, and the borrowing, lending, and investment of money.

Moses once again becomes something of an exhorter. His caution is that Israel "Take heed lest there be a base thought in your heart" (15:9). This is rather close to earlier warnings: "Beware lest you say in your heart, 'My power . . .' " (8:17) and "do not say in your heart, . . . 'It is because of my righteousness . . .' " (9:4).

There is more to the sabbatical year than the cancellation of debts. It is not sufficient simply to erase the financial obligations others owe. There must be a sharing of one's possessions with the poor (15:7–8). This becomes particularly important as a sabbatical year approaches (15:9). It would be possible at this time to refuse a loan to someone in need. But Deuteronomy says: if a person in need requests a loan on the last day of the sixth year, the eve of the sabbatical year, meet his needs, even if it means you have to cancel the debt the next day.

From a discussion of the sabbatical year we turn to a law about slavery, verses 12–18. At many points it is similar to the law of Exodus 21:2–11. But at other points it is distinctly different. In the first place the Exodus law treats male slaves and female slaves separately (Exod. 21:2–6 and 7–11). Here they are treated together—"a Hebrew man or a Hebrew woman" (15:12). Second, the version in Exodus holds out release for the male slave after six years, but not for the female slave, Exodus 21:2, 7—"she shall not go out as the male slaves do."

Third, should the male slave decide to remain he has that option in Exodus 21:5. In Deuteronomy 15:17 that privilege is extended to the female slave. Fourth, and an extension of the third point, the male slave who agrees to stay with his master is to have his ear pierced, Exodus 21:6. That ceremony is also for the remaining female slave in Deuteronomy 15:17b, "and to your bondwoman you shall do likewise." Fifth, in Exodus 21:6 the master pierces his servant's ear only after "he has brought him to God" (the KJV has "judges" for *'elōhîm*). This note is absent in this account.

More light (or complication?) is thrown on the whole area of slavery by the emphatic note in Leviticus 25:39b that an Israelite could not make a fellow Israelite serve as a slave. Slaves were to be taken only from the nations and non-Israelites in Canaan (Lev. 25:44–45). In only two instances could an Israelite become the servant of an Israelite: voluntarily, if "he sells himself" because of abject poverty (Lev. 25:39a); or compulsorily, in the case of the thief who is unable to make restitution ("he shall be sold for his theft," Exod. 22:3).

Two ramifications follow from this. First, the law of

Exodus 21:2ff., "When you buy a Hebrew slave," may not refer to a Hebrew slave, but to a Habiru slave, those second-millennium B.C. migratory groups of peoples who often hired themselves out as mercenaries or servants. Certainly Israelites could "buy" slaves from this stock.

Second, the emphasis of Leviticus 25:39a, "he sells himself," demonstrates that the RSV and KJV translation of Deuteronomy 15:12, "if your brother, a Hebrew man or a Hebrew woman, is sold to you," is definitely incorrect. It can only be, "if your brother . . . sells himself to you." The Hebrew—*yimmākēr*—translates naturally with reflexive nuance, rather than passive nuance in this instance.

Thus, the slave law of Deuteronomy 15 is concerned with the Israelite who has reached the bottom rung on the poverty scale. He must sell himself to his brother. But he is not to become automatically the wealthier brother's permanent ward or possession. In seven years he is to be free, and provided for liberally. So the slave law perpetuates the theme, started in this chapter by the teaching about the sabbatical year, that the covenant community is to make a special place within her gates for the poor. They must not be abused. They must not be abandoned. They are to be helped financially, and not with parsimonious pinches.

The third paragraph deals with the sacrifice of firstlings of the herd and flock, verses 19–23. Why place this law here, especially when there has already been a reference to firstlings in 12:17? S. Kaufmann makes three interesting associations. Only Deuteronomy mentions that the firstling is not to be "worked" (15:19), an appropriate reference on the heels of the law about slaves who have "worked" for their brother (15:12, 18). Deuteronomy 15:19 limits the firstlings of the "herd and flock," the same animals to be used in the Passover (16:2). (Exodus 12:5 limited the animals to yearling sheep or goats.) Deuteronomy 15:21 prohibits the consecration of animals that are, among other things, "lame."[13] The Hebrew word for "lame" is *pissē^{a}ḥ*, very close in sound to *pesaḥ*, that is, passover, the item under discussion in the next chapter, 16.

Three Sacred Feasts (16)

Clusters of three are frequent in this immediate section of Deuteronomy. We have seen three references to years: every year, every third year, every seventh year (chaps. 14 and 15). Clean and unclean animals are from the categories of land creatures, birds, and fish (chap. 14). Three possible sources of idolatry are presented (chap. 13). There are three references to not eating the blood (12:16, 23; 15:23). In both chapters 12 and 16 there are six uses of the phrase "the place which the LORD your God will choose" (also three times in chap. 14).

Chapter 16 continues this emphasis by again drawing attention to the three major festivals to be observed throughout the year: the feast of passover and unleavened bread, verses 1–8; the feast of weeks, verses 9–12; the feast of tabernacles, verses 13–15. There follows a summarizing statement in verses 16–17, "Three times a year all your males shall appear before the LORD. . . ." Just as one is not to let his slave leave the home "empty-handed" (15:13), neither is one to appear before the Lord "empty-handed" (16:16). Giving to the poor (15:7ff.) is matched by giving to the Lord (16:17). Not only is there a triennial tithe for the Levite, the sojourner, the fatherless, and the widow (14:28–29), but there is also the celebration together of the Lord's feasts (16:11, 14). There is the offering for the poor, but there is also joint worship with the poor. Male and female, free and servant, rich and poor, married and single are all together under one roof in worship.

13. S. Kaufmann, "The Structure of the Deuteronomic Law," *Maarav* 1 (1979), p. 132.

The actual description of the festivals in this chapter is fairly close to that in other books of the Pentateuch. In the Passover, Moses' directions about the employment of the blood of the lamb, spelled out quite clearly in Exodus 12, are omitted from this chapter, but so are a number of other items. Commentators such as Moshe Weinfeld use such comparisons to buttress their point that Deuteronomy represents a move to secularization. On the other hand, if indeed Deuteronomy demonstrates this trend, what is to be said for the fact that Deuteronomy repeats what Exodus 23:17 and 34:24 mention about Passover being an observance limited to the place God shall chose, instead of a home observance as spelled out in Exodus 12:3ff.? This hardly seems to be a move toward secularization.

The chapter concludes with two brief paragraphs that might more appropriately be discussed under chapter 17. One paragraph is about the appointment of judges, verses 18–20; the other one is a note about avoiding pagan worship practices, verses 21–22.

Indeed verses 18–20 deal partly with the selection of judges who are to "judge the people with righteous judgment." But most of the paragraph is about the people themselves, not the judges; "you" and not "they." All Israel is to be judgelike in her behavior, above partiality or bribes, and followers of justice.

Public Officials (17)

As we saw, the laws about administrative personnel began in 16:18 with the directive to appoint judges and officers. Then come three statements about false worship: do not plant a tree as an Asherah, 16:21; do not set up a pillar, 16:22; do not sacrifice a blemished animal, 17:1. This is followed by a statement about the penalty for idolatry after a thorough investigation of the allegation and the testimony of at least two witnesses, 17:2–7; next is the description of a supreme tribunal which is to handle cases too involved and complex for local judges, 17:8–13.

Thus the order is the appointment of judges; forbidden pagan methods of worship; the trial, conviction, and sentencing of idolaters; a tribunal, with both clergy and lay persons as members, to adjudicate complex legal disputes. The progression is quite logical: the appointment of judges, a list of cultic infractions, and judicial procedures in cases of such infractions and difficult situations. S. Kaufmann also observes that the Asherah and the pillars, because they were divine emblems for the Canaanites, may have played a role in judicial procedures in that society; hence, the placement of the notice of their illegality in a context dealing with matters of justice.[14]

The last few verses of the chapter, verses 14–20, constitute Deuteronomy's law of the king. The first official described in this unit is the judge. He is to be appointed by the people (16:18). He is voted into office. By contrast the king is chosen by the Lord (17:15).

It seems unnecessary to say that this unique law could have been composed only long after the Judean and Israelite monarchy was in existence, and in a decaying state at that. This is, of course, the position taken by almost all critical scholars. Is it not reasonable that somewhere in the space of his 120 years Moses had ample opportunities, both inside and outside Egypt, to observe the theatrics of oriental despots who reveled in their luxurious lifestyles? This observation of Moses becomes the basis and the background for the qualifying restrictions placed on the Israelite monarch whose activity is described first negatively, verses 15–17, then positively, verses 18–20.

Von Rad observes correctly, "Deuteronomy sees in kingship not an office which Yahweh could use for the welfare of the people, but only an institution in which the holder

14. *Ibid.*, p. 155, n. 88.

must live in a sphere of extreme peril because he is tempted by his harem or his wealth either to turn away from Yahweh or 'to lift up his heart above his brethren.' "[15] A heart turned away from the Lord will normally produce a heart lifted up above one's people. Earlier Israel as a whole had been warned about saying in her heart: my power has gotten me this wealth (8:17). Both Israel and its head of state are potentially vulnerable at this point.

Positively, the king is to write, then read, regularly from "a copy of this law" (v. 18). P. C. Craigie suggests three possibilities for "this law": the law of Deuteronomy, Deuteronomy as a whole or a certain section of it, or the original document of the Sinai covenant, Exodus 20–24.[16] Regardless of which it is, the purpose of such a document is to remind the king of his subordinate status. He is not autonomous. He is an instrument of God, not God.

This law about the king is structured much like the law about worship in chapter 12.[17] In these two instances the people, once in the land, will make public an intention or request: "I will eat flesh" (12:20); "I will set a king over me" (17:14). God grants permission: "you may eat as much flesh as you desire" (12:20b); "you may indeed set as king over you . . ." (17:15). But there is a qualification attached to the permission: "Only you shall not eat the blood" (12:16); "Only he must not multiply horses" (17:16). Thus some continuity is provided between these laws and the order and structure of their formulation. Carmichael calls it "repetition."

Priests and Prophets (18)

From the "secular" offices of judge and king Deuteronomy now turns to a discussion of the "religious" offices

15. *Deuteronomy: A Commentary*, p. 120.

16. *The Book of Deuteronomy*, New International Commentary of the Old Testament series (Grand Rapids: Eerdmans, 1976), p. 256.

17. Carmichael, *The Laws of Deuteronomy*, pp. 104ff.

of priest, verses 1–8, and prophet, verses 9–22. All four of these positions illustrate the two ways in which individuals entered upon prominent positions: charismatic (judge); hereditary (king); hereditary (priest and Levite); charismatic (prophet).

Unlike the previous two chapters, which emphasized mostly the necessary qualities of those holding the position of judge or king, chapter 18 says nothing about the quality of life for the priest and Levite. Instead the preoccupation of these verses is how these religious workers will be provided for. Since they have no patrimony how will they live? As such, a word is spoken about all Levites (vv. 1–2), Levites who are also priests at the sanctuary (vv. 3–5), and nonpriestly provincial Levites (vv. 6–8). Consistently the emphasis is on their privileges of ministry and what the people are to give them as their dues. Elsewhere Deuteronomy does spell out the responsibilities of the Levite. He is to carry the ark (10:8; 31:9, 25), and he has charge of the written law which guides the king (17:18). The closest the actual law of the priest or Levite comes to outlining specific responsibilities is: "he may minister in the name of the LORD his God" (18:7). But principally the law is for the benefit of the laity, not the clergy.

Before discussing the law of the prophet, Deuteronomy first lists various techniques employed by paganism for obtaining divine oracles, verses 9–14. These are not the ways by which Israel shall detect the voice of her Lord. For what these banned items have in common is that they fall into the category of human wisdom and ingenuity. Yehezkel Kaufmann rightly calls divination "a science of cosmic secrets" and the diviner "a 'scientist' who can dispense with 'divine revelation.' "[18]

By contrast, the Lord will raise up as His medium of

18. *The Religion of Israel*, trans. Moshe Greenberg (Chicago: University of Chicago Press, 1960), p. 43.

revelation a prophet. Like the king he is to be "from your brethren" (18:15 and 17:15). He is able to speak only because God has put His word in his mouth (17:19, and quite close to what the Lord would say later to a balking Jeremiah, Jer. 1:9).

This prophet will resemble Moses. Here is one of the very few instances in the legal section of Deuteronomy where Moses speaks about himself: "The LORD your God will raise up for you a prophet like me. . . . I [God] will raise up for them a prophet like you" (18:15, 18). This is the one office described by Moses in which he specifies a particular model—himself. He is the prototype. Moses is here either exhibiting the height of arrogance, or indeed he is telling the truth about himself, his uniqueness, and his influence as a model on future generations. Understandably then Peter's preaching at Pentecost points to the second Moses (Acts 3:20ff.). And just as the people dare not at their peril ignore the first Moses (Deut. 18:19), so to turn against the second Moses will bring even a greater retribution, but a retribution that can be mitigated by repentance.

Dealing with Crime and Violence (19)

Verses 1–13 prescribe the setting up of six cities of refuge, three on each side of the Jordan. This phenomenon has already been described briefly in Exodus 21:12–14 and at greater length in Numbers 35:9–34. These cities provide asylum for the manslayer but not for the murderer. The previous chapter had distinguished between the true prophet and the false prophet, who is to be put to death. This idea of distinction is then carried into chapter 19, the distinction being between the unintentional murderer and the intentional murderer for whom, as with the presumptuous prophet, the penalty is death.

Weinfeld makes much of the fact that Deuteronomy, unlike Numbers 35, does not specify how long the manslayer must remain in the city of refuge: "and he shall live in it until the death of the high priest" (Num. 35:25, 28). Not only does Weinfeld see this as further secularization in Deuteronomy, but he also speculates that the silent assumption of the Deuteronomic law is that the individual must remain in asylum "until the rage of the avenger subsides."[19] But what if that never happens? Can the subjective mood of a person provide the basis for a law? May not Deuteronomy simply reproduce the law concerning asylum without also reproducing the high priest's part?[20]

From its discussion of the law about asylum Deuteronomy proceeds to a one-sentence law about not removing a neighbor's landmark, verse 14, and a law about the evidence of witnesses, especially malicious witnesses, verses 15–21.

The law about removing landmarks (an attempt by the rich to oppress the poor?) is found again in 27:17 and also in wisdom literature, Proverbs 22:28; 23:10. But how can it be related to the law that precedes and follows, and do the three laws in this chapter—asylum, removing landmarks, and witnesses—fit together?

Perhaps in the case of the first two laws there is some common vocabulary to tie the two together. "You shall prepare the roads and divide into three parts the area *(g^{e}bûl)* of the land" (19:3), and "you shall not [re]move your neighbor's landmark *(g^{e}bûl)*, which the men of old have set *(gābal)*" (19:14).

S. Kaufmann suggests the following organization: how to deal with homicide, verses 1–13; how to prevent homi-

19. *Deuteronomy and the Deuteronomic School*, pp. 236–237.

20. Jacob Milgrom, "The Alleged 'Demythologization and Secularization' in Deuteronomy," *IEJ* 23 (1973), p. 159.

cide, verse 14; how to deal with the accusation of homicide, verses 15–21.[21] Obviously both the laws about asylum and witnesses have a common concern, that innocent blood not be shed, either by the avenger of blood or by the witness who perjures himself against the defendant.

War Exemptions and Executions (20)

Chapter 19 discussed the taking of life when one kills his neighbor unintentionally or in hate, and as a civil procedure against the malicious witness. The theme now continues into chapter 20, in which the general theme is war.

The first half of the chapter, verses 1–9, is composed primarily of an exhortation by the priest—here in a unique role outside the sanctuary—to the soldiers to be courageous (vv. 2–4), and an offer by the officers to allow some to disqualify themselves for military service (vv. 5–9).

The list of those exempted from serving in the army is interesting: a man who has recently built a new house that is not dedicated; a man who has planted a vineyard and has not enjoyed its harvest yet; a man who is engaged to be married; and those who are fearful and fainthearted (see Judg. 7:3 and Gideon's words to the fearful). The first three categories of exemption are quite normal. It is somewhat unexpected to find a able-bodied man reclassified as unfit for service simply on the basis of being afraid. But who would want to serve in the trenches with a man given to panic under duress? He is best exempted from duty, or assigned to a noncombat position.

Of particular interest is the possible impact of this part of Deuteronomy on the Gospel of Luke. In *Studies in the Gospels*, C. F. Evans suggested that Luke 9:51—18:14 is a Christian Deuteronomy, patterned on the material in Deu-

21. "Structure of the Deuteronomic Law," p. 137.

teronomy 1–26.[22] The suggestion has been applied specifically to Deuteronomy 20:5–8 and Luke 14:16–20.[23]

The parallel is the list of those exempted from military service in Deuteronomy and the list of excuses given by those who declined the invitation to the banquet. See Table 16.

But why use a battle or war (Deut. 20) in association with a banquet (Luke 14)? Is it possibly because a good bit of Scripture points to two phenomena at the end of the age, a battle and a banquet, the great and terrible day of our Lord and the marriage supper of the Lamb?

The last two paragraphs move from military personnel to military strategies. The non-Palestinian city is first offered by Israel the chance to surrender (vv. 10–15). The city within Palestine is to be completely destroyed (vv. 16–18). In any siege, trees that bear edible fruit are not to be cut down (vv. 19–20). Interestingly, in verses 10–18 victory is assumed. There is no indication that defeat or stalemate is a possibility. Israel is pictured as a powerful nation that will either intimidate her opposition into submission or else will stride unmolested and unchallenged

Table 16

Deuteronomy 20	Luke 14
house built, not yet dedicated (20:5)	field bought, not yet seen (14:18)
vineyard planted, fruit not yet enjoyed (20:6)	oxen bought, not yet examined (14:19)
man engaged to be married (20:7)	man recently married (14:20)

22. (Oxford: Basil Blackwell, 1955), pp. 37–53.

23. See, for example, the studies by P. H. Ballard, "Reason for Refusing the Great Supper," *JTS* 23 (1972): 341–350, and J. A. Sanders, "The Ethic of Election in Luke's Great Banquet Parable," in *Essays in Old Testament Ethics*, eds. James Crenshaw and John T. Willis (New York: Ktav, 1974), pp. 245–271, especially pp. 254–259.

into the cities of her opposition and destroy "everything that breathes."

The chapter began with a list of those exempted from military service. The chapter concludes with a designation of what is to be spared from military destruction, and that is the land's natural resources.

Life and Death (21)

I suggested at the beginning of this chapter that the last few chapters of the Deuteronomic legal corpus may be the most amorphous of all. Some scholars have been content to put everything in chapters 21–25 under the one heading of miscellaneous laws. Chapter 21 seems to confirm that. For we find the following: a law about the expiation of homicide when the murderer has not been apprehended, verses 1–9; a law about marrying a woman captured in war, verses 10–14; a law about the inheritance upholding the right of the first-born, verses 15–17; a law about a stubborn and rebellious son, verses 18–21; a law about the burial of the body of an executed criminal, verses 22–23.

Carmichael contends that what all these laws have in common is that they dramatically associate death with life: the unworked heifer, the unplowed land, and the man slain in the open country. The woman captured in war is forcibly removed from her parents for whom she mourns for one month, for presumably she will see them no more. But then she becomes the wife of an Israelite, a celebration of a new life. A father approaching death must not sidestep his eldest son's future well-being, his life. Wise parents try to preserve life through concern over and chastising of the son, but they must turn him over for the punishment of death when all hope is gone and the problem is incorrigible. The interment of the impaled criminal before nightfall will mean an undefiled land for Israel, a land that is alive, not sterile or stained. It is obvious that this particular polarity—life and death—is held out to the Israelites throughout all of Deuteronomy.[24]

The first law in this chapter addresses the community. The last law is also directed to the community. Both deal with a corpse in open view, for which immediate action must be taken. In the first law the body is that of a victim. In the last it is the body of a criminal.

In the case of the unsolved murder a ritual is mandated, all parts of which are not apparent to us in terms of their significance. The heifer is no substitute for anybody's sin. Its blood is not shed; only its neck is broken. This must be the case, for the elders, after they break the heifer's neck, say, "our hands did not shed this blood." To make sense the "blood" has to be the blood of the victim, not of the heifer. All this does not mean that Deuteronomy has a unique view of sacrifice,[25] but simply that the ceremony is *not* sacrificial. That is why the priests perform no ritual, and why in the ceremony the priests enter the story *after* the neck is broken.

The ceremony concludes with a handwashing ritual (v. 6) which probably amounts to a symbolic expression of innocence (cf. Pilate's handwashing at the trial of Jesus, Matt. 27:24); and with a liturgical recitation (vv. 7–8) which amounts to a negative confession of innocence.

The next three laws of this chapter are concerned with the family and the progression is interesting: wife (vv. 10–14); wife and son (vv. 15–17); son (vv. 18–21). The first of these three laws repeats Deuteronomy 20:10–15, where we discovered that in a battle against a non-Palestinian city the women, children, and livestock were to be taken captive, not killed. Here it is added that the Israelite may take a wife from such a city. Presumably she is

24. "A Common Element in Five Supposedly Disparate Laws," *VT* 29 (1979), pp. 131ff.

25. As argued by Weinfeld, *Deuteronomy and the Deuteronomic School*, pp. 210ff.

unmarried, for she is allowed to mourn for one month for her parents, not a husband. She is not to be treated like a slave.

The second law of this section forbids a man who has two wives, of whom one is the more favored, from arbitrarily assigning the inheritance to the first-born of the favored wife even if he is not the first-born. Undoubtedly the law reflects the incident in Genesis in which Jacob bypasses his first-born by Leah, Reuben (although Jacob did not bypass Reuben's first-born rights arbitrarily).

This law stipulates that the first-born, regardless of who his mother is, is to receive a "double portion." That particular phrase is the same as the one that Elisha uses to Elijah—"let me inherit a double share of your spirit" (II Kings 2:9). The phrase is often mistakenly interpreted and has Elisha asking for twice as much of the spirit as Elijah had. He is asking Elijah—and here is his boldness—to declare him his primary successor. If there are two successors Elisha requests two-thirds of Elijah's spirit, with one-third to go to the other. If there are three successors then Elisha is requesting one-half of Elijah's spirit, with one-fourth each for the other two successors, and so forth.

The third law in this subunit deals with the case of the son who is stubborn, rebellious, and refuses correction. He is to be turned over to the authorities and stoned to death. But both parents must agree that this is the only course of action left. Few laws in Deuteronomy have as striking parabolic application to Israel as does this one. For the terms used here to describe the son—"stubborn and rebellious"—are consistently applied elsewhere in Scripture to Israel![26] Does Israel too reach the incorrigible state where God has no choice but to exile her (but ultimately to purify and redeem her)?

26. E. Bellefontaine, "Deuteronomy 21:18–21: Reviewing the Case of the Rebellious Son," *JSOT* 13 (1979), pp. 18ff.

Lawful and Unlawful Relationships (22)

There are between fifteen and twenty laws in this chapter. At least all the laws in verses 13–30 fall into one general category, laws of chastity. The first twelve verses, however, cannot be so neatly packed together. These twelve verses include a law about one's responsibilities if he comes upon something lost and belonging to his brother, verses 1–4 (and perhaps a law that provides Old Testament background for Jesus' parable about lost things);[27] transvestism, verse 5; discovery of a bird's nest, either fallen or in a tree, with the mother bird and her young ones in it, verses 6–7; how to properly build a house, verse 8; avoiding certain kinds of mixtures, verses 9–11; how to ornament one's cloak, verse 12.

There are three possibilities here. One possibility is to view verses 1–12 as a collection of heterogeneous laws. A second approach is to attempt to relate some of the laws at least to each other by a common word or theme. Thus 22:3, "so shall you do with his garment," and 22:5, "nor shall a man put on a woman's garment." The emphasis on garments is continued into the law about wool and linen, 22:11; tassels on the cloak, 22:12; and the menstrual garment, 22:17. Or one can make this connection: 22:4, a fallen animal; 22:6, a fallen nest; 22:8, a fallen person.[28]

A third possibility advanced by Carmichael is that 22:1–8 deals with procedures of wartime.[29] When you are at war don't take your anger on your enemy or brother out on his animals. You are not at war with them. And treat the occupants of a bird's nest as you would the fruit-producing trees. Spare them. The interesting law about

27. See J. D. M. Derrett, "Fresh Light on the Lost Sheep and the Lost Coin," *NTS* 26 (1979): 36–60.

28. "Structure of the Deuteronomic Law," p. 136.

29. "A Time for War and a Time for Peace: The Influence of the Distinction upon some Legal and Literary Material (in Dt)," *JJS* 25 (1974), pp. 51ff.

transvestism Carmichael takes to mean that a woman shall not put on the weapons of a man of war, or dress like a man in order to try to gain admission clandestinely into the army. Nor are men to attempt to avoid military conscription by dressing as women. Finally, in a time of peace, prized as those moments are, one does not want blood on his hand through careless house construction. Carmichael's equations are quite ingenious, especially his explanation of the law about transvestism. But in my judgment his explanation is unlikely. Why does the author of Deuteronomy 22 not speak more directly if indeed his concern is with wartime conduct? There is no indication in the first half of the chapter that the laws refer to wartime. In previous chapters (20:1, for example) the author specifically wrote, "When you go forth to war."

The majority of the chapter is about sexual relations, or more accurately, the violation of those relations. Perhaps the three brief laws about not mixing (two kinds of seeds, the ox and the ass, and wool and linen, vv. 9–11) serve as a prelude to these laws on chastity that also deal with unlawful mixing at the sexual level. In all, six situations are discussed: charges brought by a husband against a wife suspected of infidelity, verses 13–19; procedures to be followed if the charge is substantiated, verses 20–21; adultery, verse 22; intercourse with an engaged virgin in the city, verses 23–24; intercourse with an engaged virgin in the countryside, verses 25–27; intercourse with a virgin, verses 28–29. The first three of these have as their focus the married woman. The last three are concerned with the unmarried woman.

We may note three things about the penalties imposed. First, to whom is culpability attached? In only one instance is the woman alone punished—number 2. Twice both man and woman are condemned—numbers 3 and 4. Three times the man alone is judged—numbers 1, 5, and 6.

In arranging the violations in this particular order a

deliberate literary sequence is created in which the punishments are arranged chiastically:[30]

A damages of one hundred shekels to woman's father
B woman executed
C woman and man executed
C[1] woman and man executed
B[1] man executed
A[1] damages of fifty shekels to woman's father

There is a significant difference between adultery and fornication. The penalty for adultery for both people is death (vv. 21–22). For fornication there is no death penalty. Instead the man must pay a fine to the woman's father of fifty shekels (v. 29). For that reason the man and a *betrothed* virgin are also stoned to death if they cohabit (v. 24), the exception being rape in the countryside. The explanation in the difference of the penalty is that Scripture treats the marriage relationship most seriously and honorably. The two have indeed become one flesh and nothing is allowed to become a wedge in that unity.

Exclusion, Cleanliness, and Possessions (23)

There is in this chapter a potpourri of laws without perhaps an overarching theme. The first eight verses deal with who may enter and who may not enter God's community. Membership is not open to everybody. Excluded are Ammonites and Moabites, both of whom are products of an incestuous relationship (see Gen. 19:30–38), as is the "bastard" of verse 2. Included are the Egyptians (?) and Edomites.

30. G. J. Wenham and J. G. McConville, "Drafting Techniques in some Deuteronomic Laws," *VT* 30 (1980), p. 250.

Verses 10–14 discuss the need for physical cleanliness in the camp, and to that end, who needs to go outside the camp—those who have to relieve bodily needs. It is unlikely that there is anything more than a hygienic concern here.

Cleanliness in the camp is required because "the LORD your God walks in the midst of your camp" (v. 14). Also, the community is to allow the escaped slave to "dwell . . . in your midst" (v. 16). Provocatively, the slave is allowed to dwell "in the place which he shall choose." We recall that this is a divine prerogative throughout Deuteronomy. Is Israel, then, to welcome the slave, while excluding the Ammonites and Moabites and tolerating the Egyptians and Edomites ("the third generation")?

A law forbidding religious prostitution (vv. 17–18), part of which is concerned with money (v. 18), is followed by one that prohibits loans to fellow Israelites with interest (vv. 19–20). The next law also is in the general area of money and possessions (vv. 21–23). A vow to the Lord needs to be paid in the right way. Verse 18 tells the wrong way to finance the vows! In a sense the last law of this chapter is in the same area. Do not turn an act of good will by your neighbor, says this law, into an act of thievery by yourself. There is to be no "what is yours is mine" (vv. 24–25).

Marriage and Poverty (24)

The first law in this chapter, verses 1–4, is one that has evoked considerable discussion. Its subject is divorce, and more specifically, the remarriage of the woman to her first husband after either the death of her second husband or a divorce from her second husband. The crux in this passage is the explanation of the reason for the divorce: "he has found some indecency in her," literally, "the nakedness of a thing." Does this refer to adultery or some other type of mischievous sexual conduct on the part of the wife? If that is the case, then why are the woman and her companion not stoned to death, as 22:22 stipulated? We would expect execution, not divorce.

Also, the Hebrew phrase for "some indecency" is found in 23:14 in a context dealing with proper toilet facilities in the camp, "that he may not see anything indecent among you." Clearly no moral connotation is attached to the phrase there—it refers to what is unbecoming, but certainly not what is immoral. There is no evidence in the Old Testament that human excrement is itself defiling.

What then are the options if sexual indulgence is ruled out? Perhaps we can adopt the other extreme and suggest that the ambiguity of the phrase gave to the husband the right to divorce his wife for whatever reason he wished.[31] This is not to suggest that the husband had license to dissolve a marriage Hollywood-style. Rather it suggests that divorce is a domestic issue, not a concern of the courts, and therefore no legal body is able to issue or impose criteria on individual persons vis-à-vis divorce regulations.

There is nothing in the law to indicate that divorce is illegal. Nor is there anything to suggest that the remarriage of a divorcée is illegal. What is anathema is the remarriage of two people formerly married to each other. Again no reason is stated for the prohibition. Those who interpret a second marriage as adultery per se appeal for that meaning in the words, "she has been defiled." To remarry one who is defiled is out of the question. That idea may be echoed in Jeremiah 3:1a.

G. J. Wenham has suggested that the reason for prohibiting remarriage has nothing to do with adultery but instead is concerned with incest.[32] To become a bride is to become

31. A. Phillips, "Some aspects of family law in pre-exilic Israel," *VT* 23 (1973), p. 355.

32. "The Restoration of Marriage Reconsidered," *JJS* 30 (1979), p. 40.

a sister. To marry her a second time is therefore tantamount to marrying one's sister. There are certainly possibilities in Wenham's suggestion but his explanation skirts the emphasis in the law on the second marriage to somebody else. The concern of the law is neither the first nor second marriage, but the third. And having said that, it is reasonable to ask how prevalent such a custom would be. In very few societies, at least in the West, does a remarriage of spouses take place.

Those who have explored the role of women in the Old Testament have drawn attention to the fact that nowhere does Scripture permit the woman to take the initiative in divorce proceedings. This observation becomes more significant and critical when we realize that pagan cultures around Israel permitted both man and woman to start the proceedings. For instance, Law 142 of the Code of Hammurabi says: "If a woman so hated her husband that she declared, 'you may not have me' her record shall be investigated at her city council, and if she was careful and was not at fault, even though her husband has been going out and disparaging her greatly, that woman, without incurring any blame at all, may take her dowry and go off to her father's house."[33]

Are we to conclude from this that a woman in other cultures had a greater degree of independence than a woman did in Israel? Was the woman a person in Mesopotamian society, but only a possession in Israelite society?

I am persuaded that the answer to that query is a definite no, a conclusion that is borne out by a full examination of all the literary evidence in both civilizations. What, then, are we to make of the divorce procedure?

33. James B. Pritchard, *Ancient Near Eastern Texts Relating to the Old Testament*, second edition (Princeton, NJ: Princeton University Press, 1955), p. 172.

The best answer to that question may be found in the interesting remark of Walther Eichrodt:

> In general, it may indeed be said, that wherever a highly developed culture dissolves, or merely loosens, the cement of family and clan, then intensified legal protections for the individual normally become necessary. The Israelite kingdoms, however, were for the greater part of their existence peasant, agricultural states. . . . In such simpler conditions the strength of the family and clan affords the individual a powerful support, which takes the place of many legal measures. . . . If this great importance of the clan right into the monarchical period is borne in mind, then the absence of these Babylonian-type legal stipulations in Israel becomes easier to understand.[34]

Interestingly, a divorce law is followed by a law on the maintenance of marriage, verse 5. A man is allowed to spend the first year of marriage completely with his wife. Although the next law moves to the subject of taking a millstone as a pledge, verse 6, the sexual imagery of the two preceding laws is not hard to miss here. Just as the newlywed is not to be separated from his wife, neither is the "upper millstone," the one that moves over the one underneath, to be separated from its partner. S. Kaufmann notes the association of the word for "mill" with "bridegroom" and "groom" in Jeremiah 25:10.[35]

The following catena of laws rounds out the chapter: kidnaping, verse 7; leprosy—remember Miriam—verses 8–9; another word on loans and treatment of the debtor, verses 10–13; oppression of the poor, verses 14–15; individual responsibility, verse 16; justice for the defenseless, verses 17–18; leaving food for the poor, verses 19–22. This

34. *Theology of the Old Testament*, Old Testament Library, trans. J. Baker, 2 vols. (Philadelphia: Westminster, 1961), vol. 1, p. 81.

35. "Structure of the Deuteronomic Law," p. 156, n. 108.

last law parallels the last law of chapter 23. When you are a guest do not presume on your host's hospitality (23:24–25). When you are the host, or gathering in your crops, do not harvest the fields clean. The majority of this last part of the chapter is concerned with laws concerning the poor (vv. 6, 7, 10–15, 17–22). Any attempt to control them, manipulate them, oppress them, or starve them puts one's relationship to God in jeopardy.

Litigation and Justice (25)

This chapter contains mostly laws about pairs: a dispute between two men, verses 1–3; "If brothers dwell together," verses 5–10; two men fighting, verses 11–12; two kinds of weights, verses 13–16; Israel and Amalek, verses 17–19.

The first law involves a legal dispute between two contestants. The purpose of the law is not primarily to prescribe corporal punishment, but to limit it. The maximum number of blows on the guilty party is not to exceed forty (cf. Paul's thirty-nine lashes, one less than the limit, II Cor. 11:24).

Verse 4, a separate law, is about the illicit muzzling of an ox, a verse that is quoted by Saint Paul in I Corinthians 9:9 and I Timothy 5:18. Unlike the laws around it, it is not concerned with something about two parties. But it may indeed serve as an introduction to the law that follows, verses 5–10. Just as the ox is entitled to eat while it works in the fields, so is a childless widow entitled to bear a son who will carry on the name of her deceased husband.[36]

Clearly the law of verses 5–10 is a reflection of levirate marriage. The concern is not with a widow, but with a childless widow. Also the concern is that the woman not remarry "outside the family to a stranger." The law does leave some questions unanswered. For example, what is

36. Carmichael, *The Laws of Deuteronomy*, p. 239.

meant by the phrase "if brothers dwell together"? Do we take it literally, that is, under the same roof? Is the levirate marriage limited only to the first-born son? What if the other brothers are already married? If after a man fathers a child by his sister-in-law (a relationship normally forbidden, see Lev. 18:16), is he allowed to marry another woman? What if there were no other brothers? The story of Genesis 38 has the father-in-law as the levir, and in Ruth it is Boaz, one of her relatives, who "redeems" her.

One thing this law does make clear is that a man could not be forced against his will to impregnate his sister-in-law. To be sure, refusal did bring public humiliation—she "shall . . . spit in his face"—but nothing beyond that. Additionally this act of the woman was performed "in the presence of the elders," but they function only as interrogators and observers. Beyond that they play no role (unlike the judges in the law of vv. 1–3). As with the divorce law of 24:1–4, we may have another instance of family law. For the court to act would be for it to venture into unauthorized areas.

The fourth law in this chapter is also concerned with a family situation. A wife comes to the rescue of her husband who is being assaulted. She tries to put a stop to things—following her instincts—by grabbing the antagonist's genitalia. For that she is to lose her hand, of special interest because only here in biblical law is mutilation mandated as a fit punishment for a crime. It is hard to believe that this law was implemented regularly.

The fifth law in verses 13–16 shifts from people to possessions, in this instance, two kinds of weights and measures. What is forbidden here is deception. Or perhaps more accurately, what is forbidden is even the *possession* of such fraudulent items: "you shall not *have* . . . two kinds of weights" (italics mine). The best way to fight temptation is to avoid situations where the temptation most easily can move from thought to act. Thus even the appearance of evil is to be shunned.[37]

The last paragraph in the section, verses 17–19, ought to be included perhaps with the next chapter. It is Moses' reminder to Israel to show no mercy to the Amalekites, and as such is not really one of the laws of the Deuteronomy corpus. What is found here, but not in Exodus 17:8–15, is the fact that Amalek attacked only the weary and faint of Israel, those most helpless and defenseless. May the simple addition of the fact be a parable without commentary to Israel? She runs the risk of perpetually inciting God's wrath if she offends one of these of her group.

Obedience: This Day! (26)

The legal corpus of Deuteronomy concludes with this chapter, and it may be divided quite transparently into three sections. First is a liturgy for the presentation of the first fruits, verses 1–11. A substantial part of this unit is comprised of the credo Israel is to proclaim once she is settled in Palestine, verses 5–10. Essentially Moses says to Israel: in your future do not forget your past.

The second part of the chapter is another liturgy for the presentation of the triennial tithe, verses 12–15 (cf. the previous discussion of this in 14:28–29). The confession of verses 5–10 emphasized what God had done for Israel, for "us." The confession within this liturgy, verses 13–15, emphasizes what each person has done or not done. Apparently the believer is expected to be able to live a life of obedience and purity, to be able to stand before his Lord and say: I have lived by your standards, Master.

The last paragraph, verses 16–19, is the third section and is a concluding challenge of Moses to the people. Of

37. S. Kaufmann, "Structure of the Deuteronomic Law," p. 144.

special interest here is the emphasis on the "this day." "This day the LORD your God commands you. . . . You have declared this day. . . . And the LORD has declared this day" (vv. 16–18).

The phrase is a crucial one throughout all Deuteronomy. The expression, or one very close to it, appears at least fifty-nine times in Deuteronomy, almost half of which are in the formula, "the commandments which I am commanding you this day."

Simon DeVries has made an interesting study of this word. His conclusion regarding the urgency evoked by the formula is worthy of comment: "His revelation is *now*. He is very alive and present. Israel must respond one way or another, because the voice of God is near. The word they must obey is not far off in the heavens or belonging to remote antiquity. Therefore, do not defer your choice to still another 'today.' "[38]

Bibliography

Chapter 12

Claburn, W. G. "The Fiscal Basis of Josiah's Reforms." *JBL* 92 (1973): 11–22.

Gutmann, J. "Deuteronomy: Religious Reformation or Iconoclastic Revolution." In *The Image and the Word: Confrontations in Judaism, Christianity and Islam*. Edited by Joseph Gutmann. Missoula, MT: Scholars Press for the American Academy of Religion, 1977, pp. 5–25.

Kaufmann, S. "The Structure of the Deuteronomic Law." *Maarav* 1 (1979): 105–158.

Kaufmann, Y. *The Religion of Israel*. Translated by Moshe Greenberg. Chicago: University of Chicago Press, 1960, pp. 180–182.

Milgrom, J. "Profane Slaughter and a Formulaic Key to the Composition of Deuteronomy." *HUCA* 47 (1976): 1–17.

Rofé, A. "The Strata of the Law about the Centralization of Worship in

38. "The Development of the Deuteronomic Promulgation Formula," *Bibl* 55 (1974), p. 316.

Deuteronomy and the History of the Deuteronomic Movement." *SVT* 22 (1972); 221–226.

Roth, M. W. "The Deuteronomic Rest Theology. A Redaction-Critical Study." *BRes* 21 (1976): 5–14.

Wenham, G. J. "Deuteronomy and the Central Sanctuary." *TB* 22 (1971): 103–118.

Chapter 13

Polzin, R., *Moses and the Deuteronomist: A Literary Study of the Deuteronomic History*. New York: Seabury, 1980, pp. 57–65.

Chapter 14

Craigie, P. C. "Deuteronomy and Ugaritic Studies." *TB* 28 (1977): 155–169.

Chapter 15

Lemeche, N. P. "The manumission of slaves—the fallow year—the sabbatical year—the jobel year." *VT* 26 (1976): 38–59, esp. pp. 43–45.

Weingreen, J. "The Deuteronomic Legislator—A Proto-Rabbinic Type." In *From Bible to Mishnah*. Manchester: Manchester University Press, 1976, pp. 132–142.

Chapter 17

Daube, D. "One from among Your Brethren Shall You Set King Over You." *JBL* 90 (1971): 480–481.

Weingreen, J. "Deuteronomy, A Proto-Mishna." In *From Bible to Mishnah*. Manchester: Manchester University Press, pp. 143–154.

Chapter 18

Abba, R. "Priests and Levites in Deuteronomy." *VT* 27 (1977): 257–267.

Polzin, R. *Moses and the Deuteronomist: A Literary Study of the Deuteronomic History*. New York: Seabury, 1980, pp. 57–65.

Tigay, J. H. "Empirical Basis for the Documentary Hypothesis." *JBL* 94 (1975): 329–342.

Chapter 20

Palmor, H. "Just Married, Cannot Come (Matt. 22, Lk. 14, Thomas 44, Dt. 20)." *NT* 18 (1976): 241–257.

Chapter 21

Bellefontaine, E. "Deuteronomy 21:18–21: Reviewing the Case of the Rebellious Son." *JSOT* 13 (1979): 13–31.

Carmichael, C. "A Common Element in Five Supposedly Disparate Laws." *VT* 29 (1979): 129–142.

Watson, P. "A Note on the 'Double Portion' of Dt 21:17 and 2 Ki 2:9." *RestQ* 8 (1965): 70–75.

Wilcox, M. " 'Upon the Tree'—Deut 21:22–23 in the New Testament." *JBL* 96 (1977): 85–99.

Zevit, Z. "*ʿegla* Ritual of Deuteronomy 21:1–9." *JBL* 95 (1976): 377–390.

Chapter 22

Carmichael, C. "A Time for War and a Time for Peace: The Influence of the Distinction upon some Legal and Literary Material (in Dt)." *JJS* 25 (1974): 50–64.

Derrett, J. D. "2 Cor 6:14: A Midrash on Dt 22:10." *Bibl* 59 (1978): 231–250.

Fishbane, M. "Biblical Colophons, Textual Criticism and Legal Analogies." *CBQ* 42 (1980): 438–449, esp. pp. 447–449.

Wenham, G. J., and McConville, J. G. "Drafting Techniques in some Deuteronomic Laws." *VT* 30 (1980): 248–252.

Chapter 23

Craigie, P. C. "Deuteronomy and Ugaritic Studies." *TB* 28 (1977): 155–169.

Phillips, A. C. "Uncovering the father's skirt." *VT* (1980): 38–43.

Wevers, J. W. "The Earliest Witness to the LXX Deuteronomy." *CBQ* 39 (1977): 240–244.

Chapter 24

Hobbs, T. R. "Jeremiah 3:1 and Deuteronomy 24:1–4." *ZAW* 86 (1974): 23–29.

Wenham, G. J. "The Restoration of Marriage Reconsidered." *JJS* 30 (1979): 36–40.

Wevers, J. W. "The Earliest Witness to the LXX Deuteronomy." *CBQ* 39 (1977): 240–244.

Chapter 25

Carmichael, C. "Ceremonial Crux: Removing a Man's Sandal As a Female Gesture of Contempt." *JBL* 96 (1977): 321–336.

Kaiser, W. C., Jr. "Current Crisis in Exegesis and the Apostolic Use of Deuteronomy 25:4 in I Cor 9:8–10." *JETS* 21 (1978): 3–18.

Noonan, J. T. "The muzzled ox." *JQR* 70 (1980): 172–175.

Wevers, J. W. "The Earliest Witness to the LXX Deuteronomy." *CBQ* 39 (1977): 240–244.

Chapter 26

Millard, A. "A Wandering Aramean." *JNES* 49 (1980): 153–155.

Rice, G. "Egypt, the Desert, and Canaan (Three Themes in Dt 26:5–10)." *JRelTht* 18 (1961): 23–25.

Wevers, J. W. "The Earliest Witness to the LXX Deuteronomy." *CBQ* 39 (1977): 240–244.

22

Blessings and Curses

Deuteronomy 27–30, 31:1–6

The four chapters to be studied in this unit constitute the last two chapters of Moses' second address (chaps. 27–28), and Moses' brief third address (chaps. 29–30, plus the first six verses of chap. 31).

Moses has finished placing before Israel the law of the Lord. Toward this law no believer can be neutral. Either he will choose to live by it or he will choose to ignore it. What Moses is interested in establishing here is the fact of consequences, or retribution, a divine response that is commensurate with the choice made by the individual.

If that choice is obedience the consequence is blessing. If that choice is disobedience the consequence is curse. And particularly in the third address the curse includes a future exile from the land, a theme first sounded in 4:27–31. Robert Polzin has captured the shift in emphasis from Moses' second to third address: "The emphasis there [the second address, 5–28] was on the immediate future and what Israel had to do to *remain* in the land God was giving them. Here in the third address, emphasis is on the far-distant future of the exile and on what Israel has to do to *regain* the land."[1]

We may outline this section as follows:

1. *Moses and the Deuteronomist: A Literary Study of the Deuteronomic History* (New York: Seabury, 1980), p. 70.

1. 27:1–10, a covenant-renewal ceremony at Shechem
2. 27:11–26, a proclamation by the Levites of twelve prohibitions, with appropriate congregational response
3. 28:1–14, blessings
4. 28:15–68, curses
5. 29:1–29, an exhortation to commitment and faithfulness
6. 30:1–10, hope for restoration even in exile
7. 30:11–20, the options: life and death—choose!

It is obvious, when looking at the sections involving results or consequences, that far more space is devoted to curse than to blessing. In chapter 27 we note that representatives of six of the tribes stand on Mount Ebal to curse (v. 13) and representatives of the remaining six tribes stand on Mount Gerizim to bless (v. 12). Yet we read of no blessings in the last half of the chapter, only curses. (This is one of the reasons why many interpreters think that chapter 27 is an insertion that separates chapter 26 from 28, and one that has undergone a long literary development. The arguments on this question can be followed in the commentaries.)

This imbalance between curse and blessing is not unexpected. P. C. Craigie quotes Kenneth A. Kitchen on this phenomenon in other corpora. In the Lipit-Ishtar laws, curses outnumber blessings by approximately 3:1. In the Code of Hammurabi the proportion of curses to blessings is approximately 20:1. This emphasis continues into the first-millennium B.C. Assyrian treaties (for example, the seventh-century B.C. treaty of Esarhaddon), in which 250 of 674 lines are given to curses.[2]

2. *The Book of Deuteronomy*, New International Commentary of the Old Testament series (Grand Rapids: Eerdmans, 1976), p. 340, n. 15.

The theological issue that is being sounded in these chapters is one that provided a basis for serious theological reflection in Scripture itself, and is an issue that continues into the present day. I refer here to what is commonly called Deuteronomic theology. That is, those who follow the Lord may anticipate blessing in the form of children, health, prosperity, conquest over the enemy, or ideal climatic conditions in which to produce one's agricultural crops. Conversely, the absence of these factors, or their antithesis, is a result of disobedience to covenantal norms. Thus, Deuteronomy 28 puts the curses of God on Israel's disobedience into the categories of sickness and drought, verses 20–24; military defeat, verses 25–26; diseases of mind and body and loss of one's wife and livestock, verses 27–35; a dreary, nonproductive life in exile, verses 36–46; and siege by the enemy, verses 47–57.

The system then appears simple, straightforward, and black and white. Those who follow the Lord rightly may instantly expect blessings at every material level. Those who repudiate Yahweh's lordship over their lives can expect heartaches, setbacks, sterility, and so forth.

The question I wish to pursue is to what degree Deuteronomic theology informs the rest of the Old Testament. Are there sections of the Old Testament that challenge too easy of an equation at this point? Does Deuteronomy itself forbid its reader from oversimplifying the relationship between one's character and one's circumstances? What about the teachings of Jesus and Paul?

Or, if the Deuteronomic emphasis is perverted what are the possibilities for ruin, harm, and misrepresentation? G. K. Chesterton speaks to this. "When once people have begun to believe that prosperity is the reward of virtue, their next calamity is obvious. If prosperity is regarded as the reward of virtue, it will be regarded as the symptom of virtue. Men will leave off the heavy task of making good men successful. They will adopt the easier task of making out successful men good."[3]

I have already had occasion to refer to the studies of Martin Noth and his contention that the narratives in Joshua and Kings function primarily as a historical witness to the truthfulness of Deuteronomy's theology vis-à-vis obedience, disobedience, and consequences.

To these historical books we may also add much from the oracles of the prophets. It is, for example, not an exaggeration to say that almost all the preaching of the eighth-century B.C. Amos is based on Deuteronomy 28, or something very close to it. Such a backdrop makes even more intelligible his rhetorical questions such as: "Does evil befall a city, unless the LORD has done it?" (3:6b). In the very next chapter (4:6–11) Amos lists the following as illustrations of God's trying to bring Israel to an awakening: a shortage of food, no rains for the harvest, a lack of adequate drinking water, disease that wiped out the precious produce of gardens and vineyards, and war and pestilence. Thus, every conceivable misfortune is the product of the Lord's wrath.

A second support of this emphasis is a number of the Psalms. One has only to think of passages such as Psalm 1, a contrast between the righteous man who prospers in all that he does, and the wicked man who is perishing. Again, one recalls David's testimony: "I have not seen the righteous forsaken or his children begging bread" (Ps. 37:25); or "Many are the pangs of the wicked, but steadfast love surrounds him who trusts in the LORD" (Ps. 32:10).

Parallel to some of these "wisdom Psalms" are similar reverberations in Proverbs. The first nine chapters alone provide ample illustrations of the rewards for those who fear the Lord. They will be delivered but the wicked will

3. Quoted in *The Dimensions of Job: A Study and Selected Readings*, ed. Nahum N. Glatzer (New York: Schocken, 1969), pp. 236–237.

be cut off and rooted out (2:12, 21–22). To fear the Lord is a guarantee that "your barns will be filled with plenty, and your vats will be bursting with wine" (3:10). One may add to these longer units aphoristic sayings in Proverbs such as, "He who sows injustice will reap calamity" (22:8). (I am not concerned here with the debate on whether wisdom literature views the retribution to be something imposed on the person from outside or above, or something that is inward and necessary, growing out of the act itself. I am simply establishing the fact of the principle that each act has a consequence.)

So deeply entrenched was this idea that it was still prevalent among Jesus' disciples. Viewing a man with congenital blindness, they asked, "who sinned, this man or his parents, that he was born blind?" (John 9:2). After His conversation with the rich young ruler Jesus added the following for the benefit of His disciples: "it will be hard for a rich man to enter the kingdom of heaven." A camel will squeeze through the needle's eye first (Matt. 19:23–24). Their response? "Who then can be saved?" For had not wealth been considered one of the prime evidences of God's blessing? Their theology also explains why they could not accept the Lord's forthcoming crucifixion.

Yet we need to observe that, for all the truthfulness of the treaty curses and blessings of Deuteronomy, they present only a part of the picture. Any conclusions we may want to draw need to be tempered by a study of all Scripture. The following observations are important.

First, the historical books themselves present something of a mixed picture. In war "the sword devours now one and now another" (II Sam. 11:25), so that the innocent suffer along with the guilty. Witness the untimely death of Abner (II Sam. 3:33–34), the priests of Nob (I Sam. 22:18), and the brothers of Abimelech (Judg. 9:5). These are instances in which death has nothing at all to do with retributive justice. On the other side of the ledger one has only to think of the many kings, both Judean and Israelite, who basked in luxury and opulence, and all this in spite of a God-defying lifestyle.

Second, the prophets do not baptize the Deuteronomic theology uncritically. In an emphasis reminiscent of parts of Deuteronomy, Hosea reminds Israel that in spite of her infidelity He has given her "the grain, the wine, and the oil, and who lavished upon her silver and gold" (Hos. 2:8). Here are gifts of divine blessing, although by all accounts such gifts should have been withheld. Perhaps the parade example in prophetic literature is the "suffering servant" of Isaiah 53. The servant of the Lord is rejected, afflicted, and treated with contempt. He does not prosper. And this is simply an extension, but in much greater intensity, of the suffering experienced by most of the prophets. Few, if any, escaped persecution and harassment. But at no point is the suggestion made that these trials are a divine rebuke leveled at His spokesmen.

Third, indeed some Psalms do support a traditional understanding of reward and punishment. But as many, if not more, challenge the traditional view. Limiting himself to the wisdom psalms, J. K. Kuntz divides these psalms into three categories in what they espouse about the doctrine of reward and punishment. These categories are the traditional; the realistic; and the futuristic, which hopes in the prospects of immortality.[4] Add to this the large number of lament psalms (almost one-third of the Psalter), a few of which move into imprecation, and we are forced to take a deeper look at too facile an understanding of the act-and-consequence relationship.

Fourth, some entire books within the Old Testament canon protest against a frozen interpretation of Deuteronomy. The best examples are Ecclesiastes and Job. As the writer of Ecclesiastes observed, one fate comes to both the

4. "The Retribution Motiv in Psalmic Wisdom," *ZAW* 89 (1977), p. 232.

wise and the fool (2:14; 9:2). Both are forgotten quickly (2:16). Man has no advantage over the beast (3:19). God gives wealth and honor, but others who do not deserve them eat from them like scavengers (6:2). The experience of Job is well known. Job's friends were reflecting the theology of Deuteronomy accurately, but their application of it to Job was inaccurate and thus irrelevant.

Fifth, the witness of the New Testament is interesting. Jesus certainly taught the *eventual* relationship of character to destiny. What He repudiated was the *immediate* relationship of character and circumstance. Thus, the case of the lad being born blind had nothing at all to do with sin. The eighteen who were crushed to death by the falling tower in Siloam were not quintessential sinners (Luke 13:1–5). He taught that God sends rain and sunshine on unbeliever and believer alike (Matt. 5:45), a point especially interesting in light of Deuteronomy 28:12, which pinpoints rain as one of God's blessings on the obedient.

Two experiences from Paul's life buttress the instances taken from the Gospels.[5] Paul's experience on the Mediterranean during a storm may be compared with Jonah's experience much earlier on the same sea and in the same kind of weather. For Jonah the storm is sent from God to break down his disobedience and reluctance to go to Nineveh. For Paul the storm is simply a phenomenon of weather.

The second illustration revolves around Romans 8:31–39. Paul lists certain experiences that Deuteronomy 28 precisely lists as treaty curses—tribulation, distress, persecution, famine, nakedness, peril, and sword. In the midst of his argument Paul quotes Psalm 44:22—"For thy sake we are being killed all day long"—but does *not*

5. Both examples are taken from D. L. Thompson's perceptive article, "The Godly and the Good Life: The Relationship Between Character and Circumstance in Biblical Thought," *AsSem* 34 (April 1979): 28–46.

need to quote 44:23, "Rouse thyself! Why sleepest thou, O Lord?" Paul can say: "in all these things we are more than conquerors." The basis for Paul's assurance is not his experiences, but the death and resurrection of Christ (8:32–34).

A final point that can be made is that Deuteronomy itself gives us something of a double picture. Moses reminds Israel that God humbled Israel in the wilderness, not because of any specific sin, but to teach her and to test her (Deut. 8:2–3). It was a way of disciplining her (Deut. 8:5). Moses also reminds Israel that she has been given wealth, but it is all a gift of God, and is not something earned (Deut. 8:18). God is not giving the blessing of land and conquest to Israel because she is more righteous than the other nations (Deut. 9:4–6). And finally, Israel avoided the wrath of God in the episode of the golden calf only because Moses prayed (Deut. 9:25–29). She is spared by virtue of another, not because of any virtue in herself.[6] So even the Book of Deuteronomy cautions us against oversimplifying a very complex area of walking with God.

Bibliography

Bellefontaine, E. "The Curses of Deuteronomy 27: Their Relationship to the Prohibitives." In *No Famine in the Land*. Studies in honor of John L. McKenzie. Missoula, MT: Scholars Press for the Institute for Antiquity and Christianity, 1975, pp. 49–61.

Brichto, H. C. *The Problem of "Curse" in the Hebrew Bible*. Philadelphia: Society of Biblical Literature, 1963, pp. 77ff.

Budd, P. J. "Priestly Instruction in pre-exilic Israel." *VT* 23 (1973): 1–14.

Eichrodt, W. *Theology of the Old Testament*. Old Testament Library. Translated by J. Baker. 2 vols. Philadelphia: Westminster, 1967, vol. 1, pp. 258ff.

Gammie, J. G. "The Theology of Retribution in the Book of Deuteronomy." *CBQ* 32 (1970): 1–12.

6. See J. G. Gammie, "The Theology of Retribution in the Book of Deuteronomy," *CBQ* 32 (1970), pp. 10–12.

Kaufmann, Y. *The Religion of Israel*. Translated by Moshe Greenberg. Chicago: University of Chicago Press, 1960, pp. 329–338.

Kearney, P. J. "The Role of the Gibeonites in the Deuteronomic History." *CBQ* 35 (1973): 1–19.

Kuntz, J. K. "The Retribution Motiv in Psalmic Wisdom." *ZAW* 89 (1977): 223–233.

Patrick, D. "The Word Is Near At Hand." *Encounter* 33 (1972): 385–392.

Polzin, R. *Moses and the Deuteronomist: A Literary Study of the Deuteronomic History*. New York: Seabury, 1980, pp. 69–71.

Rad, G. von. *Wisdom in Israel*. Translated by James D. Martin. Nashville: Abingdon, 1973, pp. 128–137.

Thompson, D. L. "The Godly and the Good Life: The Relationship Between Character and Circumstance in Biblical Thought." *AsSem* 34 (April 1979): 28–46.

Towner, W. S. "Retribution Theology in the Apocalyptic Setting." *USQR* 26 (1971): 203–214.

Weinfeld, M. *Deuteronomy and the Deuteronomic School*. Oxford: Clarendon Press, 1978, pp. 104–146.

Wolff, H. W. "The Kerygma of the Deuteronomic Historical Work." Walter Brueggemann and Hans W. Wolff. *The Vitality of Old Testament Traditions*. Atlanta: John Knox, 1974, pp. 93–100.

23

Moses' Farewell

Deuteronomy 31:7—34:12

Two major chapters of this unit are poems—the "song of Moses," chapter 32, and "the blessing of Moses," chapter 33. Prefacing these poems is a list of a few events towards the end of Moses' life: the writing of the law, a concern for its periodic reading, the presentation of Joshua before the Lord (chap. 31). Following the poems is a final chapter, mostly about the death of Moses (chap. 34).

No small amount of ink has been expended on the two poems. For one thing, they are replete with translation problems and some unusual vocabulary and Hebrew grammar. The reader can easily check the verse-by-verse treatment in the commentaries or the study of Frank M. Cross and D. N. Freedman in order to see some of the issues here.

Another concern has been the dating of these poems. The theories suggest the time of Samuel as the earliest possibility to the time of the exile as the latest possibility. I know of no critical scholar who has suggested a pre-Samuel or Mosaic date for composition (except for Umberto Cassuto, who dates both poems to the time of the Judges). Nor am I aware of any critical scholar who does not endorse the idea that most of this latter unit is secondary, added much later to Ur-deuteronomy.

The conservative response would be at least threefold. First, the critical reconstruction, if plausible, must simply avoid the witness of these chapters themselves about their origin: "Then Moses spoke the words of this song" (31:30); "Moses came and recited all the words of this song" (32:44); "This is the blessing with which Moses the man of God blessed the children of Israel before his death" (33:1). Can such a witness be so easily ignored?

Second, the language of the poems is sufficiently archaic to be viewed as an authentic representation of late second-millennium B.C. Canaanite. George E. Mendenhall even goes so far to suggest a number of linguistic correlations between Deuteronomy 32 and the syllabic texts from Byblos which he dates to not much later than 2000 B.C., if not earlier![1]

Third, as the "final" text stands, we have an almost perfect structure for a second-millennium B.C. covenant. These last few chapters would include the following parts of that structure: the deposition of the text ("Take this book of the law, and put it by the side of the ark of the covenant of the LORD your God," 31:26); the periodic, public recital of the contents of the covenant ("At the end of every seven years . . . read this law before all Israel in their hearing," 31:10–11); the presence of witnesses to observe the covenant event ("that this song may be a witness for me against the people of Israel," 31:19; "this song shall confront them as a witness," 31:21; "this book of the law . . . that it may be there for a witness against you," 31:26; "and call heaven and earth to witness against them," 31:28). The question is: which is more likely, a homogeneous creation by an individual cognizant of contemporary patterns of expression and covenant making, or the creation by bits and pieces of a perfect structure patterned nostalgically after forms that essentially have long ceased to exist?

1. "Samuel's 'Broken *Rîb*': Deuteronomy 32," in *No Famine in the Land*, Studies in honor of John L. McKenzie (Missoula, MT: Scholars Press, 1975), p. 66.

Joshua the Successor (31)

This chapter contains seven speeches, four by Moses and three by the Lord:

1. Moses to Israel, verses 1–6: Israel will conquer Canaan, even without Moses
2. Moses to Joshua, verses 7–8: Away with fear! The Lord will be with you
3. Moses to the priests and elders, verses 9–13: Read this law every seven years
4. the Lord to Moses, verses 14–15: You are about to die. Bring Joshua before me
5. the Lord to Moses, verses 16–21: Israel will forsake me in Canaan
6. the Lord to Joshua, verse 23: I will be with you, Joshua
7. Moses to Levites, verses 24–29: Israel will rebel, as she already has

In three of these speeches Joshua is present (numbers 2, 4, and 6). Once he is spoken to by Moses (v. 7) and once by the Lord (v. 23); once he is spoken about (v. 14). One might expect verse 23 to follow verse 15; that is, the fourth speech leads naturally into the sixth speech. Thus we read: " 'Call Joshua, and present yourselves in the tent of meeting, that I may commission him.' And Moses and Joshua went and presented themselves in the tent of meeting" (v. 14); "And the LORD appeared" (v. 15); and then, "the LORD commissioned Joshua" (v. 23). However, coming between the summoning of Joshua and his actual commissioning is a speech by the Lord to Moses.

The point of this speech is that Israel, once in the land of promise, will follow other gods and force God into hiding (His face). To this prophecy Joshua is listening, or at least eavesdropping. This speech is really more for his benefit than for Moses'. It is God's way of saying, indirectly, to Joshua: Be prepared for the worst; your leadership over Israel will not deter her from disobedience. It is significant that throughout these events Joshua never speaks. He only listens. It is a chilling experience to be informed beforehand that your mission will meet only with mixed results. Even the reading of the law every seven years, designed to bring people to "fear the LORD," will not be a deterrent. For we note that the Lord speaks not of the possibility of apostasy, but of its inevitability. Apparently Moses is in agreement with the Lord at this point (vv. 27, 29)! He at least viewed himself as a restraining influence, a shadow his successor would not be able to cast.

The Song of Moses (32)

This poetic composition is, more than anything, a graphic contrast between the nature of God and the nature of His people. He is the Rock (vv. 4, 18, 30, 31). They are on the rocks, or following the wrong rock (v. 37).

The extensive study of G. E. Wright laid the foundation for subsequent understandings of this poem. It was his suggestion that the composition is a "covenant lawsuit" with a summons to witnesses (v. 1); an accusation in the form of a question (v. 6); the plaintiff's (God) benefits to the accused (vv. 7–14); a statement of breach of covenant (vv. 15–18); and subsequent sentencing and judgment on the guilty (vv. 19ff.).[2]

This analysis has been accepted more or less by most commentators. Only recently has a distinctive alternative been raised. Mendenhall suggests the poem is not a covenant lawsuit but rather a prophetic oracle. He states, "here

2. "The Lawsuit of God: A Form-critical Study of Deuteronomy 32," in *Israel's Prophetic Heritage*, essays in honor of James Muilenburg, Bernhard W. Anderson and Walter Harrelson, eds. (New York: Harper and Row, 1962), pp. 26–67.

Yahweh is *not* suing anyone for breach of covenant; instead the breach *had* taken place, the consequences *had* been suffered, and the issue is whether or not Yahweh would be a reliable refuge for the future."[3]

This interpretation has the advantage of shifting the major part of the poem from a diatribe against the people to a doxology to God. In the past God may have "hid his face" (v. 20). Now Moses will try to let Israel see that face again. Whether they will see it is uncertain. Moses himself is not sure of that. For that reason, in the introduction to the poem he can speak only wishfully, "May my teaching drop as the rain, my speech distil as the dew" (v. 2).

It is a waste of time to attempt to identify specific historical events to which the writer is alluding, although essentially the poem is a résumé of Israel's history. Even phrases that perhaps are identifiable seem strange. For example, we are struck by the phrase, "He found him in a desert land" (v. 10a; compare an echo of this in Hosea 9:10, "Like grapes in the wilderness, I found Israel"). The "desert land" can hardly be Egypt, although the equation is possible. Did God "find" Israel in the wilderness? Equally futile is the attempt to identify the enemies of verses 27–43. Are they Arameans, Assyrians, Babylonians, Samaritans, or perhaps some one other than these candidates?

The timelessness of the poem is accented not only by the vagueness of language but also by the constant change of pronominal subject throughout. To illustrate, "They have dealt corruptly with him, they are no longer his children. . . . Do you thus requite the LORD, you foolish and senseless people?" (vv. 5–6). Or, "you waxed fat, you grew thick, you became sleek; then he forsook God who made him. . . . They stirred him to jealousy" (vv. 15–16).

I pointed out that the prevalent metaphor in this chapter for God is "rock." Obviously the idea that is conveyed is

3. "Samuel's 'Broken *Rîb*,' " p. 70.

stability, permanence, refuge and security. But Moses is concerned to go beyond God's Gibraltar-like qualities. The parental metaphors, for instance, are interesting. At one point we read, "Is he not your father, who created you?" (v. 6). Later the writer changes to gynomorphic language: "You were unmindful of the Rock that begot you, and you forgot the God who gave you birth" (v. 18). (Jeremiah may parody this verse when he speaks to his backslidden contemporaries, those who say to a tree, "You are my father," and to a stone, "you gave me birth," Jeremiah 2:27, and in Jeremiah perhaps an ironic shift of sex roles.)

He is a God who has kept Israel as "the apple of his eye" (v. 10b). The phrase is particularly pregnant. The Hebrew reads literally, "he kept them as the 'little man' of his eye." How close do you have to get to another person before you see yourself reflected, diminutively, in that person's eyes? God has gotten that close to Israel. Israel too He has known face to face.

Verses 23–33 are especially interesting. God is about to unleash the ultimate punishment on His people—annihilation—but then He stops after further reflection. Here we have an instance of God deliberating with Himself. Of these verses Gerhard von Rad says, "This section is therefore an interlude which takes us out of the turmoil of historical processes and allows us to overhear a soliloquy within the depths of the divine heart."[4] His decision is to exercise restraint, not because Israel is meritorious, but because His honor is at stake.

But if the Lord exercises restraint on Israel's behalf, Israel's neighbors cannot expect to receive the same treatment. Against them the Lord will move with a vengeance (used four times in this section, vv. 35, 41, 43). Before we dismiss this notion as much too primitive and un-Chris-

4. *Deuteronomy: a Commentary*, Old Testament Library (Philadelphia: Westminster), p. 198.

tian let us recall similar sentiments that appear in the New Testament: "O Sovereign Lord . . . how long before thou wilt judge and avenge our blood on those who dwell upon the earth?" (Rev. 6:10), and "he has avenged on her the blood of her servants" (Rev. 19:2). Both of these verses from the Apocalypse are remarkably similar to Deuteronomy 32:43.

The Blessing of Moses (33)

This second poem also is addressed by Moses to Israel. But unlike the one in chapter 32, this one is directed mostly to individual groups, rather than to the whole. The whole community is addressed only in the preface, verses 1–5, and in the conclusion, verses 26–29. In between there is an individual word of Moses to Reuben, Judah, Levi, Benjamin, Joseph, Zebulun, Gad, Dan, Naphtali, and Asher.

This is not the first time in the Pentateuch that such oracles have been addressed to the tribes of Israel. The best parallel to this chapter is Genesis 49, the blessing of Jacob.

But in comparing the two one notices a crucial difference. The oracles in Genesis 49 are sometimes judgmental, sometimes salvific. By contrast, the oracles of Deuteronomy 33 are consistently salvific and promissory. They promise continued existence (v. 6); priestly prerogatives (v. 10); safety (v. 11); choice gifts (vv. 13–16); affluence (vv. 18–19); reward of land (vv. 20–21); possessions (v. 23); prosperity and strength (vv. 24–25).

We need only to contrast Jacob's word to Reuben with Moses' word to Reuben. "Reuben . . . Unstable as water, you shall not have pre-eminence because you went up to your father's bed; then you defiled it" (Gen. 49:3–4). But to the Reubenites Moses says, "Let Reuben live, and not die, nor let his men be few" (Deut. 33:6).

Observing that this chapter contains no exhortations but

rather invocations of future blessings, Brevard Childs remarks,

> The canonical function of ch. 33 serves to place the law fully within the perspective of divine sovereignty, shifting the focus from Israel's behaviour to God's ultimate purpose. The Mosaic legislation is thus subordinated to the overriding purpose of God for his people and the final eschatological realization of his will is attested to in spite of the nation's failure.[5]

The blessings on the tribes are framed by eulogies spoken about God. Verses 1–5 are an introductory praise of God. The poem ends with the same emphasis: "There is none like God, O Jeshurun" (v. 26). Thus the order is the Blesser (vv. 2–5), the blessings (vv. 6–25), the Blesser (vv. 26–29).

The Death of Moses (34)

Moses received orders from the Lord to walk to the top of Pisgah (32:48–52). That was delayed by the blessing of Moses (chap. 33). Now begins the ascent. He is given one last kaleidoscopic view of the land his people will inherit, and then he dies. He is buried in a grave of which only the general location was known (v. 6).

He lived to be 120 years old. He maintained until his death excellent vision (to "show" the land to a blind man would be absurd) and the use of his faculties (v. 7), although old age did hamper him—"I am no longer able to go out and come in" (31:2).

Throughout Deuteronomy, and especially in the last few chapters, it is he who has been blessing Israel. Now it is time for someone to bless him (vv. 10–12).

5. *Introduction to the Old Testament As Scripture* (Philadelphia: Fortress, 1979), pp. 220–221.

Joshua recognizes his limitations. He is no Moses nor an alter ego for Moses. For Moses alone the Lord knew face to face (see Exod. 33:11). To be sure, there is no attempt to apotheosize Moses. No one is allowed to say, "I am of Moses" or "I am of Joshua." Moses does not become a cult hero. Joshua is not Moses, and Moses is not God.

The emphasis that is made in these concluding verses is not on Moses' knowledge of the Lord, but the Lord's knowledge of Moses. To Moses the Lord will never to able to say: "I never knew you; depart from me" (Matt. 7:23). Can anything less be the hope of every believer?

Bibliography

Blenkinsopp, J. *Prophecy and Canon: A Contribution to the Study of Jewish Origins*. Notre Dame, IN: University of Notre Dame Press, 1977, pp. 80–95.

Cassuto, U. "The Son of Moses (Deuteronomy Chapter XXXII, 1–43)." In *Biblical and Oriental Studies*. Translated by Israel Abrahams. 2 vols. Jerusalem: Magnes Press, the Hebrew University, 1974, vol. 1, pp. 41–46.

———. "Deuteronomy Chapter XXXIII and the New Year in Ancient Israel." In *Biblical and Oriental Studies*. Jerusalem: Magnes Press, vol. 1, pp. 47–70.

Childs, B. *Introduction to the Old Testament As Scripture*. Philadelphia: Fortress, 1979, pp. 219–221.

Coats, G. W. "Legendary Motifs in the Moses Death Reports." *CBQ* 39 (1977): 34–44.

Crenshaw, J. "High Places of Earth." *CBQ* 34 (1972): 39–53.

Cross, F. M., and Freedman, D. N. *Studies in Ancient Yahwistic Poetry*. Missoula, MT: Scholars Press for the Society of Biblical Literature, dissertation series, no. 21, 1975, pp. 97–122.

Dahood, M. "Northwest Semitic Notes on Dt 32, 20." *Bibl* 54 (1973): 405–406.

Gordis, R. "Critical Notes on the Blessing of Moses (Dt. 33:21)," and "Additional Note on Dt. 33:27." In *The Word and the Book: Studies in Biblical Language and Literature*. New York: Ktav, 1976, pp. 337–339.

Grossfeld, B. "Neofiti 1 to Deut. 31, 7. The Problem Re–analyzed." *ABR* 25 (1976): 30–34.

Hidal, S. "Some Reflections on Deuteronomy 32." *ASTI* 11 (1978): 15–21.

Klein, M. "Deut. 31:7, *Tby'* or *tbw'*?" *JBL* 92 (1973): 584–585.

Labuschagne, C. J. "The Tribes in the Blessing of Moses." *OTS* 19 (1974): 97–112.

Lundbom, J. R. "Lawbook of the Josianic Reform." *CBQ* 38 (1976): 293–302.

McCarthy, D. J. "Installation Genre?" *JBL* 90 (1971): 31–41.

Mendenhall, G. E. "Samuel's 'Broken *Rîb*': Deuteronomy 32." In *No Famine in the Land*. Studies in honor of John L. McKenzie. Missoula, MT: Scholars Press for the Institute for Antiquity and Christianity, 1975, pp. 63–74.

Polzin, R. *Moses and the Deuteronomist: A Literary Study of the Deuteronomic History*. New York: Seabury, 1980, pp. 71–72.

Weisman, Z. "A Connecting Link in an Old Hymn. Deuteronomy XXXIII, 19A, 21B." *VT* 28 (1978): 365–368.

Wittstruck, T. "So–called Anti–Anthropomorphisms in the Greek Text of Deuteronomy." *CBQ* 38 (1976): 29–34.

Wright, G. E. "The Lawsuit of God: A Form-critical Study of Deuteronomy 32." In *Israel's Prophetic Heritage*. Essays in Honor of James Muilenburg. Edited by Bernhard W. Anderson and Walter Harrelson. New York: Harper and Row, 1962, pp. 26–67.

Index of Authors

Abba, R., 263, 330, 451
Abrahams, I., 240
Ackermann, J. S., 160
Aḥiṭuv, S., 294
Albright, W. F., 127, 137, 160, 282, 360, 371, 387
Althann, R., 223
Andersen, F., 75, 82
Anderson, B. W., 54, 75, 76, 82, 127
Andrews, M. E., 223
Archer, G. L., 112, 157, 160, 180, 330

Bailey, J., 54
Bailey, L. R., 241
Ballard, P. H., 436
Baltzer, K., 387
Barclay, W., 223
Barnard, A. N., 83
Barr, J., 54, 146, 179
Bartlett, J., 355, 370, 401
Basset, F. W., 77, 83
Battenfield, J. R., 137
Baumgarten, A. L., 83
Beegle, D., 159
Bellefontaine, E., 439, 452, 462
Bigger, S., 309
Blenkinsopp, J., 54, 234, 240, 399, 473
Bonneau, N., 113
Borass, R. S., 370
Breasted, J. H., 179
Bretscher, P., 160
Brichto, H. C., 256, 263, 309, 323, 331, 462
Bright, J., 197, 223
Brin, G., 282, 349
Brisco, T., 183
Brow, R., 83
Brownlee, W. H., 160
Brueggemann, W., 54, 83, 88, 113, 191, 232, 310, 390, 400
Budd, P. J., 462
Bush, F., 160
Butler, T. C., 348
Butterworth, M., 160

Caine, I., 329, 342
Campbell, E. F., Jr., 160
Carlson, G. I., 54
Carmichael, C. M., 224, 399, 417, 431, 437–438, 440, 441, 447, 452, 453
Cassuto, U., 53, 74, 83, 137, 159, 201, 204, 465, 473
Cazelles, H., 400
Charny, I. W., 113
Chesterton, G. K., 53, 457–458
Childs, B., 32–33, 54, 83, 92, 146, 149, 153, 159, 160, 176, 183, 187, 198, 203, 209, 215, 228, 238, 240, 262, 315, 329, 336, 379, 399, 413, 472, 473
Chilton, B. D., 113
Christensen, D. L., 370
Claburn, W. G., 419, 450
Clark, W. M., 54, 83, 224
Clarke, E., 127
Clements, R. E., 159, 262, 399
Clifford, R. J., 113
Clines, D. J. A., 54, 60, 82, 83, 94
Coats, G. W., 83, 108–109, 113, 129, 137, 138, 159, 160, 183, 191, 192, 241, 337, 348, 349, 350, 356, 359, 371, 372, 473
Cody, A., 267, 272, 330
Cohen, C., 160, 183

Cohen, M. B., 223
Cohn, H. H., 224
Cole, R. A., 159
Collins, J. J., 263
Coote, R., 127
Craigie, P. C., 183, 371, 378, 387, 399, 431, 451, 452, 456
Crenshaw, J., 436, 473
Cross, F. M., 183, 333, 335–336, 465, 473
Crump, W., 414
Culley, R. C., 371
Cunliffe-Jones, H., 399

Dahlberg, B., 134, 135, 138
Dahood, M., 184, 473
Daube, D., 451
Davies, D., 263
Davies, G. H., 236
Davies, G. I., 192, 373, 400
Davies, J. D., 54
Davies, P. R., 113
Dentan, R. C., 315, 316, 329
Derrett, J. D. M., 309, 440, 452
DeVries, S. J., 182, 348, 450
Douglas, M., 275–276, 282
Dumbrell, W., 160
Duncan, R., 54
Dunn, J. D. G., 241

Eakin, F. E., Jr., 182
Eakins, J. E., 160
Eichrodt, W., 172–173, 195, 204–205, 240, 263, 268, 294, 308, 310, 331, 446, 462
Eissfeldt, O., 309
Elder, W. E. H., 182
Ellison, H. L., 224
Emerton, J. A., 113, 138
Eslinger, L., 63
Etkin, W., 350
Evans, C. F., 435–436

Faur, J., 223
Fearghail, F., 294
Feinberg, C. L. 229, 240, 294
Feliks, J., 160, 192
Fensham, F. C., 127, 224, 241
Ferris, P. W., 192
Finkelstein, L., 399
Fishbane, M. A., 118, 127, 128, 331, 397, 400, 452
Fisher, E., 83
Fisher, L. R., 54, 128, 372, 373
Fitzmyer, J. A., 288, 294
Flanagan, J. W., 349, 393
Foh, S. T., 54
Fokkelman, J. P., 128
Fox, M. V., 113, 349
Francisco, C. T., 184
Frankena, R., 128
Freedman, D. B., 223
Freedman, D. N., 160, 184, 390, 400, 465, 473
Freedman, R. D., 113
Freeman, H. E., 263
Fretheim, T. E., 54, 128, 371, 412, 414
Frymer, T. S., 331
Fukita, S., 83

Gabriel, M. L., 123
Gager, J. G., Jr., 160
Gammie, J. G., 113, 414, 462
Gamoran, H., 310
Gehman, H. S., 311
Gehrke, R., 54
Geisler, N. L., 245, 416
Gevirtz, S., 113, 138
Gilbert, M., 54
Gilmer, H. W., 159
Ginsberg, H. L., 113
Ginsburg, C. D., 188
Glueck, N., 240
Goldin, J., 138
Good, E., 184
Gordis, R., 473–474
Gordon, C. H., 74, 82, 113, 133, 150, 154, 160, 212, 301–302, 379
Gray, G. B., 263, 316
Grayson, A. K., 113
Greeley, A. M., 223
Greenberg, M., 128, 144, 146, 154, 159, 182, 223, 373
Greengus, S., 113

Gronigen, G. Van, 184
Grossfeld, B., 474
Gunn, D. M., 371
Gutmann, J., 240, 450
Gutzke, M. G., 159

Habel, N. C., 55, 83, 113
Haggerty, B. A., 223
Hallo, W. W., 214–215
Halpern, B., 241
Hamlin, E. J., 161
Hanson, A., 241
Hanson, H. E., 349
Hanson, P. D., 224
Hanson, R. S., 55
Haran, M., 182, 224, 231–232, 240, 271, 272, 299, 309
Harris, R. L., 161
Harrison, R. K., 278, 282, 378, 399
Hartmann, T. C., 83
Hasel, G. F., 55, 84
Hauge, M. R., 113
Heinemann, J., 262
Hertz, J. H., 293, 378
Heschel, A. J., 202
Hidal, S., 474
Higgins, J. M., 55
Hobbs, T. R., 452
Hoenig, S., 282
Hoffner, H. A., Jr., 214, 309
Hoftijzer, J., 371
Honeycutt, R. L., Jr., 241
Hooker, M. D., 241
Horowitz, H. L., 414
Horton, F. L., 309
Houtman, C., 128
Huey, F. B., Jr., 159
Huffmon, H. B., 224
Hulse, E. V., 278, 282
Hummel, H., 262
Hyatt, J. P., 159

Isbell, C., 150, 161
Ishida, T., 414

Jackson, B. S., 220, 224, 225
Jacobsen, T., 37, 66, 391
Janzen, J. G., 161
Jensen, J., 161
Jobling, D., 337, 348
Jocz, J., 182, 282
Joenig, S., 310
Joines, K. R., 55, 371

Kaiser, W. C., Jr., 51, 80, 309, 453
Kapelrud, A., 55
Kaufmann, S., 417–418, 427–428, 430, 434–435, 440, 446, 449, 450
Kaufmann, Y., 41, 237, 258, 263, 268, 286, 293, 294, 300, 303, 310, 329, 359, 371, 381, 399, 432, 450, 463
Kearney, P. J., 233–234, 240, 463
Kensky, T. F., 84
Kessler, M., 84, 128
Kickasola, J., 263
Kidner, F. D., 34, 53, 130, 262
Kikawada, I. M., 55, 84
Kimbrough, S. T., Jr., 225
Kinlaw, D. F., 262, 277–278
Kitchen, K. A., 74, 130, 138, 158, 161, 181, 184, 378, 386, 398, 399, 400–401, 456
Klein, M., 184, 474
Kline, M., 63, 84, 113, 161, 225, 378, 386, 399
Klostermann, A., 297
Knight, G. A. F., 152, 155, 159, 181
Kraus, H. J., 294, 310, 373
Kselman, J. S., 348
Kuntz, J. K., 460, 463
Kuyper, L. J., 182

Labuschagne, C. J., 474
Lachs, S. T., 161
Lambert, W. G., 37, 40, 84
Landman, L., 263
Larson, G., 84
Laughlin, J. C. H., 271, 272
Laurin, R. B., 84
Leiman, S. Z., 348
Lemeche, N. P., 225, 310, 451
Levine, B. A., 256, 263, 289, 293, 294, 310, 315, 329, 348
Lewis, C., 55

Lewis, C. S., 48, 338–339
Lewis, J., 128, 241
Lilley, J. P. U., 401
Limburg, J., 55
Lindars, B., 401
Lipinski, E., 241, 268, 272
Loewenstamm, S. E., 114, 182, 184, 225, 237, 241
Lohfink, N., 383, 399
Long, B. O., 371
Longacre, R., 84
Longenecker, R., 114
Lowenthal, E. I., 136, 138
Lundbom, J. R., 474
Lust, J., 371
Lyonnet, S., 294

MacIntosh, A. A., 183
MacRae, A., 339–340
Magonet, J., 161
Maimonides, M., 159
Maloney, R., 310
Manley, G. T., 378, 388, 389, 399
Mann, T. W., 184
Margolis, M., 378–379
Margulis, B., 182
Martens, E. A., 161
Martin, R. A., 55
Mayes, A. D. H., 330
McBride, S. D., 414
McCarthy, D. J., 114, 161, 183, 263, 399, 474
McConville, J. G., 442, 452
McCurley, F. R., Jr., 389
McEvenue, S. E., 84, 114, 241, 339, 349
McKay, J. W., 183, 225, 414
McKeating, H., 309
McKenzie, J. L., 128, 401
Mendenhall, G. E., 55, 142–143, 178, 198, 223, 330, 361, 362, 369, 372, 387, 466, 468–469, 474
Milgrom, J., 178, 254, 257, 261–262, 263–264, 266, 271–272, 276, 279, 282, 286, 295, 301, 306, 309, 310, 311, 319, 328, 329, 330, 331, 345–346, 347, 349, 363, 385, 421, 434, 450
Millard, A. R., 84, 453
Miller, J. M., 55, 84
Miller, P. D., 184, 331
Miscall, P. D., 128
Mitchell, J. J., 114
Mittwoch, H., 310
Mondin, B., 55
Moran, W. L., 55, 400, 413, 414
Moriarty, F. L, 316, 330
Motyer, J. A., 241
Muraoka, T., 309
Myers, J., 114

Naidoff, B., 55
Napier, B. D., 159, 204
Neff, R., 114
Neiman, D., 55
Neusner, J., 279, 280–281, 282
Neve, L., 348
Nicholson, E. W., 159, 223, 225, 382, 400
Nielsen, E., 55, 75, 84
Nixon, R., 161
Noonan, J. T., 453
North, R., 310
Noth, M., 151, 160, 262, 286, 316, 330, 337, 389, 390, 391–392, 401, 458

O'Connell, K. G., 264
Ogden, G. S., 183
Olson, W. S., 84
Oppenheim, A. L., 214
Orlinsky, H. M., 161
Oswalt, J., 241, 302, 330
Otto, R., 23
Otwell, J. H., 282
Ovadiah, A., 349

Palmor, H., 451
Parker, S. B., 184
Patrick, D., 184, 225, 463
Paul, S., 225
Peacock, H. F., 414
Peck, W. J., 114, 138
Peckham, B., 412, 414

Perdue, L. G., 241, 264
Petersen, D. L., 84
Petrie, F., 178
Phillips, A. C., 223, 331, 400, 444, 452
Phillips, J. B., 47
Phipps, W. E., 56
Piper, J., 56
Plaut, W. G., 161
Ploeg, J. P. M. Van der, 225
Polzin, R., 97, 114, 379, 397, 400, 401, 406, 414, 451, 455, 463, 474
Porter, J. R., 262
Premsager, P., 114
Pritchard, J. B., 445

Rabinowicz, H., 283
Rad, G. von, 32, 45, 47, 53, 71–72, 79, 92, 105, 123, 138, 223, 264, 283, 290, 295, 358, 372, 382, 398, 400, 410, 412, 416, 419, 430–431, 463, 470
Rainey, A., 250, 251, 257, 264, 331, 368
Ramm, B., 160, 183
Rand, H., 161
Rast, W. E., 128
Redford, D. B., 136, 138
Reif, S. C., 372
Reist, I. W., 184
Rice, G., 56, 453
Riemann, P., 84, 326
Riggs, J. R., 183
Ringgren, H., 264
Robinson, G., 271, 272, 349
Rofé, A., 384, 450–451
Rogers, C. L., 114
Rotenberry, P., 114
Roth, M. W., 114, 128, 451
Rowley, H. H., 264
Ruger, H. P., 56
Ryken, L., 21, 56, 114

Sabourin, L., 184, 272, 294
Sakenfeld, K. D., 349
Sanders, J. A., 436
Sandmel, S., 84
Sarna, N., 53, 131, 136
Sasson, J., 85, 323, 330, 331
Sawyer, J., 56, 278, 283
Schaeffer, F., 53
Schmidt, W. H., 160
Schultz, J. P., 114
Schultz, S. J., 378, 400
Scott, R. B. Y., 228
Scullion, J. J., 56
Seerveld, C. G., 360, 372
Segal, M. H., 378
Seybold, D. A., 138
Shanks, H., 56
Shea, W. H., 56
Sheehan, J. F. X., 388
Sider, R. J., 307, 310
Simpson, W. K., 215
Sklba, R. J., 225
Smick, E. B., 372
Smith, E. C., 223
Smith, G. V., 85
Smith, R. H., 114
Smith, R. L., 225
Snaith, N. H., 56, 225, 264, 309, 330, 349, 372
Soltis, T., 184
Speiser, E. A., 31, 37, 53, 96
Stamm, J. J., 223
Stern, E., 372
Stott, J. R. W., 46, 47, 56
Sturdy, J., 330
Sumner, W. A., 401
Swindell, A. C., 114

Tate, M., 226
Thompson, D. L., 461, 463
Thompson, J. A., 378, 400
Thompson, P., 56
Thompson, T. L., 115
Tigay, J. H., 152, 161, 192, 451
Toeg, A., 349
Tomes, R., 184
Toombs, L., 283
Tosato, A., 372
Towner, W. S., 463
Tozer, A. W., 109, 353
Trible, P., 45, 56

Trudiger, L. P., 56, 224
Trueblood, E., 203
Tsevat, M., 224
Tucker, G. M., 128

Uitti, R. W., 226
Uphill, E. P., 161

Vannoy, J. R., 226
Van Seters, J., 113, 115, 128, 355–356, 371, 401
Van Unnik, W. C., 372
Vaux, R. de, 255, 264, 267, 272, 285–286, 295, 310, 330, 331, 349, 355, 362, 371, 372, 373, 401
Vawter, B., 54
Vermès, G., 192
Vos, G., 91, 281–282
Vriezen, T. C., 226

Wagner, N. E., 115
Waldman, N., 184
Walsh, J. T., 184
Walsh, M. F., 414
Waltke, B., 56
Ward, E. F. de, 331
Watson, P., 452
Weeks, N., 85, 115
Weinfeld, M., 224, 378, 380, 381, 383, 384, 385, 387, 388, 400, 416, 419–420, 429, 434, 438, 463
Weingreen, J., 310, 451
Weisman, Z., 474
Wellhausen, J., 227, 228, 381, 392
Wenham, G. J., 75, 76, 85, 226, 250, 263, 266, 293, 300, 310, 311, 420, 442, 444, 451, 452
Wenham, J. W., 330
Westbrook, R., 311
Westermann, C., 19, 49, 52, 54, 56, 141, 331, 372
Westphal, M., 311
Wette, W. M. L. De, 379, 380, 383, 385
Wevers, J. W., 452, 453
White, H. C., 101, 115, 128
Whybray, R. N., 138
Wickham, L. R., 85
Wifall, W. R., 0, 56, 372
Wijngaards, J. N. M., 400
Wilcox, M., 452
Wilkinson, J., 278, 283
Williams, A. J., 56
Williams, J. G., 224
Willis, J. T., 414
Willoughby, B. E., 414
Wilson, R. R., 167, 183
Wilson, S. G., 56
Wiseman, D. J., 115
Wittstruck, T., 474
Wold, D. J., 350
Wolff, H. W., 88, 89, 113, 135, 198, 390, 401, 463
Woudstra, M. H., 56, 241
Wouk, H., 204
Wright, G. E., 400, 468, 474
Wright, G. R. H., 138

Yohanan, A., 371

Zannoni, A. E., 359, 372
Zevit, Z., 166, 183, 452
Ziskind, J., 311
Zimmerli, W., 161, 224, 264, 311

Index of Scripture Passages

Genesis

1–2—18–42, 166
1:1—2:3—20, 24
1:1—24, 30–33
1:2—23, 25, 234
1—2:4a—397
1:3—166
1:6—166
1:9—166
1:10—166
1:11—166
1:14—166
1:16—28
1:20—166
1:21—24, 25, 32
1:22—89
1:24—166
1:26—22, 26, 27, 166
1:27—24, 26, 32
1:26–29—21, 28
1:26–31—29
1:28—28, 72, 89, 166
1:29—166, 275
1:29–30—28
1:30—275
2:1–3—26
2:3—26, 32, 89
2:4–25—20–21
2:5—52
2:7—20, 24
2:8—29, 81
2:14—29
2:15—30, 52, 59
2:15–17—29
2:16–17—45
2:17—30
2:18–25—28
2:19—21, 28
2:20—28
2:22—21, 24
2:23—29, 52, 72
2:24—29, 106
3—29, 42–53, 352
3:1—44
3:2–3—45
3:3—44
3:4—44
3:4–5—47
3:5—134
3:6—44
3:7—48, 58, 275
3:8–11—48
3:10—122
3:12–13—48
3:14—89
3:14–15—48
3:15—48–51
3:16—29, 48, 58, 71
3:17—61, 62, 71, 89
3:17–19—48
3:20—52
3:21—48, 60, 275
3:22—30, 61
3:22–24—52, 60
3:24—58, 81
4:1—51, 58
4:6—326
4:7—58, 59
4:8—58–60
4:9—59
4:11—89
4:14—58
4:15—60
4:16—58, 60, 81
4:17–22—61
4:19—62
4:21–22—60
4:23–24—60–62
4:25—50
4:25—5:32—61
5:1—26
5:1–2—32
5:1–32—61
5:2—89
5:4, 7, 10, 13, 16, 19, 22, 26, 30—62
5:24—61
5:29—61, 62, 89
5:32—80
6:1—63
6:1–4—62–65, 361
6:1–8—80
6:2—62, 63
6:3—64–65
6:5—53, 70, 71
6:5–7—64
6:5—9:27—65–80
6:6–8—73
6:7—32
6:9—71, 253
6:9–10—80
6:11, 12—70
6:13b—70

6:14—71
6:19–20—72, 74
7:1—71
7:2—72, 275
7:4—73
7:6–17—75
7:9—75
7:9, 15—72, 74
7:11—73
7:12—73
7:15—75
7:17—73
7:24—73
8:6—73
8:20–22—73
8:21—71–72
9:1–18—73
9:1—72, 82, 89
9:2–6—72
9:3–5—275
9:5—46
9:5–6—218
9:9—46
9:11—72
9:12–17—72
9:18—78, 79
9:18–19—80
9:20ff.—71
9:20–27—77–80
9:21—78
9:22—77, 79
9:24—77, 79
9:25—89
9:27—80
10—82
10:5, 20, 31—81
10:6—79
10:20—29
10:21–31—80
10:30—81
11—30, 82
11:1–9—80–82
11:2—81
11:4—81, 88
11:7—23
11:9—81
11:10–32—80
11:22—29
11:31—96
12—51, 88, 96, 97, 98, 102, 108, 109, 135, 181
12:1—102, 121, 157
12:1–3—89, 92, 93
12:2—88, 107
12:3—97
12:4—92, 94, 102, 107
12:7—94, 95, 177
12:8—157
12:10–20—96–97
12:15—97, 103
12:16—96, 123
12:17—97
12:20—102
13—102–103
13:5ff.—127
13:6–7—103
13:14–18—93
13:15—94
13:17—94
14—102, 103–104
14–17—94
14:12—103
14:15—104
14:18—104
14:20—104
14:21–24—104
15—102, 104–107
15:1—95, 104
15:1–6—93, 94, 106
15:2—104
15:2–3—99
15:4—104
15:5—104
15:6—105, 112
15:7—104, 157
15:7–21—94, 106
15:8—104
15:9—104
15:12–16—95
15:13—104, 157
15:16—70, 104, 157
15:17–21—106
15:18—95, 104
15:18–21—104
16—100, 105, 108
16:2—99
16:3—99
16:6—100
16:10—50
16:16—100, 106
17—102, 104–107, 154
17:1—93, 94, 104, 106, 253
17:2—104
17:3—105
17:4–8—104
17:5—106
17:8—104
17:9—93, 105
17:9–14—106
17:15—105
17:16—104
17:18—104
17:19—104, 105
17:23–27—106
17:25—100
18—107
18–19—103, 107, 108
18:8—188
18:10—94
18:19—93
18:22—188
19:1–11—107
19:30–38—77, 78, 442
20—107
20:1ff.—97
20:3—97
20:4, 6—97
20:12—302
20:14–16—97
20:17—107, 117
21—100
21–22—107–109
21:1—136
21:4—100, 107
21:5—107

21:9ff.—99
21:11—100
21:14—100
21:15—100, 101
21:18—94
22—96, 109, 112, 351
22:1—185
22:3, 5—108
22:5, 12—108
22:6—108
22:7—108
22:12—109
22:13—269
22:14—109
22:15–18—93, 94, 109
23—95
23:1—108
24—109–110
24:1—97
24:7—110
24:12–14—110
24:12, 42, 48—80
24:14, 44—110
24:60—50
25—96
25:19–26—119–120
25:19—28:9—119–121
25:19–26—119–120
25:20—117
25:21—117
25:23—121
25:26—117
25:27–34—120
25:28—129
25:33—120
26—120
26:1ff.—97
26:3—94
26:4–5—93
26:4, 24—94
26:8—97
27:1ff.—120–121
27:1–45—120
27:35—126
27:46—120
27:46—28:9—120–121
28:1–9—120
28:10–22—121–122, 147
28:10—32:21—121–124
28:13–15—122, 148
28:13, 15—94
28:14—94
28:17—121, 147
29–31—122–124
29:2–10—148
29:13—122
29:14—29, 122
29:15—122
29:16–30—302
29:19—122
29:23—77
29:25—77, 126
29:28—148
29:34–35—123
30:2—117
30:3—117
30:25–43—123
30:37–39—123
31:9—123
31:12—123
31:16—123
31:22–55—123
31:30—124
31:31—121
31:34–35—124
32—127
32:1–21—124
32:7, 11—121
32:16—126
32:22–32—124–125
32:24—124
32:25—125
32:26—119, 125
32:27—125
32:28—125, 156
32:29—125, 127, 150
32:30—125
32:31—125
33—127
33–36—126–127
33:3—126
33:10–11—126
34—107
34:5—126
34:13—126
34:30—126
35:2–3—271
35:2–4—126
35:5–8—127
35:7—127
35:9–10—127
35:10—156
35:11—94
35:12—94
35:16–21—127
35:22—78, 127
35:27–29—127
36—127
36:1–43—118
36:2—361
37—130, 133, 136, 137
37:2—108, 132
37:3—129
37:5–7—129
37:9—129
37:9–36—130–132
37:20, 22, 24—101
37:28—130
38—136–137, 448
38:9—136
39—136, 137
39–41—130–132
39:5—135
40—132
40:8—132
40:14–15—131
40:23—131
41—132
41:1—132
41:16—132
41:41—132
41:46—132
42—133
42–50—132–136
42:7—134
42:9—133
42:15–17—133

42:18ff.—133
44:1ff. — 133
44:14–34—133
45:5—134
45:5–8—134
46:3—94
46:4—94
46:8—143
47:9—137
48:4—94
48:10—167
48:13–14—255
49—471
49:3–4—78, 471
49:5–7—126
50:19—134
50:20—134
50:23—158
50:24–25—136
50:26—143

Exodus

1–2—143–147
1:1—143
1:6—158
1:7—143, 144
1:8–14—144
1:9—180
1:16—144
1:22—144
2:6—108
2:10—145–146
2:11–12—146
2:14—146
2:15b–17—148
2:17—146
2:21—148, 336
3–5—147–155
3:1—4:17—155
3:1–6—147
3:5—231
3:6—147
3:7–10—148
3:11—149
3:12—149
3:12a—150
3:12b—150
3:13—149
3:14—150–151
3:21, 22—228
4:1—149
4:2–9—152
4:10—149, 167
4:13—149, 150
4:14—152
4:14, 16—236
4:18–26—155
4:21—168, 169
4:24—153–155
4:25—345
4:27–31—155
5:2—148, 155, 163
5:3—155
5:14–18—148, 155
5:19–21—148, 155
5:22–23—148
6—156–159
6:1—7:7—148
6:3—156–157
6:7—163
6:12, 30—156
6:14–27—157–158
6:23—158
6:25—158
7–11—163–174
7:1—163, 236
7:3—168, 169
7:4—163
7:5—163
7:13—168
7:14—168, 170
7:17—163
7:19—166
7:22—168
8:8—171, 352
8:15—168, 170
8:19—168, 170, 171
8:22—164
8:25–28—171
8:28—171
8:32—168, 170
9:7—168, 170
9:12—168, 170
9:14—164
9:16—174
9:27—171, 172
9:28—171
9:29—164
9:34—168, 171, 172
9:35—168, 171
10:1—168, 171
10:2—164
10:16—172
10:17—171
10:20—168, 171
10:24—171
10:27—169, 171
11:2–3—228
11:7—164
11:10—169, 171
12—175, 176
12:1–13—176
12:1—13:16—175–177
12:3—195
12:3ff.—429
12:5—427
12:7, 13—175
12:12—165
12:13—175
12:21–27—176
12:23—175
12:27—175
12:29–32—163
12:35–36—228
12:37—177, 333
12:38—176
12:40–41—157
12:43–49—176
12:46—176
13:3–10—177
13:5, 11—177
13:8, 14—177
13:11–16—177
13:15—169
13:17—15:21—177–182
13:20—333
14:2—195, 333
14:4—164, 169

14:8—169
14:15—190
14:17—169
14:18—164
14:31—181
15:1—181
15:1–5—181
15:2—181
15:3—181
15:6—181
15:6–17—181
15:11—181, 182
15:13—182
15:13–18—182
15:16—181
15:17—181
15:18—181
15:18–21—181
15:21—181
15:22—333
15:22–27—185
15:23—188
15:24—186
15:25—185, 186, 190
16—187, 410
16:1—333
16:1–36—185, 186
16:2—186
16:2–3—181
16:4—185, 186
16:5—187
16:6, 12—164
16:7–8—186
16:16, 18—186
16:19—186
16:20—186
16:22—187
16:25–26—187
16:27—187
17:1—333
17:1–7—185, 186, 188, 347, 411
17:2, 7—185
17:4—190
17:6—188, 189, 239
17:8—189
17:8–14—340
17:8–15—449
17:8–16—185, 189, 317
17:9—189
17:12—185
17:13—190
18:1–27—185
18:5—190
18:8—190
18:13—185
18:13ff.—395
18:25—393
19—193–195, 198, 222, 239, 397
19:1—142
19:2—333
19:3—193
19:3–6—193
19:4—193
19:5—193, 194, 222
19:6—195, 222, 299
19:7—193
19:8—194, 221
19:9—193
19:10–13—194
19:14—193, 194
19:16—194
19:18—194
19:20—193, 195
19:24—195
19:25—193
20—198, 210, 397
20–23—222
20:1—196
20:1–17—404
20:1–20—195–209
20:2—151, 199
20:2–6—196
20:3—199
20:3–6—199
20:4—196
20:4–6—199
20:7—199
20:7–17—196
20:11—200
20:17—200, 209
20:20—185, 198
20:21ff.—196
20:21—23:33—209–221
20:22—196, 209, 220
20:22–26—211, 212, 220
20:24—220
21–23—197, 210, 388
21:1—211, 220
21:1–11—219
21:2—221, 426
21:2ff.—427
21:2–11—426, 427
21:1—22:17—212
21:2—23:19—417
21:5—426
21:6—426
21:7—426
21:7–11—215
21:12—208, 211, 221
21:12–14—433
21:12, 15–17—211
21:13—220, 370
21:14—44
21:15—211
21:15, 17—208
21:16—208, 211
21:17—211
21:20—221
21:20–21—219
21:23–24—306
21:24–25—219–220
21:26–27—219, 221
21:27—221
21:28—218
21:28–36—217
21:29—218
21:30—218
21:32—219
22:1–3—208
22:3—426
22:7, 10—101
22:17—211
22:18—212
22:18—23:19—212
22:20—207
22:20—23:19—220

22:23—220
22:24—220
22:27—220
22:31—276, 299
23:4–5—219
23:7—221
23:10–11—306, 425
23:10–19—366
23:13—221
23:15—221
23:17—221, 366, 429
23:19—212
23:20—221
23:29–30—177
24:1–18—221–223
24:3, 7—236
24:3a, 7—222
24:3b, 7b—222
24:4—222
24:7—209
24:9—222
24:10–11—222
24:12—222
24:16—234
24:18—235
25–31—227–235, 265, 266
25:1—196, 233
25:1–7—231
25:11—233
25:15—233
25:16, 21—187
25:17—231
25:22—187
25:24—233
25:31–40—327
25:31, 36, 38, 39—233
26:1—233
26:7—233
26:31—233
26:32—233
26:33–34—187
27:2, 4, 6—233
27:10—233
27:20–21—327
28–29—231, 265
28:6–12—229
28:15–30—229
28:30—268
28:31–35—229
28:36–38—229
28:40–42—229
28:41—267
29—265
29:7—325
29:9, 33, 35—267
29:19–34—266
29:42–43—236
29:43–46—235
30:1–10—231
30:3—233
30:11—233
30:17—233
30:22—233
30:34—233
31:1—233
31:3—234
31:12—233
31:15—207
31:18—187
32—152, 207, 222, 236, 238, 266, 269, 410
32–33—234
32–34—227, 236–240, 410–412
32:2–3—237
32:4—237
32:5–6—237
32:10—154
32:11–14—411
32:12—237, 412
32:14—237
32:15—187
32:20—238
32:22—237
32:24—237
32:29—267
32:30—238, 363
32:32—412
32:34—238
33—238
33:1–5—238
33:3—238
33:7–11—229, 238
33:11—473
33:13—238
33:14—238
33:18—238
33:19—151
33:23—239
34—197, 411
34–40—234
34:2–5—239
34:6—239
34:9—239
34:10–26—239
34:17, 21—239
34:18–24—366
34:23—366
34:23, 26—239
34:24—429
34:28—199
34:29—187
34:29–30—240
35–40—227, 229, 265
35:1—196
35:2–3—271
35:31—234
36:2–7—231
38:21–31—180, 228
38:26—177
39—265
40—265
40:17—327
40:34—233
40:35—233

Leviticus

1:1—6:7—249, 265
1:2—249
1:3–5—254
1:4—248, 254
1:5—248
1:5, 11, 15—249, 256
1:6–9—256
1:9, 13—259
1:9, 13, 17—247, 257
1:10—254
1:12–13—256

1:14—254
2—59
2:2—267
2:2, 9, 12—247
2:2, 9, 16—257
2:3, 10—259
3—266
3:2, 8, 13—249, 254, 256
3:3–5—259
3:5, 16—247
3:5, 11, 16—257
3:17—259, 300
4:2—248
4:2, 13, 22, 27—259
4:3, 14—254
4:4, 15, 24, 29, 33—254
4:5–7—249, 256
4:8–10—259
4:10, 19, 26, 31, 35—257
4:11, 12, 21—259
4:12, 21—258
4:16–18—249
4:20, 26, 31, 35—248
4:23—254
4:25—249
4:28—254
4:30, 34—249
4:31—247
4:32—254
5:1–13—259
5:5—291
5:7—254
5:10, 13—248
5:11ff.—59
5:14—260
5:14—6:7—260–261
5:14–16—261
5:14, 18—259
5:15—248
5:16—261
5:16, 18—248
5:17–19—261
6:1ff.—261
6:1–7—261
6:3—261
6:5—261
6:7—248
6:8—7:38—249, 250, 265
6:9—250
6:15, 21—247
6:16, 18—259
6:26, 29—271
6:30—249, 259
7:8—259
7:15–21—259
7:26—300
7:26, 27—259
7:31–35—259
8—251, 265–268, 269
8–9—266
8–10—246
8:3–4—268
8:4, 5, 9, 21, 29, 34, 36—266
8:5–9—268
8:10–13—265, 268
8:14–17—251
8:14–21—269
8:14–35—265, 268
8:17—258
8:18–21—251
8:22ff.—251
8:22–35—266
8:33—266–267
9—269–270
9:1–14—269
9:2, 8—269
9:4, 6, 23—270
9:8–11—251, 269
9:11—258
9:12–14—251, 269
9:15—251
9:15–21—269
9:16—251
9:17—251, 267
9:18–21—251
9:24—270
10—270–271, 273
10:1–2—266
10:6—270, 325
10:9—325
10:10–11—273
10:11—271, 273
10:16–20—266, 271
10:17—271
11—273–277, 299
11:44—276
11:44–45—298
12—277–278
12:2—277
12:4—277
12:6—277
13—273
13–14—278–280
13–15—304
13:46—321
14—273
14:2–8—279
14:3—279
14:9—279
14:10–32—279
15—280–282
15:13–15—277
15:14–15—280
15:18, 21—280
15:29–30—277, 280
15:31—280
16—246, 249
16:5, 10, 20—291
16:6—286
16:6–10—286
16:6, 11, 17, 24—287
16:8, 10—291–293
16:10—293
16:11—286
16:11–28—286
16:12–15—289
16:14–15—249
16:16—288
16:16, 21—289, 290
16:18—288
16:19—288
16:20—288
16:21—255, 291
16:29—287
16:29, 31—294
16:29–34—286

16:32—267
16:33—288, 289
17—297, 299–301
17:1–9—384
17:1–16—257
17:3ff.—300
17:3–4—300
17:5—257
17:7—292, 293
17:10, 12, 14—259
17:11—256, 257
18—78
18–20—301–304
18:3—301
18:6–18—302
18:9—302
18:16—448
18:18—302
18:19–23—302
19–27—246
19:2—298, 385
19:3—303
19:4–8—303
19:9–10—303
19:11–18, 35–36—303
19:15—303
19:18b—303
19:19—303
19:19, 23–25—303
19:20–22—303
19:26—301
19:26–28, 30–31—303
19:29—303
19:32—303
19:33–34—303, 304
20—78
20:2–5—301
20:6—301
20:7—298
20:10–16—301
20:17—78
20:17–19—301
20:20–21—301
20:25–26—276
20:26—298
21—297
21—297
21–22—304
21:1–4—325
21:1–9—304
21:1—22:16—246
21:6–7—325
21:8, 15, 23—304
21:10—267, 325
21:10–15—304
21:11—325
21:16–24—304
22—297
22:1–9—304
22:9, 16, 32—304
22:10–16—304
22:17–30—304
23—287, 297, 304–305, 366
23:3—305
23:4–8—305
23:5–8—175
23:9–14—305
23:15–22—305
23:23–24—305
23:26–32—285, 305
23:27–32—294
23:33–44—305
23:40—305
24—305–306
24:1–4—306
24:2–4—327
24:5–9—306
24:10–16—306
24:14—255
24:14, 16—306
24:19–20—306
24:22—306
25—306–307
25:1–7—306, 425
25:2—425
25:6—425
25:8–55—306
25:9—307
25:10—307
25:11–12—307
25:23—307
25:25ff.—307
25:25–55—307
25:35ff.—307
25:35–38—307
25:39–46—307
25:39b—426, 427
25:43—28
25:44–45—426
25:47ff.—307
26—307, 308
26:3–13—307
26:4—307
26:6—307
26:11—307
26:14–46—307
26:16—307
26:17—28
26:23–39—307
27—297, 308
27:13, 15, 19, 27, 31—308

Numbers

1—363
1–2—317–318, 321
1:1—6:21—326
1:1—10:10—317, 338
1:3—108, 178, 317
1:26–27—179
1:36—267
1:45—108
1:46—177
1:50–51—318
1:51—318, 319, 334
1:53—318, 328
1:54—321
2:32—177
2:34—321
3–4—318–320, 321
3:3—267
3:4—318, 319
3:10, 38—319, 344, 363
3:14–39—319
3:51—321
4:1–15—327

4:1–49—319
4:3—319, 320
4:4–20—320
4:4, 23, 24, 27, 30, 31, 33, 35, 43, 47—320
4:5–14—320
4:5–15—328
4:15—320
4:15, 18, 20—320
4:15–49—328
4:19—320
4:21–28—320
4:29–33—320
4:49—321
5—321–324, 347
5:1–4—321
5:2–3—347
5:3—325
5:5–10—321
5:6–8—261
5:8–10—322
5:11–31—322–324
6—321, 324–326
6:2—325
6:4—325
6:7—325
6:9–12—324
6:10–11—277
6:13–20—325
6:14–15—251
6:16–17—251
6:21–27—324, 325–326
7—327
7:1—327
7:1—10:10—326–329
7:1–11—327
7:6—385
7:12–88—327
7:89—327
8:1–22—327
8:9–10—255
8:16, 18—255
9:1–14—175, 328
9:3, 5, 11—328
9:5–7—329
9:10—328
9:15–23—329
10:1–10—329
10:1–35—333
10:11—142
10:11—12:16—333–337
11—334, 336, 340, 348
11–14—347
11:1–3—334, 336, 411
11:2—334, 411
11:2ff.—190
11:4–34—334
11:10—334
11:13—190
11:14–17—395
11:15—334
11:16—335
11:16ff.—334
11:24—335
11:26—335
11:28—335
11:31–34—411
11:33—334, 335
12—279, 334, 335, 336, 340
12:1—335, 336
12:6–8—336
12:10—334
12:11–13—336
12:15, 21—384
13–14—395
13:1—14:15—337–341
13:21, 22—338
13:23, 24, 27b—340
13:25–33—340
13:28, 31, 33—340
13:30—338
13:33—356
14:1–5—340
14:2—341
14:2, 21—385
14:6—338
14:6–9—340
14:10—341
14:11–12—340
14:13–19—341, 343, 395
14:18—239
14:19—341
14:22–23—340
14:24—338, 340
14:27—341
14:27, 30—340
14:28–31—341
14:29–30—340
14:30—338, 340
14:29, 32, 34—341
14:31, 33—341
14:37—340, 341
14:39–45—190, 342
15–18—341–346
15:1–16—342
15:15, 21, 23—347
15:17–21—342
15:22–26—342, 343
15:22–31—342
15:27–31—260
15:27–39—343
15:30—343
15:32–36—271, 342
15:37–41—342
15:40—343
16:3—343
16:5–7—343
16:7—345
16:8—343
16:8–10—344
16:16—420
16:21—344
16:22—343, 344
16:31–33—344
16:34—393
16:35, 49—346
16:40, 41—344
16:46–48—344, 363
16:48—346
17:5—345
17:12–13—345, 346
18:1—345
18:1–7—345
18:3—344, 346

18:5—328, 345
18:7—344, 346, 363
18:21–23—345, 346
18:32—346
19:1—20:21—346–348
19:11–13—346
19:14—346
19:17–19—347
19:21—347
20:1—333, 347, 351
20:1–4—385
20:2–13—190
20:10–12—362
20:12—190, 348, 351, 356
20:13—316
20:14–21—395
20:21—354
20:22—333
20:22—21:35—352–356
20:22–29—347, 351
20:24—351
20:29—359
21—359
21:2—352
21:4–9—352
21:7—352, 357
21:9—42, 316
21:10—333
21:10–20—353
21:10–32—352
21:13—316
21:14–15—353
21:17–18—353
21:21—355
21:21ff.—356
21:23—354
21:27–30—354
21:33–35—352
22–24—356–360
22:1—316, 333
22:5—357
22:7, 17—357
22:9, 12, 20—358
22:18—358
22:22—43
22:27—361
22:31—357, 358, 361
22:32—43
23:5, 16—358
23:7–10—357
23:16—358
23:18–24—357
24:1, 2—358
24:3–9—357
24:4—361, 362
24:5—361
24:6–15—362
24:8—362
24:9—361, 362
24:10—361
24:14–24—357
24:17—360
25—359, 360–363, 397
25:4, 5—361
25:6–15—362
25:8, 9—362
25:13—363
25:14, 15—362
26—366
26–27—363–365
26:10—420
26:51—177
26:52–56—363
27—366
27:1—364
27:1–2—364
27:1–11—366
27:8–11—364
27:12–14—396
27:12–23—365
27:15–23—396
27:16–18—365
27:21—268
28–30—365–368
28:16–25—175
30—352
30:3–8—366
31–36—368–370
31:2–3—369
31:16—359, 360
31:19–24—369
31:25–54—369
31:50—369
32:11–12—268
32:50—351
33—369
33:38–39—351
34—369
35—370
35:11—205
35:25, 28—434
35:27—205
36—370

Deuteronomy

1–3—393, 394, 397
1–4—389, 392, 406
1:1—385, 393, 403
1:1–5—386, 392
1:3–9—397
1:5—386, 393, 403, 415
1:6—4:40—392, 393
1:6—4:49—386
1:9—395
1:9–18—395
1:16–17—397
1:20–21—397
1:29–31—397
1:36—267
1:37—395, 396
1:37b–40—397
1:38—188
2—355
2:3–7—397
2:5—395
2:9—395, 397
2:13—397
2:18–19—397
2:24–25—397
2:24, 25, 30, 31, 33, 36—355
2:26—355
2:26–37—355
2:27–29—397
2:30—396
2:31—397

3—394
3:2—397
3:18–28—397
3:26—395, 396
3:28—396
4—393, 397
4–6—394
4:1—397
4:3—397
4:9–14—397
4:12—398
4:13—199
4:15–19, 23, 25—397
4:16–19—397
4:21—395, 396
4:22—398
4:24—398
4:25ff.—398
4:27—398
4:27–31—455
4:30—399
4:31—398, 404
4:35—398
4:38—398
4:40—398
4:41–43—403
4:42—205
4:44—415
5—415, 417
5ff.—392
5–6—403–409
5–11—387, 392, 413
5–26—418, 455
5–26, 28—379, 389
5–28—393, 455
5:1—393, 403
5:2—406
5:2–3—404
5:3—404
5:6–10—407
5:6–21—200
5:10—407
5:12—200
5:15—200
5:16—200
5:21—200, 209
5:22ff.—410
5:23–27—405
5:28–29—405
6:1–9—408
6:4—406–408
6:4–9—408
6:5—201, 407, 408
6:6—408
6:6–8—413
6:7–9—408
6:10–11—408
6:12—407
6:14—407
6:15—407
6:16—185
6:17—407
6:20–23—408
7–11—409–413
7:1–5—409
7:6—385, 409
7:7—409
7:8–9—409
7:17—409
7:17–26—409
7:18—410
7:20–24—409
7:25—208
8:2—185, 410
8:2–3—462
8:5—462
8:7–10—410
8:14–18—410
8:16—185
8:17—410, 425, 431
8:18—431, 462
9:1—10:11—410–412
9:4—411, 425
9:4–6—462
9:7–17—411
9:18–20—411
9:18–21—411
9:20—411
9:22—411
9:22–24—411
9:25—412
9:25–29—411, 462
10:1ff.—411
10:4—199
10:5—412
10:8—188, 432
10:12–15—413
10:16—413
10:17–18—413
10:20—29
11—415, 423
11:18–21—413
11:22—29
11:26–32—413
11:26–28—413
11:32—413
12—413, 418–421, 429, 431
12–13—423
12–26—381, 387, 388, 403, 413, 415
12:1—16:17—416
12:2–4—421
12:3—423
12:5—388, 421
12:5, 11, 14, 18, 21, 26—418
12:5, 21—418
12:6—419
12:7, 8, 12—421
12:11—418
12:15, 21—300, 384, 421
12:15–28—421
12:16—431
12:16, 23—300, 421, 428
12:17—427
12:18—421
12:20—431
12:29–31—421
13—421–422
13:1–5—422
13:6–11—422
13:12–18—422
13:14—422
13:17–18—424
14—423–424, 428
14:1—423
14:2, 21—385
14:3—423

14:3–21—423
14:17—423
14:21—276
14:22—424
14:22–27—424
14:22–29—423
14:23—424
14:24—418
14:25—424
14:26—424
14:28—424
14:28–29—424, 428, 449
14:29—424
15—424–428
15:1—425
15:1–11—306, 424
15:2—425
15:7–8—425
15:7ff.—428
15:9—425
15:12—426, 427
15:12–18—424, 426
15:13—428
15:17—426
15:18—426
15:19—427
15:19–23—427
15:21—424, 427
15:23—428
16—428–429
16:1–8—175, 428
16:1–17—366
16:2—427
16:9–12—428
16:11, 14—428
16:13–15—428
16:16—366, 420, 428
16:16–17—428
16:18—429, 430
16:18–22—429
16:18—18:22—416
16:18—20:20—416
17—429–431
17:1—429
17:2–6—386
17:2–7—429
17:8–13—385, 430
17:14—431
17:14–20—430
17:15—430, 431, 433
17:16—431
17:18—432
17:19—433
18—431–433
18:1–8—432
18:7—432
18:9–14—432
18:9–22—432
18:15—433
18:15, 18—433
18:19—433
19—433–435
19:1—21:9—416
19:1–13—434
19:1–21—416, 434–435
19:3—434
19:14—434, 435
19:15–21—434, 435
19:18–19—208
20—416, 435–437
20–24—431
20–26—416
20:1—441
20:1–4—385
20:1–9—435
20:5–8—436
20:10–15—438
20:10–18—436
20:12—396
20:19–20—436
21—416, 437–439
21:1–9—437
21:6—438
21:7–8—438
21:10—22:30—416
21:10–14—437
21:10–21—438
21:15–17—364, 437
22—416, 417, 440–442
22:1–8—440
22:5—417
22:6–7—417
22:9–11—441
22:13–29—441
22:17—440
22:21–22—442
22:22—208, 444
22:24—442
22:29—442
23—442–443
23–26—416
23:2—442
23:10–14—443
23:14—420, 443, 444
23:16—420, 443
23:17–25—443
23:24–25—446
24—443–447
24:1–4—386, 443–446, 448
24:5, 6—446
24:7–22—446
24:6, 7—447
24:10–15—447
24:17–22—447
25—447–449
25:1–3—447, 448
25:4—386, 447
25:5—446
25:5–10—136, 447–448
25:6—446
25:11–12—447, 448
25:13–16—447, 448–449
25:17–19—447, 449
26—449–450
26:1–11—449
26:10—420
26:12–15—449
26:16–18—450
26:16–19—449
27–28—387, 455
27:12, 13—456
27:14—396
27:17—434
28—413
28:12—461

28:17–18—98
28:20–57—457
28:22–24—98
29—389
29–30—393, 455
29:2—393
30—389
30:19—387
31—412, 465, 467–468
31:2—472
31:6—393
31:7—467
31:7–29—393
31:9—378, 386
31:9–13—387
31:9, 25—432
31:10–11—466
31:14—467
31:15—467
31:19—387, 466
31:21—466
31:23—467
31:26—387, 466
31:27—468
31:28—466
31:29—468
31:30—466
32—465, 468–471
32–33—393
32:1—468
32:2—469
32:4—468
32:5–6—469
32:6—468, 470
32:7–14—468
32:10—469, 470
32:15–16—469
32:15–18—468
32:18—468, 470
32:19ff.—468
32:20—469
32:23–33—470
32:27–43—469
32:30, 31—468
32:35, 41, 43—470
32:37—468
32:43—471
32:44—466
32:48–52—472
32:50—351
33—465, 471–472
33:1—466
33:1–5—471, 472
33:2–5—472
33:6–25—472
33:8—185, 268
33:26–29—471, 472
34—412, 472–473
34:1–12—393
34:6—472
34:7—472
34:10–12—472

Joshua

5:10–12—175
5:14—357
5:15—231
6:23—108
14:8, 9, 14—268
17:4—364
18:1—228
19:51—228
20:3, 5—205

Judges

5:1—335
6:15—178
7:3—435
8:22—130
9:2—29
9:5—459
16:21—219
11—355
11:19–26—355
17:5, 12—267

I Samuel

1:7—228
2:22—228
2:30—205
11:2—219
10:19, 21—178
14:32–33—301
14:41—268
15:22—237
16:22—188
17:26, 31—129
22:18—459
23:13—150
28:6—268
29:4—43
31:9–10—219

II Samuel

1:20, 24—361
3:33–34—459
5:1—29
7—63
7:12—50
9–20—90
10:4—219
11:25—459
13:13—302
17:23—206
18:17—101
19:12–13—29
19:22—43
24:3—318
24:15, 17—63

I Kings

1–2—90
5:4—43
5:16—28
7:13ff.—228
8:46—53
11:14—43
11:23—43
11:25—43
13:33—267
18—343

II Kings

2:9—439
13:21—101
16:10–16—383
18:4—42
23:21–23—175

I Chronicles

7:20–29—158
21:1—43
21:3—318

II Chronicles

11:15—292
20:7—95–96
29—251
30:1–27—175
35:1–19—175

Ezra

2:63—268
6:19–22—175

Nehemiah

7:65—268
9:17, 31—239

Job

1–2—43
1:6—63
2:1—63
5:12—44
9:17—49
12:4—253
15:5—44
38:7—63
42:8–9—326
42:15—364

Psalms

1—458
8—240
15:2—253, 266
22:23—205
24:3—266
24:4—266
28:2—189
29:1—63
32:10—458
37:25—458
44:22—461
44:23—462
50:15—205
50:23—205
51:5—53
51:7, 10—281
51:16–17—253
63:4—189
72:8—28
72:9—50
74:12—26
74:13—25
74:13–14—25, 26
86:9—205
86:12—205
86:15—239
89:4—50
89:6—64
89:23—50
89:29—50
89:36—50
103:8—239
106:15—335
109:6—43
110:1—50
134:2—189
139:11—49
145:8—239

Proverbs

1:4—44
1:15–16—197
2:12—459
2:21–22—459
3:9—205
3:10—459
12:15—191
12:16—43
12:23—43
13:10—191
13:16—43
14:8—43
14:15—43
14:18—43
22:3—43
22:8—459
22:28—434
23:10—434
27:12—43

Ecclesiastes

2:14—461
2:16—461
3:19—461
4:13—191
6:2—461
9:2—461
12:12—377

Isaiah

1:11–17—253
3:16—361
6:2—352
6:8—23
6:10—167
14:12–14—410
24:15—205
27:1—25
29:13—205
34:14—292
41:8—96
43:20, 23—205
45:4—358
46:1–2—203
51:9—25
51:10—25
53—253, 460
53:4—291
53:12—96, 291
55:6—143

Jeremiah

1:9—433
1:16—29
2:27—470
3:1a—444
3:12—326
6:20—253
7:1–15—253
12:5—156
25:10—446
31:33—413
32:18—239
38:6—101
41:7—101
44:15–23—271

Ezekiel

1, 10—27
1:28—270
3:23—270
4:14—276
8:14—45
12:25—151
16:49, 50—107
28:2–10—410
33:25—301
34:4—28
36:33—281

Daniel

1:18—276
6:10—134
8:17—270

Hosea

2:8—460
6:6—253
9:10—469
11:9—22

Joel

2:13—239

Amos

3:2—348
3:6—458
4:6–11—458
5:21–24—253
9:7—396

Jonah

3:4—65
4:2—239

Micah

2:2—208
6:6–8—253

Nahum

1:3—239

Habakkuk

3:7—336

Malachi

1:6—253
1:8—253
2:17—253
3:8—253

Matthew

1:3—137
3:8—172
5:21–26—206
5:27–30—206
5:38ff.—219
5:43—303
5:45—461
5:48—298–299
6:25, 34—187
7:23—473
9:20—342
10:16—44
10:37—205
12:43—292
15:4—205
19:8—386
19:19—303
19:23–24—459
22:36–38—201
22:39—201, 303
23:5—342
24:24—422
27:24—437

Mark

1:41—321
5:9—125
5:25–34—281
7:10—205
7:11—252
12:25—64
12:31, 33—303

Luke

1:15—324
2:9–10—198
2:52—125
3:38—52
9:49—335
9:51—18:14—435
9:51–56—354
9:56—354
10:27—303
13:1–5—461
14:16–20—436
16:8—191

John

1:14—236
1:29—291
2:9—186
3—124
3:14–15—353
9:2—459
17:6—157
19:17—108
19:22—151
19:36—176

Acts

3:20ff.—433
5:4—186
6:1–6—191
7:2—102
7:22—152
7:23—142
7:23, 30—142
7:30—142
7:35—146
7:52—146
8:18–19—357
9:4—270
10:14—276
15:9—280
27:9—285
27:23—149

Romans

1:3—50
2:24, 26, 28—70
3:21–31—408
3:22, 27, 28, 30—110
3:30—408
4:1–8—110
4:9–12—110
4:13–15—110

4:16ff.—110
4:17–20—110–111
5:12ff.—53
5:19—53
5:20—260
8:28—134
8:31–39—461
8:32—110
8:32–34—462
9–11—173–174
9:3—238
12:1—254
13:9—303
16:20—49

I Corinthians

5:7—176
7:5—194
9:9—386, 447
10:1, 3–4—188
13:6—107
15:22—53
15:25—50

II Corinthians

7:1—280
11:24—447

Galatians

3:6ff.—111
4:4—50
5:14—303

Ephesians

2:3—53
5:2—258
5:26—280
6:2—205

Philippians

1:12–14—134
2:3—207
4:11—209
4:19—206

Colossians

1:19—236

II Thessalonians

2—65

I Timothy

2:14—45
5:18—447

Hebrews

3:7–13—186
6:4–6—262
6:19–20—291
9:7–14—291
9:11—236
9:11–14—287
10:26—262
10:28—386
11—101, 112
11:4—59
11:8–22—112
11:9–10—95

James

2:8—303
2:21–23—112
2:23—96
4:8—280

I Peter

1:15–16—298
1:19—177, 253
2:6—420
3:19–20—64

II Peter

1:21—210
2:4—64

I John

1:7—299
1:7, 9—280
2:1—199
2:6—299
3:3—299
3:7—299
3:12—59
3:23—299
4:20—303

Jude

6, 7—64
11—59

Revelation

1:17—270
6:10—471
12:9—42
19:2—471
20:2—42

Nazarene Theological College
B30518